"This new translation, noteworthy for both its accuracy and its sympathy for Gregory's endeavours, will make his thinking on The Song of Songs far better known. It is extremely welcome."

> —John Moorhead
> McCaughey Professor of History, Emeritus
> University of Queensland
> Author of *Gregory the Great*

"This is the most exhaustive treatment in modern scholarship for the Commentary on the Song of Songs attributed to St. Gregory the Great and the legacy of that text for medieval exegetes. The careful translation and exhaustive commentary of this overlooked text is an important contribution to Gregorian scholarship and a boon to all those interested in Biblical interpretation during the Middle Ages."

> —George Demacopoulos
> Associate Professor of Historical Theology
> Co-Founding Director, Orthodox Christian Studies Program
> Fordham University

"Anyone wanting to learn pre-modern exegesis by walking through a lively example of it should take firm hold of this book. The accessible translation pays due scholarly attention to the channels through which Gregory came to us (Paterius, Bede, William of St Thierry). Those medieval fans of Gregory on the Song show us what a classic it became, and this should encourage us to see it in the same way. In the full Introduction we are given both a basic primer in figural reading and allegorizing which promoted contemplation, and also a platform for research (not least in footnotes which reflect the state of the question in patristic-medieval exegesis). Priceless!"

> —Mark W. Elliott
> Senior Lecturer in Church History, School of Divinity
> University of St Andrews

CISTERCIAN STUDIES SERIES: NUMBER TWO HUNDRED FORTY-FOUR

Gregory the Great On the Song of Songs

Translation and Introduction

by *Mark DelCogliano*

Cistercian Publications
www.cistercianpublications.org

LITURGICAL PRESS
Collegeville, Minnesota
www.litpress.org

A Cistercian Publications title published by Liturgical Press

Cistercian Publications
Editorial Offices
Abbey of Gethsemani
3642 Monks Road
Trappist, Kentucky 40051
www.cistercianpublications.org

© 2012 by Order of Saint Benedict, Collegeville, Minnesota. All rights reserved. No part of this book may be reproduced in any form, by print, microfilm, microfiche, mechanical recording, photocopying, translation, or by any other means, known or yet unknown, for any purpose except brief quotations in reviews, without the previous written permission of Liturgical Press, Saint John's Abbey, PO Box 7500, Collegeville, Minnesota 56321-7500. Printed in the United States of America.

Library of Congress Cataloging-in-Publication Data

Gregory the Great on the Song of Songs / translation and introduction by Mark DelCogliano.
    p.   cm. — (Cistercian studies series ; no. 244)
   Includes bibliographical references and index.
   ISBN 978-0-87907-244-5
   1. Gregory I, Pope, ca. 540–604. Expositio in Canticum canticorum. 2. Bible. O.T. Song of Solomon—Criticism, interpretation, etc.—Early works to 1800.   3. Gregory I, Pope, ca. 540–604.   I. DelCogliano, Mark. II. Gregory I, Pope, ca. 540–604. Expositio in Canticum canticorum. English. 2012.

BS1485.52.G74   2012
223'.907—dc23   2011051221

To the Monks of Saint Joseph's Abbey
in Spencer, Massachusetts:
fratribus quondam in conversatione,
nunc et semper in Christo

CONTENTS

Preface   xi

List of Abbreviations   xv

A Note on References to Primary Sources   xvii

Introduction   1

    I. The Life of Gregory the Great and His Writings   1
        A. Rome in Late Antiquity   1
        B. Gregory's Early Years   5
        C. Deacon and Papal *Apocrisiarius*   10
        D. Gregory's Papacy   15
        E. Gregory's Writings   20
        F. Gregory's Death and Legacy   24

    II. Gregory's Writings on the Song of Songs   29
        A. Gregory's *Exposition on the Song of Songs*   29
            1. The Question of Authenticity   29
            2. The Date and Circumstances of Composition   33
            3. The Scope of the *Exposition*   43
        B. The Excerpters of Gregory   48
            1. Paterius's *Book of Testimonies*   50
            2. Bede's *Commentary on the Song of Songs*   52
            3. William of Saint Thierry's *Excerpts from the Books of Blessed Gregory on the Song of Songs*   54

III. Gregory's Exegesis of the Song of Songs   57
  A. Gregory in the History of Interpretation   57
  B. Gregory's Method of Scriptural Exegesis   65
    1. Gregory's Exegetical Motivation   66
    2. Grammatical Reading Techniques   67
    3. Gregory's Figural Approach to
       the Song of Songs   73
    4. Gregory's Exegetical Practice   79

IV. Gregory's Sources   84
  A. Origen   85
  B. Augustine   87
  C. Apponius   89
  D. Ambrose of Milan   92
  E. John Cassian   98

V. Two Notes to the Reader   99
  A. Note on References to the Song of Songs   99
  B. Note on the Translations   101

Translations   103

  I. Gregory the Great's *Exposition on
      the Song of Songs*   105
    Introduction   107
    Translation   109

  II. Excerpts from the Works of Gregory the Great on the
      Song of Songs Compiled by Paterius and Bede   145
    Introduction   147
    Bede's Preface to *Commentary on
      the Song of Songs* VI   149
    Translation of the Compilations of
      Paterius and Bede   150

III. William of Saint Thierry's *Excerpts from the Books of Blessed Gregory on the Song of Songs* 181
    Introduction 183
    Translation 186

IV. Supplemental Texts 241
    Introduction 243
    Translation 244

Appendices 249

    Appendix One: Gregory's Citations of the Song of Songs 251

    Appendix Two: Table of Correspondences among Paterius, Bede, and William 257

    Appendix Three: Textual Notes on Gregory the Great's *Exposition on the Song of Songs* 275

    Appendix Four: Textual Notes on the Compilations of Paterius and Bede 279

    Appendix Five: Textual Notes on William of Saint Thierry's *Excerpts from the Books of Blessed Gregory on the Song of Songs* 287

Bibliography 295

Scriptural Index 309

General Index 315

PREFACE

At a certain point in my life I became enamored with the Cistercian Fathers. For a lengthy period I immersed myself in their writings and was deeply affected by their thought, particularly their exegesis of the Song of Songs. Inquisitive about the origins of their ideas, I naturally gravitated toward Gregory the Great, whose influence on the Cistercian Fathers, I learned, was pervasive. In Gregory I found a man of rare humanity and insight whose struggles to integrate the exigencies of his own life with his spiritual aspirations and contemplative ideals so resonated with my own. I was attracted to Gregory because of his utter faith in Christ, because of his honesty about himself and the world he lived in, and above all because of his deep-rooted nobility of soul that pervaded everything he said and did.

The translations that appear in this volume are born of my devotion to Gregory and my desire to share him with others. In his literary corpus Gregory encapsulated the best of patristic theology and spirituality and in so doing bequeathed this rich legacy to generations of Christians who lived after him. Nowhere is this more clearly seen than in Gregory's exegesis of the Song of Songs. Gregory's interpretation of this popular Old Testament book not only owes much to Christian exegetes that preceded him, such as Origen, but also profoundly influenced later Western Latin exegetes of the Song, such as Bernard of Clairvaux. In Gregory's exegesis of the Song of Songs, then, we encounter a recapitulation of the best of what preceded and a harbinger of the riches that were to follow.

This volume includes all that Gregory had to say on the Song of Songs. It is intended as the major sourcebook for anyone with an interest in Gregory's exegesis of this biblical book. Students of patristic and medieval scriptural exegesis will find in this volume the work of a master of the exegetical art whose interpretations are methodologically fascinating, theologically profound, and historically influential. This volume will also be of interest to students of patristic and medieval Christian thought more generally, for Gregory frequently uses the Song of Songs to expound upon some of the classic themes of patristic theology, and Gregory's influence on medieval Christianity is all-encompassing. Those interested in monastic spirituality in general and in Cistercian spirituality in particular will find in this volume the source from which many monastic writers such as Bernard of Clairvaux and William of Saint Thierry developed their own interpretations of the Song of Songs and their own teachings on the spiritual life. Finally, this volume will be of particular interest to students of William of Saint Thierry since it contains a translation of one of the few parts of his corpus that has remained hitherto unavailable in English, thus enabling the evaluation of his thought with more accuracy and greater insight.

As I look back over the decade or so it took for this project to come to fruition, I am awed by the generosity of so many people. Each of the following helped me in a unique way, and I thank each of them: Bernard Bonowitz, OCSO; Timothy Scott, OCSO; Bob Power; Edward Vodoklys, SJ; Gabriel Weaver, OCSO; Peter Schmidt, OCSO; Phillipe Makram, OCSO; and Lewis Ayres. I offer my thanks as well to Basil Pennington, OCSO (R.I.P.); Casimir McCambly, OCSO; Albert James, OCSO; and Maureen McCabe, OCSO, each of whom read an early version of my translation of Gregory's *Exposition on the Song of Songs* and offered helpful feedback. I would especially like to thank James Palmigiano, OCSO, who for many years undoubtedly heard me talk about Gregory more than anyone else yet never gave a hint of boredom, even when I discussed the intricacies of Gregory's Latin—no one could ask for a more supportive, devoted, and caring friend. E. Rozanne

Elder was a source of encouragement from the moment I mentioned the project to her, and I wish we could have collaborated until its happy conclusion. Thomas Humphries was my expert reader in the final stages of this project, graciously reading through the entire manuscript and offering constructive criticism. I thank him for his help and wish to add that my own understanding of Gregory has been enriched by reading Gregory's writings together with him during our time at Emory. Karen Levad kindly offered her copyediting services to me, and my prose is more comprehensible because of her careful attention: thank you. I also owe a debt of gratitude to Mark Scott, OCSO, who guided me through the editorial process with care and expertise. I would also like to thank my parents, Edward and Patricia DelCogliano, for their support throughout my life but especially in the last twenty years in which I have made one transition after another. Finally, a thousand thanks to my wife Amy Levad. Though her feminist sensibilities may make her somewhat suspicious of patristic interpretations of the Song of Songs, her love and encouragement have been unwavering.

This book is dedicated to the monks of Saint Joseph's Abbey in Spencer, Massachusetts, among whom I spent an unforgettable seven years in their midst as one of them. Though now separated in way of life, I remain joined with them longing for "the kiss of his mouth, the very fullness of interior peace: whenever we attain it, nothing more remains for us to seek" (Gregory the Great, *Exposition on the Song of Songs* 19).

Mark DelCogliano
Minneapolis, Minnesota

ABBREVIATIONS

Series

CCCM   Corpus Christianorum Continuatio Mediaevalis
CCSL   Corpus Christianorum Series Latina
CF   Cistercian Fathers Series
CS   Cistercian Studies Series
CSEL   Corpus Scriptorum Ecclesiasticorum Latinorum
MGH   Monumenta Germaniae Historica
PL   Patrologia Latina
SChr   Sources Chrétiennes
SRM   Scriptores rerum Merovingicarum

The Works of Gregory the Great

Dial.   *Dialogorum libri IV de miraculis patrum italicorum*
Exp.   *Expositio in Canticis canticorum*
H.Ev.   *Homiliae in Evangelia*
H.Ez.   *Homiliae in Hiezechihelem prophetem*
Mor.   *Moralia in Iob*
Reg. ep.   *Registrum epistularum*
Reg. past.   *Regula pastoralis*

The Works of the Excerpters
(followed by book and line numbers)

Cant.   *In cantica canticorum*
Exc.   *Excerpta ex libris beati Gregorii super cantica canticorum*
Test.   *Liber testimonium*

The Works of the Excerpters
(followed by the excerpt number)

B	Bede, *In cantica canticorum*
P	Paterius, *Liber testimonium*
W	William, *Excerpta ex libris beati Gregorii super cantica canticorum*

Other Works

C. Cant.	*Commentaria in cantica canticorum*
H. Cant.	*Homiliae in cantica canticorum*
HE	*Historia ecclesiastica*
HF	*Historia Francorum*
LP	*Liber pontificalis*
VG	*Vita Gregorii*

A NOTE ON REFERENCES TO PRIMARY SOURCES

In general, references to primary sources have the following format: *Reg. past.* 3.25. The name of work (or its abbreviation) is followed by the book and section numbers, separated by a period. Works not divided into books simply have the section number, as in *VG* 33. When citations from primary texts are made, the line numbers of the edition are added (if there are any), separated from what precedes by a comma; for example, *Reg. past.* 3.25, 71–72.

Complicating the issue is the fact that writings from the patristic, late antique, and early medieval periods acquired a variety of divisions in the course of their editing through the centuries. Each book of the *Moralia*, for example, has two separate divisions into sections. One (the older) breaks each book into larger sections, whereas the other (the more recent) divides the book into smaller, manageable sections. Yet the standard edition of this work assigns line numbers according to the older division. This has necessitated references to the *Moralia* in the following format: *Mor.* 17.27 [39], 24–32. The second number, the one after the period, refers to the section number according to the older division, whereas the number in square brackets refers to the section number according to the more recent division. The line numbers after the comma therefore refer to the line numbers of sections according to the older division. All this information is included to make looking up passages as easy as possible.

A similar, but less complicated, method of division is found in the standard editions of Gregory's homilies. Each homily is divided into sections, but line numbers are assigned consecutively from the beginning to the end of the homily. Thus references to the homilies take the following form: *H.Ez.* 2.2 [4], 95–106. The "2.2" refers to the second homily of the second book. The number in square brackets refers to the section number of the homily. Finally, the numbers after the comma refer to the line numbers. Other primary texts have similar formats for similar reasons. In general, any number within square brackets refers to a section that lies outside of the line numbering used in the edition, and whatever follows a comma refers to line numbers.

INTRODUCTION

I. THE LIFE OF GREGORY THE GREAT AND HIS WRITINGS

A. ROME IN LATE ANTIQUITY

Gregory the Great lived in a time of acute crisis in the West.[1] The city of Rome, once the center of the Roman Empire, had ceased to be the capital of Western civilization when Constantine relocated the imperial government to Constantinople in 330. Yet through the fourth century the city's politics remained heated, her economy booming, and her intellectual activities vibrant. The imperial promotion of Christianity led to a program of building in Rome on a scale not seen since the days of Trajan in the early second century, but it was churches that were built, not forums,

---

1. In the following sketch of the historical context of Gregory, I am particularly indebted to the following works: Averil Cameron, *The Later Roman Empire. AD 284–430* (Cambridge, MA: Harvard University Press, 1993); Averil Cameron, *The Mediterranean World in Late Antiquity. AD 395–600* (London: Routledge, 1993); A. H. M. Jones, *The Later Roman Empire, 284–602* (Baltimore, MD: Johns Hopkins University Press, 1986); and Mark Humphries, "Italy, A.D. 425–605," in *Late Antiquity: Empire and Successors, A.D. 425–605*, ed. Averil Cameron, Bryan Ward-Perkins, and Michael Whitby, 525–51 (Cambridge: Cambridge University Press, 2000). See also Jeffery Richards, *Consul of God: The Life and Times of Gregory the Great* (London: Routledge & Kegan Paul, 1980), 4–24; and Andrew J. Ekonomou, *Byzantine Rome and the Greek Popes: Eastern Influences on Rome and the Papacy from Gregory the Great to Zacharias, A.D. 590–752* (Lanham, MD: Lexington Books, 2007), 1–5.

markets, and other civic structures. Rome became, at least externally, a Christian city.

After the reign of Theodosius the Great (379–95), the Roman Empire was definitively split into Western and Eastern halves, each governed by its own emperor. The Western emperors were for the most part too young, too short-lived, or simply too incompetent to devise creative responses to the new problems that faced the Western empire. The most pressing of these were the barbarians—peoples from the periphery of the Roman world not fully integrated into the empire but desiring to be so. Barbarian peoples were not the invading marauders they are sometimes portrayed to be but rather groups joined together by common interests struggling to share in the advantages and opportunities that accompanied being part of the economic, military, and political systems of the Roman Empire. The sack of Rome by Alaric and his Visigoths in 410 epitomizes the failure of Western emperors to deal effectively with the barbarians.[2]

With the weakening of imperial power in Rome, the Western empire became increasingly ruled piecemeal by the leaders of various barbarian peoples. Typically these leaders had been given high military commands by the imperial government. They headed armies made up of soldiers loyal to them, not to the empire. At times they fought for the Romans, at times against them, not out of fickleness, but because of political expediency and the need to make a living. Their military lifestyle was not so much due to an innate martial character but rather to the lucrative nature of a military career. It was also the best way to reach the upper echelons of power within the Roman political system. Successful barbarian generals were assigned (or simply took over) the security of various regions, eventually establishing independent rule in them when imperial authority evaporated. In 418 the Visigoths, after leaving Italy, founded a kingdom in Gaul centered at Toulouse. By 442 the

---

2. Thomas S. Burns, *Barbarians within the Gates of Rome* (Bloomington: Indiana University Press, 1994); Thomas S. Burns, *Rome and the Barbarians, 100 B.C.–A.D. 400* (Baltimore, MD: Johns Hopkins University Press, 2003).

Vandals, after moving through Gaul and Spain, had established a kingdom in North Africa, depriving the Western empire of one of its most wealthy and cultured regions. In the latter part of the fifth century, the Franks fought the Visigoths for control of Gaul. In 507, the Frankish king Clovis won a decisive battle at Vouillé, securing Frankish supremacy. The Visigoths fled to Spain and slowly recouped, establishing a kingdom centered at Toledo in 568. The Western Roman Empire had become dismembered into several successor kingdoms.[3]

In this period Italy was ruled *de facto* by a series of barbarian military commanders. They set up various puppet emperors who represented the last gasp of imperial power in the West. But the line of Western emperors came to an end when, in 476, one of these barbarian military commanders, Odoacer, deposed the last emperor, the boy Romulus Augustulus, who was in fact a usurper not recognized by the Eastern emperor. Odoacer set himself up as the *rex* (king) of Italy. Though his bid for recognition by the court in Constantinople was rejected, he had the support of the Roman senate and presented himself as ruling in the stead of the emperor. Odoacer ruled ably and peacefully until 487/8 when his invasion of Illyricum gave the Eastern emperor Zeno a pretext for invading Italy. The task was entrusted to Theoderic, a Roman patrician, one of Zeno's military commanders, and the leader of the Ostrogoths in Pannonia. Here is a prime example of how difficult it is to draw sharp distinctions between Romans and barbarians in this period. Theoderic had his foot in both worlds, or rather, in him the Roman and barbarian worlds were blended together. After the final defeat of Odoacer in 493, Theoderic was proclaimed "king of the Goths" by his troops. Like Odoacer, Theoderic sought to establish good relations with the Eastern empire and in 497/8 was recognized by Emperor Anastasius as ruling in the emperor's stead. Theoderic's strong rule over the Ostrogothic kingdom that he had established

---

3. Roger Collins, *Early Medieval Europe*, 2nd ed. (New York: Saint Martin's Press, 1999).

in Italy lasted until his death in 526. He presented his government as a legitimate continuation of the Roman Empire in the West and saw himself as the ruler of two nations, Goth and Roman, who were nonetheless one people, joined together, mutually interdependent, and ruled by Roman law.[4]

In the two hundred years after Constantine's relocation of the capital of the Roman Empire in 330, the city of Rome itself was utterly transformed. No longer the center of power in the Roman world, a diminished Rome had increasingly become solely a Christian city. As imperial power faded in the West, Rome came to be ruled by barbarian kings who nonetheless brought stability in otherwise uncertain times. Theoderic's long reign definitively transformed Italy from empire to kingdom with minimal disruptions to its social, political, and economic stability. It is only after the death of Theoderic in 526 and the ensuing dynastic instability of the Ostrogothic royalty that Italy entered into a time of severe crisis.

When Justinian became the Eastern emperor in 527, he resolved to reconquer the provinces of the Western empire that had been lost to barbarian kings in the last century. After the Vandals were easily driven out of North Africa in 533–34, Justinian began a war for the reconquest of Italy in 535. If he had expected another quick victory, it was gross miscalculation. The war lasted for twenty years, devastating Italy in the process. Further degrading an already dire situation, in 542–43 plague broke out in Italy and elsewhere around the Mediterranean, killing off about a third of the population. In 550, for the first time in its history, Rome was abandoned when the Ostrogothic king Totila drove the city's population to the Campanian countryside. Italy south of the Po River was restored to imperial rule only in 555, with the new administrative center at Ravenna, headed by a new official called the exarch. Italy north of the Po was not secured until 562. Twenty years of war had destroyed the economy and regular government in Italy. The sena-

---

4. Patrick Amory, *People and Identity in Ostrogothic Italy* (Cambridge: Cambridge University Press, 1997).

torial order, its members now either dead, dispersed, or impoverished, played a vastly reduced role in Italian civic life and eventually ceased to be an active force in it altogether. Most of the functions of civil government were gradually taken over by military and clergy. Many Italians resented being "liberated" by imperial forces, since it had come with so much loss of life and property.

The slow process of rebuilding had only begun when in 568 another barbarian people, the Lombards, occupied northern Italy, first conquering cities such as Milan and Pavia. A depleted Italy lacked the means to resist. During the next few years, the Lombards took over areas south of the Po, so much so that by 584 they controlled most of the Italian peninsula except for the southernmost tip of Italy and a swath of land that ran from Aquileia to Ravenna and then to Rome. Tensions ran high between the imperial administration and the Lombards as each government jockeyed for control of Italy by encroaching upon the territories of the other. The civil government was no more; Italy, whether imperial or Lombard, was ruled by a military aristocracy whose governmental centers were essentially strongholds. The loyalties of Italians were divided in this time of political instability. Areas loyal to the empire, which included Rome, lived in near-constant fear of attack by the Lombards. Such was the situation when Gregory became bishop of Rome in 590. A homily Gregory delivered in 593 during a period of Lombard attacks paints a bleak picture. "Everywhere we see weeping," writes Gregory, "on all sides we hear groaning. Our cities are ruined; our fortresses are overthrown; our fields are ravaged; our land is reduced to a desert. No one lives in the country; there remains hardly anyone living in the cities."[5]

B. GREGORY'S EARLY YEARS

Nothing definite is known of Gregory's childhood, as he rarely speaks of his life before becoming pope. He was born around 540, in the midst of the empire's war of reconquest in Italy, and his

---

5. *H.Ez.* 2.6 [22], 524–28 (CCSL 14:310).

earliest childhood would have been marked by the outbreak of the plague in 542–43 and by Totila's depopulation of Rome in 550.[6] He was the scion of a wealthy and prominent Roman family that had a long reputation for Christian piety. The family owned large estates in Rome, in her environs, and in Sicily. Gregory's great-great-grandfather (*atavus*) was Pope Felix III (483–92),[7] and Pope Agapitus (535–36) may have been a distant relative of his.[8] Gregory's father, Gordianus, was an official in the Roman Church, serving in an administrative and legal capacity.[9] Three of his paternal aunts (named Tarsilla, Æmiliana, and Gordiana) adopted the ascetic life, though Gordiana later abandoned it for marriage, scandalizing Gregory.[10] His mother, Silvia, also adopted the ascetic life after the death of her husband, retiring to Cella Nova near the Basilica of Saint Paul.[11] Gregory also mentions a maternal aunt named Pateria,[12] and had at least two brothers, Palatinus and another whose name is not known.[13] Gregory's earliest biographers assumed that Chris-

---

6. There are several excellent short sketches of Gregory's life before becoming pope: Richards, *Consul of God*, 25–43; Ekonomou, *Byzantine Rome*, 6–13; Carole Straw, *Gregory the Great* (Aldershot: Variorum, 1996), 1–8; R. A. Markus, *Gregory the Great and His World* (Cambridge: Cambridge University Press, 1997), 8–14; John R. C. Martyn, *The Letters of Gregory the Great* (Toronto: Pontifical Institute of Mediaeval Studies, 2004), 1–13; John Moorhead, *Gregory the Great* (London and New York: Routledge, 2005), 1–9. See also Pierre Riché, *Petite vie de saint Grégoire le Grand (540–604)* (Paris: Desclée de Brouwer, 1995).

7. *H.Ev.* 38 [15], 392 (CCSL 141:375); *Dial.* 4.17. Note that *atavus* may simply mean "ancestor."

8. Agapitus was the son of a priest named Gordianus, a name found in Gregory's own family, suggesting a relation to him; see *LP* 59.

9. In *VG* 1.1 John the Deacon anachronistically calls Gordianus a *regionarius* (PL 75:63a), but in all likelihood he was a *defensor*.

10. *H.Ev.* 38 [15], 361–435 (CCSL 141:373–76); *Dial.* 4.17.1–2.

11. John the Deacon, *VG* 1.1 (PL 75:63a) and 1.9 (PL 75:66a).

12. *Reg. ep.* 1.37 (CCSL 140:44).

13. For Palatinus, see *Reg. ep.* 11.4.5 (CCSL 140A:862); for the unnamed brother, see *Reg. ep.* 9.201 (CCSL 140A:759). On both, see John R. C. Martyn, "Six notes on Gregory the Great," *Medievalia et Humanistica*, n.s. 29 (2003): 1–25, at 12–15.

tian piety was strong in him from his childhood. Gregory of Tours, a contemporary of Gregory, wrote that he was "devoted to God from his youth."[14] A later biographer, Paul the Deacon, expresses a similar sentiment when he writes, "His devotion to God and yearning with all desire for the homeland of the life above began in his youthful years, a period of life in which young men usually enter upon the ways of the world."[15]

While Justinian's war of reconquest and the invasion of the Lombards made a classical literary education harder to attain, it was still possible, and Gregory was well trained in grammar and rhetoric.[16] He does not display the sheer erudition of the educated elite in Italy from earlier in the century, such as that of Boethius (ca. 480–ca. 525) or Cassiodorus (ca. 490–ca. 585), but still stands out as one of the greatest literary figures in the West at this time, both in output and in rhetorical skill. Indeed, Gregory of Tours, writing around 593/4, beamed that Gregory "was so learned in grammar, dialectic, and rhetoric that he was regarded as second to none in the City."[17] His works evince a knowledge of classical authors such as Cicero, Vergil, Seneca, and Juvenal, though he hardly ever mentions them by name. He also shows an interest in the natural sciences, astronomy, history, arithmetic, medicine, and music. Gregory was less interested in philosophy and refers to philosophical tenets most often to denounce them. It was the Christian literary tradition that had the most influence on him, and no text more profoundly

---

14. *HF* 10.1 (MGH-SRM 1/1: 478, 14): *ab adulescentia devotus Deo*.

15. *VG* 2 (PL 75:42a–43a): *Hic in annis adolescentiae in quibus solet ea aetas vias saeculi ingredi Deo coepit devotus existere, et ad supernae vitae patriam totis desideriis anhelare*.

16. On the state of education in Lombard Italy and Gregory's own learning, see Pierre Riché, *Education and Culture in the Barbarian West* (Columbia: University of South Carolina Press, 1976), 139–76. See also Claude Dagens, *Saint Grégoire le Grand: culture et expérience chrétiennes* (Paris: Études augustiniennes, 1977), 16–24 and 31–34; and Martyn, *Letters*, 2–3 and 101–14.

17. *HF* 10.1 (MGH-SRM 1/1: 478, 8–9): *Litteris grammaticis dialectisque ac rethoricis ita est institutus ut nulli in Urbe ipsa putaretur esse secundus*.

than the Scriptures. Gregory's grammatical and rhetorical education had a decisive influence on how he interpreted the Bible (his exegesis is discussed in part 3 of the introduction). His thought is also deeply imbued with the writings of Latin Christian authors such as Ambrose, Jerome, John Cassian, and especially Augustine. It seems that Gregory knew some Greek, though to what extent it is hard to say.[18] Nonetheless, Gregory had some contact with Greek patristic writers, whether in translation or in the original.[19]

Gregory first embarked upon a career of public service, attaining by 573 high political office, most likely that of urban prefect.[20] In this capacity Gregory would have been responsible for law and order in Rome and her environs and would have overseen the defense and provisioning of the city. The Roman government in Gregory's day was loyal to the emperor in Constantinople and the exarch in Ravenna; however, the exarch was often preoccupied with the Lombards elsewhere in Italy and the emperor with other concerns far from Rome. Despite good intentions, they could manage little

---

18. The issue of Gregory's Greek has attracted much scholarly attention; G. J. M. Bartelink, "Pope Gregory the Great's Knowledge of Greek," in *Gregory the Great: A Symposium*, ed. John C. Cavadini, 117–36 (Notre Dame, IN: University of Notre Dame Press, 1995), provides the best summation. See also the recent summaries of Martyn, *Letters*, 102–3; and Ekonomou, *Byzantine Rome*, 14–15.

19. E.g. *Reg. past.* 3.praef., where Gregory uses Gregory of Nazianzus.

20. *Reg. ep.* 4.2.10–11 (CCSL 140:218). The mss. read both *urbanam praefecturam* (urban prefect) and *urbanam praeturam* (urban praetor), and the latter reading is found in the better mss. (F. Homes Dudden, *Gregory the Great: His Place in History and Thought*, 2 vols. (London: Longmans, Green, and Co., 1905), 1.101 n. 1; and Martyn, *Letters*, 3). At *VG* 1.4 John the Deacon also says that Gregory was urban praetor (PL 75:64b): *sub praetoris urbani habitu*. Most scholars reject the reading *praeturam* and the witness of John the Deacon since the office of praetor was defunct by Gregory's time (Dudden, *Gregory the Great*, 1.101 n. 1; Straw, *Gregory the Great*, 20 n. 6; see Markus, *Gregory the Great and His World*, 8 n. 35). The reading *praeturam* could also be a textual corruption, a scribe accidentally omitting *-fec-* from *praefecturam* due to skipping from the letter *f* to letter *t*. Martyn, however, adopts the minority position and prefers the reading *praeturam* and holds that Gregory became urban praetor in 573 and urban prefect a year later in 574 (Martyn, *Letters*, 3).

tangible support for the Romans, who were more or less left to their own resources. As urban prefect, Gregory would also have been the president of the senate when it convened, which was rare, since that august body had long been on the wane in civic life.

Gregory was in office as urban prefect in the dying days of the Roman senate, on the verge of extinction after existing for nearly one thousand years. His political career spanned a time in which the traditional verities of civilian life and government in Rome were quickly fading away. The transitoriness and unreliability of the world and its failure to provide security made a deep impression on Gregory. The longer he pursued a career of public service, the more distant he felt from God and the more anxious he grew over the salvation of his soul. He was torn between his sense of obligation to serve others and his own desire to focus on the eternal realities of God in contemplative retreat. After much inner torment, Gregory resolved to abandon his secular career and enter a monastery. Long after the decisive event, Gregory reflected on his conversion to the monastic life in this way:

> For a very long time I delayed the grace of conversion, and after I had been inflamed with a desire for heaven I thought it better to wear secular clothing. For what I should seek concerning the love of eternity was already being revealed to me, yet long-established custom had so cast its chains upon me that I could not change my outward attire. And while my mind still obliged me to serve this world in outward activity, many of the cares for this same world began to threaten me so that I was in danger of being engulfed in it no longer in outward activity alone, but, what is more serious, in my own mind. At long last being anxious to avoid all these dangers, I sought the haven of the monastery, and having left all that is of the world, as at that time I vainly believed, I came out naked from the shipwreck of this life.[21]

---

21. *Mor.* ad Leandrum [1], 5–15 (CCSL 143:1); trans. [modified] Martyn, *Letters*, 379–80.

Gregory never fully resolved this tension between action in the world in service of others and the life of contemplation. Gregory recognized the need for both, and it is a theme that frequently recurs in his writings.[22]

Because he had the faculties to dispose of his family property as he pleased, we know that Gregory converted to the monastic life soon after or concurrently with the death of his father.[23] Gregory built six monasteries on the family estates in Sicily and a seventh at his family home within the walls of Rome on the Caelian Hill, at the Clivus Scauri near the Basilica of Saints John and Paul.[24] This monastery was dedicated to Saint Andrew. The foundation of monasteries by wealthy men and women was a common enough event in late antiquity, but unlike most, Gregory actually entered the monastery he founded as a simple monk. Gregory was never the abbot but served under two different abbots during his monastic career, first Valentio, then Maximian.[25] Gregory always looked on his initial years in the monastery with great fondness. But his contemplative repose was not to last.

C. Deacon and Papal *Apocrisiarius*

Gregory was too talented to remain sequestered in a monastery. Either Pope Benedict I (575–78) or his successor Pope Pelagius II (578–90) made Gregory one of the seven deacons of Rome. Gregory missed the monastery acutely, but his sense of obedience to the Church left him unwilling to let the pope's call go unheeded. Soon after his ordination as deacon, in 579 or 580, Pope Pelagius II sent Gregory to Constantinople as his ambassador (*apocrisiarius*). He may have traveled with a Roman delegation sent to the emperor to seek help against the Lombards.[26] Desiring only to be a

---

22. See Markus, *Gregory the Great and His World*, 17–26.
23. John the Deacon, *VG* 1.5.
24. Gregory of Tours, *HF* 10.1; Paul the Deacon, *VG* 3; John the Deacon, *VG* 1.5–6.
25. Valentio: *Dial.* 4.22.1; Maximian: *Dial.* 3.36.1; 4.33.1; and *H.Ev.* 34.18.
26. Ekonomou, *Byzantine Rome*, 5 and 8.

monk, Gregory was thrust into the cauldron of ecclesiastical politics in the imperial capital.

Gregory spent about six years in Constantinople representing the interests of Rome and the papacy (579/80–585/86). From the shreds of evidence from this period in Gregory's life, we know that his duties included requesting help against the Lombards. The emperors in the period of Gregory's tenure as *apocrisiarius* were largely preoccupied with campaigns against the Persians in the east and the Avars and Slavs in the north and were thus unable to allocate substantial military support for Italy. Gregory managed to wrangle only a small contingent of soldiers from Emperor Tiberius (578–82), which proved to be of little help.[27] He had even less success at securing help from Tiberius's successor Maurice (582–602), who preferred diplomacy and attempted to enlist the Franks to combat the Lombards.[28] Gregory's inability to reverse this entrenched imperial policy toward Italy and Rome highlights his unproductive tenure as *apocrisiarius*. "His tenure as papal representative," according to Andrew Ekonomou, "appears to have accomplished few, if any, of the things for which Pelagius II had sent him to the imperial city."[29]

During his tenure as *apocrisiarius* Gregory also became embroiled in a controversy with Eutychius, the Patriarch of Constantinople, over the status of the resurrection body. In doing so, Gregory was sucked into a theological debate that had been raging in Constantinople for several decades.[30] In brief, Gregory defended the notion that the resurrection body was a truly corporeal reality, just like the mortal body, except that it was made immortal. Eutychius was accused of denying this and of arguing instead that the resurrection body would be lighter and more beautiful, that

---

27. Ekonomou, *Byzantine Rome*, 5.
28. Pelagius, *Ep.* 1 (PL 72:703d); see Ekonomou, *Byzantine Rome*, 5 and 9–10.
29. Ekonomou, *Byzantine Rome*, 11.
30. For a history of the debate before Gregory became involved, see Yves-Marie Duval, "La discussion entre l'aprocrisaire Grégoire et la patriarche Eutychios au sujet de la résurrection de la chair: l'arrière-plan doctrinal oriental et occidental," in *Grégoire le Grand*, ed. Jacques Fontaine et al., 347–66 (Paris: CNRS, 1986).

is, essentially different, from the mortal body. According to Gregory, the debate was resolved only by the intervention of Tiberius. Debating before the emperor, Gregory refuted his enemy simply by citing Christ's word in Luke 24:39: "Touch and see; a ghost does not have flesh and bones, as you see I have." In Gregory's mind, this verse proved that all resurrection bodies, on the model of Christ's resurrection body, are corporeal in the same way that mortal bodies are. Gregory says that the affair left both parties seriously ill, with Eutychius dying shortly thereafter, recanting on his deathbed.[31]

Andrew Ekonomou has rightly suspected the veracity of Gregory's account and has suggested that Gregory used and tailored it for ideological purposes.[32] First of all, Gregory depicted Eutychius as a simpleminded heresiarch; from other sources we know that Eutychius was an intelligent theologian and pastorally minded patriarch, despite his tendency to controversy. Second, no Eastern source records Gregory's refutation of Eutychius and the deathbed recantation. Ekonomou proposes that one purpose of the account was to demonstrate the orthodoxy of Rome against "the East's unremitting tendency to lapse into heresy through vain speculation."[33] In his account of the controversy, Gregory's distaste for theological speculation and debate is clear. The affair also enabled Gregory to boast of at least one success in an otherwise unproductive tenure as *apocrisiarius*. Finally, Ekonomou suggests that Gregory used the story "to show that a simple appeal to the Bible, which for him was the ultimate repository for all virtues and the final defense against all vices, was able to achieve what all the treatises and disputations of the religious philosophers could not."[34] Recounting this incident in some detail affords us an

---

31. For Gregory's account, see *Mor.* 14.56 [72–75] (CCSL 143A:743–6).
32. Ekonomou, *Byzantine Rome*, 11–12.
33. Ekonomou, *Byzantine Rome*, 12.
34. Ekonomou, *Byzantine Rome*, 12.

opportunity to see perhaps the earliest example of Gregory's thoroughgoing biblicism.

During his stay in Constantinople, Gregory also made useful political contacts, perhaps in the hope of advancing Rome's interests through their influence, given his own ineffectiveness before the emperor. Though these contacts appear to have done nothing to help Gregory in his role as *apocrisiarius*, they would later serve him well after he became pope. He developed intimate friendships with Constantia, the wife of Emperor Maurice; Theoctista, Maurice's sister; Narses, the patrician and general; and many other elites in the East. In 584 Gregory was also the baptismal sponsor of the imperial couple's son, Theodosius.[35]

Gregory's residence in Constantinople was not entirely consumed with political turmoil, doctrinal controversy, and socializing. At some point an entourage of monks from Saint Andrew's arrived in Constantinople in order to provide him a haven of peace and contemplation in the midst of his burdensome activities at the imperial court. Other clerical visitors to Constantinople joined him, such as Leander of Seville, the elder brother of Isidore, who was on a diplomatic mission from the Visigothic kingdom in Spain; they became lifelong friends. Gregory and his companions lived in common away from the court at the Placida Palace; in this way he was able to maintain a modicum of contemplation in the midst of his duties. Once again, Gregory's account, written years later to Leander, best captures how valuable this "traveling monastery" was to him:

> Many of my brethren from the monastery followed me there, bound by their brotherly love. And I see that this was done according to divine dispensation, so that by their example, I might always be tethered to a placid shore of prayer, as with the rope of an anchor, when I was tossed to and fro under the incessant pressure of secular cases. Indeed, I used to flee the

---

35. For Gregory's more "social" activities in Constantinople, see Markus, *Gregory the Great and His World*, 11–12; and Martyn, *Letters*, 7–11.

> great volume of earthly business and disturbances to join their fellowship, as if to a bay in the safest of ports, and although that ministry had removed me from my monastery and former life of peace, and had destroyed me with the sword of its occupation, yet among those brethren, through a daily discussion of a learned reading, I was revived by a feeling of remorse.[36]

It was in this context of reading texts together and discussing them that Gregory, clearly the expert of the group, began to give lectures on the exegesis of the book of Job. The brothers asked him not only to comment on the historical sense but also to deliver an allegorical reading of the text that emphasized its moral sense. At first Gregory made his commentary orally, and notes were taken by stenographers. For the latter parts, he dictated to a scribe. He undertook a revision of the whole after his return from Constantinople. Entitled *Moralia in Iob*, it eventually filled six volumes and was divided into thirty-five books. The work did not attain its completed form until after Gregory became pope.

Pope Pelagius recalled Gregory to Rome in 585/6, where he resumed his office of deacon. In this period Gregory lived at Saint Andrew's and was engaged in revising the *Moralia*. He devoted himself to reading, contemplation, and fasting but also remained in the service of the Roman Church and advised the pope. This was among the happiest periods of his life.[37] But all was not well outside the monastery. War with the Lombards resumed in 587. In 589 northern Italy experienced particularly heavy rainfall that caused catastrophic flooding. In autumn the Tiber overflowed in Rome, flooding the city and the papal granaries and destroying some old churches. Plague broke out in January. One of its victims was Pope Pelagius II, who died on February 8, 590.[38]

---

36. *Mor.* ad Leandrum [1], 33–43 (CCSL 143:2); trans. Martyn, *Letters*, 380.
37. *Dial.* 1, prol. 3–5.
38. Gregory of Tours, *HF* 10.1.

D. Gregory's Papacy

With the city in turmoil, faced with floods, disease, and possible attacks from the Lombards, a papal election was soon held. The electors—clerics, nobles, and people—unanimously chose Gregory. His unique combination of administrative and diplomatic experience, together with his ascetic piety and pastoral skill, made him the obvious choice. Gregory, once again heavily reluctant to forego the quiet of the monastery for the bustle of pastoral service, immediately wrote to Emperor Maurice, requesting that he withhold his consent to the election. Apparently, the letter was intercepted and replaced by a letter acclaiming Gregory's unanimous election. Maurice would soon heartily confirm Gregory's election.[39]

In the meantime, control of the city passed to the archpriest, the archdeacon, the *primicerius notariorum*, and the pope-elect, as custom decreed.[40] Gregory chose to address the crisis of the plague by preaching a sermon in the Basilica of Saint John Lateran.[41] He proclaimed that the plague was the scourge of God (*flagellum Dei*) meant to call people to conversion. He exhorted the people to repent and do penance for their sins. He instructed the people to pray for forgiveness and sing psalms for three days, after which seven different processions would set off from various churches and converge upon Saint Maria Maggiore. Tradition has it that this took place on April 25. As they processed, the people sang *Kyrie eleison* in supplication to the Lord. The gravity of the situation and the desperation of the massive intercession with God that Gregory orchestrated is underscored by the fact that, in the space of one hour, eighty people dropped dead as they walked in procession. The plague ravishing the city had yet to abate.[42]

---

39. Gregory of Tours, *HF* 10.1; Paul the Deacon, *VG* 10; John the Deacon, *VG* 1.39–40.

40. Richards, *Consul of God*, 41.

41. The text is preserved in Gregory of Tours, *HF* 10.1.

42. Gregory of Tours, *HF* 10.1; Paul the Deacon, *VG* 11–12; Paul the Deacon, *Historia Langobardorum* 3.24; John the Deacon, *VG* 1.41–43.

In time, however, the waters receded, the plague subsided, and Emperor Maurice's diploma approving the election arrived in Rome. Gregory was consecrated as pope on September 3, 590. It is reported that Gregory was thwarted in a plan to go into hiding before his consecration; whether the story is true or not, it underscores his apprehension over assuming the office.[43] "Resistance to episcopal consecration," writes Robert Markus, "was a well-established convention, and not only in literature; but Gregory's aversion was deeply felt. He felt unequal to the responsibilities of his new office; and, more important in his own mind, it plunged him back into the tempestuous sea of worldly affairs from which he had long been seeking to extricate himself."[44] The letters written by Gregory soon after his consecration—the earliest letters of his we possess—are replete with sentiments of his insufficiency for the burdensome office, of his reluctance at once again being cast into the whirlwind of activity, and of his profound sorrow over the loss of his monastic contemplation, which, he realized, would never be his again.[45]

But Gregory did not slip into a quagmire of depression; ever obedient to the will of God, it did not take long for him to be reconciled to his vocation. By early 591, he could write, "I admit that I have taken on the burdens of this office with a heavy heart. But because I was not able to fight against divine decrees, I have by necessity recalled my mind to a happier state."[46] A month later, he wrote, "Because it is not possible to oppose the decision of

---

43. Gregory of Tours, *HF* 1.10, records that Gregory planned to go into hiding to avoid being consecrated but was abducted before he had the chance. This account was later embellished: Paul the Deacon, *VG* 13; and John the Deacon, *VG* 1.44. See Richards, *Consul of God*, 42 and Markus, *Gregory the Great and His World*, 13. There seems to be some truth to it, since Gregory refers to his planned escape from the papacy by hiding himself away (*delitescendo*) in *Reg. ep.* 1.24a.

44. Markus, *Gregory the Great and His World*, 13.

45. The best example is *Reg. ep.* 1.5, to Theoctista, but also see *Reg. ep.* 1.3; 1.4; 1.6; 1.7; 1.24; 1.25; 1.29; and 1.30.

46. *Reg. ep.* 1.20, 7–9 [January 591] (CCSL 140:19); trans. (slightly modified) Martyn, *Letters*, 133.

the Lord who disposes, I have obediently followed what the merciful hand of the Lord wished to be done concerning me."[47] And so began one of the most dynamic and influential papacies in history.[48]

Gregory is credited with inaugurating the medieval papacy. But the authority he secured for the bishop of Rome was born of necessity. Soon after Gregory's accession, Agilulf became the king of the Lombards, and new Lombard dukes gained control of two towns near Rome: (1) Spoleto, one hundred kilometers to the north of Rome on the road to the exarch in Ravenna; and (2) Benevento to the south of Rome. Thus, Rome was surrounded by Lombards and for practical purposes cut off from Ravenna. Since the ineffective exarch ignored Rome's plight, Gregory was forced to oversee the defense of the city, the movement of troops, and the organization of supplies. In July 592 Gregory himself concluded a peace treaty with the duke of Spoleto, paying the ransom from Church funds. When this move brought Agilulf south to Rome to besiege the city in 593, Gregory eventually prevailed upon him to leave. During the next few years, Gregory continued to oversee the ransoming of hostages, the organization of supplies, the payment of the imperial troops, and the care of refugees, as the exarch in Ravenna repeatedly failed to make peace with the Lombards. Toward the end of 598, with a new exarch in office, peace was finally concluded with the Lombards, though occasional conflicts would arise. Gregory's dealings with the Lombards were born of his frustration with the imperial government and the necessity of defending Rome in the absence of imperial support. Still, Gregory remained loyal to the emperor and continually tried to convince the imperial government to fulfill its obligations to defend Rome.

---

47. *Reg. ep.* 1.26, 9–11 [February 591] (CCSL 140:34); trans. Martyn, *Letters*, 148–49.

48. Essential studies of Gregory's papacy are Dudden, *Gregory the Great*; Richards, *Consul of God*; and Markus, *Gregory the Great and His World*. Good summations can be found in Moorhead, *Gregory the Great*, 5–9; and Straw, *Gregory the Great*, 14–41.

Nonetheless, Gregory's extraordinary involvement in Rome's political and military affairs set a precedent for future popes.

Gregory also devoted much energy to the reorganization of the papal patrimony, the administration of which had fallen into disarray. The Roman Church owned vast estates, which had been accumulated throughout the preceding centuries. They were located mostly in southern Italy and in Sicily but also in other parts of Italy, Gaul, and North Africa. These estates were farmed directly by the Church or leased to tenants for either lifetime or fixed-term leases. Gregory corrected abuses in the administration of the estates to ensure their efficient management. He also sought to improve the quality of the lives of the peasants who worked on these farms. Under Gregory's tenure, the estates increased in production and thus in value, tenants made a profit, and the Roman Church was enriched by the share of the revenues it received.[49]

As the occupant of one of the ancient patriarchal sees, Gregory intervened in ecclesiastical affairs in the East and West, with varying degrees of success.[50] His papal correspondence includes letters to contacts in Antioch, Jerusalem, Constantinople, Alexandria, Dalmatia, Illyricum and the Balkans, North Africa, Gaul, Britain, and Spain. On the whole, Gregory had little direct influence in churches outside of Italy. Perhaps his greatest achievement was the conversion of the English. In 595 he sent a group of forty monks led by Augustine to the royal court at Kent; they converted King Æthelbert and many others, thereby establishing Roman Christianity in England. The monk Augustine was soon made bishop of Canterbury, and a strong bond was forged between the English and Roman

---

49. On the papal patrimony, see Richards, *Consul of God*, 126–39; Straw, *Gregory the Great*, 16–20; and Markus, *Gregory the Great and His World*, 112–24.

50. On Gregory's intervention in ecclesial affairs outside the Roman church, see Dudden, *Gregory the Great*, 1.402–76; 2.43–159, and 201–37; Richards, *Consul of God*, 195–227; Straw, *Gregory the Great*, 26–37; and Markus, *Gregory the Great and His World*, 143–202.

Churches that lasted until the Reformation. Indeed, the country considered Gregory "the Apostle of the English."[51]

Gregory's political activity in his dealings with the Lombards, Franks, and the imperial court; his administration of the papal patrimony; and his intervention in the Churches around the East and West constitute only a small subset of his activities as pope. As bishop of Rome, Gregory was the shepherd of countless Christians in the eternal city and throughout Italy. It is in Italy and particularly in Rome that he had his greatest impact. Nowhere is this more clearly seen than in his reform of the Roman Church, leading to its "monasticization." First of all, Gregory re-created a monastic environment in the Lateran Palace, much as he had earlier done in Constantinople at the Placida Palace, to keep him "tethered to a placid shore of prayer, as with the rope of an anchor, when . . . tossed to and fro under the incessant pressure of secular cases." As during his tenure as *apocrisarius*, the pope's inner circle of monks was the setting for a collective study of the Scriptures, again with Gregory taking the lead.[52] As will be argued below, Gregory's extant exposition of the Song of Songs (translated in this volume) is a transcription of comments on the biblical book that Gregory delivered to his monastic intimates in the Lateran Palace.

Gregory's inner circle of confidants at the Lateran Palace was much more than a fellowship of like-minded ascetics and contemplatives.[53] It was also the pool from which Gregory drew candidates for appointment to crucial positions in the papal administration. This preference for placing monks in the important positions of the administration of the Roman Church was a move that alienated members of the Roman clerical aristocracy who had traditionally fulfilled such functions. This caused an anti-monastic backlash in the Roman Church after Gregory's papacy, leading to the election of Sabinian, the preferred candidate of the clerical party.

---

51. *Whitby VG* 6; Bede, *HE* 2.1.
52. See *Reg. ep.* 12.6, discussed below.
53. On Gregory's inner circle, see Richards, *Consul of God*, 70–84.

Gregory also promoted monasticism more generally throughout Italy.[54] Gregory was not a monastic innovator or legislator but an enthusiastic advocate of the monastic way of life, which he regarded as the supreme form of Christian living. While all his writings are imbued with monastic principles and ideals, it is perhaps his *Life of Saint Benedict*, the second book of his *Dialogues*, that is his most sustained effort to popularize monasticism. He also gave practical support to the movement, encouraging others to found and endow monasteries as he had done and giving subsidies to monasteries that were in financial straits. Gregory also concerned himself with the reform of lax monasteries, the maintenance of monastic discipline, the preservation of monastic seclusion, and the protection of monasteries from arbitrary secular and episcopal interference. And so, Gregory was devoted to monasticism not only by preference in how he lived his life but also by policy in how he shaped the Church entrusted to him.

E. Gregory's Writings

Gregory was extraordinarily busy as pope. So much is known about his papacy because there is a massive amount of literary evidence for his tenure. The bulk of this evidence comes from the collection of his letters that spans the fourteen years of his papacy, called the *Registrum epistularum*. There are 854 letters that survive.[55] In these letters, particularly those to individuals, another side of Gregory emerges: that of friend, spiritual advisor, and pastor. Despite Gregory's countless engagements in the political, military, and administrative affairs of his day, at heart he remained a monk devoted to Christian piety. As pope, he continued to struggle to balance his contemplative aspirations with his papal obligations. Yet Gregory wrote much more than letters; in fact, he is one of the

---

54. Dudden, *Gregory the Great*, 2.173–200; Richards, *Consul of God*, 251–8; Markus, *Gregory the Great and His World*, 68–72.

55. For a description of the collection, see Markus, *Gregory the Great and His World*, 14–15; Moorhead, *Gregory the Great*, 16–17; Straw, *Gregory the Great*, 47–9; and Martyn, *Letters*, 13–14.

most prolific authors of the late antique period.[56] Gregory's other writings reveal him most fully as a thinker, ascetic theologian, contemplative, spiritual expert, and moral reformer. These facets of Gregory can be seen in his short *Exposition on the Song of Songs* as well as in his major writings.

Mention has already been made of Gregory's chief major writing, the *Moralia in Iob*. It is based on lectures Gregory delivered while he was the papal *apocrisiarius* in Constantinople in the years 579/80 to 585/86. Gregory seems to have begun revising these when he had more leisure after his return to Rome from Constantinople.[57] The revision appears to have been completed shortly after his election as pope by early 591.[58] It is Gregory's *magnum opus*. Being a line-by-line commentary on the book of Job, it is not a systematic treatise but rather a treasurehouse of moral, ascetic, theological, christological, and spiritual teachings. It was enormously popular in the Middle Ages.[59]

Early in his papacy Gregory wrote the *Regula pastoralis liber*, or *The Book on Pastoral Care*. Written between his installation in

---

56. Descriptions of Gregory's works can be found in Markus, *Gregory the Great and His World*, 14–16; Straw, *Gregory the Great*, 41–60; Moorhead, *Gregory the Great*, 10–18. A list of editions and translations can be found in the bibliography.

57. *Mor.* ad Leandrum [2], 72–90 (CCSL 143:3).

58. *Reg. ep.* 1.41, 51–58 [April 591] (CCSL 140:49). See also Paul Meyvaert, "Uncovering a Lost Work of Gregory the Great: Fragments of the Early Commentary on Job," *Traditio* 50 (1995): 55–74 at 63–64; and Markus, *Gregory the Great and His World*, 186 n. 99.

59. For example, the copying of Gregory's *Moralia* at the New Monastery at Cîteaux was completed on December 23, 1111 (the codex is now at Bibliothèque Municipale in Dijon, mss. 168–170, 173, cat. nos. 24–25). It was the first book copied after the liturgical books (1099) and the Stephen Harding Bible (1109). It deeply influenced the first Cistercians. On the illumination of this codex, see Conrad Rudolph, *Violence and Daily Life: Reading, Art, and Polemics in the Cîteaux Moralia in Job* (Princeton, NJ: Princeton University Press, 1997). On Gregory's influence on the Middle Ages more generally, see Jean Leclerq, *The Love of Learning and the Desire for God*, 3rd ed. (New York: Fordham University Press, 1982), 25–36; and Terryl Kinder, *Cistercian Europe: Architecture of Contemplation* (Kalamazoo, MI: Cistercian, 2002), 27.

September 590 and February 591, in this book Gregory reflects on the nature of the episcopal ministry, an issue suddenly of vital importance for him. Robert Markus has suggested that the process of writing this book played a crucial role in Gregory's gradual interior acceptance of his new office.[60] In it the tension between the active and contemplative forms of life boils beneath the surface and continually erupts. The book is divided into four parts: the qualifications of the pastor, the pastor's way of life, how the pastor's teaching and admonition of his flock must be according to a diversity of individual characters, and how the pastor should return to contemplation after exercising his ministry. Even in Gregory's lifetime the book gained wide circulation throughout Europe and made its way—in a Greek translation—to the major cities of the East such as Constantinople, Jerusalem, Antioch, and Alexandria. It was immensely influential in the formation of ecclesial ministers at all levels. This oft-repeated opinion contains no exaggeration: "What Benedict's Rule was to monks of the Middle Ages, the Pastoral Rule of Gregory the Great was to the clergy of the world."[61]

In the early years of his papacy, Gregory delivered two series of homilies. The first was on the gospels, in the years 590 to 592.[62] These homilies were preached to the clergy and the people during the liturgy in various churches in Rome and revised for circulation shortly after their delivery, around 593.[63] There are forty altogether: the first twenty were dictated by Gregory and then read out by his secretary; the last twenty Gregory preached himself, caving in to

---

60. Markus, *Gregory the Great and His World*, 14.

61. Hubertus R. Drobner, *The Fathers of the Church: A Comprehensive Introduction* (Peabody, MA: Hendrickson Publishers, 2007), 518.

62. For the date, see Raymond Étaix, *Gregorius Magnus: Homiliae in Evangelia*, CCSL 141 (Turnhout: Brepols, 1999), lvix–lxix.

63. This is the date to which Paul Ewald and Ludwig Hartmann assign Gregory's prefatory letter to Bishop Secundinus of Taormina in Sicily; see the comments in their edition on *Ep.* 4.17a (*Gregorii I papae registrum epistolarum*, MGH, 1.251); this letter is not included in Norberg's CCSL edition but is found in Étaix's edition of *H.Ev.* (CCSL 141:1–2).

the wishes of the people. Some consider these homilies among his most charming, written as they are in plain, unadorned language and lacking the complicated exegeses and digressions that characterize Gregory's other works. They emphasize moral reform and deal with issues of Christology. The second set of homilies was on the book of the prophet Ezekiel, given in late 593.[64] They were delivered to a small group of monks and clerics and revised for dissemination only eight years afterward, in 601, at their request.[65] In these homilies Gregory discusses the allegorical meaning of Ezekiel 1:1–4:3 and 40:1-47; the latter narrated Ezekiel's vision of the temple, considered by Gregory to be the prophet's most obscure passage. Given the subject, these homilies make more demands on the reader, but those who persevere are rewarded.

One of Gregory's most widely read works were his *Dialogues*, written around 593/4. The work is presented as a discussion with his subdeacon Peter, a member of his inner circle. It relates the stories of about two hundred Italian holy men working miracles in their day. Consisting of four books, the second is devoted entirely to the life of Saint Benedict, the author of the monastic rule bearing his name. The fourth book deals with eschatology. The book is successful in depicting a consistent ideal of holiness based on the virtues of the ordinary Christian life, such as humility, obedience, love, and self-discipline.[66] The work was translated into Greek, and in the

---

64. This date is inferred from internal evidence: these homilies seem to have been preached as the Lombard Agilulf was approaching Rome in 593; see *H.Ez.* 2, praef. (CCSL 142:205), and 2.10.24 (CCSL 142:397). Note that the first book of homilies may have been delivered earlier in 591–92.

65. *H.Ez.* praef., 5 (CCSL 142:3).

66. The best analysis of the *Dialogues* can be found in the first volume of Adalbert de Vogüé's edition: *Grégoire le Grand. Dialogues, Vol. 1*, SChr 251 (Paris: Cerf, 1978). Also see Joan M. Petersen, *The Dialogues of Gregory the Great in the Late Antique Cultural Background* (Toronto: Pontifical Institute of Mediaeval Studies, 1984); William D. McCready, *Signs of Sanctity: Miracles in the Thought of Gregory the Great* (Toronto: Pontifical Institute of Mediaeval Studies, 1989); and Adalbert de Vogüé, *The Life of Saint Benedict—Gregory the Great* (Petersham, MA: Saint Bede's Publications, 1993).

Greek Church Gregory's fame rests upon it, being called the "Dialogist." Since the sixteenth century, the authenticity of this work has been disputed, and quite vigorously recently; yet the majority of Gregorian scholars continue to affirm its attribution to Gregory.[67]

A *Commentary on the First Book of Kings* is also attributed to Gregory. Though it had a long history of being suspected as inauthentic, scholars mostly considered it to be genuinely Gregorian—that is, until recently. In a 1996 article, Adalbert de Vogüé uncovered that its true author was Peter of Cava, a twelfth-century Italian abbot.[68] Other works attributed to Gregory are considered doubtful or spurious.[69]

F. Gregory's Death and Legacy

After becoming pope, Gregory never enjoyed good health. Hard work, stress, and ascetic discipline undoubtedly took their toll. His letters are filled with references to his various illnesses.[70] He had a weak stomach and suffered from gout. He was susceptible to fever in the summer. From 598 onward he was mostly confined to his sickbed, rising only to celebrate Mass. He lived in what seems to have been constant pain. He died on March 12, 604. It is recorded in the *Liber pontificalis* that he served as pope for thirteen years, six months, and ten days.[71] He was buried on the same day

---

67. The most recent debate was sparked by the work of Francis Clark, most fully argued in his *The Pseudo-Gregorian Dialogues* (Leiden: Brill, 1987) and his *The "Gregorian" Dialogues and the Origins of Benedictine Monasticism* (Leiden: Brill, 2003). For summaries of the debate and references to further literature, see Straw, *Gregory the Great*, 54–55; Markus, *Gregory the Great and His World*, 15–16; and Moorhead, *Gregory the Great*, 160 n. 22. For the latest reports, see Terrence Kardong, "Who wrote the *Dialogues of Saint Gregory*? A Report on a Controversy," *Cistercian Studies Quarterly* 39, no. 1 (2004): 31–39; and Adalbert de Vogüé, "Is Gregory the Great the Author of the *Dialogues*?" *American Benedictine Review* 56, no. 3 (2005): 309–14.

68. Adalbert de Vogüé, "L'auteur du Commentaire des Rois attribué à saint Grégoire: un moine de Cava?" *Revue Bénédictine* 106 (1996): 319–31.

69. See Straw, *Gregory the Great*, 53–54, for details.

70. See Dudden, *Gregory the Great*, 1.243; Martyn, *Letters*, 5–7.

71. *LP* 66.

in Saint Peter's Basilica.[72] His epitaph, written by Peter Oldradus, the bishop of Milan, and recorded by John the Deacon, gives us some sense of Gregory's legacy in the centuries after his death. The poet commends Gregory's corpse to a personified Earth, lauding the pope's character and deeds, and concludes with a direct address to the departed pope himself:

> O Earth, receive this body taken from your body,
> To do with it what you can, until God raises it to new life.
> His spirit seeks the stars; the powers of hell will not harm him.
> For him death is the way to another, better life.
> The limbs of the high priest are enclosed in this sepulcher.
> Wherever he lived he always did immeasurable good.
> He overcame hunger with feasts, cold with clothing;
> And with holy advice he protected souls from the enemy.
> And he fulfilled in deed what he taught in word;
> He was like an example that spoke mystical words.
> He converted the English to Christ through the teachings
>   of piety,
> Thereby acquiring a faithful army from this new people.
> This toil, this zeal, this care of yours, you undertook
>   as pastor,
> That you might offer to the Lord a much increased flock.
> And by these triumphs you were made to rejoice, O Consul
>   of God,
> For now you hold the reward of your work without end.[73]

The appellation "Consul of God" fittingly encapsulates Gregory's integration of his Roman heritage and his Christian faith. While he struggled to reconcile his *Romanitas* and his *Christianitas*, the leadership he exercised in both political and ecclesiastical domains, and the literary legacy he bequeathed to subsequent ages, stand nonetheless as remarkable achievements.

---

72. See Dudden, *Gregory the Great*, 2.273–76, for an account of Gregory's relics and their frequent translation.
73. John the Deacon, *VG* 4.68 (PL 75:221bc).

Accounts of Gregory's life began to be written soon after his death. He did not lack hagiographers, and the facts of his life soon became embellished with legends. Most of these legends appear to stem from the English Church. Three of the most popular are worth relating. The first is that Gregory's "weeping" for the condemned soul of Emperor Trajan (AD 98–117) secured his release from the torments of hell.[74] The theological ramifications of this incident—namely, the dubious orthodoxy of praying for dead pagans—troubled not only John the Deacon but even Saint Thomas Aquinas.[75] Dante employed a modified form of the story in his *Divine Comedy*.[76]

The second legend concerns a Roman lady who doubted that the bread she herself had baked and donated for liturgical use could be consecrated into the Body of Christ.[77] When she grinned before receiving Communion, Gregory withheld the host from her and reposed it upon the altar. He then led the people in a prayer that Christ show the woman the true nature of the sacrament. Thereupon the host assumed the appearance of a piece of a bloody pinky finger (*digituli auricularis particulam sanguilenti*). Gregory had the people pray that the host's pristine form be restored, and so it happened. The story ends with the astonished woman taking Communion in full belief. By the high Middle Ages this story had been transformed: one day when Gregory elevated the host at the consecration of the Mass, Christ appeared to him as the Man of Sorrows surrounded by the instruments of the passion. The depiction of this scene, called the *Mass of Saint Gregory*, became widespread

---

74. *Whitby VG* 29; Paul the Deacon, *VG* 27; John the Deacon, *VG* 2.44. For discussion, see Dudden, *Gregory the Great*, 1.43; Bertram Colgrave, *The Earliest Life of Gregory the Great by an Anonymous Monk of Whitby* (Lawrence: University of Kansas Press, 1968), 161–63.

75. ST Suppl. q. 71 a. 5. Saint Thomas derived his information from John of Damascus's *Oratio de his qui in fide dormierunt* 16 (PG 95:261d–64a).

76. *Purgatorio* 10, 73–93; *Paradiso* 20, 106–17.

77. *Whitby VG* 20; Paul the Deacon, *VG* 23; John the Deacon, *VG* 2.41. See also Dudden, *Gregory the Great*, 2.272.

in the late medieval and early modern periods, especially the fifteenth and sixteenth centuries.[78]

The third legend also had a pervasive influence on how Gregory was depicted in art. According to this story, Peter the subdeacon recounted that he had seen the Holy Spirit in the form of a dove dictating to Gregory as he wrote his homilies on Ezekiel.[79] This account of Gregory's clear inspiration by God was intended to contradict those who sought to discredit Gregory after his death. Accordingly, one of the most common representations of Gregory has him seated at a writing table with a dove nearby interpreting the Scriptures for him as he writes or dictates his commentary on Ezekiel. The legend indicates the esteem in which Gregory was held as an inspired exegete of Scripture.

Many more legends could be recounted, but these suffice to give a sense of their content and extensive influence. Fortunately, there are more sober elements in the accounts of Gregory's life, and fact can generally be teased from fiction. There are several late antique texts useful for retrieving the historical Gregory. The first was written soon after his consecration as pope. Gregory of Tours included a chapter on Gregory in his *History of the Franks*, based on reports he heard from one of his deacons who had just returned from Rome.[80] Gregory of Tours narrates Gregory's accession to the papacy and records the sermon he delivered during the plague

---

78. See Patricia DeLeeuw, "Unde et Memores, Domine: Memory and Time and the Mass of Saint Gregory," in *Memory and the Middle Ages*, ed. Nancy Netzer and Virginia Reunburg, 33–42 (Boston: Boston College Museum of Art, 1995); and Caroline Walker Bynum, "Seeing and Seeing Beyond: The Mass of Saint Gregory in the Fifteenth Century," in *The Mind's Eye: Art and Theological Argument in the Middle Ages*, ed. Jeffrey F. Hamburger and Anne-Marie Bouché, 208–40 (Princeton, NJ: Department of Art and Archaeology, Princeton University in association with Princeton University Press, 2005). Both articles include numerous examples of the scene.

79. *Whitby VG* 26; Paul the Deacon, *VG* 28 (this is actually an interpolated text and is not original to Paul); John the Deacon, *VG* 4.69. See Dudden, *Gregory the Great*, 2.269–70 and 272; and Colgrave, *The Earliest Life*, 157.

80. Gregory of Tours, *HF* 10.1. See above, p. 15.

in early 590. The first account of Gregory's life written after his death was undoubtedly the short entry in the *Liber pontificalis*, likely composed in 604.[81] It lists his major writings, mentions his mission to England, his addition of a line to the Canon used at Mass, his redecoration of the interiors of various Roman churches, and how many he ordained. Around 625, Isidore of Seville wrote a brief chapter on Gregory in his *De viribus illustribus*, basically listing the Gregorian writings known in Spain at the time.[82] Ildefonsus of Toledo expands upon Isidore's chapter in his *De virorum illustrium scriptis*, from about 650.[83] Venerable Bede sketched Gregory's life around 731 in his *Ecclesiastical History* and provided a more extensive account of Gregory's life than either Isidore or Ildefonsus.[84] Bede's chapter unsurprisingly focuses on Gregory's missionary activities in England.

Besides these accounts of Gregory's life inserted in works of wider scope, there are three early medieval biographies completely devoted to Gregory. The first is the so-called *Whitby Life of Gregory*, composed by an unknown monk of Whitby around 713. It is based on English materials and is mostly the stuff of legend.[85] The Lombard historian Paul the Deacon used the *Whitby Life* as well as other sources for his own *Life of Gregory*, composed around 775 or so, and it is more reliable historically. John, a deacon in the Roman Church under Pope John VIII (872–82), wrote the final and the longest early medieval biography of Gregory. While he used the earlier biographies and Gregory's own writings, John also had access to the papal archives. "He read his documents with care and sympathy," writes Robert Markus, "and succeeded in producing one of the finest of early medieval biographies."[86]

---

81. *LP* 66.
82. Isidore of Seville, *De viris illustribus* 40 [53–56] (PL 83:1102a–3a).
83. Idefonsus of Toledo, *De virorum illustrium scriptis* 1 (PL 96:198c–99b).
84. Bede, *HE* 2.1.
85. Edition: Colgrave, *The Earliest Life*.
86. Markus, *Gregory the Great and His World*, 2.

II. Gregory's Writings on the Song of Songs

A. Gregory's *Exposition on the Song of Songs*

1. The Question of Authenticity. Gregory's *Exposition on the Song of Songs* is not one of his major works, nor was it well-known in his lifetime, nor has it attracted much attention in modern times, save for a handful of devoted scholars. At times, the Gregorian attribution of the *Exposition* has even been doubted. This is due partly to its stylistic differences from Gregory's genuine works and partly to the fact that this work is not mentioned in the early medieval biographies compiled in the decades and centuries after his death.[87] It is not mentioned in the *Liber pontificalis*, nor do Isidore of Seville, the *Whitby Life*, Bede, Paul the Deacon, or John the Deacon list it explicitly in their catalogues of Gregory's works. The stylistic differences and absence from these catalogues can be explained. The *Exposition on the Song of Songs* is a notary's copy of an oral discourse which was circulated without his approval. This accounts for its stylistic differences and its exclusion from the official lists.

Yet the text was not completely excluded from all lists of Gregory's works. Explicit mention *is* made of Gregory's *Exposition* in early medieval texts such as *Epistle* 1 of the Irish abbot Columbanus (ca. 600), Gregory's own *Reg. ep.* 12.6 (January 602), and Ildefonsus of Toledo's *De virorum illustrium scriptis* 1 (ca. 650). (These three texts will be discussed in more detail below.) Furthermore, early medieval biographies mention other writings by Gregory not explicitly named but which could include the *Exposition*. For example, after listing the major works of Gregory, the *Liber pontificalis* says that he wrote "many others we cannot enumerate."[88] Isidore of Seville: "He wrote other books on morals."[89] Paul the Deacon:

---

87. For convenience, I refer to all the early accounts of Gregory's life and writings, both the chapters included in longer works and the biographies devoted exclusively to him, as the "early medieval biographies."

88. *LP* 66.

89. Isidore of Seville, *De viris illustribus* 40 [55] (PL 83:1103a): *et alios libros morales scripsisse.*

"Moreover he wrote several others, and also quite a number of letters."[90] Such notices *could* refer to Gregory's *Exposition*, though these passages are hardly sufficient evidence. At the least, they furnish evidence that other works of Gregory were known to exist.

The attribution of the *Exposition on the Song of Songs* to Gregory was disputed for another reason as well: it was transmitted in the manuscripts in a corrupt form. Scholars are now able to recognize that, in the centuries after the death of Gregory, his *Exposition* circulated in both genuine and corrupt forms. At the dawn of critical scholarship in the seventeenth century, some scholars rejected the Gregorian authorship of the *Exposition* because they knew the text only in its corrupt form. While others continued to argue for attribution to Gregory, the authorship of the text remained in doubt until the pioneering work of Dom Bernard Capelle in 1929, who definitively identified the primitive and genuine form of the exposition and distinguished it from its corrupt medieval form.[91]

Capelle determined that the genuine form of Gregory's *Exposition on the Song of Songs* comments only upon the first eight verses of the Song. In the late eleventh century or soon thereafter, this primitive "incomplete" exposition was "completed" by a commentary on the Song of Songs composed by Robert of Tombelaine, a commentary conspicuous for its brevity and conciseness.[92] In other words, Robert's commentary on Song 1:9f. was appended to Gregory's exposition on Song 1:1-8 to form a complete commentary on the entire biblical book. It was in this "mixed" or

---

90. Paul the Deacon, *VG* 14 (PL 75:48c): *Scripsit praeterea et alia nonnulla, sed et epistolas complures.*

91. Dom Bernard Capelle, "Les homélies de saint Grégoire sur le Cantique," *Revue Bénédictine* 41 (1929): 204–17. See also Rodrigue Bélanger, *Grégoire le Grand: commentaire sur le Cantique des cantiques*, SChr 314 (Paris: Cerf, 1984), 15–21.

92. Robert was born at Tombelaine, became a monk at Mont-Saint-Michel, and was made abbot of Saint-Vigor near Bayeux. He died before 1090. His commentary can be found in PL 150:1361–70.

"medieval" form that the text was first printed around 1473 in Cologne by Ulrich Zell (without any discussion of authenticity).[93]

In his edition of the mixed form of Gregory's exposition in 1675, Pierre de Goussainville was the first to raise the issue of the text's authenticity.[94] Goussainville was struck by the vast stylistic difference between the prolix commentary on Song 1:1-8 and the terse commentary on Song 1:9f. and accordingly rejected attribution to Gregory. Initially the Maurists accepted Goussainville's opinion,[95] but in their 1705 edition of the exposition in its mixed form they reaffirmed the Gregorian authorship.[96] The Maurists explained the stylistic divergence between the commentary on Song 1:1-8 and Song 1:9f as due to redactional activity: the prolix section on Song 1:1-8 bore the mark of revision by Gregory, while the remainder was the slipshod editorial work of one Claudius,

---

93. Patrick Verbraken, "La tradition manuscrite du commentaire de saint Grégoire sur le Cantique des cantiques," *Revue Bénédictine* 73 (1963): 277–88, at 285. This mixed text was printed again in 1496 at Bâle and in 1498–99 at Paris, also without discussion of authenticity.

94. Pierre de Goussainville, *Sancti Gregorii Papae Primi cognomenato Magni Opera in tres tomos distributa* (Lutetiae Parisiorum: Impensis Societatis Typographicae, 1675).

95. Dom Denys de Saint-Marthe, *Histoire de S. Grégoire le Grand, Pape et Docteur de l'Église* (Rouen: Behourt, 1697), 555–58.

96. *Sancti Gregorii Papae I cognomento Magni Opera omnia*, t. III (Paris, 1705), Part 2, cols. 397–414. This text was reprinted by Migne: PL 79:471–547, along with the Maurist preface at PL 79:467–71. One of their key arguments for the Gregorian authorship of the text was the discovery of an excerpt from the exposition in the florilegium of Gregorian texts compiled by Paterius, the notary of Gregory (see PL 79:1060b-d). But this argument was subsequently proven to be without merit when it was determined that the excerpt in question is found only in the medieval elaboration of the florilegium of Paterius. See André Wilmart, "Le recueil grégorien de Paterius et les fragments wisigothiques de Paris," *Revue Bénédictine* 39 (1927): 81–104, and Raymond Étaix, "Le Liber testimonium de Paterius," *Revue des Sciences Religieuses* 32 (1958): 66–78. Hence, the Maurist argument for attribution to Gregory rests solely on the widespread attribution to him in the mss. tradition.

whom we will meet again below.[97] In his 1722 edition of the commentary of Robert of Tombelaine, Casimir Oudin was the first to recognize that the commentary on Song 1:9f. in the mixed form of the Gregorian exposition was in fact Robert's.[98] Following a suggestion of Goussainville, he attributed the commentary on Song 1:1-8 to Richard of Saint Victor. No one seriously examined the question of authenticity after Oudin until Capelle in 1929.[99]

Capelle was able to recognize the authentic Gregorian exposition and distinguish it from its mixed corrupt form by examining the manuscript tradition. He identified four pertinent versions in the manuscripts.[100] The first version is the primitive Gregorian exposition on Song 1:1-8 preceded by a long prologue. There are manuscripts of this version dating from the ninth century, two centuries before Robert. The second version is the original commentary of Robert preceded by Jerome's prologue to his commentary on Ecclesiastes.[101] The third version is the mixed medieval form of the exposition discussed above: the primitive Gregorian commentary on Song 1:1-8 supplemented by Robert's commentary on Song 1:9f. The fourth is Robert's commentary preceded by a summary of the authentic Gregorian prologue.

The first and third versions transmit the authentic exposition of Gregory on the Song of Songs—the first in its primitive and independent "unmixed" form, the third is its corrupt medieval "mixed" form. Capelle corroborated his attribution of the primitive

---

97. PL 79:471.

98. Casimir Oudin, *Commentarius de Scriptoribus Ecclesiae Antiquis* (Frankfort and Leipzig, 1722), t. II, cols. 768–76.

99. In the early 1890s, J. Barthélemy Hauréau adopted the views of Oudin; see his *Notices et extraits de quelques manuscrits latins de la Bibliothèque Nationale* (Paris: Klincksieck, 1890–93), t.V, pp. 15–19.

100. See Capelle, "Les homélies," 207–10, with the elaborations and corrections of Verbraken, "La tradition manuscrite," 277–88; and Bélanger, *Gregoire le Grand*, 16–21.

101. The Hieronymian provenance of the prologue to Robert's commentary was first detected by P. A. Vaccari, "De scriptis S. Gregorii Magni in Canticum Canticorum," *Verbum Domini* 9 (1929): 306 n. 3.

exposition to Gregory based on external criteria with an internal critique. He adduced eleven examples in which the exegesis of particular verses of the Song had close parallels in the other works of the Gregorian corpus.[102] Claiming that such passages could easily be doubled, he deemed that the eleven citations he produced were sufficient for proving the Gregorian authorship of the exposition. No one has contested Capelle's view, and it is generally accepted by scholars.

2. The Date and Circumstances of Composition. The text of Gregory's *Exposition on the Song of Songs* itself offers no clue to the time and circumstances of its composition. Gregory's only reference to the exposition appears in a letter written to the subdeacon John, Gregory's *apocrisiarius* in Ravenna, in January 602:

> Furthermore, the same most dear Claudius, who was once my son, had heard me when I discoursed on Proverbs, the Song of Songs, the Prophets, and the books of the Kings as well as the Heptateuch. Since I was unable to put what I had said into writing due to sickness, he dictated it according to his own understanding lest it perish in oblivion. He did this planning to bring it to me when the time was right, so that it could be dictated more correctly. When it was read to me, I found that the sense of what I had said had been most unsuitably altered. This is why it is necessary for Your Experience to leave aside every excuse and delay, to go to his monastery, to convene the brothers, and, under the authority of All Truth, to have them produce whatever papers on the various Scriptures he brought there. Get these papers and send them to me as quickly as possible.[103]

---

102. Capelle, "Les homélies," 210–14.

103. *Reg. ep.* 12.6, 31–42 (CCSL 140A:975): *Praeterea quia isdem carissimus quondam filius meus Claudius aliqua me loquente de prouerbiis, de canticis canticorum, de prophetis, de libris quoque regum et de eptatico audierat, quae ego scripto tradere prae infirmitate non potui, ipse ea suo sensu dictauit, ne obliuione deperirent, ut apto tempore haec eadem mihi inferret et emendatius dictarentur. Quae cum mihi legisset, inueni dictorum meorum sensum ualde inutilius fuisse permutatum. Unde necesse est ut tua experientia, omni excusatione atque more cessante, ad eius monasterium accedat, conuenire fratres faciat*

Scholars have justifiably not hesitated to see Gregory's *Exposition on the Song of Songs* as ultimately rooted in these lectures on various books of the Old Testament. Yet this brief excerpt presents scholars with a host of interpretive issues that bear decisively upon our understanding of the nature and composition of Gregory's *Exposition*. Until quite recently, the interpretation of this excerpt had been seriously undermined due to the erroneous assumption that the extant *Commentary on the First Book of Kings* was genuinely Gregorian, an attribution definitively proved false only in 1996.[104] Along with Gregory's exposition on the Song of Songs, this commentary on 1 Kings was thought to be the only other discourse mentioned in this letter that was still extant.[105] Since the commentary on 1 Kings has long sections in which the author speaks as a monk to other monks, scholars who assumed the Gregorian authorship of the text drew two erroneous conclusions from the letter cited above. First, they dated the scriptural commentaries mentioned in the letter to the years 586–90, when Gregory was still a monk in the monastery of Saint Andrew, just before becoming bishop of Rome. The basis for this date was the assumption that it was in this period that Gregory most likely spoke as a monk to other monks. Second, they held the abbot Claudius mentioned in this letter to have been a member of Gregory's monastic community in this period, since Claudius had been present at Gregory's monastic discourses.[106]

---

et sub omni ueritate quantascumque de diuersis scripturis chartulas detulit, ad medium deducant, quas tu suscipe et mihi celerrime transmitte.

104. Vogüé, "L'auteur du Commentaire des Rois." The true author was Peter of Cava, a twelfth-century Italian abbot. In Vogüé's own six-volume edition and translation of this commentary, *Grégoire le Grand (Pierre de Cava): Commentaire sur les Premier Livre des Rois*, 6 vols., SChr 351, 391, 432, 449, 469, 482 (Paris: Cerf, 1989–2004), he recognizes the true author from vol. 3 onward.

105. Patrick Verbraken edited the text along with the *Exposition on the Song of Songs* in his *Sancti Gregorii Magni Expositiones in Canticum Canticorum, in Librum Primum Regum*, CCSL 144 (Turnhout: Brepols, 1963).

106. This opinion ultimately goes back to the Maurist edition of 1705 (repr. in PL 79:471–548; see their introduction at PL 79:467–71). It was followed by

Both of these conclusions are mistaken, as demonstrated independently by Paul Meyvaert and Adalbert de Vogüé.[107] By examining all the available evidence on Claudius from Gregory's letters, Meyvaert and Vogüé found no evidence that Claudius, who during Gregory's papacy was the abbot of the monastery of Saints John and Stephen in Classe in Ravenna, had ever been a monk with Gregory at Saint Andrew's.[108] Furthermore, Meyvaert determined that Claudius had spent an extended sojourn in Rome with Gregory from late 594 or early 595 to April 598.[109] Therefore, we can safely assume that Gregory's *Exposition on the Song of Songs* first saw the light of day as an oral discourse delivered in Rome in the years 594–98 during Gregory's pontificate, with Claudius

---

Dudden, *Gregory the Great*, 1.187–222; Pierre Batiffol, *Saint Grégoire le Grand*, 2nd ed. (Paris: J. Gabalda, 1928), 47–51; O. Porcel, *La doctrina monastica de San Gregorio Magno y la 'Regula Monachorum'* (Washington, DC: 1951), 36–57; Capelle, "Les homélies"; and Verbraken, *Sancti Gregorii Magni Expositiones*, vii.

107. Paul Meyvaert, "The Date of Gregory the Great's Commentaries on the Canticle of Canticles and on I Kings," *Sacris Erudiri* 23 (1978–79): 191–216; Adalbert de Vogüé, "Les vues of Grégoire le Grand sur la vie religieuse dans son commentaire des Rois," *Studia Monastica* 20 (1978): 17–63; English translation: "The Views of St Gregory the Great on the Religious Life in His Commentary on the Book of Kings," *Cistercian Studies Quarterly* 17 (1982): 40–64 and 212–32. Both Meyvaert and Vogüé assumed the Gregorian authorship of the commentary on 1 Kings, but their arguments against the older opinion of the date of the exposition on the Song is not otherwise affected by this.

108. Meyvaert, "The Date," 197–98; Vogüé, "The Views," 43–44.

109. Meyvaert, "The Date," 192–98; Vogüé, "The Views," 44–45, limits Claudius's visit to Rome to the years 597–98. We know for certain that Claudius stayed in Rome for an indeterminate yet extended period, leaving in April 598 (*Reg. ep.* 8.18). Vogüé assumes a visit of less than a year. Meyvaert's argument for a visit of around three years is based on his interpretation of Gregory's letter to Marinianus, Bishop of Ravenna, written in January 596 (*Reg. ep.* 6.24), which he sees as implying that Claudius was already in Rome appealing to the pope before the death of Bishop John of Ravenna, the successor of Marinianus with whom Claudius had jurisdictional problems, a length of time also implied by Gregory's letter to Marinianus in April 598 (see Meyvaert, "The Date," 193–94).

in attendance.[110] These discourses on the various books of the Old Testament were probably delivered to a small group of Gregory's intimates and visitors, both clerics and monks, a venue which Gregory found less demanding and exhausting than public sermons in church before large groups of people.[111]

Claudius's precise role in the composition of the *Exposition* in the form that we now possess it has been the subject of much scholarly debate. Besides the excerpt from *Reg. ep.* 12.6 cited above, there is one other bit of evidence that helps evaluate Claudius's role. In Gregory's letter to Marinianus of Ravenna in April 598 (*Reg. ep.* 8.18), which Claudius himself carried from Rome to Ravenna, the pope said that Claudius had been "a great help with the word of God" (*magnum . . . erat in verbo Dei solatium*). This is a typical Gregorian expression that denotes that Claudius assisted Gregory in his exegesis of the holy Scriptures.[112] In the excerpt of *Reg. ep.* 12.6 cited above, Gregory speaks more precisely on the nature of their exegetical collaboration.[113] In order to understand this passage, one must first differentiate between the two distinct methods of composition mentioned in it: *loquere* and *dictare*.

On the one hand, when Gregory says that he had discoursed (*aliqua me loquente*) on various books of the Old Testament, he

---

110. Bélanger, *Grégoire le Grand*, 27–28; and K. Suso Frank, *Origenes und Gregor der Grosse. Das Hohelied* (Einsiedeln: Johannes, 1987), 81, also accept this date. Meyvaert, "The Date," 198–202, advances the further argument that Gregory's inability to dictate due to the sickness best corresponds to what is known of the middle and later years of his pontificate.

111. See Meyvaert, "The Date," 201–7.

112. See Meyvaert, "The Date," 198; Vogüé, "The Views," 44–45. Here Vogüé also speculates, based on Gregory's earlier collaboration with the Deacon Peter in the *Dialogues*, on the nature and form of the exegetical collaboration between Gregory and Claudius. He suggests that Claudius "conversed with Gregory, in the presence of a few companions or even one to one, on scriptural texts whose meaning they sought to penetrate together. In these conversations Claudius played the role of the disciple who helps the master's developments by his intelligence, modesty, and receptivity" (45). But this remains conjecture.

113. Meyvaert, "The Date," 198.

meant that he had delivered an oral lecture which was recorded by a notary in shorthand with the intention of later transcribing it in longhand. The goal of *loquere* was the oral discourse; the written transcription of it was secondary. On the other hand, by *dictare* Gregory meant that he dictated to a scribe or notary with the specific intention of producing a written text. It was a question of composing a literary work rather than having his oral discourse simply recorded. In the composition of texts such as the *Moralia*, Gregory reworked and revised the notary's transcription of his original spoken discourse into a more literary composition.[114]

Meyvaert notes that "one may legitimately presume" that whenever Gregory discoursed on Scripture it was recorded by notaries,[115] so we may suppose that when Gregory discoursed on the Song of Songs and the other Old Testament books there was a notary present who recorded the proceedings. In *Reg. ep.* 12.6 Gregory says that when poor health prevented him from producing a written version of his discourse (*aliqua me loquente . . . de Canticis canticorum . . . quae ego scripto tradere prae infirmitate non potui*), Claudius "dictated it according to his own understanding lest it perish in oblivion" (*ipse ea suo sensu dictauit, ne obliuione deperirent*). Claudius did what Gregory's health prevented him from doing: he dictated a revised text from the notary's transcription to produce a literary composition.

Two issues raised by Gregory's description of Claudius's activity warrant comment. First, Gregory says that Claudius dictated "lest it perish in oblivion." Does this imply that there was a danger of losing Gregory's discourse altogether had not Claudius dictated? It seems that the notary's copy itself would have been sufficient to ensure the survival of the discourse. Rather, Gregory's expression "lest it perish in oblivion" appears to mean nothing more than "lest it be forgotten." In other words, it seems that Gregory and Claudius realized that unless the notary's transcription was reworked by

---

114. Meyvaert, "The Date," 207–8.
115. Meyvaert, "The Date," 209.

Claudius soon after the oral discourse, it would remain in that form, since Gregory at this stage of his life and papacy would never have the time or energy to take on the arduous task of recasting the recorded notation into a literary composition, as he had done earlier in his papacy for the *Moralia*. Hence, Claudius's dictation was a pragmatic action aimed at producing a literary composition based on an oral discourse deemed worthy of preservation. Second, Claudius dictated the written version "according to his own understanding" or, more literally, "with his own mind" (*suo sensu*). What this phrase seems to mean is that Claudius, in recasting the rough copy of the notary, filled out the text and turned it into prose, undoubtedly aiming to be faithful to the thought of Gregory, but inevitably importing a good bit of his own thought and concerns into it.

We also learn from *Reg. ep.* 12.6 that Claudius's dictation was done with the intention of bringing it to Gregory for final revisions, when Gregory himself would dictate the corrected version of Claudius's work (*ut apto tempore haec eadem mihi inferret et emendatius dictarentur*). But when Claudius's dictation was read to Gregory, he was very dissatisfied with the result, claiming that the sense of what he had said had been grossly misrepresented (*Quae cum mihi legisset, inueni dictorum meorum sensum ualde inutilius fuisse permutatum*). When did Claudius prepare his dictation and read it to Gregory? While Claudius may have begun to prepare his provisional edition of the exposition while still with Gregory in Rome in the years 594–98, it appears that at least some of his editorial activity was undertaken after his return to Ravenna in April 598. For in the same letter, written in January 602 after Claudius had died (probably in late 601), Gregory ordered the subdeacon John to retrieve Claudius's copies from his monastery in Classe (*Reg. ep.* 12.6), no doubt to prevent the dissemination of texts Gregory deemed unfaithful to his own ideas.[116] We also know that in July

---

116. Meyvaert, "The Date," 214–15; Vogüé, "The Views," 45; Bélanger, *Grégoire le Grand*, 28.

599 Gregory invited Claudius back to Rome for a stay of five or six months (*Reg. ep.* 9.179), though there is no evidence that Claudius did, in fact, return to Rome at this time. Meyvaert and Vogüé argue that Claudius did make such a visit in late 599 through early 600 and claim that during this period Claudius read his dictation to Gregory.[117] Accordingly, the most likely scenario is that Claudius began reworking the notary's transcriptions in Rome before 598, completed this work after returning to Ravenna in April 598, and in late 599 returned to Rome, where he read his dictation to Gregory, albeit to his dissatisfaction. Gregory never mentions whether he had the time to correct Claudius's edition before his own death in 604.

And so, this raises the vexed question: whose version is the text that has come down to us as Gregory's *Exposition on the Song of Songs*? Gregory's? Claudius's? The notary's? The fact that the *Exposition* was not included in the lists of Gregory's works drawn up soon after his death has led no scholar to claim that the version of it that we now possess corresponds to the correction made by Gregory after being dissatisfied with the work of Claudius.[118] On the evidence of *Reg. ep.* 12.6, most scholars have seen Claudius as responsible for the text as we possess it, being a reworked version of the notary's copy that preserved the undeniably "spoken-character" of the text.[119] But Meyvaert has argued most forcibly that the *Exposition* in the form that we know it is simply the unrevised notary's transcription.[120] Meyvaert's position seems the most persuasive.

---

117. Meyvaert, "The Date," 215; Vogüé, "The Views," 45–46; Bélanger, *Grégoire le Grand*, 28. Vogüé even speculates that Gregory, dissatisfied with Claudius's work, sent him back to Ravenna recommending that he not circulate the exposition.

118. Verbraken, *Sancti Gregorii Magni Expositiones*, vi.

119. This was the position first expressed in the Maurist Life of Gregory, published by Thomas Gals in 1698 (*Sancti Gregorii Papae I Vita* VI, 9; repr. PL 75:447–48) and was followed and developed by subsequent scholars such as Capelle, "Les homélies," and Verbraken, *Sancti Gregorii Magni Expositiones*, vii.

120. Meyvaert, "The Date," 212 and 215. Robert Markus, *Gregory the Great and His World*, 16 n. 72, appears to agree with Meyvaert.

Meyvaert bases his argument on the fact that the exposition bears all the marks of being a *spoken* discourse that was recorded by a notary.[121] For example, Gregory frequently uses expressions like "as we said earlier" (*sicut prius diximus*)[122] and engages his hearer (*auditor*),[123] not his reader. In addition, the frequent syncopated and poorly connected phrases and sentences reflect an oral style.[124] A line from the prologue provides another indication that his exposition was originally delivered orally and copied by a notary: "In this book here, in which the Song of Songs is written" (*in hoc libro, qui in Canticis canticorum conscriptus est*).[125] In using the demonstrative adjective *hoc* (*this book here*), Gregory may be pointing to the book in front of him and telling his audience which text has been copied into it. Therefore, as the text that has come down to us seems to be more or less a verbatim record of Gregory's oral discourse and seemingly untouched by an editorial hand, it seems that Meyvaert is correct in claiming that it corresponds to the notary's transcription.

Besides Meyvaert's arguments, the case for attributing the text as we possess it to Claudius is weak. Those who hold this opinion base their claim on two arguments: (1) that there are signs of the hand of Claudius in the text of the exposition, and (2) that the most primitive title given to the work in the manuscripts indicates that Claudius was the redactor.[126] Both of these arguments fail to convince upon further scrutiny.

It was Capelle who detected the hand of Claudius in the text we now possess. But he cites only a single instance: the exegesis of Song 1:6 in the *Exposition* diverges from Gregory's exegesis of the

---

121. For the evidence, see Meyvaert, "The Date," 212 n. 46 and 214 n. 48.

122. For example, *Exp.* 16.

123. For example, *Exp.* 43.

124. A point well made by Bélanger, *Grégoire le Grand*, 25; see, for example, *Exp.* 22–24 and 37.

125. *Exp.* 3.

126. These arguments were laid out by Capelle, "Les homélies," and have been followed by Bélanger, *Grégoire le Grand*; and Frank, *Origenes und Gregor der Grosse*, 81–82.

same verse elsewhere in his corpus. At *Exp.* 41, Gregory interprets the "at midday" of *where you lie down at midday* (Song 1:6) as a reference to the "fervor of charity" (*fervor charitatis*), whereas elsewhere he interprets it pejoratively, connecting it with the fervor of the passions (e.g., *H.Ev.* 33 [7], 189–206; *Mor.* 30.26 [79], 33–36).[127] Yet at *Exp.* 41 Gregory is simply following Augustine.[128] It seems more likely that Gregory would draw upon Augustine, one of his principle sources for interpreting the Song,[129] than that Claudius would insert a text that contradicted Gregory. Therefore, there is no evidence for "the hand of Claudius" in the exposition.

It was also Capelle who argued that the most primitive title given to the work in the oldest manuscripts comes from the hand of Claudius. According to Capelle, Claudius's authorship of the title proves that he is the redactor of the text as we have it. The most primitive title runs: *Expositio in canticis canticorum a capite de exceda relevata domni gregorii papae urbis romae.* Capelle clarified the meaning of the obscure phrase *expositio . . . a capite de exceda relevata*; it means that the exposition was retrieved or restored (*relevata*) from the notary's transcription (*exceda*).[130] Capelle claimed that this title

---

127. Capelle, "Les homélies," 216; followed by Patrick Verbraken, "Le commentaire de Saint Gregoire sur le Premier Livre des Rois," *Revue Bénédictine* 66 (1956): 159–217, at 213; see also Meyvaert, "The Date," 214 n. 48. Capelle also noted that the *Exposition* contained citations of the Song in the Vulgate form which varied from Gregory's Old Latin citations elsewhere, e.g., the exposition's Vulgate Song 1:7 (*Si ignoras te*) differs from the Old Latin version elsewhere cited by Gregory (*Nisi cognoveris te*). Capelle saw in this an indication of the hand of Claudius, but I prefer Bélanger's explanation of this, that Gregory simply used the scriptural version of his sources (*Grégoire le Grand*, 63).

128. Augustine, *Sermon* 295.5 (PL 38:1351): *Nam videte quid dicat sponsus dilectae suae in Cantico canticorum, quando ei dixit sponsa, «Annuntia mihi, quem dilexit anima mea, ubi pascis, ubi cubas in meridie; ne forte fiam sicut operta, super greges sodalium tuorum»* [Song 1:6]. *Annuntia, inquit, mihi, ubi pascis, ubi cubas in meridie, in splendore veritatis, in fervore charitatis.*

129. See below p. 87.

130. Capelle, "Les homélies," 214–15. Bélanger, *Grégoire le Grand*, 68 n. 2, also follows Capelle's interpretation.

went back to Claudius himself on three grounds: (1) it corresponds to what we know about Claudius's role in the composition of the text as described in *Reg. ep.* 12.6; (2) the omission of Claudius's name and mention of his role in the recasting of the notary's copy is best explained by attributing the title to Claudius, not to another editor who would have mentioned Claudius if he had known about him; and (3) the fact the Gregory is called "Lord Gregory" (*domni gregorii*) points to a date during the lifetime of the pope, who shortly after his death began to be called *sanctus* or *beatus*.[131] Bélanger follows Capelle's attribution of the title to Claudius and accepts it as a sign that the text of the exposition that has come down to us is Claudius's version.[132]

Here, the claims of Capelle are tenuous. It is not as necessary as Capelle suggests that the author of the title was Claudius. The title is receptive of alternate explanations. The attribution of the text to "Lord Gregory" does seem to suggest that the title was affixed during the lifetime of Gregory. But anyone with access to the papal archives during Gregory's lifetime or shortly thereafter could have come across the notary's copy of the exposition on the Song of Songs. Whether or not he knew Claudius's role as described in *Reg. ep.* 12.6, he could have made a clean longhand copy from the notary's transcription, affixed the primitive title to it, and circulated it. It does not logically follow from the omission of Claudius's name that he is the author of the title. The best explanation of the primitive title is that it is another indication that the text as we possess it is simply a longhand version of the notary's shorthand transcription.

By way of summary, I find Meyvaert's conclusions the most persuasive: the version of Gregory's *Exposition on the Song of Songs* that we now possess is the unrevised notary's transcription, not Claudius's revision. We do not possess the dictation of Claudius, which Gregory found so dissatisfactory. In fact, Gregory's ninth-

---

131. Capelle, "Les homélies," 215–16.
132. Bélanger, *Grégoire le Grand*, 26.

century biographer, John the Deacon, records an ancient tradition that Gregory had the work of Claudius burned lest it be disseminated.[133]

3. The Scope of the Exposition. The extant *Exposition* comments on only Song 1:1-8. This raises the question of its original scope. Did Gregory comment on the entire biblical book? If so, then we possess only the beginning of this commentary due to some accident in the manuscript tradition. Or did he comment on only the first eight verses? There are five pieces of evidence that collectively indicate that Gregory commented on the entire Song of Songs.

The first piece of evidence stems from a letter that the Irish abbot Columbanus (who was at the time residing in Gaul) wrote to Gregory in the year 600.[134] The pertinent section runs as follows:

> I read your book containing the Pastoral Rule, brief in style, prolix in learning, packed with holy mysteries. I confess that the work is sweeter than honey to one in need, and so, in my thirst, I pray you through Christ, bestow on me your works that, as I have heard, you wrote on Ezekiel with amazing talent. I read Jerome's six books on it, but he did not cover even half. But if you think me worthy, send me something from your readings in Rome; namely the final expositions of the book. Send too the Song of Songs, from where it says: *I shall go to the mountain of myrrh and hill of frankincense* [Song 4:6] until the end, briefly treated with others' comments, or yours, I ask. And to expound all the obscurity of Zechariah, make his secrets public, so that a Western blindness may thank you over this. My demands are unfit and I ask for too much, as anyone would

---

133. John the Deacon, *VG* 4.70 (PL 75:222–23).
134. Columbanus, *Ep.* 1; edition: G. S. M. Walker, ed., *Sancti Columbani Opera*, Scriptores Latini Hiberniae, v. 2 (Dublin: Dublin Institute for Advanced Studies, 1957), 2–12. For the date of this letter, see p. xxxvi. For a discussion of this letter, see John R. C. Martyn, "Pope Gregory the Great and the Irish," *Journal of Australian Early Medieval Association* 1 (2005): 65–83.

know. But you too have so much, as you well know less can be lent from a small sum, more from a big one.[135]

This citation is taken from near the conclusion of the letter. His thirst aroused from reading Gregory's book *Pastoral Care*, Columbanus requests Gregory's expositions on Ezekiel, the Song of Songs, and Zechariah. It seems that Columbanus has heard of Gregory's homilies on Ezekiel but has not read them. He does not explicitly say that he has heard that Gregory wrote an exposition on the Song of Songs. But the very fact that Columbanus is asking Gregory for comments on it suggests that he at least knows that Gregory had expounded on it.

It is significant that Columbanus asks only for an exposition of Song 4:6–8:14. It implies that he already has in his possession an exposition on Song 1:1–4:5. In all likelihood, the exposition on Song 1:1–4:5 that Columbanus already possessed was Gregory's.[136] This claim needs to be elaborated in some detail. The goal of Columbanus was to procure Gregory's own interpretations of the three biblical books mentioned. If the exposition on Song 1:1–4:5 was not Gregory's, why wouldn't he also ask him for his exposition on Song 1:1–4:5 in addition to that on Song 4:6–8:14? If the exposition on Song 1:1–4:5 was Gregory's, it makes sense for Columbanus to request of Gregory only an exposition on Song 4:6–8:14. Columbanus's appeal for the Song of Songs "briefly treated with others' comments, or yours" (*aut aliorum aut tuis brevibus . . . tracta sententiis*) means that he was inviting Gregory to compose or already knew that Gregory had composed a commentary on Song 4:6–8:14, either drawn from the commentaries of others or comprised of original interpretations. Columbanus was not asking for an exposition on Song 4:6–8:14 composed either by Gregory or by someone else; Columbanus wanted Gregory's own commentary.

---

135. *Ep.* 1 (Walker, 10, 11–23); trans. Martyn, "Pope Gregory the Great and the Irish," 82.
136. See Verbraken, "La tradition manuscrite," 279–80; and Bélanger, *Grégoire le Grand*, 21–22.

In fact, Gregory's *Exposition on the Song of Songs* is a mixture of both original interpretations and those drawn from other ecclesiastical fathers.[137] Columbanus did not need to ask the pope in order to obtain a non-Gregorian commentary on Song 4:6–8:14.

The letter of Columbanus to Gregory from 600 appears to indicate that Columbanus had in his possession a version of Gregory's exposition that ran through Song 4:5. Either Columbanus knew of a continuation of this work through Song 8:14 or he was inviting Gregory to complete it. How did this exposition come into the possession of Columbanus? Undoubtedly, he had obtained an unauthorized copy of the notary's transcription of Gregory's oral exposition on the Song when, after its delivery in the years 594–98, it was put in circulation without the pope's consent. In any event, Columbanus's letter indicates that Gregory's original exposition commented on more than Song 1:1-8, at least to Song 4:5, and quite possibly to the end (Song 8:14).

The second piece of evidence is the extant exposition's abrupt ending after the exegesis of Song 1:8. It is more likely that an authentic Gregorian exegesis on Song 1:9f. has been lost than that Gregory purposely concluded his exposition in such a brusque manner. Indeed, such a way of concluding would be uncharacteristic of Gregory, who in his other commentaries on Job and Ezekiel brought his interpretations to an end with protestations of his insufficiency, the wish only to benefit his readers, and suchlike.[138] Admittedly, conclusions such as these are found in works that were heavily revised by Gregory for dissemination after their initial oral presentation, whereas the exposition on the Song of Songs never achieved such a state. Nonetheless, it seems likely that even when delivering an exposition orally Gregory would have followed his usual practice of concluding his exegesis with some appropriate

---

137. See the discussion of sources below.
138. See *Mor.* 35.20 [49] (CCSL 143B:1810–11); and *H.Ez.* 2.10 [24] (CCSL 142:397).

comments as found in his revised works. The abrupt ending to the exposition appears to indicate that it was originally longer.

Another indication—the third—of the truncated nature of the extant exposition may be the addition of the words *libri duo* to the title in the most ancient manuscripts.[139] These words may signal that a complete exposition on the entire Song was originally distributed in two books. Such an interpretation of the words *libri duo* is supported by the letter of Columbanus, who noted that the commentary he had in his possession stopped at Song 4:5, roughly the middle of the biblical book. Columbanus may have possessed only the first book which commented on Song 1:1–4:5 and was therefore requesting the second book which dealt with Song 4:6–8:14. Further indication of an original distribution in two books is found in the usual manuscript division of the extant exposition on Song 1:1-8 into two *omeliae* or *sermones*, the second *omelia* beginning at Song 1:3.[140] Patrick Verbraken explains this curious division as the result of copyists or readers who, when confronted with the primitive title that included the words *libri duo*, split the extant exposition on Song 1:1-8 into two sections despite the fact that the two sections flow seamlessly together. Accordingly, the title that includes the words *libri duo* and the division of the text into two *omeliae* or *sermones* may indicate that our extant exposition on the Song of Songs originally covered the entire biblical book.

The fourth indication that Gregory commented on the entire biblical book is reflected in the most primitive title. As mentioned above, this title runs, *Expositio in canticis canticorum a capite de exceda relevata domni gregorii papae urbis romae*. The relevant words here are *a capite*, and it is unclear whether they are to be construed with *expositio in canticis canticorum* (i.e., "the exposition on the Song of Songs from the beginning, restored from the notary's transcrip-

---

139. For this argument, see Verbraken, "La tradition manuscrite," 280–81; and Verbraken, *Sancti Gregorii Magni Expositiones*, viii, and the critical apparatus on p. 3. Note that Verbraken excises these words from his critical text.

140. See the critical apparatus on pp. 3 and 27.

tion") or with *de exceda relevata* (i.e., "the exposition on the Song of Songs restored from the beginning of the notary's transcription"). Capelle, Verbraken, and Denys Turner prefer the latter construal, though Verbraken considers the expression "quelque peu énigmatique."[141] But as Verbraken notes, why would a scribe draw attention to the obvious fact that the exposition of the Song begins at the beginning of the Song? Rather, it seems more likely that the words *a capite* were inserted to signal to the reader that exposition was "restored from the beginning of the notary's transcription." If what we have is the "beginning" of the notary's transcription, there must have been another part that constituted its "ending," or at least its continuation. If this interpretation is correct, then the words *a capite* are another indication that the original exposition of Gregory on the Song of Songs commented on more than Song 1:1-8, since it would seem that the extant exposition constitutes only the "beginning" of a longer transcription.

The fifth—and clearest—indication that Gregory's original exposition on the Song of Songs ran through the entire biblical book is found in the *De virorum illustrium scriptis* of Ildefonsus of Toledo (ca. 607–67).[142] In the first chapter, which is on Gregory, he says, "How wonderfully he wrote upon the book of Solomon, whose title is the Song of Songs, running through the entire work by an exposition on its moral sense."[143] The description of Ildefonsus, that the commentary was "an exposition on its moral sense" (*morali sensu . . . exponendo*), corresponds exactly to the extant Gregorian exposition and furthermore indicates that Ildefonsus likely possessed and had read a copy of it. If this is correct, the fact

---

141. Capelle, "Les homélies," 215; Verbraken, "La tradition manuscrite," 279; and Denys Turner, *Eros and Allegory: Medieval Exegesis of the Song of Songs*, CS156 (Kalamazoo, MI: Cistercian, 1995), 248 n. 2.

142. See Verbraken, "La tradition manuscrite," 280; and Bélanger, *Grégoire le Grand*, 22.

143. *De virorum illustrium scriptis* 1 (PL 96:198d–99a): *Super librum Salomonis, cui titulus est Canticum canticorum, quam mire scribens morali sensu opus omne exponendo percurrit.*

that the bishop of Toledo attests that Gregory commented on the Song in its entirety (*opus omne . . . percurrit*) is one of the strongest pieces of evidence that the original Gregorian exposition commented on more than Song 1:1-8 and in fact the entire biblical book.[144]

Collectively these five pieces of evidence appear to indicate that the extant Gregorian *Exposition on the Song of Songs* is, in fact, a truncated version of an originally more extensive commentary that probably interpreted the entirety of the biblical book. One can therefore legitimately conjecture that the loss of bulk of the exposition from Song 1:9 onward was due to some irregularity or accident in the manuscript tradition.[145] While one may lament this loss, it is equally appropriate to marvel that this unrevised notary's transcription survived at all.

B. THE EXCERPTERS OF GREGORY

In addition to the *Exposition*, Gregory commented on the Song of Songs elsewhere in his literary corpus. We possess three medieval collections of his comments on the Song drawn from his other

---

144. Though Ildephonsus lived in Spain and wrote within sixty years of Gregory's death, he was in a good position to know the corpus of Gregory. See Markus, *Gregory the Great*, 164–68, for Gregory's relationship with the Spanish church. This relationship was fostered through Leander, bishop of Seville from 579 to 601, whom Gregory had befriended when both were residents of Constantinople in the early 580s. At the request of Leander, Gregory revised his lectures on Job and dedicated and sent the finished composition, the *Moralia*, to him. Leander was succeeded as bishop of Seville by his brother, Isidore, who served from 601 to 636. In his *De viris illustribus* 40, on Gregory, Isidore proves that the *Regula pastoralis*, the *Moralia*, and *Homilies on the Gospels* were known in Spain during his lifetime (PL 83:1102). The *De virorum illustrium scriptis* of Ildephonsus was a conscious continuation of his contemporary Isidore's similar work. He explicitly alludes to the Gregorian works mentioned by Isidore and lists several other works that were known in Spain at the time: the *Homilies on Ezekiel*, the *Exposition on the Song of Songs*, the *Dialogues*, and the *Register of Letters* (PL 96:198–99).

145. Verbraken, "La tradition manuscrite," 280; and Bélanger, *Grégoire le Grand*, 22.

works. The massive literary output of Gregory—his *Moralia in Job* alone runs to 1,880 pages in the modern critical edition—and its unsystematic nature resulted in its excerption. This was a fairly common scholarly practice from antiquity through the Middle Ages. Such collections of excerpts were organized either by theme or by scriptural book. Scholars would comb through the entire corpus of a particular writer, say Augustine or Ambrose or Gregory, and excerpt every passage that commented on the chosen theme or scriptural book. For example, a scholar could collect passages on love or on the book of Romans. Clerical and monastic readers who did not have time or the willpower to read the entire corpus of important authors like Augustine, Ambrose, and Gregory could then become familiar with their ideas in a far more efficient and systematic way. It is thought that many writers of the Middle Ages, both in monasteries and in the emerging universities, gained their basic understanding of the fathers through such collections of excerpts.[146]

Some authors relied heavily but not exclusively on Gregory's writings for their collections, such as Isidore (d. 636) in his *Sententiae* and the late seventh-century Defensor of Ligugé in his *Liber scintillarum*. But there are several late antique and medieval scholars who produced collections of excerpts exclusively from the works of Gregory. For example, Taio of Saragossa went to Rome in 642 to consult the best copies of Gregory's works in the papal archives for his *Liber sententiarum*. Taio systematizes Gregory's thought in five books: he begins with the Trinity, then proceeds with the foundation of the world and the creation of humanity; he next deals with the incarnation of Christ and all aspects of the Christian life, and then concludes with Gregory's teaching on the

---

146. One could think of these collections of excerpts as the precursors of today's textbooks on the thought of particular ancient Christian writers, which present their doctrine in a systematic way and are essential for introducing these figures to a new audience. The most famous versions of such collections were Peter Abelard's *Sic et non* and Peter Lombard's *Libri quatuor sententiarum*.

consummation of the world. Each of the five books has numerous chapters, each of which is devoted to a particular subtheme.[147]

Paterius, Bede, and William of Saint Thierry compiled excerpts of Gregory's exegesis of the Song of Songs not found in the *Exposition*. Susanne Müller has identified ninety-two places in the corpus of Gregory where he cites and comments on verses of the Song of Songs outside of the *Exposition*.[148] This number, however, needs to be adjusted. Five are from the spurious *Commentary on First Book of Kings*. Two are counted twice.[149] In addition, Müller has overlooked four passages.[150] Therefore, there are eighty-nine Gregorian passages that deal with verses from the Song of Songs. Knowing the number of possible texts that could have been excerpted will allow one to judge the comprehensiveness of the work of Paterius, Bede, and William. Appendix 1 contains a list of all the Gregorian citations of and allusions to the Song of Songs outside of the *Exposition* and provides references to the location of the passage within the florilegia of Paterius, Bede, and William. Appendix 2 lists the precise texts of Gregory excerpted by Paterius, Bede, and William and shows the correspondences among them.

1. *Paterius's* Book of Testimonies. Paterius was a notary (*notarius*) of the Roman Church during the pontificate of Gregory. In this era, while notaries on the papal staff took down the pope's dictation, they also played a more elevated role as administrative officials of the papal secretariat.[151] Paterius was a cleric, presumably in minor

---

147. PL 80:727–990. Taio notes that he supplemented Gregory with Augustine when he could not find Gregorian passages on the subject at hand (praef. 4 [PL 80:729b]).

148. Susanne Müller, *"Fervorem discamus amoris": das Hohelied und seine Auslegung bei Gregor dem Grossen* (Saint Ottilien: EOS Verlag, 1991), 49–229.

149. *Mor.* 27.2 and *H.Ev.* 25 are listed for both Song 3:1-2 and 3:3-4. Gregory's comments on Song 3:1-4 should be considered together.

150. *Reg. ep.* 7.23 on Song 1:3; *H.Ev.* 33 [7] on Song 2:9a; *Mor.* 27.2 on Song 5:7; and *Reg. past.* 1.11 on Song 7:4.

151. See Markus, *Gregory the Great*, 112–22. See *Reg. ep.* 5.26; 6.12; and 9.98 for instances of Gregory dictating to Paterius.

orders since he is never called deacon, and was part of Gregory's inner circle of intimates and confidants.[152] Paterius served Gregory as a notary at least from February 595 and quite possibly from the beginning of his papacy.[153] At some point after September 595, Paterius was appointed *secundicerius notarius*, or deputy to the head of the papal secretariat, and presumably served in that capacity for the remainder of Gregory's pontificate.[154]

Of Paterius, John the Deacon says, "Paterius the notary, whom Gregory appointed *secundicerius*, plucked the most beneficial passages from his books."[155] Here John is referring to Paterius's *Book of Testimonies (Liber testimonium)*, a collection of Gregory's interpretations of particular passages of Scripture excerpted from his writings, especially the *Moralia*, and arranged according to their biblical sequence. Paterius undertook this task during the lifetime of Gregory[156] and aimed to produce from the writings of Gregory a kind of running commentary on Scripture. Originally consisting of three parts (two for the Old Testament and one for the New Testament), all that survives is the first part, from Genesis to the Song of Songs.[157] The first part consists of thirteen books, the final of which

---

152. John the Deacon, *VG* 2.11. On Gregory's intimates, see Richards, *Consul of God*, 70–84.

153. The earliest reference to Paterius in Gregory's letters is in *Reg. ep.* 5.26 (February 595). He is mentioned in three others: 6.12 (September 595); 9.98 (January 599); and 11.15 (5 October 600).

154. Paterius is named as *secundicerius* in *Reg. ep.* 9.98 and 11.15; see also John the Deacon, *VG* 2.11.

155. John the Deacon, *VG* 2.11 (PL 75:92a): *Paterium aeque notarium, qui ab eo secundicerius factus, ex libris ipsius aliqua utillima defloravit.*

156. Paterius, *Liber testimonium*, prooem. (PL 79:683–86). The undertaking of the compilation during the lifetime of Gregory is further supported by the fact that Paterius preserved numerous extracts from earlier editions of *Mor.* and *H. Ez.* that were not incorporated into the final editions (Étaix, "Le *Liber testimonium* de Paterius," 78).

157. PL 79:683–916. The two following parts printed in Migne (PL 79:917–1136) are not the work of Paterius but of an anonymous twelfth-century compiler. Neither is the preface to the three parts (PL 79:681–84) Paterius's but rather that of someone named Bruno.

is that on the Song of Songs, translated in this volume.[158] Paterius excerpted forty-four out of eighty-nine possible Gregorian passages on the Song of Songs.

2. *Bede's* Commentary on the Song of Songs. Bede (ca. 635–735) was a monk—from the age of seven!—at the dual monasteries of Wearmouth and Jarrow in northeastern England and is considered the greatest scholar of Anglo-Saxon England.[159] One of the best-educated men in Europe in his generation, he wrote works on orthography, poetic meter, natural phenomena, a chronology of the history of the world, and a book on the calculation of the date of Easter. Bede also composed hagiography, most notably his two lives of Saint Cuthbert, one in verse and another in prose. He is also the author of the *Ecclesiastical History of the English Nation*, the chief source for studying the English Church in the Anglo-Saxon period. Because of this book Bede is best known today as a historian. But in his lifetime and throughout the Middle Ages he was best known as an exegete of Scripture. He commented on many books of the Old and New Testaments, including the Song of Songs. His exegesis relies heavily on the earlier Latin tradition, particularly Augustine, Jerome, Ambrose, and Gregory the Great. While he produced original work, some of Bede's commentaries were, in fact, simply collections of excerpts from one particular author, such as Augustine.[160]

Bede's *Commentary on the Song of Songs* consists of six books.[161] The first five contain his running commentary on the entire text

---

158. The thirteen books cover Genesis, Exodus, Leviticus, Numbers, Deuteronomy, Judges, 1 and 2 Samuel, 1 and 2 Kings, Psalms, Proverbs, and the Song of Songs.

159. For a good overview of Bede's life and writings, see Benedicta Ward, *The Venerable Bede*, CS 169 (Kalamazoo, MI: Cistercian, 1998).

160. For example, David Hurst, trans. *Bede the Venerable: Excerpts from the Works of Saint Augustine on the Letters of the Blessed Apostle Paul*, CS 183 (Kalamazoo, MI: Cistercian, 1999).

161. While Bede considered his *Commentary on the Song of Songs* to consist of seven books, the editors of the modern critical edition of the text have organized it into six books preceded by a long introduction, despite the fact that Bede

of the Song. The sixth is a kind of appendix in which he collected excerpts on the Song gathered from the works of Gregory. As we learn from the preface to the sixth book, Bede seems to have done this in case readers were dissatisfied with his own commentary: "We have composed a sixth[162] book on the Song of Songs. It is a collection of texts made through our very own efforts, but one which brings together the words and thought of Blessed Gregory. So if there should perhaps be anyone who judges that there is good reason to scorn our work, he may have ready access to those statements of Gregory that ought to be read, which all agree are not to be scorned in any way."[163] The reverence that the English Church had for Gregory is apparent here.

Later in the preface Bede also reveals that, while he has heard of the existence of Paterius's collection, it was not available to him.[164] His work of collation is therefore his own. Bede excerpted fifty out of eighty-nine possible Gregorian passages on the Song of Songs. Therefore, Bede was slightly more thorough than Paterius. Bede and Paterius have thirty-seven excerpts in common: he missed seven of the passages excerpted by Paterius[165] and located an additional thirteen Gregorian passages that have no parallel in Paterius.[166] In thirteen of the thirty-seven passages cited in common, Bede cites the exact same text as Paterius.[167] Otherwise, Bede generally cites a bit more than Paterius. As a result, Bede's florilegium gives the reader a better impression and understanding of Gregory's exegesis of the Song of Songs than Paterius's.

---

himself considered the introduction to be the first book. While this move on the part of the editors seems dubious, I adopt their division of the work to facilitate easy reference to their edition.

162. The text here actually reads "seventh." See the preceding note.
163. *Cant.* 6, 10–14 (CCSL 119B:359).
164. *Cant.* 6, 17–21 (CCSL 119B:359).
165. P1.2; P18; P20; P21; P31; P34B; and P39.
166. B1; B3; B5; B16; B20; B21; B24; B26; B29; B33; B34; B38; and B47.
167. P2, B4; P5, B7; P6, B8; P24, B24; P28, B31; B37, P34; P36, B40; P38, B42; P43, B46; P44, B48; P45, B49; P46, B50; and P49, B53.

3. William of Saint Thierry's Excerpts from the Books of Blessed Gregory on the Song of Songs. William of Saint Thierry (ca. 1075/80–1148) is considered, along with Bernard of Clairvaux, Guerric of Igny, and Ælred of Rievaulx, one of the four evangelists of Cîteaux.[168] He belongs to that second generation of Cistercian Fathers (the first being the three founders of the New Monastery at Cîteaux: Saints Robert, Alberic, and Stephen Harding) whose writings contributed to the flourishing of Cistercian spirituality and the rapid spread of the Order. William became a Cistercian only in 1135 after a long career as a Benedictine. Around 1100 he entered the Benedictine monastery of Saint Nicasius after being educated in the liberal arts at Reims. Around 1121 he was elected the abbot of the monastery of Saint Thierry. In 1135 he resigned his abbacy and joined the new Cistercian foundation at Signy. Perhaps his best-known writing from his Cistercian period is his Golden Letter, the *Epistle to the Brethren of Mont-Dieu*, a compendium of ascetical and contemplative doctrine. William remained a simple monk at Signy until his death in 1148.[169]

William viewed the Song of Songs as a kind of textbook of the contemplative experience of God and had a passionate interest in it. Whatever his original interest in the Song of Songs may have been, it deepened through his friendship with Bernard of Clairvaux. The two met in 1118, when William visited Clairvaux.[170] William

---

168. This designation appears to have been popularized by Dom Anselme Le Bail (1878–1956), a Cistercian monk of Scourmont Abbey in Belgium who is largely responsible for renewed interest in the Cistercian Fathers in the twentieth century; see Louis Bouyer, *The Cistercian Heritage* (Westminster, MD: Newman Press, 1958), 13.

169. Though dated, Jean Marie Déchanet, *William of Saint Thierry: The Man and his Work*, CS 10 (Kalamazoo, MI: Cistercian, 1972), remains a basic introduction to William's life and thought. Déchanet overstates William's reliance on the Greek fathers. For a more recent introduction to William's thought, see David N. Bell, *Image and Likeness: The Augustinian Spirituality of William of Saint Thierry*, CS 78 (Kalamazoo, MI: Cistercian, 1984). Also recommended as an overview: M. Basil Pennington, *The Last of the Fathers*, Studies in Monasticism 1 (Still River, MA: Saint Bede's Publications, 1983), 109–80.

170. William, *Vita Bernardi* 1.7, 32–34 (PL 185:246b–47d).

made subsequent visits to Clairvaux. On one such visit, when both William and Bernard were convalescing in the infirmary, they spoke about the Song of Songs. William recalls:

> It was then, so far as the length of my illness allowed, that he expounded the Song of Songs to me; though only in its moral sense, without launching upon the mysteries with which the book abounds. This was what I hoped for, what I had asked him to do. Every day, for fear of forgetting the things I had heard, I put them down insofar as God enabled me to and my memory served me. Thus I shared the insights of the man of God. As good-natured and disinterested as you please, he disclosed his ideas to me as they came to mind and the meanings that his experience enabled him to make out. He outdid himself enlightening my utter ignorance of things that can only be known from personal experience. I could not as yet grasp all that he told me; but listening to him I realized as never before how far above me those lofty truths still soared.[171]

The notes that William made of these conversations have been preserved as the so-called *Brief Commentary* (*Brevis commentatio*).[172] During his abbacy (1121–35), William composed two florilegia of patristic interpretations of the Song, one drawn from the works of Ambrose of Milan[173] and the other from the works of Gregory the Great.[174] Finally, he wrote the *Exposition on the Song of Songs* in his early days as Cistercian monk at Signy, in the years 1135 to 1138.[175]

---

171. William, *Vita Bernardi* 1.12, 59 (PL 185:259bc); trans. Déchanet, *William of Saint Thierry*, 26–27.

172. Paul Verdeyen, Stanislaw Ceglar, and Antonius van Burink, *Guillelmi a Sancto Theodorico Expositio super Cantica canticorum, Brevis commentatio, Excerpta de libris beati Ambrosii et Gregorii super Cantica canticorum*, CCCM 87 (Turnhout: Brepols, 1997), 155–96.

173. Verdeyen et al., *Guillelmi a Sancto Theodorico*, 207–384.

174. Verdeyen et al., *Guillelmi a Sancto Theodorico*, 387–444.

175. Verdeyen et al., *Guillelmi a Sancto Theodorico*, 19–133.

In his preface to the *Golden Letter*, in the course of enumerating the books he has written and compiled, William of Saint Thierry describes his two florilegia on the Song of Songs in this way: "I have excerpted from the books of Saint Ambrose whatever he discussed in them about the Song of Songs. It is a work that is large and remarkable. I did the same from the books of the Blessed Gregory, but more extensively than Bede did. For Bede, as you know, made these excerpts into the final book of his commentary on the Song."[176] From this we know that William used the extracts made by Bede but did not limit himself to Bede's collection. Of the eighty-nine possible texts that William could have cited, he found eighty of them. He cited every text that both Paterius and Bede excerpted, thereby adding thirty texts to Bede's florilegium. William appears to have verified the Gregorian provenance of Bede's excerpts, and demonstrable traces of Bede's work are discernable in William's collection.[177] He is thus the most diligent, thorough, and accurate of the three Gregorian excerpters, his use of Bede notwithstanding. The nine Gregorian passages on the Song of Songs that William missed are translated in this volume as "supplemental texts."

In composing his *Excerpts from the Books of Blessed Gregory on the Song of Songs*, William of Saint Thierry adopted a unique methodology whereby he produced self-contained units of Gregorian commentary.[178] Unlike Paterius and Bede, who cited blocks of texts and arranged them in sequence, William interweaves all the available Gregorian passages on a particular Song verse (or at least all

---

176. William, *Epistula ad fratres de monte Dei*, praef., 11 (SChr 223:138 Déchanet): *Excerpsi enim ex libris sancti Ambrosii quicquid in eis disseruit super Cantica canticorum, opus grande et inclytum; similiter et ex beati Gregorii, sed diffusius quam Beda fecerit. Nam idem Beda, ut nostis, ultimum in Canticis suis librum hanc ipsam exceptionem constituit.*

177. Mark DelCogliano, "The Composition of William of Saint Thierry's *Excerpts from the Books of Blessed Gregory on the Song of Songs*," *Cîteaux: Commentarii cistercienses* 58 (2007): 62–64.

178. For a detailed discussion of William's methodology, see DelCogliano, "The Composition of William of Saint Thierry's *Excerpts*," 64–76.

those he could find) to produce a single self-contained unit of Gregorian commentary, resulting in a composition that is a kind of running commentary on the Song. This is not to say that William has not altered or added to Gregory's original text. He has, but the goal of such changes in general appears to have been the clarification of texts torn from their original context and mixed together with other texts on the same Song verse. His alterations and additions indicate a concerted effort to make decontextualized and rearranged Gregorian passages as clear as possible. William chose this method of producing his florilegium probably in order to make it something more than a kind of reference work of Gregory's exegesis of the Song of Songs, as Paterius and Bede had done. Rather, William composed a thoroughly Gregorian commentary on the Song of Songs using Gregory's own words.

Despite the rearrangement of the original Gregorian texts and the minor alterations to them, the *thought* of Gregory has been preserved. The changes are merely *structural*. No ideas foreign to Gregory are imported on the part of William. The document William composed is thus a reliable presentation of Gregory's exegesis of the Song of Songs, and it can be read on its own since there is a single unit of commentary for each verse of the Song. William of Saint Thierry's *Excerpts from the Books of Blessed Gregory on the Song of Songs* is a stand-alone work produced by his meticulous attention to detail and editorial genius, perhaps to fulfill his desire to hold in his hands a genuine Gregorian commentary devoted to the Song of Songs.[179]

III. GREGORY'S EXEGESIS OF THE SONG OF SONGS

A. GREGORY IN THE HISTORY OF INTERPRETATION

There is a vast difference between Gregory's exegesis of the Song of Songs and modern scholarly interpretations. Gregory stands in a

---

[179] William seems to have been ignorant of the extant fragment of Gregory's own commentary on the Song of Songs.

long tradition of Christian allegorical interpretation of the Song of Songs that emerged in the third century, flourished for well over one thousand years thereafter, began to wane only in the early modern period, but still has a small number of adherents today.[180] For now, we may provisionally define allegorical exegesis as an interpretation of a text that privileges its deeper, spiritual meaning rather than its more obvious, literal meaning. Gregory is one of the major contributors to the tradition of allegorical exegesis of the Song of Songs and, more important, one of the key innovators within it. This tradition may have its origins in early Rabbinic allegorical interpretations of the Song.[181] Yet it received its decisive impetus from Origen's pioneering work. Though the relationship between the man and the woman is never defined in the text of the Song itself, Origen was the first to identify the Song as an *epithalamium*, or wedding song, that consisted of dramatic dialogue between a bride and bridegroom, with occasional lines by minor characters. He developed a twofold figurative interpretation of the Song wherein the bride and bridegroom were variously understood either as the Church and Christ

---

180. The following survey of the history of interpretation is highly selective. For more comprehensive surveys, see Friedrich Ohly, *Hohelied-Studien: Grundzüge einer Geschichte der Hoheliedauslegung des Abendlandes bis um 1200* (Wiesbaden: Franz Steiner, 1958); Marvin H. Pope, *Song of Songs* (Garden City, NY: Doubleday, 1977), 89–229; Roland E. Murphy, *The Song of Songs* (Minneapolis, MN: Fortress Press, 1990), 11–41; and Duane Garrett, *Song of Songs* (Nashville, TN: Thomas Nelson Publishers, 2004), 59–91. See also the classic essay of H. H. Rowley, "Interpretation of the Song of Songs," in his *The Servant of the Lord and Other Essays on the Old Testament*, rev. ed. (Oxford: Basil Blackwell, 1965), 197–245.

181. The influence of early Rabbinic allegorical exegesis of the Song on early Christian exegesis is more often assumed than proven. There is evidence for first-century Rabbinic dispute over the canonicity of the Song, but clear evidence for its allegorical interpretation emerges only in the seventh and eighth centuries, even if it developed earlier. See Roland E. Murphy, "Patristic and Medieval Exegesis— Help or Hindrance?" *Catholic Biblical Quarterly* 43 (1981): 505–16, at 506; and Garrett, *Song of Songs*, 60. For a discussion of Rabbinic exegesis of the Song, see Daniel Boyarin, "The Song of Songs: Lock or Key? Intertextuality, Allegory, and Midrash," in *The Book and the Text: Bible and Literary Theory*, ed. Regina M. Schwartz, 214–30 (Cambridge, MA: Basil Blackwell, 1990).

or the individual soul and the Word of God. Most commentators subsequent to Origen employ elements of both the ecclesiastical and individual-soul interpretations. Gregory knew and used Origen's writings on the Song of Songs in Latin translation, and the influence of the Alexandrian's exegesis upon Gregory is pervasive.

The allegorical interpretation of the Song of Songs flourished in the centuries after Gregory. New allegorical approaches were developed as well, such as the interpretation of the woman in the Song as the Virgin Mary (the Mariological interpretation). It could be argued that this ancient tradition of exegesis reached its apex in the Cistercian homilies on the Song of Songs in the twelfth and early thirteenth centuries.[182] The greatest of these are the eighty-six homilies by Saint Bernard of Clairvaux, who in his exegetical exuberance managed to discuss the Song only through verse 3:1.[183] The popularity of Bernard's homilies can be seen in the efforts to continue his work after his death in 1153. The English Cistercian abbot Gilbert of Hoyland wrote forty-eight sermons covering Song 3:1–5:10 before his own death in 1172.[184] John of Ford, also an English Cistercian abbot, composed 120 sermons covering the remainder of the book before his own death in 1214.[185] Nor ought we omit William of Saint Thierry, whose exegetical works on the Song were discussed above.[186] For the most part, Cistercian exegesis of the Song explores the love between God and the individual soul as the Christian advances toward mystical union. Indeed, Bernard's sermons on the Song of Songs "are widely recognized to be at once the crowning achievement of the approach to the Song

---

182. On Cistercian exegesis of the Song of Songs, see Ohly, *Hohelied-Studien*, 135–205; Matter, *Voice of my Beloved*, 123–33.

183. Killian Walsh and Irene Edmonds, trans., *Bernard of Clairvaux: Sermons on the Song of Songs*, 4 vols., CF 4, 7, 31, and 40 (Spencer, MA: Cistercian, 1971–80).

184. Lawrence C. Braceland, trans., *Gilbert of Hoyland: Sermons on the Song of Songs*, 3 vols., CF 14, 20, and 26 (Kalamazoo, MI: Cistercian, 1978–79).

185. Wendy Mary Beckett, trans., *John of Ford: Sermons on the Song of Songs*, 7 vols., CF 29, 39, 43, 44, 45, 46, and 47 (Kalamazoo, MI: Cistercian, 1978–84).

186. See p. 55.

initiated by Origen and the superlative contribution of monastic theology to Christian spirituality."[187]

In the early modern period, Reformation theologians initiated new approaches to the Song of Songs. For example, Martin Luther interpreted the Song of Songs as a political allegory.[188] The ancient tradition of allegorically interpreting the Song began to decline in the Enlightenment era with the rise of rational criticism. Nascent critical scholarship in the late eighteenth and early nineteenth centuries began to make the Song of Songs the subject of literary and historical-critical analysis, uninterested in its religious or theological significance. Nonetheless, allegorical interpretations of the Song of Songs continued to be produced by Catholic and Protestant exegetes alike from the sixteenth century (perhaps most notably Saint John of the Cross) through the middle of the twentieth century, when the modern critical approaches came to dominate.[189] Even though today allegorical interpretations have been mostly abandoned, there have been recent critical attempts to retrieve the Song's spiritual meaning and even interpret it as a celebration of God's love for humanity.[190]

---

187. Murphy, *The Song of Songs*, 25.
188. E. Kallas, "Martin Luther as Expositor of the Song of Songs," *Lutheran Quarterly* 2 (1988): 323–41.
189. A few twentieth-century Catholic scholars have produced allegorical interpretations, such as: Paschal P. Parente, "The Canticle of Canticles in Mystical Theology," *Catholic Biblical Quarterly* 6 (1944): 142–58; and Alfonso de Rivera, "Sentido mariológico del Cantar de los Cantares" *Ephemerides mariológicas* 1 (1951): 437–68 and 2 (1952): 25–42. For a critique of Rivera, see Roland E. Murphy, "The Canticle of Canticles and the Virgin Mary," *Carmelus* 1 (1954): 18–28; and Pope, *Song of Songs*, 188–92. There is also a French Catholic school of "midrashic" allegorical interpretation; see the following: André Robert and Raymond J. Tournay, with André Feuillet, *Le Cantique des Cantiques: Traduction et commentaire* (Paris: J. Gabalda, 1963); Raymond J. Tournay, *Word of God, Song of Love: A Commentary on the Song of Songs* (New York: Paulist, 1988); and André Feuillet, *Comment lire le Cantique des Cantiques: Étude de théologie biblique et réflexions sur une méthode d'exégèse* (Paris: Téqui, 1999).
190. André LaCocque, *Romance She Wrote: A Hermeneutical Essay on Song of Songs* (Harrisburg, PA: Trinity International Press, 1998); Corey Ellen Walsh, *Exquisite Desire: Religion, the Erotic and the Song of Songs* (Minneapolis, MN: Fortress Press,

In contrast to Gregory and the wider tradition of the Song's allegorical interpretation, modern exegetes of the Song of Songs generally consider it a poem that celebrates human love—and only human love. The opening line of J. Cheryl Exum's 2005 commentary on the biblical book expresses this attitude well. "The Song of Songs," she writes, "is a long lyric poem about erotic love and sexual desire—a poem in which the body is both object of desire and source of delight, and lovers engage in a continual game of seeking and finding in anticipation, enjoyment, and assurance of sensual gratification."[191] Most modern commentary on the Song of Song adopts this approach. As a result, the focus of such exegetes is more on the literary aspects of the biblical text than its theological or religious meaning.[192] In the late nineteenth and early twentieth centuries, for example, scholars interpreted the Song of Songs as a love-drama, with two or three characters. Because of the Song's lack of plot and its undeveloped characters, this dramatic approach has since dropped out of favor, though it still has some adherents.[193] More significantly, the discovery of ancient Near Eastern texts in the nineteenth century has sparked a comparative literature interest in the Song of Songs, setting it within the wider context of ancient Near East love poetry.[194] Such scholarship reflects a purely historical

---

2000); Christos Yannaras, *Variations on the Song of Songs* (Brookline, MA: Holy Cross Orthodox Press, 2005); and Larry L. Lyke, *I Will Espouse You Forever: The Song of Songs and the Theology of Love in the Hebrew Bible* (Nashville, TN: Abingdon Press, 2007).

191. J. Cheryl Exum, *The Song of Songs* (Louisville, KY: Westminster John Knox Press, 2005), 1.

192. Good summaries of modern scholarship on the Song of Songs include: E. Ann Matter, "Song of Songs, Book of," in *Dictionary of Biblical Interpretation*. vol. 2, ed. John H. Hayes, 495–96 (Nashville, TN: Abingdon, 1999); and Exum, *The Song of Songs*, 78–86.

193. For example, Michael D. Goulder, *The Song of Fourteen Songs* (Sheffield: JSOT, 1986); and Iain W. Provan, *Ecclesiastes, Song of Songs* (Grand Rapids, MI: Zondervan, 2001).

194. The best example of this is Michael V. Fox, *The Song of Songs and the Ancient Egyptian Love Songs* (Madison: University of Wisconsin Press, 1985).

interest in the Song. Most scholars concentrate on interpreting the Song of Songs as an affirmation of the goodness, dignity, and even sanctity of human love and sexuality.[195]

In recent years, feminist biblical criticism has proved to be one of the most fruitful approaches to the Song of Songs. Feminist critics have noted the gender and sexual equality of the man and the woman in the Song of Songs, the mutuality of their sexual desire, and even the gynocentricity of the poem.[196] Not all agree with these interpretations, not even all feminist scholars, and these issues remain a subject of lively scholarly debate. Feminist criticism of the Song of Songs is currently one of the most thought-provoking avenues of interpretation.

Many modern exegetes of the Song of Songs denigrate its allegorical interpretation, finding the methodology arbitrary, unverifiable, and implausible. The most contemptuous of these can be found in the famous 1974 essay by William E. Phipps titled "The Plight of the Song of Songs," in which he bemoans the stifling influence of allegorizations of the Song that he believes were the product of early Christian disgust for sex. "It is one of the pranks of history," he writes, "that a poem so obviously about hungry passion has caused so much perplexity and has provoked such a

---

195. Such is the thrust of the commentaries of Murphy and Exum. See also Ariel Bloch and Chana Bloch, *The Song of Songs: A New Translation with an Introduction and Commentary* (New York: Random House, 1995).

196. For example, Phyllis Trible, "Love's Lyrics Redeemed," in *God and the Rhetoric of Sexuality*, 144–65 (Minneapolis, MN: Fortress Press, 1978); repr. in Harold Bloom, ed., *The Song of Songs* (New York: Chelsea House Publishers, 1988), 49–66; Renita J. Weems, "Song of Songs," in *Women's Bible Commentary*, ed. Carol A. Newsom and Sharon H. Ringe, 156–60 (Louisville, KY: Westminster John Knox Press, 1992); Renita J. Weems, "Song of Songs," *The New Interpreter's Bible* (Nashville, TN: Abingdon, 1997), 5:361–434; Athalya Brenner, ed., *A Feminist Companion to the Song of Songs* (Sheffield: Sheffield Academic Press, 1993); and Athalya Brenner and Carole R. Fontaine, eds., *The Song of Songs: A Feminist Companion to the Bible* (Sheffield: Sheffield Academic Press, 2000).

plethora of bizarre interpretations."[197] But this is a woefully inadequate explanation of the patristic allegorical approach to the Song of Songs. In describing such "one-dimensional" assessments, Roland Murphy has said, "A preoccupation with eroticism is rather boldly projected onto the ancient Church, while allegory is reduced to a sort of exegetical alchemy for transmutation or spiritualization of the Song's ostensibly sexual themes." Rather, continues Murphy, allegory "facilitated construction and maintenance of a Christian worldview, providing the intellectual mechanism to effect a synthesis between Old Testament witnesses to God's providential love for humankind and what was confessed to be the preeminent display of that love in the Christ event."[198] We will return to the theme of the function and purpose of allegorical interpretation below.[199]

While rejecting the allegorical method and viewing the Song as only a poem about sexual love, most scholars offer a more balanced perspective on the history of allegorical interpretation. As Dianne Bergant writes,

> This book is now regarded as a collection of love poetry, and it is usually interpreted as such. Its sensuous imagery and its depiction of an erotic affair celebrate the passion of heterosexual love. Three features set the Song of Songs apart from other biblical works. First, the sexuality within it is explicit and erotic, and it makes no excuses for this. Second, there is no mention of God in any of the poems. Third, while the focus of the Song of Songs is human behavior, it neither passes judgment on that behavior nor offers any moral teaching. These features may have

---

197. William E. Phipps, "The Plight of the Song of Songs," *Journal of the American Academy of Religion* 42 (1974): 82–100; repr. in Harold Bloom, ed., *The Song of Songs* (New York: Chelsea House Publishers, 1988), 5–23. Citation from pp. 5–6.
198. Murphy, *The Song of Songs*, 16.
199. See pp. 73–79.

contributed to its early allegorical interpretation, but such an interpretive approach is no longer promoted by scholars.[200]

J. Cheryl Exum offers a similar perspective: "The Song is not an allegory; there is no indication that the poet ever intended it to be given an esoteric interpretation. . . . Although the Song is not an allegory, it may be admitted that it lends itself to allegorical interpretation. Ironically, some of the features that helped make the Song a great love poem . . . were the very features that facilitated its allegorical interpretation."[201]

Exum also helpfully points out how the allegorical method can limit exegetical possibilities when reading the biblical text. The equality of the lovers in the poem and the absence of subordination or hierarchy between them are hard to reconcile with the unequal, hierarchical relationship between Christ and the individual soul or Church that is present in allegorical interpretations. "Furthermore," she adds, "the Song of Songs presents its readers with not one but two subject positions from which to read or with which to identify: the female's and the male's, either or both of which readers are free to adopt. In allegory, however, only one subject position is available to the reader: with few exceptions, that of the female. In the long history of allegorical interpretation of the Song, male readers have identified themselves with the woman who desires, seeks, suffers for, and rejoices in her beloved, who is identified with God."[202] Modern critiques of the allegorical interpretation of the Song are useful not least of all because they help those interested in the ancient methodology realize its limitations.[203]

---

200. Dianne Bergant, *The Song of Songs* (Collegeville, MN: Liturgical Press, 2001), xi.
201. Exum, *The Song of Songs*, 76.
202. Exum, *The Song of Songs*, 77.
203. See Elizabeth A. Clark, "The Celibate Bridegroom and His Virginal Brides: Metaphor and the Marriage of Jesus in Early Christian Ascetic Exegesis," *Church History* 77, no. 1 (March 2008): 1–25.

The lesson to be taken from this survey of the history of interpretation is that each exegetical methodology, whether ancient or modern, has the potential for opening new perspectives on the Song of Songs. No single method can exhaust the text's exegetical possibilities. No single interpretation can claim exclusive insight into the text's meaning. The Song of Songs is polyvalent and demands a variety of exegetical approaches to plumb its meaning. However committed to modern critical exegesis a modern reader of the Song may be, he or she should not neglect the abundance of wisdom that is to be found in premodern exegesis of the Song. A critical reading of the Song can only be enriched by familiarity with the kind of exegesis that predominated until quite recently. And there is hardly a better writer from which to gain this familiarity than Gregory the Great.

B. GREGORY'S METHOD OF SCRIPTURAL EXEGESIS

Gregory the Great's exegesis of Scripture has been the object of many studies. In this introduction it is impossible to give a full account of their findings. Bibliographical references are supplied for readers interested in a greater treatment of the subject. The work of the Italian scholar Vincenzo Recchia is fundamental for understanding Gregory's exegesis.[204] What follows situates Gregory's approach to Scripture by drawing upon recent studies of patristic exegesis. Its goal is to facilitate an informed and fruitful reading of his comments on the Song of Songs.

---

204. Vincenzo Recchia, *L'esegesi di Gregorio Magno al cantico dei cantici* (Torino: Società Editrice Internazionale, 1967); Vincenzo Recchia, *Gregorio Magno papa ed esegeta biblico* (Bari: Edipuglia, 1996); and Vincenzo Recchia, *Lettera e profezia nell'esegesi di Gregorio Magno* (Bari: Edipuglia, 2003). Other recent studies include: Stephan Ch. Kessler, *Gregor der Grosse als Exeget: eine theologische Interpretation der Ezechielhomilien* (Innsbruck: Tyrolia, 1995); Giuseppe Cremascoli, *L'esegesi biblica di Gregorio Magno* (Brescia: Queriniana, 2001); and Angela Russell Christman, *What did Ezekiel See? Christian Exegesis of Ezekiel's Vision of the Chariot from Irenaeus to Gregory the Great* (Leiden: Brill, 2005).

1. Gregory's Exegetical Motivation. Before discussing Gregory's exegetical approach and practice, it will be helpful to understand his motivation for interpreting Scripture in the first place. Gregory was convinced that Scripture contained different levels of meaning, such that everyone who read it, regardless of training, intelligence, spiritual insight, or lack thereof, could benefit from it. In his letter to Leander of Seville that was prefaced to the *Moralia*, Gregory writes, "For as the divine word exercises the understanding of the wise by the mysteries it contains, so usually it comforts the simple by its surface meaning. It lays open what can nourish the little ones; it keeps in secret what lifts up the minds of loftier men in admiration. It is like a kind of river, so to speak, which is both shallow and deep, in which both the lamb may walk and the elephant may swim."[205] Gregory was clearly an elephant. He knew that plumbing the depths of Scripture and searching into its mysteries required exegetical effort. Scripture's obscure passages would nourish only if their meaning could be wrestled from them. Thus, he also conceptualized scriptural exegesis as a kind of digestion. "For sacred scripture," writes Gregory, "is sometimes food to us, sometimes drink. It is food in the more obscure passages because in a certain sense it is broken in pieces by being explained and swallowed after chewing. But it is drink in the plainer passages because it is imbibed just as it is found. . . . Few attain a knowledge of the mighty and hidden meanings, but many understand the plain sense of the narrative."[206] Lambs are more plentiful than elephants. Yet the elephant does not swim in the depths of Sacred Scripture merely for his own enjoyment: those possessing the wisdom and requisite skill to penetrate the deep mysteries of Scripture have a responsibility to communicate their insights to the simple lambs. Elephants enable lambs to be nourished by the obscure passages of Scripture; lambs should be given access to all the Scriptures, not simply the plain passages.

---

205. *Mor.* ad Leandrum [4], 173–78 (CCSL 143:6).
206. *Mor.* 1.21 [29], 7–9 and 21–22 (CCSL 143:40).

In the opening lines of one of his homilies on Ezekiel, Gregory explains the specific purpose for which an understanding of the Scriptures is given.[207] During private reading, scriptural insight is given for the sake of the individual's spiritual advancement, either in compunction (one's own moral improvement) or in contemplation (insight into the mystery of God). But the understanding of Scripture given in private reading is meant to be shared in the communal setting. The real purpose of scriptural insight is to edify the community; hence, individual understanding must be communicated to a wider audience. This was Gregory's principle motivation in the bulk of his exegetical corpus, and he had a strong sense of responsibility to use the gift he had received for the benefit of others. His commentaries and homilies on the books of Job, Ezekiel, and the Song of Songs—all considered particularly obscure to the simple reader—were meant to break open the hidden insights they contained and communicate them to others, so that they too could be nourished by the word of God. Gregory believed that one of the primary tasks of the preacher was to communicate insight into the Scriptures.

2. *Grammatical Reading Techniques.* Gregory's interpretation of Scripture relies heavily on grammatical reading techniques.[208] Recent scholarship on patristic exegesis has highlighted the role of such techniques in determining the meaning of the scriptural text. In the Greco-Roman educational system the primary role of the grammarian (*grammaticus*) was to impart to students a command of correct language, a mastery of a selection of classic texts, and the skills needed to interpret them properly.[209] Grammatical studies provided students

---

207. *H.Ez.* 1.2.1.

208. In his *L'esegesi di Gregorio Magno al cantico dei cantici*, Vincenzo Recchia has stressed the grammatical and rhetorical methodologies that inform Gregory's exegesis of the Song of Songs. Though he considered the spurious commentary on 1 Kings as genuinely Gregorian, in my estimation his overall argument is not marred by his liberal use of it.

209. On the teaching of grammarians, see Quintilian, *Institutio oratio* 1.4–9; H. I. Marrou, *Education in Antiquity* (Madison: University of Wisconsin Press, 1956),

not only with the fundamental techniques and skills for good reading but also with a sense of the appropriate order in which to apply these techniques.[210] Unsurprisingly, Christian exegetes trained in these grammatical techniques applied them when reading Scripture.[211] These techniques were used to determine what Lewis Ayres calls "the plain sense of scripture," by which he means "the way the words run," that is, "the sense that a text had for a Christian of the period versed in ancient literary critical skills."[212] This plain sense as determined by grammatical reading techniques was the point of departure for all interpretations, including figurative.[213] As a member of an aristocratic Roman family, Gregory was able to obtain a solid formation in grammatical reading techniques as part of his education, even though such training was becoming increasingly rare in the sixth century.[214] At the same time, by Gregory's day grammatical reading techniques had been used by Christian exegetes for centuries, and Gregory would have encountered them in the exegetical traditions with which he was familiar. Undoubtedly, Gregory learned how to interpret the Bible grammatically, at least in part, by reading the leading lights of the Christian exegetical tradition: Origen, Ambrose, Augustine, Jerome, and so forth.

160–85 and 274–91; and Martin Irvine, *The Making of Textual Culture: Grammatical and Literary Theory 350–1100* (Cambridge: Cambridge University Press, 1994). On ancient education, see Teresa Morgan, *Literate Education in the Hellenistic and Roman Worlds* (Cambridge: Cambridge University Press, 1998); and Raffaella Cribiore, *Gymnastics of the Mind: Greek Education in Hellenistic and Roman Egypt* (Princeton, NJ: Princeton University Press, 2001). On the role of grammarians in society, see Robert A. Kaster, *Guardians of Language: The Grammarian and Society in Late Antiquity* (Berkeley: University of California Press, 1988).

210. Lewis Ayres, *Nicaea and Its Legacy: An Approach to Fourth-Century Trinitarian Theology* (Oxford: Oxford University Press, 2004), 35–36, provides a good summary.

211. Bernhardt Neuschafer, *Origenes als Philologe*, 2 vols. (Basle: Friedrich Reinhardt, 1987); Frances Young, *Biblical Exegesis and the Formation of Christian Culture* (Cambridge: Cambridge University Press, 1997).

212. Ayres, *Nicaea and Its Legacy*, 32.

213. See Ayres, *Nicaea and Its Legacy*, 31–40.

214. See above p. 7.

The most basic reading techniques learned from the grammarian were aimed at the preliminary analysis of the letter of the text.[215] Preliminary analysis, called *methodike*, begins with the establishment of the correct text (textual criticism) and the proper construal of the text once established. In an age of *scripta continua*, the reader had to determine where the words began and ended, how to punctuate sentences, where to place the stress, and so forth. In his comments on the Song of Songs, Gregory does not often engage in this sort of preliminary analysis since there was wide consensus on these issues.[216] Next, the exegete paid very close attention to the grammar, vocabulary, and syntax of sentences. Sentences were parsed, homonyms identified, the meaning of unfamiliar words determined, figures of speech discussed, and the significance of the grammatical characteristics of verbs, nouns, and the other parts of speech discussed.[217] A great deal of Gregory's exegesis takes up issues such as these. Indeed, he viewed the Song of Songs as a whole as an extended figure of speech. But preliminary analysis was not limited to basic philological concerns. For example, it was important to identify who was speaking, who was spoken to, and who was spoken about in a particular passage when it was disputed, each of which was recognized as a *persona*, that is, a distinct character in the narrative. Scholars now call this technique "prosopographic exegesis," and it was particularly influential in the development of trinitarian and christological terminology.[218] Gregory uses prosopographic exegesis abundantly in his

215. Young, *Biblical Exegesis*, 77–78.

216. For examples elsewhere in Gregory's corpus, see Recchia, *L'esegesi di Gregorio Magno al cantico dei cantici*, 46–47.

217. For a fourth-century example of the significance of a verb's tense in exegesis, see my "Basil of Caesarea, Didymus the Blind, and the Anti-Pneumatomachian Exegesis of Amos 4:13 and John 1:3," *Journal of Theological Studies* n.s. 61 (2010), 644–48.

218. Michael Slusser, "The Exegetical Roots of Trinitarian Theology," *Theological Studies* 49 (1988): 461–76, provides a good introduction to the method; see also Hubertus R. Drobner, *Person-Exegese und Christologie bei Augustinus* (Leiden: Brill, 1986); Hubertus R. Drobner, "Grammatical Exegesis and Christology in Saint Augustine," *Studia Patristica* 18 (1990): 49–63.

exegesis of the Song of Songs, specifying who speaks each verse and to whom it is spoken. Preliminary analysis concluded with an analysis of the style. And so, "reading a classic in school meant analyzing its sentences into parts of speech and its verses into metre, noting linguistic usage and style, discussing different meanings of words, elucidating figures of speech or ornamental devices."[219]

Once the basic linguistic analysis was complete, the exegete could advance to the explanation of the content of the text, *historia*. Frances Young has described *historia* as "the enquiry that produces as much information as possible with respect to the elements, actions, characters, and background of the text."[220] It is *not* a reconstruction of the historical facts that the text reports; rather, it is an explanation of narrative that the text itself presents. Gregory uses his preliminary analysis of the Song of Songs to understand its content *as an extended figure of speech*. In other words, Gregory viewed that plain sense of the Song of Songs as figural, as pointing to a deeper, spiritual sense. Figural interpretation will be discussed in more detail below, but for now it suffices to say that Gregory believed that the Song of Songs could nourish spiritually only when interpreted as an extended figure. Through his use of grammatical reading techniques, then, Gregory determined that the plain sense of the Song of Songs *was* its figural interpretation. Thus, grammatical reading techniques are used to explain the figural, spiritual content of the text. Fundamental for understanding the meaning of a text in grammatical analysis was discerning the reference of words and sentences.[221] Determining the reference meant answering questions such as: What are the extratextual realities to which the words of the text refer? What are the extratextual reali-

---

219. Young, *Biblical Exegesis*, 78.

220. Young, *Biblical Exegesis*, 87.

221. I am indebted to Young's exposition of reference and cross-reference in *Biblical Exegesis*, chap. 6. As Young notes, this sort of approach is rooted in the ancient assumption that language referred to something other than itself, that there was a correspondence between words and reality; see Young, *Biblical Exegesis*, 119–20.

ties about which the sentence is talking? Discerning the reference plays a crucial role in Gregory's exegesis. Since the Song of Songs is interpreted figurally, words are symbols that point to realities of the spiritual life. Gregory takes great pains to clarify that to which figurally interpreted words and passages refer.

In cases where reference was disputed, two other grammatical reading techniques were used to resolve the issue. The first is cross-referencing. Cross-referencing by either quotation or allusion was not understood as purely ornamental but as a reinforcement of the point being made.[222] The use of cross-references corroborated a claim by showing that the same was said elsewhere. Therefore, in cases of disputed reference, a cross-reference could clarify or even establish reference. Frances Young has noted that "the principle of looking for the reference and exploiting cross-reference in order to substantiate proposed exegesis in a rational way remains crucial throughout the [patristic] period."[223] Gregory often cross-references other passages of Scripture to support his interpretation. At times, the cross-reference provides the essential link between the verse of the Song of Songs and his interpretation.

The second technique for clarifying references is the identification of the *skopos* or *hypothesis* of a text—its basic plot, theme, direction, or inner coherence—and then interpreting difficult passages in light of that *skopos*. In other words, when the meaning of a passage was uncertain because of disputed reference(s), it was interpreted in light of its wider context. In biblical exegesis, the contextual unit could range from the paragraph in which the disputed passage is embedded to Scripture as a whole. The main point, however, was that any interpretation of a particular passage that was inconsistent with the text's *skopos* was deemed inappropriate.[224]

---

222. Young, *Biblical Exegesis*, chap. 5.

223. Young, *Biblical Exegesis*, 137. In his study of the use of Scripture in the *Apophthegmata Patrum*, Per Rönnegård has employed with good results Young's insight regarding reference and cross-reference; see *Threads and Images: The Use of Scripture in Apophthegmata Patrum* (Lund: Lund University, 2007).

224. Young, *Biblical Exegesis*, chaps. 1 and 2.

Gregory was heir to an exegetical tradition that viewed the reference of the Song of Songs in its entirety as disputed. If it is not about human sexual love, then about what? In the preface to the *Exposition* Gregory clearly identified the *skopos* of the Song of Songs: union with God, not erotic human love. Every passage in his exposition had to be interpreted in the light of this overarching theme. Hence Gregory considered the plain sense of the text to be an extended figure of speech about union with God. Indeed, the very title given to Gregory's commentary on the Song of Songs—*expositio*—points to his grammatical and rhetorical approach, as this term signified in grammatical and rhetorical circles a certain genre of exegetical discourse.[225] And the prologue of the *Exposition* seems to be an *accessus ad auctorem*, a literary genre with set topics used to introduce a work that became standard in the medieval period.[226] Hence Gregory's debt to grammatical exegetical practices can be seen even in the title and structure of his *Exposition*.

The preface to the *Exposition* concludes with a discussion of the characters that speak in the Song of Songs (*Exp.* 10). Gregory is not sorting out the speaking characters in a particular disputed passage or section. Rather, his identification of the extra-biblical references of these characters in the preface is meant to set the parameters for the interpretation of the entire biblical book. There are four characters: the Bridegroom, the Bride, the young girls who attend the Bride, and the companions of the Bridegroom. But to what extra-biblical realities do these characters refer? Gregory discerns the reference of the Bridegroom as the Lord and that of the Bride as the Church. The attendants are spiritual neophytes, whereas the companions are either angels or the perfect. Yet both the attendants and the companions, as members of the Church, are part of the Bride. In this way Gregory justifies his twofold interpretation of the Song of Songs, that it is a dialogue both between Christ and the Church and between Christ and the individual soul.

---

225. Recchia, *L'esegesi di Gregorio Magno al cantico dei cantici*, 2–11.
226. Recchia, *L'esegesi di Gregorio Magno al cantico dei cantici*, 13–26.

While in the *Exposition* Gregory is initially systematic about interpreting each verse of the Song of Songs in both ways, elsewhere he picks one or the other.

Gregory also recognizes another reference for these characters. An attendant is someone at the beginning of his or her spiritual quest, dedicated to doing good works. A companion is someone who is more experienced and preaches the Bridegroom in his or her words and actions. A Bride is someone who loves God perfectly. The identification of the reference of the characters in the Song of Songs and the tripartite division of the Bride harmonizes well with Gregory's overall motivation in interpreting the Scriptures: there is something for everybody in this biblical book, whether you are a novice Christian or have already attained Christian perfection, whether you are a lamb or an elephant. Every reader can identify with one of the characters and so derive some benefit from the Song of Songs. In the final lines of the preface, Gregory gives this exhortation: "So then, we are invited to be the Bride. But if we are still unable to do this, let us be companions. If even this exceeds our capacities, let us at least gather together as young girls around the marriage-bed. Therefore, since we said that the Bridegroom and the Bride are the Lord and the Church, let us as either young girls or companions listen to the words of the Bridegroom, let us listen to the words of the Bride, and from their dialogue let us learn the fervor of love" (*Exp.* 10).

3. *Gregory's Figural Approach to the Song of Songs*. As mentioned above, the Church fathers considered the Song of Songs one of the most obscure books of the Bible. Its unmistakably erotic language presented Christian interpreters with an exegetical dilemma. In the patristic era, the status of this biblical book as the inspired word of God that was meant to nourish Christians precluded the very possibility of interpreting it as a celebration of human sexual desire and love. As Augustine had written, "Anything that cannot be related to either good morals or to the true faith should be taken as figurative."[227] This resulted in the allegorical interpretation of the

---

227. *De doctrina christiana* 3.10.

Song of Songs, and as mentioned above, Gregory was a part of this tradition.[228]

Modern scholars have devoted many pages to studying ancient allegorical exegesis.[229] Earlier a few examples of modern disdain for the allegorical interpretation of the Song of Songs were mentioned. Too often modern scholars use "allegorical" as code for exegesis that is devoid of objectivity, unconnected with what the text "actually" says, and subject to flights of fancy. Allegorical exegesis is often contrasted with another kind of figurative exegesis, called "typological," which is supposedly tied to the "historical" meaning of the text itself and has an objectivity that presages modern historical-critical exegesis. Yet there is a growing recognition that the terms "allegorical" and "typological" have acquired meanings in modern scholarship that diverge quite significantly from how they were used in antiquity.[230] Patristic exegetes did not divide figurative exegetical

---

228. Helmut Riedlinger, *Die Makellosigkeit der Kirche in den Lateinischen Hoheliedkommentaren des Mittelalters* (Münster: West. Aschendorff, 1958), 64–68; Recchia, *L'esegesi di Gregorio Magno al cantico dei cantici*, 35–43; Recchia, "*Invigilata Lucernis*: L'esegesi di Gregorio Magno ai simboli del «Cantico dei Cantici»," *Invigilata Lucernis* 23 (2001): 207–21; Domingo Ramos-Lisson, "En torno a la exégesis de San Gregorio Magno sobre el 'Cantar de los Cantares,'" *Teología y vida* 42 (2001): 241–65.

229. The standard work is Henri de Lubac, *Medieval Exegesis*, trans. Mark Sebanc, 2 vols. (Grand Rapids, MI: Eerdmans, 1998). Traditional accounts of allegorical exegesis and references to the important studies can be found in Robert M. Grant with David Tracy, *A Short History of the Interpretation of the Bible*, 2nd ed., rev. and enlarged ed. (Philadelphia, PA: Fortress Press, 1984); Bertrand de Margerie, *Introduction to the History of Exegesis* (Petersham, MA: Saint Bede's Press, 1993–94); Manilo Simonetti, *Biblical Interpretation in the Early Church* (Edinburgh: T & T Clark, 1994). John J. O'Keefe and J. J. Reno, *Sanctified Vision: An Introduction to Early Christian Interpretation of the Bible* (Baltimore, MD: The Johns Hopkins University Press, 2005) represents a good recent attempt to describe patristic exegesis and its theological assumptions.

230. For new approaches, see James L. Kugel and Rowan A. Greer, *Early Biblical Interpretation* (Philadelphia, PA: Westminster Press, 1986); Young, *Biblical Exegesis*; and Peter W. Martens, "Revisiting the Allegory/Typology Distinction: The Case of Origen," *Journal of Early Christian Studies* 16 (2008): 283–317.

approaches into two basic categories but rather used a variety of words—such as "allegory" and "type"—to describe what has been called in modern scholarship "figural reading practices."[231]

Figural reading practices are those techniques used by Christian exegetes, especially when interpreting the Old Testament, to illustrate aspects of God's action in Christ. Patristic authors believed in the unity and the coherence of the Scriptures: the Old and New Testaments narrate a single story of salvation history that begins with creation and culminates in Jesus Christ, who continues to be present in the Church through the Spirit. Hence the Old Testament needed to be interpreted in the light of Christ: Christ is the interpretive key that unlocks the meaning of the whole of Scripture.[232] A figural reading of an Old Testament book enabled such an interpretation by treating the text as a resource for describing God's action in salvation history, in the incarnation, and in the result of the incarnation, the transformation of souls in the ongoing life of the Church.[233] And so, Gregory interprets the Song of Songs allegorically—or, better, figurally—in order to gain a better understanding of the mystery of God's action in salvation history, particularly in the incarnation of Christ and in drawing souls and the Church into union with Christ.

But why the Song of Songs in particular and not some other Old Testament book? Several studies have been devoted to trying to understand Christian figural exegesis of the Song of Songs and Gregory's place within this wider context.[234] Dennis Turner has

---

231. David Dawson, *Allegorical Readers and Cultural Revision in Ancient Alexandria* (Berkeley: University of California Press, 1992); David Dawson, *Christian Figural Reading and the Fashioning of Identity* (Berkeley: University of California Press, 2002).

232. For a good discussion, see Greer, *Early Biblical Interpretation*, 155–76; and O'Keefe and Reno, *Sanctified Vision*, 24–44.

233. For a good summary, see Ayres, *Nicaea and Its Legacy*, 37–38.

234. E. Ann Matter, *The Voice of My Beloved: The Song of Songs in Western Medieval Christianity* (Philadelphia: University of Pennsylvania Press, 1990); Ann W. Astell, *The Song of Songs in the Middle Ages* (Ithaca, NY: Cornell University Press, 1990); and Turner, *Eros and Allegory*.

argued that late patristic and medieval allegorical interpretation of the Song of Songs is a fusion of "erotic metaphysics" derived from the pseudo-Dionysius and ascetical monastic eschatology. Indeed, the eroticism of the Song provided an argument for the very necessity of interpreting the books of the Old Testament figurally. Hence patristic and medieval commentaries on the Song of Songs are not merely instances of figural exegesis but justifications for it. Turner argues that celibate Christians chose to interpret the Song of Songs *because of* its eroticism, not *in spite of* it, since their own worldview was so thoroughly informed by a biblical, eschatological theology suffused with yearning and desire for mystical and contemplative union with God in Christ.[235] He situates Gregory at the very head of this tradition (while acknowledging Origen's influence).[236] This tradition views the erotic love of the man and the woman in the Song of Songs as the best likeness available for understanding the love and union between Christ and the Church, between Christ and the individual soul.[237] And so, Gregory considered the Song of Songs the best textual resource for describing and understanding God's action in the whole of salvation history, provided that it was interpreted figurally.

One of the remarkable features of Gregory's *Exposition* is that it begins with a preface devoted to justifying why the Song of Songs should be read figurally. Simply put, humanity's fallen condition has made it necessary for God to communicate the loftiest spiritual truths through symbolic language.[238] In their fallen condition human beings now lack the ability to understand spiritual

---

235. E. Ann Matter has argued that Song of Songs commentaries constitute a distinct subgenre of the genre of biblical commentaries since this biblical book "provided an extraordinarily rich ground for the elaboration of allegory and therefore provided an unparalleled opportunity for finding the truth hidden beneath the figures of the text" (*The Voice of My Beloved*, 10).

236. See Turner, *Eros and Allegory*, 38, 85–87, and 111.

237. Turner, *Eros and Allegory*, 153.

238. This idea is a crucial aspect of Gregory's doctrine of God's condescension in the incarnation; see Rodrigue Bélanger, "Anthropologie et parole de Dieu dans

truths that are directly communicated by God. Therefore, such truths need to be mediated. As Gregory puts its, God communicates what humans do not know by means of what they do know (*Exp.* 1). Therefore, it is the divine intention that the Scriptures contain what Gregory variously calls enigmas or allegories. These figurative devices use language that a person already understands to communicate something not yet understood: "Allegories are produced by clothing divine thoughts in what we know. When we recognize the exterior language, we attain interior understanding" (*Exp.* 2). They act "as a kind of crane" that lifts the soul up to God (*Exp.* 2). They facilitate the search for wisdom and exercise the mind, enabling purification and spiritual progress (*Exp.* 4).[239] A figural reading of the enigmas and allegories employed by God in the Scriptures allows the exegete to access the spiritual truths they contain mediated through mundane language. Enigmas and allegories thus play a purely pedagogical and instrumental role in Gregory's exegesis: they are means to interior, spiritual understanding. Hence the passage from letter to spirit mirrors the path of spiritual progress from exteriority to interiority, from ignorance of divine truths to knowledge of them. Allegories and enigmas mediate not mere information but rather an experience of God. In other words, they facilitate contemplation. The Song of Songs not only is about contemplation but also is the privileged resource for attaining it. Gregory conceives of contemplation as the transcendence of knowledge by faith and a kind of incipient, if fleeting, grasp of God that obtains in the afterlife (*Exp.* 19).

But enigmas and allegories only function as intended when the exegete can recognize them for what they are. The exegete should not immediately reject the Song of Songs because of its erotic

---

le commentaire de Grégoire le Grand sur la cantique des cantiques," in *Grégoire le Grand*, ed. Jacques Fontaine et al., 245–54 (Paris: Éditions du CNRS, 1986).

239. Origen saw the spiritual senses of the Song of Songs as intended to exercise the soul to facilitate spiritual progress; see O'Keefe and Reno, *Sanctified Vision*, 135–39. While Gregory adopts this view, he places much more emphasis on God's condescension to humanity through the scriptural text.

language; rather, God uses such language out of mercy. "He has gone so far as to embrace the language of our vulgar love in order to enkindle our heart with a yearning for that sacred love. . . . We learn from dialogues of the love here below with what intensity we should burn in the love of Divinity" (*Exp.* 3). The eroticism of the Song of Songs, when properly interpreted as a figure of speech, teaches Christians about the love and desire they should have for God. One of the main purposes of the preface is to help readers of the Song of Songs recognize that it must be interpreted figurally.

Gregory is well-aware that exegetes of the Song of Songs can become fixated on its erotic language. Therefore, the surface meaning of the "exterior" words must be passed by in order to attain their "interior" meaning. The interpreter has to adopt a hermeneutic of divine charity and abandon reading the Song of Songs through the lens of physical, bodily love. Here, Gregory employs a number of analogies to help his readers pass beyond the external form of the words to arrive at their interior, spiritual content. Focusing on the external words while ignoring their meaning is like looking at the colors of a painting while missing the subject depicted; it is like eating husks instead of the kernel (*Exp.* 4). In order to avoid such a mistake, an interpreter of the Song of Songs must purify himself and be filled with love of God (*Exp.* 5). Therefore, correctly interpreting the Song of Songs requires moral preparation. This prerequisite explains why the Song of Songs is placed third among the books traditionally ascribed to Solomon: Proverbs, Ecclesiastes, and the Song of Songs. Proverbs teaches morality, whereas Ecclesiastes teaches the transience of natural goods. Only when prepared by these two biblical books can the exegete properly understand the spiritual content of the Song of Songs (*Exp.* 7).[240] Thus, proper exegesis for Gregory (as for many of the Church fathers) is not merely an intellectual exercise but must take place in a nexus of ascetical, liturgical, and communal practices.

---

240. Here, Gregory draws upon a traditional view of the so-called Solomonic corpus.

The Song of Songs represents a high point of God's condescension to humanity in Scripture. Gregory notes that the very title of this biblical book—the Song of Songs—signifies something quite superlative, a solemn mystery (*Exp.* 6). There are many songs in the Old Testament, each with their own character, but the Song of Songs is the most sublime of all because it is about humanity's union with God: "through this song the Lord is embraced with an intimate love" (*Exp.* 7). The fact that the Lord calls himself "Lord" and "Father" elsewhere in the Scriptures but "Bridegroom" in the Song of Songs is also significant. The first two titles are used to convey that the Lord should be feared and honored, but the latter that he should be loved: "In this book, then, when 'Bridegroom' is said, something quite sublime is being conveyed since it reveals our bond of union with him" (*Exp.* 8).

Gregory's explanation of the purpose and function of scriptural allegories and enigmas in *Exp.* 1–5 is unparalleled in patristic literature. In the preface he not only justifies reading the Song of Songs figurally but also argues that such an interpretation grants access to the most sublime mysteries of God. The Song of Songs is special and unique. Though seemingly utterly inappropriate for inclusion within the Bible because of its exuberant eroticism, a figural interpretation reveals that it is perhaps the most profound of all biblical books because it teaches about mystical union with God. For this reason, it should be approached with due caution, after significant preparation and purification, "lest we linger over exterior meanings when we hear the words of exterior love [and] the very crane employed to lift us will instead burden us and thus not lift us" (*Exp.* 4).

4. Gregory's Exegetical Practice. By way of conclusion to this introduction to Gregory's exegesis of the Song of Songs, it will be helpful to give some examples of the concrete grammatical reading techniques he employs.[241] Prosopographic exegesis plays a fundamental

---

241. For more examples, see Recchia, *L'esegesi di Gregorio Magno al cantico dei cantici*, 43–65.

role. It is crucial for Gregory to determine first whether the verse under discussion is spoken by the Bridegroom to the Bride or by the Bride to the Bridegroom. In most cases Gregory explicitly identifies the *personae*, as for example: "And note the words of the Bridegroom when he replies to the Bride: *If you do not know yourself, O beautiful among women, set out and follow the tracks of the flocks, and pasture your young goats near the tents of the shepherds* [Song 1:7]" (*Exp.* 44). Other times he names just the speaker, and the one spoken to can be easily inferred: "Hence the Bride says in the Song: *Bolster me with flowers, surround me with apples, for I grow faint with love* [Song 2:5]" (B10, W14). Often Gregory identifies the Church herself as one of the *personae*, passing to its figural interpretation: "it is said to the holy Church in the voice of the Bridegroom: *Honey and milk are under your tongue* [Song 4:4]" (B29, W30), and "In the voice of the Bride the holy Church plainly desires to see him in the present time, saying: *Lo! He stands behind our wall* [Song 2:9]" (B14). Undoubtedly, Gregory's prosopographic exegesis has been influenced by previous interpreters of the Song of Songs, such as Origen.

Another key technique employed by Gregory is the discernment of reference. Given his figural exegesis, he must specify to what extra-biblical reality the words of any given verse of the Song of Songs refer. In most cases Gregory explicitly names the references. For example, in his interpretation of Song 3:8b, he writes, "A 'blade is placed upon the thigh' when a wicked suggestion of the flesh is subjugated by the sharp edge of holy preaching. But the term 'night' refers to the blindness that characterizes our enfeebled state. For we do not see the forces of opposition that threaten us at night. Therefore, *everyone's blade is on their thigh on account of nocturnal fears* because it is clear that holy men, while they dread the dangers they do not see, are always prepared to ward off an attack" (B24). Two references in this verse needed to be determined: the blade on the thigh and the nocturnal fears. The first refers to the resistance to carnal desire enabled by edifying preaching; the second, to the moral and intellectual blindness of the human condition. Once these two references have been discerned,

Song 3:8b can be interpreted figurally: holy men, though unable to foresee temptations, are always ready to resist them through previous preparation.

But a single word can have multiple references. In this case, the appropriate reference must be discerned in the particular verse. An example of this situation can be seen in Gregory's interpretation of Song 5:2, *I sleep but my heart is awake*. He writes, "In Sacred Scripture, the figurative use of 'sleep' or 'slumber' can be understood in three ways. Sometimes 'sleep' expresses the death of the flesh, sometimes the numbness of indifference, but sometimes the calmness of life that ensues when earthly desires are trod underfoot" (W35). Gregory then justifies these different references by cross-referencing concrete scriptural passages. Sleep denotes the death of the flesh as in 1 Thessalonians 4:13-14, the numbness of indifference as in Romans 13:11 and 1 Corinthians 15:34, and the calmness after fleshly desires are subdued as in Song 5:2. Once the reference of 'sleep' is established in Song 5:2, Gregory explains how the Bride can be asleep but her heart awake.

At the same time, Gregory does not feel compelled to identify only a single reference for any given word in a particular verse. A word can have numerous references, each providing additional insights into God's action in salvation history. For example, Gregory discerns three distinct references for the Bride in Song 1:4-5: (1) the Church of Jewish converts, (2) the Church of Gentile converts, and (3) the whole Church in the present time (*Exp.* 32–40). Accordingly, when the Bride says, *the sons of my mother fought against me* (Song 1:5c), three references can be discerned: (1) Jews who persecuted Jewish converts to Christianity, (2) the apostles who converted the Gentiles to Christianity (here, the 'fighting' is interpreted positively as the struggle to turn Gentiles from error to belief), and (3) the fallen angels who tempt Christians. The polyvalence of the scriptural text is virtually inexhaustible in the hands of Gregory.

Sometimes Gregory needs to provide a cross-reference in order to support his identification of the reference of a verse. For example, when interpreting *All are holding swords and they are very skilled in warfare* (Song 3:8a), Gregory cross-references Ephesians 6:17 to clarify the reference of 'sword.' He writes, "What the 'sword' represents in the Divine Scripture, Paul laid open when he said: *And the sword of the Spirit, which is the Word of God* [Eph 6:17]" (P22, B22). In this context, another facet of Gregory's grammatical approach can be seen when he says, "Now Solomon did not say, 'All have swords,' but: *All are holding swords*, clearly because is it wonderful not only to know the Word of God, but also to do it." Gregory finds meaning in the use of one verb instead of another: the Word of God must not only be possessed but also put in practice. Such detailed attention to verbs and nouns is characteristic of Gregory's grammatical exegesis.

Gregory also uses formal analogies to discern the reference of the text. These analogies are typically expressed in terms of "as a is to b, so c is to d." For example, a formal analogy is employed in his interpretation of *Your lips are like a scarlet headband* (Song 4:3). As a headband binds together the hairs of the head, so a pious exhortation binds together the wandering thoughts of the mind (P26, B28). Thus, the reference of the 'headband' is a holy exhortation. Another example of the use of formal analogy can be found in Gregory's interpretation of *Your shoots are a garden of pomegranates* (Song 4:13). As a pomegranate protects many seeds within it, so the unity of the faith shelters many people within the Church (B33). Thus, the reference of 'pomegranate' is 'the unity of the faith.' Gregory employed formal analogy in many of his figural interpretations of the Song of Songs.

Gregory does not limit himself to using a single method to discern the reference. Often several techniques are used to strengthen his exegesis. For example, in interpreting *Your name is ointment poured-out* (Song 1:2b), Gregory claims, "'Ointment poured-out' is the incarnate divinity" (*Exp.* 21). He justifies the incarnate divinity as the reference of the poured-out ointment by a formal analogy between ointment and the divinity. When ointment is in the bottle, you can't smell it, but when it is poured out, you can perceive it. Likewise, the divine nature is invisible, but when incarnate it is perceptible. Gregory then supports this interpretation by cross-referencing Philippians 2:6-7, which speaks of Christ "emptying himself." Gregory writes, "Paul called 'emptying' what Solomon called 'pouring-out.'" By means of this cross-reference Gregory suggests that the divine kenosis is variously described as God pouring himself out and emptying himself. And so, he makes a stronger case for his interpretation of Song 1:2b by employing both formal analogy and a cross-reference.

The final grammatical reading technique that Gregory employs on a regular basis is paraphrase. A good example is his interpretation of Song 8:14, *Escape, my beloved, escape!*, the last verse of the book:

> We say "it escapes me" as often as what we want to remember does not come to mind. We say "it escapes me" when we do not retain in our memory what we want to remember. So the holy Church, after narrating the Lord's death, resurrection, and ascension, cries out to him, filled with a prophetic spirit: *Escape, my beloved, escape!* It is as if she were saying: "You who were made comprehensible to us by the flesh, transcend the grasp of our senses by your divinity and remain incomprehensible to us in your very own self!" (P49, B53, W52)

Here, Gregory appeals to common expression, "it escapes me," to understand what this verse means before offering a paraphrase. He suggests that the verse is a prayer to the ascended Lord, no longer visible in the flesh and once again incomprehensible. As in this example, Gregory usually offers an interpretive paraphrase of a verse only after he has used a variety of other techniques to elucidate his interpretation. Sometimes he introduces the paraphrase without any introduction, but in most cases he begins with a formula. The three most common formulas are as follows: (1) "In other words" (*id est*); (2) "It is as if he/she were saying" (*ac si dicat*); and (3) "It is as if he/she were saying in plain speech, as if it was being said in plain speech" (*ac si aperte dicat/diceret/diceretur*). By using subjunctive forms of *dicere* Gregory indicates that the paraphrase he presents is a hypothetical reconstruction based on his interpretation, not actually what the text says. When *aperte* is added, it highlights the fact that, when paraphrasing, Gregory is engaging in figural exegesis and has uncovered the hidden, spiritual meaning that the allegory or enigma was intended to communicate. Once Gregory has penetrated the figural, "exterior," erotic language of the Song of Songs and attained the spiritual, "interior" meaning, he paraphrases the verse in plain "exterior" language in order to contribute to the edification of his audience. The allegories and enigmas have served their purpose, and now the spiritual truths God wants to convey through them can be expressed directly in an easily understandable manner. The elephant speaks plainly to the lambs.

IV. Gregory's Sources

It is notoriously difficult to pinpoint Gregory's sources. His writings are so suffused with the thought of his patristic predecessors that it is tough to demarcate where their doctrine ends and his begins. He has made the preceding patristic tradition his own. Gregory absorbed the teachings of his predecessors and reexpressed them in a way that reflected his concerns as well as those of his audience. He was no mere copyist; he digested the thoughts of others and ruminated on them in the light of his own experience as a pastor, ascetic, and contemplative. This would often transform the ideas of his sources in striking ways. Hence, we find in Gregory's writings sentiments that are simultaneously very familiar and very novel. Perhaps it is Robert Gillet who has best expressed the situation. "A reader [of Gregory]," he writes, "who is even slightly familiar with patristic literature constantly feels that he is reading things he has already come across. But what if he searches for the source of what he has just read? It is most often the case that there is no possibility of making a precise comparison. He merely finds himself in the presence of an immense communal ambience."[242]

---

242. Robert Gillet, "Introduction," in *Grégoire le Grand: Morals sur Job I-II*, ed. Robert Gillet and André de Gaudemaris, 7–133, at 13, SChr 32 bis. (Paris: Cerf, 1975).

Nonetheless, despite these difficulties in determining Gregory's sources, it is certain that he had an intimate knowledge of the Latin fathers, particularly Augustine and John Cassian, and that whatever knowledge of the Greek fathers he had came mostly through Latin translations.[243]

A. ORIGEN

In his exegesis of the Song of Songs, Gregory was most deeply influenced by Origen. One can detect his inspiration on every page.[244] Origen wrote both homilies and a commentary on the Song of Songs, and Gregory would have had contact with both through the Latin translations of Jerome and Rufinus. Whether in translation or in the original, Origen's exegesis of the Song of Songs was a decisive inspiration for the Latin fathers,[245] and Gregory is no exception. Indeed, Henri de Lubac considers Gregory one of the primary heirs of Origen's exegetical methodology. "In Gregory's case," de Lubac writes, "it is not only his manner of understanding the threefold sense that makes him reminiscent of Origen but also certain exegetical details and a likeness of mind which is perhaps connatural. Even certain words, certain expressions, or certain turns of phrase which are characteristic of Gregory's style hark back to those of his Greek predecessor, in the form, at least, which had been given them by the Latin Rufinus. . . . [I]n the end Saint Gregory depends even more on Origen than he does on Saint Augustine."[246]

---

243. See Markus, *Gregory the Great and His World*, 35, who cites the relevant studies. See also Moorhead, *Gregory the Great*, 31–32.

244. Meyvaert, "A New Edition," 220–24; Bélanger, *Grégoire le Grand*, 43–49; Joan M. Petersen, "The Influence of Origen Upon Gregory the Great's Exegesis of the Song of Songs," *Studia Patristica* 17 (1985): 343–47.

245. Elizabeth A. Clark, "The Uses of the Songs of Songs: Origen and the Later Latin Fathers," in *Ascetic Piety and Women's Faith*, 386–427 (Lewiston, NY: E. Mellen Press, 1986).

246. De Lubac, *Medieval Exegesis*, 2.153–54.

In his *Exposition* Gregory owes to Origen both the structure of the commentary and many particular points of exegesis. Like Origen, Gregory synthesizes two traditions of interpreting the Song, each of which views the Bride of the Word differently. One tradition sees the Bride as the individual soul, whereas the other as the Church. Besides this structural influence, Gregory has in many cases taken Origen's concrete ideas as the "point of departure" for his own exegesis.[247] "At times Gregory's *dicta* appear to be no more than a résumé or paraphrasing of Origen," writes Paul Meyvaert, "and elsewhere we can see how a saying of Origen gave Gregory a cue for his own development."[248] Paul Meyvaert, Rodrigue Bélanger, and Joan M. Petersen have all listed numerous parallels between Gregory and Origen found in the *Exposition*.[249] Origen's influence on Gregory is particularly evident in the latter part of the prologue of the *Exposition*, in paragraphs 6–7 and 9–10.[250]

But Origen's exegesis of the Song of Songs has also influenced Gregory in works besides the *Exposition*, such as the *Moralia*, *Pastoral Care*, and his homilies. For example, Gregory follows Origen in interpreting "the fragrant nard" of Song 1:11 as the good works or virtues of the Church's members.[251] In this context both Origen and Gregory cite 2 Corinthians 2:15 as further scriptural support of their exegesis. Another example is Gregory's adoption of Origen's interpretation of the "shadow" in Song 2:3 as the incarnation of the Lord by connecting it with Luke 1:35.[252] Gregory also follows Origen in interpreting the "young hart" of Song 2:9a as a reference to the Lord's human existence according to the flesh.[253]

---

247. Petersen, "The Influence of Origen," 346.

248. Meyvaert, "A New Edition," 220–21.

249. Meyvaert, "A New Edition," 221–23; Bélanger, *Grégoire le Grand*, 45–46; and Petersen, "The Influence of Origen," 343–46.

250. Petersen, "The Influence of Origen," 343–46, discusses these parallels in detail.

251. Origen, *H.Cant.* 2.2; Gregory, *Mor.* 35.17 [43], 29–41.

252. Origen, *C.Cant.* 3.5; *H.Cant.* 2; Gregory, *Mor.* 33.3 [5], 2–19.

253. Origen, *C.Cant.* 3; Gregory, *H.Ev.* 33 [7], 192–93.

Finally, Origen lies behind Gregory's exegesis of the "left" and "right" hands mentioned in Song 2:6, which both writers interpret by reference to Proverbs 3:16.[254] Though Gregory does not follow Origen exactly, he borrows from his predecessor's idea that the left hand refers to the Lord's incarnation and his right hand to the eternal Word. Taking Origen's exegesis as his point of departure, Gregory interprets the left hand as the present life and the right as eternal life and teaches that the prosperity of the present life should push us to seek eternal blessedness. This last instance of Gregory's use of Origen is thus a particularly good example of how Gregory both borrowed from his predecessors and transformed them.[255]

B. AUGUSTINE

Besides Origen, Augustine also had a formative and pervasive influence on the thought of Gregory. Indeed, Gregory himself expressed his high esteem for him in a letter to Innocent, the praetorian prefect of Africa: "If you desire to be nourished with delicious food, read the little works of Saint Augustine, your countryman, and do not look for our bran, in comparison with his fine flour."[256] But unlike Origen, Augustine did not write a commentary or homilies on the Song of Songs. His interpretations of the book are found scattered throughout his works.[257] So the inspiration of Augustine on Gregory's exegesis of the Song of Songs is not a question of Gregory borrowing from particular writings, as was the case with Origen. Rather, because Gregory had a thorough knowledge of the writings of the bishop of Hippo, when he encountered particular verses of the Song of Songs that Augustine had commented upon, they acted as triggers for Gregory's memory

---

254. Origen, *C. Cant.* 3.9; *H. Cant.* 2.9; Gregory, *Reg. Past.* 3.26 [50], 32–54.

255. Bélanger, *Grégoire le Grand*, 47–49, remarks on Gregory's use of Origen in the light of the condemnation of Origen at the Council of Constantinople in 553.

256. *Reg. ep.* 10.16 (trans. Martyn, *Letters*, 727). See also *Reg. ep.* 12.16a [=*H. Ez.* praef.], cited below on pp. 92–93.

257. See A. M. La Bonnardière, "Le Cantique des Cantiques dans l'œuvre de saint Augustin," *Revue des Études Augustiniennes* 1 (1955): 225–37.

to recall what Augustine said on the verse. Accordingly, the influence of Augustine's exegesis of the Song of Songs on Gregory is far less pervasive than is the case for Origen's and contributes nothing to the plan and structure of the *Exposition*. Nonetheless, one can detect several lines of influence between Augustine and Gregory in the interpretation of particular verses.

As mentioned above, one point of contact between Augustine and Gregory is their exegesis of "at midday" in Song 1:6.[258] In addition, Rodrigue Bélanger has discussed Augustine's influence upon Gregory in his exegesis of the Song of Songs in the *Exposition* and cited several examples.[259] There are also examples of Gregory basing himself on Augustine outside of the *Exposition*. For example, Gregory follows Augustine in his interpretation of the "teeth" of Song 4:2 as those in the Church who correct others by their teaching and manner of life.[260] While Augustine sees such "teeth" as convincing heathens and heretics (i.e., Donatists) to enter the Church, for Gregory, the Church's "teeth" correct sinners within the Church. Nevertheless, both Augustine and Gregory speak of these "teeth" as softening up the "toughness" (*duritia*) of sinners by chewing them.[261]

In another example, Gregory borrows from Augustine's interpretation of Song 4:16. Augustine says that the devil and the other fallen angels, having turned from the light and warmth of love, have become frozen in icy hardness and accordingly are located figuratively in the north wind. The Spirit of grace, however, is the south wind, and when it blows, the sins of the people are forgiven.[262] Taking Augustine as his point of departure, Gregory says that the north wind represents the chilliness of an evil spirit and that the devil has possessed the "frozen" minds of sinners. The south wind signifies the fervor of the Holy Spirit who, when he touches

---

258. See pp. 90–91.

259. Bélanger, *Grégoire le Grand*, 30–34.

260. Augustine, *Enarrationes in Psalmos* 3.7; *De doctrina christiana* 2.6 [7]; see *Enarrationes in Psalmos* 77.4 and 94.11; Gregory, *Mor.* 33.27 [47], 6–12.

261. Augustine, *De doctrina christiana* 2.6 [7].

262. Augustine, *Ep.* 140.22 [55].

sinners, releases them from the chilliness of their evil ways.²⁶³ In this context, both Augustine and Gregory cite 2 Corinthians 2:15 to describe what happens when the south wind, that is, the Spirit, blows.

Perhaps the most significant example is Augustine's interpretation of Song 2:2 as a reference to the Church as a necessary mixture of good and bad people.²⁶⁴ In this case, Gregory both borrowed from Augustine's exegesis of this verse and transformed it. Gregory has taken an element of Augustine's ecclesiology that was forged in the heat of the Donatist controversy and modified it into a principle of perfection in the Christian life, removing all traces of the earlier polemic. Gregory's interpretation of Song 2:2 is thus another good example of how he could both be influenced by his predecessors and yet transform them in ways that corresponded to his own experience and the pastoral needs of his audience.

C. APPONIUS

A third source for Gregory is Apponius, whose sole surviving work is a commentary on the Song of Songs, written in the first third of the fifth century.²⁶⁵ Apponius was probably a monk who lived in northern Italy, perhaps near Rome. Rodrigue Bélanger has cited several instances of Gregory's dependence on Apponius.²⁶⁶ He correctly notes that one must exercise due caution in seeing Apponius as a source for Gregory, since parallels between them

---

263. Gregory, *Mor.* 9.11 [17], 125–49; *Mor.* 27.38 [63], 6–17; *H.Ez.* 1.2 [9], 176–93.

264. Gregory, *Mor.* 1.1 [1], 1–28; *Mor.* 20.39 [76], 20–53; *H.Ev.* 38 [7], 141–84. For Augustine's use of this verse, see Michael Cameron, "Augustine's Use of the Song of Songs against the Donatists," in *Augustine: Biblical Exegete*, ed. Frederick Van Fleteren and Joseph C. Schnaubelt, 99–127 (New York: Peter Lang, 2001).

265. On the date, see Bernard de Vregille and Louis Neyrand, *Apponius: Commentaire sue le cantique des cantiques*, SChr 420, 421, and 430 (Paris: Cerf, 1997–98), 1.111–20; see also Mark W. Elliott, *The Song of Songs and Christology in the Early Church 381–451* (Tübingen: Mohr Siebeck, 2000), 40–50; and Bélanger, *Grégoire le Grand*, 35–36.

266. Bélanger, *Grégoire le Grand*, 37–40.

could be explained by a shared recourse to Origen.[267] While a shared recourse to Origen is undeniable and needs to be taken into account when determining the extent of Apponius's influence on Gregory, there are cases in which one can detect the inspiration of Apponius alongside the Alexandrian exegete.

One example of this can be found in *Exp.* 7, from the second part of the prologue. In *Exp.* 7 Gregory follows Origen in listing several different kinds of scriptural songs that culminate in the Song of Songs.[268] While there is not exact correspondence between the lists (Origen has six songs that precede the Song of Songs; Gregory has four), the influence of Origen is unmistakable. The songs enumerated by Origen in the *Homilies* are:

1. the song of Moses after crossing the Red Sea (Exod 15:1-28)
2. the song sung upon the arrival at the well (Num 21:17-18)
3. the song of Moses at the bank of the Jordan (Deut 32:1-43)
4. the song of Deborah after the overthrow of Sisera (Judg 5)
5. the song of David after escaping his enemies and Saul (2 Sam 22)
6. the song of the vineyard (Isa 5:1-7)
7. the Song of Songs

In his *Commentary*, Origen substitutes David's song of thanksgiving on the appointment of Asaph and his brethren (1 Chr 16:8-36) as the fifth song. Gregory's first song corresponds to Origen's first song, though he attributes it to Miriam, not Moses, an identification based on Exodus 15:21. His second song corresponds exactly to Origen's third. In third place Gregory substitutes the song of Hannah (1 Sam 2:1-10). His fourth corresponds to Origen's fifth.

---

267. Bélanger, *Grégoire le Grand*, 37.
268. Origen, *H.Cant.* 1.1; and *C.Cant.* prol. 4.3–14.

While clearly influenced by Origen, Gregory does not follow him in every detail. Gregory also adopts Origen's teaching that one must ascend through the songs in order before attempting to sing the Song of Songs. But Gregory places less stress on the order of the songs than Origen does and highlights, rather, the different character of each song. The song of Miriam is a song of victory. Moses' song at the Jordan is a song of encouragement and affirmation. The song of Hannah is a song of rejoicing. David's song after escaping his enemies is a song asking for help. Such categorization of the songs is not found in Origen.

In this, Gregory may have Apponius as his point of departure. Apponius, also clearly influenced by Origen, listed nine songs that preceded the Song of Songs and says that "these songs were sung by various prophets for various persons or reasons."[269] He describes the song of Moses after crossing the Red Sea as "a song in praise of victory" (*pro victoriae laude*). Though Gregory categorized this song as a song of encouragement and affirmation, he may have developed Apponius's idea that each of the songs that precedes the Song of Songs has a certain character, in that they were sung "for various persons or reasons." Gregory may have specified what Apponius suggested. Furthermore, the four songs that Gregory places before the Song of Songs are all listed in Apponius, whereas only three are found in Origen. Accordingly, Gregory may have inserted the song of Hannah into Origen's list based on his reading of Apponius. And so, the example of *Exp.* 7 shows that, even if both Gregory and Apponius independently used Origen, there is evidence that Gregory may have known and appropriated Apponius as well.

Apponius may have also influenced Gregory in *Exp.* 8. Most of the second half of Gregory's preface to the *Exposition* is based on Origen (*Exp.* 6–7 and 9–10).[270] Gregory has inserted *Exp.* 8 into the material he drew from Origen. In this paragraph he explains the significance of the names 'Lord,' 'Father,' and 'Bridegroom.' God uses

---

269. *In Canticum canticorum expositio* 1, 229–60.
270. See p. 86.

these three titles to indicate the character of the relationship he wants to have with the person who calls him by these names. 'Lord' is used in relations where the fear of God takes precedence. In this context, Gregory cross-references Malachi 1:6. 'Father' is used when honor of God is primary, 'Bridegroom' when it is a question of love, and here Gregory cites Hosea 2:19-20 and Jeremiah 2:2 as cross-references. Gregory adds that these names correspond to the stages of spiritual progress. God's own goal is to be called Bridegroom. Yet in order to attain this stage the Christian must begin with fearing God, advance to honoring God, and then arrive at loving God.

In *Exp.* 8 Gregory is not drawing on a single source but rather synthesizes the ideas of others with Apponius. Lactantius had used Malachi 1:6 to make the point that 'Lord' emphasizes God's power to punish whereas 'Father,' his kindness.[271] The appeal to this verse for the same theme is also found, for example, in Jerome and Cassian.[272] Elsewhere in his corpus Gregory explains in a similar vein how God prefers to be loved as Father rather than feared as Lord.[273] Apponius cites Hosea 2:19-20 and Jeremiah 2:2 as evidence that the Word is the Bridegroom of the Church.[274] And so, it appears that Gregory connects these two streams of thought: (1) the distinction made between 'Lord' and 'Father' by appeal to Malachy 1:6, which is found in Lactantius, Jerome, and Cassian; and (2) the significance of the title 'Bridegroom' by appeal to Hosea 2:19-20 and Jeremiah 2:2 found in Apponius.

D. AMBROSE OF MILAN

Gregory esteemed Ambrose as much as he did Augustine. In a letter to Marinianus, bishop of Ravenna, Gregory writes, "I believed it most inappropriate that you should drink despicable water [i.e., Gregory's own homilies on Ezekiel], when it is certain that you

---

271. *De vera sapientia et religione* 4.3.
272. Jerome, *Ep.* 52.7; *Commentary on Malachy* 1.6; Cassian, *Conferences* 11.10.
273. *Mor.* 9, 39–41 [62–64]; 11, 41 [55].
274. *In Canticum canticorum expositio* 1, 192f.

regularly imbibe the deep and clear streams from the springs of the blessed Fathers, Ambrose and Augustine."[275] Yet the influence of Ambrose upon Gregory in respect of his exegesis of the Song of Songs has not been much studied. The following discusses three examples in which Gregory borrowed from Ambrose's interpretation of the Song of Songs.

1. In a passage in which Ambrose is interpreting Song 2:8, he discusses the meaning of the Bridegroom's leaping upon the mountains. Gregory follows him closely, almost word-for-word:

Ambrose	Gregory
Salit de caelo in virginem, de utero in praesepe, de Iordane in crucem, de cruce in tumulum, in caelum de sepulcro. Proba mihi David salientem, proba currentem. Tu enim dixisti: «Exsultavit ut gigas ad currendam viam.»[276]	*De caelo venit in uterum, de utero venit in praesepe, de praesepe venit in crucem, de cruce venit in sepulcrum, de sepulcro rediit in caelum. Ecce ut nos post se faceret, quos pro nobis saltus manifesta per carnem Veritas dedit, quia «exsultavit ut gigas ad currendam viam.»*[277]
He leaps from heaven into the virgin, from the womb into the manger, from the Jordan onto the cross, from the cross into the grave, from the tomb into heaven. Show me, David, the one who leaps, show me the one who runs. For you have said: *he exulted like a giant to run his course* [Ps 18:6].	From heaven he came into the womb. From the womb he came into the manger. From the manger he came onto the cross. From the cross he came into the tomb. From the tomb he returned to heaven. Behold! In order to make us run after him, Truth manifested in the flesh performed for our sake a certain number of leaps and *he exulted like a giant to run his course* [Ps 18:6].

---

275. *Reg. ep.* 12.16a [=*H.Ez.* praef]; trans. Martyn, *Letters*, 821.
276. Ambrose, *Expositio psalmi cxviii* 6, 2–3 (CSEL 62:111, 18–24). Virtually the same text is found in *De Isaac et anima* 4.31.
277. Gregory, *H.Ev.* 29 [10], 231–34 (CCSL 141:253–54).

Gregory takes from Ambrose both the five leaps performed by the Bridegroom and the reference to Psalm 18:6. The heavenly Word becomes incarnate in the womb of Mary, is born and placed in the manger, dies on the cross and is buried, and after the resurrection returns to heaven: this is his "course," the course the Incarnate Word "ran." Though Gregory makes some minor alterations, his indebtedness to Ambrose is clear.

Incidentally, Ambrose is here adapting an earlier christological interpretation of Song 2:8 that views the incarnation as the descent and ascent of the Word.[278] For example, in his interpretation of Song 2:8, Hippolytus writes, "Now what is meant by 'leaping'? The Word leapt from heaven into the womb of the virgin. He leapt from the holy womb onto the tree. He leapt from the tree into hell. He leapt upward from there to the earth in this human flesh. O new resurrection! From there he leapt from the earth to heaven. Here he sits at the right hand of the Father, and from there he will leap to the earth to repay the exchange of retribution."[279] Though Hippolytus describes seven leaps of the Word, as opposed to Ambrose's five, Ambrose is clearly drawing on Hippolytus in this instance. And so, through the fourth-century Ambrose, the christological interpretation of the third-century Hippolytus has influenced the sixth-century Gregory.

2. Gregory also follows Ambrose in his "historical" interpretation of Song 1:1 that connects it with Luke 7:45 because both verses speak of kissing.

Ambrose	Gregory
«*Osculum mihi non dedisti: haec autem ex quo intravi, non cessavit osculari pedes meos*». *Osculum utique insigne est charitatis. Unde ergo Judaeo osculum, qui pacem non recognovit, qui pacem a Christo non*	«*Osculum mihi non dedisti: haec autem ex quo intravi, non cessavit osculari pedes meos*». *Osculum quippe dilectionis est signum. Et infidelis ille populus Deo osculum non dedit, quia ex caritate eum*

278. See Elliott, *The Song of Songs*, 76–77.
279. Hippolytus, *C. Cant.* 21.2 (40 Garitte).

*accepit dicente: «Pacem meam do vobis, pacem meam relinquo vobis»? Non habet Synagoga osculum; habet Ecclesia, quae exspectavit, quae dilexit, quae dixit: «Osculetur me ab osculis oris sui»; diuturnae enim cupiditatis ardorem, quem adventus Dominici exspectatione adoleverat, osculo ejus volebat stillanter exstinguere, hoc explere sitim suam munere.*³	*amare noluit, cui ex timore servivit. Vocata autem gentilitas Redemptoris sui vestigia osculari non cessat, quia in eius continuo amore suspirat. Unde et sponsae voce de eodem Redemptore sui in Canticis canticorum dicitur: «Osculetur me ab osculis oris sui». Osculum recte conditoris sui desiderat, quae se ei obsequi per amorem parat.*⁴
You have not given me a kiss, yet this woman has not ceased kissing my feet since I entered [Luke 7:45]. To be sure, a kiss is a sign of love. This is why the kiss is not given to the Jew, seeing that he has neither known peace nor received peace from Christ when he said: *My peace I give to you, my peace I leave you* [John 14:27]. The synagogue did not have the kiss. The Church has the kiss because she has waited for it and desired it when she said: *Let him kiss me with the kiss of his mouth* [Song 1:1]. For by his kiss she wished to quench bit-by-bit the burning of her long desire, which had increased as she waited for the coming of the Lord, and to satisfy her thirst with this gift.	You have not given me a kiss, yet this woman has not ceased kissing my feet since I entered [Luke 7:45]. Now a kiss is a sign of love. On the one hand, that faithless people did not give a kiss to God because they chose not to love out of charity him whom they served out of fear. But the Gentiles, on the other hand, after they were called have not ceased to kiss the feet of their Redeemer because they sigh with unceasing love for him. This is why in the Song of Songs it is said in the voice of the Bride about that same Redeemer of hers: *Let him kiss me with the kiss of his mouth*. They are right to desire the kiss of their maker since they get themselves ready to obey him through their love.

---

280. Ambrose, *Ep.* 41.14. See *On repentance* 2.69.
281. Gregory, *H.Ev.* 33 [6], 159–67 (CCSL 141:294); see *Exp.* 18.

A little before the Gregorian passage cited above, the pope had spelled out the references in Luke 7:45: "But whom does the Pharisee, presuming on his false justice, represent, if not the Jewish people? Who is represented by the woman who was a sinner but came to the Lord's feet and wept, if not converted Gentiles?"[282] Like Ambrose, Gregory connects the kissing of Song 1:1 with the kissing of Luke 7:45 and makes the point that "a kiss is a sign of love," though the terminology he uses is different. For Ambrose, the Jews did not receive the kiss because of their lack of peace, whereas for Gregory it is because of their lack of love. For Ambrose, the Church received the kiss because of her desire for the Lord, whereas for Gregory the Church received the kiss because of her love. While Gregory's indebtedness to Ambrose is clear, he has developed Ambrose such that reception of the kiss of the Redeemer is solely a matter of love.

3. The next example demonstrates how Gregory could remove a passage from its original context and make it serve his own purposes. While Ambrose's christological exegesis of Song 1:2b is part of a larger argument about the divinity of the Holy Spirit, Gregory is solely concerned with the christological exegesis of the verse, not its use in Ambrose's overall argument.

Ambrose	Gregory
«*Unguentum exinanitum est nomen tuum*». *Cuius virtute sermonis nihil potest esse praestantius. Nam sicut inclusum in vase aliquo unguentum cohibet odorem suum, qui odor quamdiu vasis illius angustiis coercetur, etsi ad plures non potest pervenire, tamen vim suam servat; cum vero de vase illo, quo claudebatur, unguentum fuerit*	«*Unguentum effusum nomen tuum*». *Unguentum effusum est diuinitas incarnata. Si enim sit unguentum in uasculo, odorem exterius minus reddit; si uero effunditur, odor effusi unguenti dilatatur. Nomen ergo dei unguentum effusum est: quia ab inmensitate diuinitatis suae ad naturam nostram se exterius fudit*

---

282. Gregory, *H.Ev.* 33 [5], 104–6 (CCSL 141:292).

effusum, longe lateque diffunditur: ita et Christi nomen ante ejus adventum in Israel populo, quasi in vase aliquo Judaeorum mentibus claudebatur: «Notus» enim «in Judaea Deus, in Israel magnum nomen ejus»: hoc utique nomen, quod vasa Judaeorum angustiis suis coercitum continebant.⁵	et, ab eo quod est inuisibilis, se uisibilem reddidit. Si enim non se effunderet, nequaquam nobis innotesceret. Effudit se unguentum, cum se et deum seruauit et homo exhibuit.⁶
Your name is ointment poured-out [Song 1:2b]. Nothing can surpass the force of this statement. For just as ointment stored in some bottle keeps in its odor, and as long as it is confined in the narrow space of that bottle it preserves its strength, even though it cannot reach many, but when the ointment is poured out of the bottle in which it was enclosed, it is diffused far and wide; so too the name of Christ before his coming among the people of Israel was enclosed in the minds of the Jews as if in some bottle. For *God is known in Judah; his name is great is Israel* [Ps 75:1], meaning that name that the bottles of the Jews used to confine in their narrow spaces.	Your name is ointment poured-out [Song 1:2b]. Poured-out ointment is the incarnate divinity. Now when ointment is stored in a small bottle, there is no odor outside of it. But when it is poured out, the odor of the poured-out ointment spreads far and wide. Therefore, the name of God is ointment poured-out because God poured himself out exteriorly from the immensity of his divinity into our nature and rendered himself visible from that which is invisible. For if he had not poured himself out, he would not have become known to us at all. He poured himself out as ointment by both preserving himself as God and displaying himself as a human being.

Before citing Song 1:2b, Ambrose had been arguing for the divinity of the Holy Spirit based on the fact that in Romans 5:5 the Spirit

---

283. Ambrose, *De spiritu sancto* 1.95.
284. Gregory, *Exp.* 21.

is said to be "poured out."²⁸⁵ Ambrose cited Song 1:2b to show that being poured out is proper only to God, as this verse speaks of Christ's pouring out, that is, his incarnation.²⁸⁶ The interpretation of Song 1:2b as a prophecy of the incarnation goes back at least to Origen, and Gregory has adopted aspects of Origen's exegesis of this verse.²⁸⁷ Yet Gregory has borrowed Ambrose's description of the two states of ointment, enclosed in a bottle or poured out of it. Ambrose himself had copied this description from Didymus the Blind.²⁸⁸ Hence, through Ambrose, Gregory has appropriated a fourth-century Greek exegesis of Song 1:2b.²⁸⁹ Gregory has no interest in Ambrose's use of this verse as part of an argument for the Holy Spirit's divinity. By Gregory's time this issue had been long settled. Gregory's interest in the verse is solely christological.

E. JOHN CASSIAN

Though Gregory was deeply influenced by John Cassian, there is virtually no evidence that Cassian's exegesis of the Song of Songs had an impact on Gregory. This is not surprising since Cassian cited the Song of Songs a mere nine times in his works. The only parallel—and it is a slight one—between the two is found in *Institutes* 5.17–18. Here Cassian cites Song 1:3b to interpret 1 Corinthians 9:26-27, in which Paul speaks of his running not without purpose so as to attain the prize. Gregory makes a similar connection between Song 1:3b and Paul, but cites 1 Corinthians 9:24 as

285. See Ambrose, *De spiritu sancto* 1.90–94.
286. See Ambrose, *De spiritu sancto* 1.95–96.
287. Origen, *C. Cant.* 1.4.4; and *H. Cant.* 1.4. Gregory's indebtedness to Origen is seen especially in the connection made between Song 1:2b with Phil 2:6-7 (*C. Cant.* 1.4.4): though Origen hints at this, it is Gregory who makes it explicit. Once again, Origen is Gregory's point of departure for his own developments.
288. See Didymus, *De spiritu sancto* 51. Didymus may owe something to Eusebius of Caesarea, *Demonstratio evangelica* 4.3. Jerome denigrated Ambrose's *De spiritu sancto* as little more than bad Latin translation of Didymus's Greek treatise; see Didymus, *De spiritu sancto*, prol.
289. See Elliott, *The Song of Songs*, 53–57, for a discussion of the christological use of Song 1:2b.

an example of running to the end in perseverance.[290] Both Gregory and Cassian view the "running" of Song 1:3b as the kind of running that obtains the ultimate prize—God. Aside from this, there is no trace of Cassian's exegesis of the Song of Songs in Gregory. Yet there are many instances in which doctrines of Cassian that are not specifically associated with the exegesis of the Song of Songs turn up in Gregory's interpretation of particular verses. For example, Gregory borrows Cassian's notion that only those who are sinners do not desire the Lord's coming as judge, as those who are confident about their good works look forward to it without fear.[291]

V. Two Notes to the Reader

A. Note on References to the Song of Songs

Because of Gregory's habit of citing snippets of what are single verses of the Song of Songs according to modern divisions, it has been necessary for reference purposes to subdivide certain verses. This happens most frequently in Song 1:1-8.

Vulgate Text	English Translation
1:1a *osculetur me osculo oris sui*	Let him kiss me with the kiss of his mouth!
1:1b *quia meliora sunt ubera tua vino*	For your breasts are better than wine.
1:2a *fraglantia unguentis optimis oleum*	The odor of your ointments surpasses all perfumes.
1:2b *effusum nomen tuum*	Your name is ointment poured-out.
1:2c *ideo adulescentulae dilexerunt te*	Therefore, the young girls have loved you.

---

290. Gregory, *Exp.* 25.
291. Cassian, *Conferences* 9.19; Gregory, *Exp.* 31.

1:3a *trahe me* **1:3b** *post te curremus in odorem ungventorum tuorum*[292]	Draw me. After you we shall run in the odor of your ointments.
1:3c *introduxit me rex in cellaria sua*	The king has brought me into his bedchamber.
1:3d *exultabimus et laetabimur in te* **1:3e** *memores uberum tuorum super vinum* **1:3f** *recti diligunt te*	We shall rejoice and be glad in you, mindful of your breasts that surpass wine. The upright love you.
1:4a *nigra sum sed formonsa filiae Hierusalem* **1:4b** *sicut tabernacula Cedar* **1:4c** *sicut pelles Salomonis*	I am black but beautiful, daughters of Jerusalem, like the tents of Kedar, like the curtains of Solomon.
1:5a *nolite me considerare quod fusca sim* **1:5b** *quia decoloravit me sol*	Do not stare at me because I am dark, for the sun has scorched me.
1:5c *filii matris meae pugnaverunt contra me* **1:5d** *posuerunt me custodem in vineis* **1:5e** *vineam meam non custodivi*	The sons of my mother fought against me. They stationed me as a guardian in their vineyards, but I have not guarded my own vineyard.
1:6a *indica mihi quem diligit anima mea ubi pascas ubi cubes in meridie* **1:6b** *ne vagari incipiam per greges sodalium tuorum*	Show me, you whom my soul loves, where you pasture, where you lie down at midday, lest I begin to wander after the flocks of your companions.
1:7a *si ignoras te o pulchra inter mulieres* **1:7b** *egredere et abi post vestigia gregum* **1:7c** *et pasce hedos tuos iuxta tabernacula pastorum*	If you do not know yourself, O beautiful among women, set out and follow the tracks of the flocks, and pasture your young goats near the tents of the shepherds.

292. For Song 1:3b the Vulgate reads only *post te curremus*.

1:8 *equitatui meo in curribus Pharaonis adsimilavi te amica mea*	I have associated you, my sweetheart, with my cavalry while you were in the chariots of Pharaoh.

B. Note on the Translations

A few words on the style and format of the following translations are necessary. *Italics* are used in the translations for scriptural citations or reminiscences; these are always followed by the scriptural reference in square brackets, for example [John 1:1]. References to scriptural allusions are given in the footnotes. Single quotation marks (' ') are used to signal when Gregory is quoting a scriptural phrase, sometimes not exactly, or even a single word from a verse of Scripture, before he offers his own interpretation. Single quotation marks are also used to signal when Gregory is talking about a word in itself, not the object that it names. Double quotation marks (" ") almost always signal one of Gregory's interpretive paraphrases of a scriptural verse. On rare occasions words are inserted in square brackets to improve the sense.

In these translations I have attempted to render Gregory as clearly as possible in English without making him clearer than he is in Latin and have refrained from making his prose more exciting than his somewhat wooden style warrants. In fact, Gregory's style varies considerably in the texts contained in this volume. In the excerpts from the *Moralia* and Gregory's other published works, Gregory's prose is elegant and terse, marked by long periods and variety in vocabulary. The style of the *Exposition* falls short of the refinement of his published works. This is not surprising given the fact that the *Exposition* is a notary's copy of an oral delivery that Gregory never polished. Here, Gregory's style is at times repetitious and unglamorous. Yet the lack of flourish in his words is counterbalanced by the profundity in his thought. In these translations I have aimed to avoid the extremes of literalism and paraphrase. On the one hand, I have strived to produce English prose that is understandable, idiomatic, and felicitous; on the other hand, I have endeavored not to stray into paraphrase so that the words and phrases of the translations could be matched with the Latin on which they are based. Dear reader, the result of my efforts is now before you.

TRANSLATIONS

GREGORY THE GREAT'S

Exposition on the Song of Songs

Introduction

The modern critical edition of Gregory the Great's *Exposition on the Song of Songs* was established for *Corpus Christianorum Series Latina* by Patrick Verbraken in 1963.[1] After examining the twenty-two extant manuscripts, he identified two major textual families, each of which could be further subdivided into groups.[2] For his edition, he favored the four manuscripts of group α of the first family, the most ancient witnesses, dating from the ninth to tenth centuries. But he noted that the six manuscripts of group δ from the second family (ninth to thirteenth centuries) were nearly as important, especially $\delta^{1,2,3}$, as their archetype's age rivaled that of α. Verbraken's edition replaced two older editions.[3] The first is the Maurist edition of 1705 (*m*), which was based on manuscripts no longer available

---

1. Patrick Verbraken, *Sancti Gregorii Magni Expositiones in Canticum Canticorum, in Librum Primum Regum*, CCSL 144 (Brepols: Turnhout, 1963), 3–46.

2. Verbraken used twenty-one mss. in his original edition. For a detailed discussion of the manuscripts, see his, "La tradition manuscrite du commentaire de saint Grégoire sur le Cantique des cantiques," *Revue Bénédictine* 73 (1963): 277–88, which he summarizes in the introduction to his edition (CCSL 144:viii–ix). Subsequent to his edition Verbraken discovered another ms. that proved to be the oldest surviving witness to the text (eighth to ninth century). Nonetheless, its readings correspond to Verbraken's family β, a text of very poor quality. See Patrick Verbraken, "Un nouveau manuscript du Commentaire de saint Grégoire sur le Cantique des Cantiques," *Revue Bénédictine* 75 (1965): 143–45.

3. *Sancti Gregorii Papae super Cantica Canticorum Expositio* in *Sancti Gregorii Papae I cognomento Magni Opera omnia*, Édition des Bénédictins de Saint-Maur, t. III (Paris, 1705), 2ᵉ part, cols. 397–414. Reprinted by Migne, PL 79:471–92; and *Commentarius Gregorio Magno adscriptus* in Gotth. Heine, *Bibliotheca Anecdotorum seu Veterum Monumentum ecclesiasticorum Collectio novissima. Pars I. Monumenta regni Gothorum et Arabum in Hispaniis* (Leipzig: Weigel, 1848), 168–86.

today, and the second is that of Gotthard Heine from 1848 (*h*) whose text largely corresponds to Verbraken's group *β* of the first family.

Both Paul Meyvaert and J. H. Waszink, in their respective reviews of Verbraken's edition, suggested many different readings based on the manuscripts.[4] Meyvaert argued that the readings of groups *δ ε* of the second family deserved "the greatest respect, particularly if they can be reinforced by the context or by what we know *par ailleurs* about Gregory's vocabulary."[5] He suggested twenty-six alternate readings based on this principle. Waszink proposed three different readings and three punctuation changes. Rodrigue Bélanger incorporated many of their suggestions in his 1984 edition of Gregory's *Exposition* in the Sources Chrétiennes series, which reprinted Verbraken's edition with fourteen emendations. He accepted five of Meyvaert's alternate readings and five of Waszink's suggested changes (three alternate readings and two punctuation changes), and he employed five different readings of his own.[6]

The translation below is based on the critical edition of Verbraken, with twenty-five emendations. I have followed Bélanger's lead in accepting the same five alternate readings of Meyvaert as well as the five that he himself employed. But I have accepted only three of the five emendations that Bélanger adopted based on the suggestions of Waszink (two alternative readings and one punctuation change). In addition, I have adopted twelve of Meyvaert's suggested readings not accepted by Bélanger. In each of these cases, the reading is witnessed to not only by the groups *δ ε* but also by Heine's edition (*h*). The emendations employed in my translation of the *Exposition* are listed in appendix 3.

The section titles in the translation below are my own.

---

4. Paul Meyvaert, "A New Edition of Gregory the Great's Commentaries on the Canticle and I Kings," *Journal of Theological Studies* n.s. 9 (1968): 215–25; and J. H. Waszink, "Sancti Gregorii Magni Expositiones in Canticum Canticorum, in Librum Primum Regum," *Vigiliae Christianae* 27 (1973): 72–74.

5. Meyvaert, "A New Edition," 217.

6. Rodrigue Bélanger, *Grégoire Le Grand: Commentaire sur le Cantique des Cantiques*, SChr 314 (Paris: Cerf, 1984), 68–140.

In the name of the Lord here begins
the Exposition on the Songs of Songs,
restored from the beginning of the notary's transcription,
by Lord Gregory, Pope of the City of Rome[1]

+

Part 1: Prologue (1–10)

Human Ignorance and the Need for Allegory

1. After its banishment from the joys of Paradise, the human race came to the pilgrimage of this present life with a heart blind to spiritual understanding. If the divine voice had said to this blind heart, "Follow God!" or, "Love God!" (as was said to it in the Law), once this was uttered, the numbing cold of its obtuseness[2] would have prevented it from grasping what it heard. Accordingly, divine speech is communicated to the cold and numb soul by means of enigmas and in a hidden manner instills in her the love she does not know by means of what she knows.

2. Allegory provides the soul set far below God with a kind of crane whereby she may be lifted to God.[3] If enigmas are placed between God and the soul, when the soul recognizes something of her own in the language of the enigmas, through the meaning of this language she understands something that is not her own and by means of earthly language hopes for eternal things.[4] For by not recoiling from what she knows, the soul comes to understand what she does not know. Allegories are produced by clothing divine thoughts in what we know. When we recognize the exterior language, we attain interior understanding.

---

1. This *incipit* is the most genuine and is found in mss. $\alpha^{1,3,4}$, $\beta^{1,4}$, ω^2.
2. Here I read *insensibilitatis* instead of *infidelitatis*.
3. Here I read *infra positae* instead of *positae*.
4. Here I read *sperantur aeterna* instead of *separatur a terra*. The alternate reading is translated: "is separated from earthly things."

3. In this book here, in which the Song of Songs is written, the language of what appears to be physical love is employed that the soul may be revived from her numbing cold by means of her usual manner of speech, so that she may grow warm again and so be spurred on to the love that is above by the language of the love here below. Now in this book there is mention of kisses, there is mention of breasts, there is mention of cheeks, there is mention of thighs. We should not ridicule the sacred narrative for using such language. Rather, let us ponder how great God's mercy is. For when he mentions the parts of the body and thereby summons us to love, note how wonderfully and mercifully he works within us. He has gone so far as to embrace the language of our vulgar love in order to enkindle our heart with a yearning for that sacred love. Yet God lifts us by understanding to the place from where he lowers himself by speaking. For we learn from dialogues of the love here below with what intensity we should burn in the love of Divinity.

4. Let us consider this book carefully lest we linger over exterior meanings when we hear the words of exterior love. Otherwise the very crane employed to lift us will instead burden us and thus not lift us. In these bodily words, in these exterior words, let us seek whatever is interior. And when we discuss the body, let us become as if separated from the body. Let us attend this sacred wedding of the Bride and Bridegroom with an understanding of the most interior kind of charity, which is to say with a wedding gown. Such attire is necessary[5] since if we are not dressed in a wedding gown, that is, if we do not have a worthy understanding of charity, then we will be cast out of this wedding banquet into the exterior darkness, which is to say into the blindness of ignorance.[6] By means of this passionate dialogue let us cross over to the virtue of impassibility.

For just as Sacred Scripture consists of words and its meaning, so too a picture consists of colors and its subject matter. And he is

---

5. Here I read *nuptiali. Necesse est, ne, si* instead of *nuptiali, necesse est: ne, si.*
6. See Matt 22:1-14.

dumber than dumb who pays such close attention to the colors of the picture that he ignores the subject depicted! So if we embrace the words expressed in an exterior way and ignore their meaning, it is as if we were ignoring the subject depicted by concentrating only upon the colors. It is written: *The letter kills but the spirit gives life* [2 Cor 3:6]. For the letter hides the spirit just like the husk covers the kernel. Yet it is beasts who feed on husks, whereas human beings eat the kernel. So then, whoever uses human reason should discard the husks of the beasts and promptly eat the kernel of the spirit. After all, it is beneficial[7] that the mysteries are veiled by being wrapped in letters, insofar as long-sought wisdom tastes better. Hence it is written: *The wise conceal the meaning* [Prov 10:14]. For surely the spiritual meaning is concealed under the veil of the letter.

Furthermore, in the same book it is said: *It is the glory of God to hide the word* [Prov 25:2a]. For God appears more glorious to the mind that seeks him the more subtly and interiorly she seeks that he appear. But could it be that we ought not demand what God hides in his mysteries? Of course we should, for it continues: *And the glory of kings is to examine the word* [Prov 25:2b]. Now they are kings who already know how to rule and examine their bodies, or rather, the stirrings of their flesh. So then, 'the glory of kings is to examine the word' because it is praiseworthy for those who live a good life to scrutinize the mysteries of God's commandments.

Therefore, when we hear the words of a human conversation, let us be like those who are above ordinary people. Otherwise by listening in a human way to what is said we might not perceive anything about the Divinity that we ought to be hearing. Paul no longer desired his disciples to be like ordinary people when he said to them: *For when envy and contention are among you, are you not ordinary people?* [1 Cor 3:3-4]. The Lord no longer considered his disciples to be like ordinary people when he said: *Who do ordinary people say that the Son of Man is?* [Matt 16:13]. When they told him what ordinary people had said, he immediately added: *But you, who*

---

7. Here I read *utile* instead of *utilis*.

do you say that I am? [Matt 16:15]. For by saying 'ordinary people' first and then adding 'you,' he was contrasting ordinary people and his disciples, surely because by inspiring them to divine things he was making them superior to ordinary people.

The Apostle states: *Therefore if anyone is in Christ, he is a new creation, the old has passed away* [2 Cor 5:17]. And we know that at our resurrection the body is so united to the spirit that everything which the passions controlled is assumed into the power of the spirit. Therefore, whoever follows God ought to imitate his own resurrection every day. In light of the fact that at that time he will have nothing subject to the passions in his body, he should now have nothing subject to the passions in his heart. In the present time he should be a new creation according to the interior man, in the present time he should trample on anything suggestive of the old man, and he should seek in old words only the power of the new.

5. Now Sacred Scripture is a kind of mountain from which the Lord comes into our hearts to give understanding. This mountain is mentioned by the Prophet: *God shall come from Lebanon and the Holy One from a shady and thickly wooded mountain* [Hab 3:3]. This mountain is 'thick' because of its meanings and 'shady' because of its allegories. But know that, when the Lord's voice echoes on the mountain, we are commanded to wash our clothes and be cleansed from every defilement of the flesh, provided that we are hastening to approach the mountain. After all, it is written that *if a beast should touch the mountain, it is to be stoned* [Heb 12:20; cf. Exod 19:12-13]. Now a 'beast touches the mountain' when those enslaved to irrational stirrings approach the lofty heights of Sacred Scripture and understand it in an inappropriate way, interpreting it irrationally according to whim. For if some fool or half-wit should be spotted around this mountain, he would be put to death by his most dreadful thoughts as if by stones.

This mountain burns because surely Sacred Scripture causes whomever it spiritually fills to be inflamed with the fire of love. Hence it is written: *Your word is fiery* [Ps 118:140]. Hence when some men walking on the road heard the words of God,[8] they exclaimed: *Did not our heart burn within us as he opened the scriptures to us?* [Luke 24:32]. Hence it is said through Moses: *In his right hand is the fiery law* [Deut 33:2]. At God's left hand are gathered the wicked who do not cross over to his right side. At God's 'right hand' are the elect who are separated from those on the left. So then, 'in God's right hand is the fiery law' because in the hearts of the elect, who will be placed at his right hand, the divine precepts are aflame and burn with the ardor of charity. So then, let this fire consume any exterior corruption and oldness that exists in us, so that our mind may be offered as a holocaust in the contemplation of God.

Explanation of the Title, "The Song of Songs"

6. Nor is it pointless to note that this book is not called "the Song" but "the Song of Songs." For just as in the Old Testament there are holy things as well as the holies of holies, and there are sabbaths as well as the sabbaths of sabbaths, so too in Sacred Scripture there are songs as well as the Songs of Songs. The holy things were kept in the tabernacle and brought outside of it; the sabbaths were celebrated each week. But the holies of holies were undertaken with a kind of more mysterious veneration and the sabbaths of sabbaths were observed only on their own feasts. Likewise, the Songs of Songs is a kind of mystery and is solemn in a more interior way. One penetrates this mystery by grasping hidden meanings. For if the exterior language is focused upon, there is no mystery.

The Genre of the Song of Songs

7. Know also that in Sacred Scripture some songs are songs of victory and others are songs of encouragement and affirmation, some are songs of rejoicing and others are songs of help received, and some are songs of union with God. Miriam sang a song of victory after the Red Sea was crossed: *Let us sing to the Lord, for he is gloriously triumphant: horse and rider he has thrown into the sea* [Exod 15:21]. Moses

---

8. Here I read *cum verba dei audirent* instead of *cum verba dei*.

sang a song of encouragement and affirmation to the Israelites as they approached the promised land: *Give heed, heaven, and let me speak: let the land hearken to the words of my mouth* [Deut 32:1]. Hanna sang a song of rejoicing when she foresaw the fecundity of the Church in herself: *My heart exults in the Lord* [1 Sam 2:1]. Therefore, she expressed the fecundity of the Church's future generations figuratively[9] when she said: *The barren woman gives birth to many, and she who has many sons is weak* [1 Sam 2:5]. After battle David sang a song of help received: *I will love you, Lord, my strength* [Ps 17:2]. But a song of union with God is that song which was sung at the marriage of the Bride and Bridegroom, which is to say the Song of Songs. It is more sublime than all other songs insofar as it is performed at a marriage of more sublime solemnity. Now by means of those other songs vices are shunned, but through this song everyone is enriched with virtues. By means of those other songs the enemy is thwarted, but through this song the Lord is embraced with an intimate love.

Explanation of the Lord's Names

8. Note too that sometimes in Sacred Scripture the Lord calls himself 'Lord,' sometimes 'Father,' and sometimes 'Bridegroom.' When he wants to be feared, he calls himself 'Lord.' When he wants to be honored, 'Father.' When he wants to be loved, 'Bridegroom.' He himself says through the Prophet: *If I am Lord, why don't you fear me? If I am Father, why don't you honor me?* [Mal 1:6]. And again he says: *I have betrothed you to myself in righteousness and fidelity* [Hos 2:19-20]. And: *I remembered the day of your betrothal in the desert* [Jer 2:2]. Now there are surely no "whens" for God.[10] But since he wants to be feared before being honored, and honored before love of him is attained, he calls himself 'Lord' on account of the fear, 'Father' on account of the honor, and 'Bridegroom' on account of the love. Thus

---

9. Here I read *figurate* instead of *figuram*.

10. Lat. *Et quidem apud deum quando et quando non est*. In other words, the use of temporal language when speaking about God does not refer to different moments of time.

through fear we come to honor, and through honor of him we attain love. Therefore, as honor is more worthy than fear, God rejoices more to be called 'Father' than 'Lord.' And as love is dearer than honor, God rejoices more to be called 'Bridegroom' than 'Father.'

In this book, then, the Lord and the Church are not called 'Lord' and 'Handmaiden' but 'Bridegroom' and 'Bride,' that he may be served not only with fear, not only with reverence, but also with love, and that an interior affection for him may be aroused by this exterior language. When he calls himself 'Lord,' he indicates that we have been created by him. When he calls himself 'Father,' he indicates that we have been adopted by him. When he calls himself 'Bridegroom,' he indicates that we have been united to him. But being united to God is greater than being created or adopted by him. In this book, then, when 'Bridegroom' is said, something quite sublime is being conveyed since it reveals our bond of union with him.

These names are frequently employed in the New Testament because it celebrates the already consummated union of Word and flesh, of Christ and the Church. Hence John says at the Lord's coming: *He who has the Bride is the Bridegroom* [John 3:29]. Similarly, the same Lord says: *The sons of the Bridegroom will not fast while the Bridegroom is with them* [Matt 9:15]. Likewise, it is said to the Church: *I have betrothed you to one man, to present you as a chaste virgin to Christ* [2 Cor 11:2]. And again: *So that he might produce a glorious Church without stain or wrinkle* [Eph 5:27]. And again in the Revelation of John: *How happy are they who have been invited to the wedding-banquet of the Lamb!* [Rev 19:9]. And again in the same place: *And I saw the Bride as if a newlywed coming down from heaven* [Rev 21:2].

THE POSITION OF THE SONG OF SONGS AMONG
THE WORKS OF SOLOMON

9. The fact that this book of Solomon is placed third among his works is not inconsistent with its great mystery. For the ancients maintained that there were three orders of life: the moral, the natural, and the contemplative—what the Greeks called the ethical, the physical, and the theoretical lives. The subject of Proverbs is the

moral life, where it is said: *My son, hear my wisdom and bend your ear to my prudence* [Prov 5:1]. The subject of Ecclesiastes is the natural life because here consideration is given to the fact that all things tend to an end, when it is said: *Vanity of vanities, and all is vanity* [Eccl 1:2]. The subject of the Songs of Songs is the contemplative life because in these songs the coming and appearance of the Lord himself is desired, when it is said in the voice of Bridegroom: *Come from Lebanon, come!* [Song 4:8].

These orders are also signified by the lives of the three Patriarchs, Abraham, Isaac, and Jacob. Abraham led the moral life by being obedient.[11] Isaac symbolized the natural life by digging wells.[12] For to dig wells in the ground is to probe meticulously into all things here below by pondering their nature. Jacob led the contemplative life, having seen angels ascending and descending.[13] But since pondering the nature of things does not reach perfection unless first the moral life is lived, it is right that Ecclesiastes follows Proverbs. And since heavenly contemplation is not gazed upon unless first transitory things here below are despised, it is right that the Songs of Songs follows Ecclesiastes.

For first we get our morals in order. After this we ponder all present things as if they were not present. In the third place we gaze upon heavenly and interior realities with pure keenness of heart. And so, it is as if a kind of ladder to the contemplation of God has been constructed with these books as its rungs. Accordingly, as a first step, we attentively carry out virtuous tasks in the world. Then as the next step we disdain even the virtuous tasks of the world. Finally at the top rung we gaze upon the interior realities of God. So in this work the voice of the Church collectively awaits the coming of the Lord in such a way that every soul in particular also watches for the entry of God into her heart as though it were the Bridegroom climbing into the marriage-bed.

11. See Gen 12:4.
12. See Gen 26:14-22.
13. See Gen 28:12.

The Characters of the Drama

10. And know that four speaking characters are introduced in this book: the Bridegroom, the Bride, the young girls attending the Bride, and the flocks of companions with the Bridegroom. The Bride is the perfect Church herself, whereas the Bridegroom is the Lord. The young girls attending the Bride are the souls of beginners and those maturing through their novice zeal. The companions of the Bridegroom are either the angels who coming from him have often appeared to people or more likely all the perfect men in the Church who know how to relate the truth to people. But those who are individually young girls or companions are together as a whole the Bride, since together as a whole they are the Church.

Yet each of these three names can also be understood in an individual sense. For the one who already loves God perfectly is the Bride. The one who preaches the Bridegroom is a companion. The one who while still young follows the way of good works is a young girl. So then, we are invited to be the Bride. But if we are still unable to do this, let us be companions. If even this exceeds our capacities, let us at least gather together as young girls around the marriage-bed. Therefore, since we said that the Bridegroom and the Bride are the Lord and the Church, let us as either young girls or companions listen to the words of the Bridegroom, let us listen to the words of the Bride, and from their dialogue let us learn the fervor of love.

Part 2: Commentary (11–46)

The First Interpretation of Song 1:1–2a (11–14)

Christ's Incarnate Presence

11. And so, the holy Church, so long awaiting the coming of the Lord, so long thirsting for the font of life,[14] let her declare in what way she wants to see her Bridegroom's presence, in what way

---

14. See Ps 35:10; Prov 13:14; 16:22; John 4:14; Rev 7:17.

she desires it: 12. *Let him kiss me with the kisses of his mouth!* [Song 1:1a]. The Lord had sent angels to her, patriarchs to her, and prophets, all bearing spiritual gifts. Yet she was not seeking to perceive gifts through the Bridegroom's servants but to perceive right now the Bridegroom himself. Let us bring before our eyes the whole human race, from the world's beginning to its end, namely the whole Church: it is the one Bride who through the Law received pledges for a spiritual gift. Nonetheless, she was seeking the presence of her spouse when she said: *Let him kiss me with the kisses of his mouth*. For the holy Church, sighing for the coming of the Mediator between God and humanity, for the coming of her Redeemer, beseeches the Father in prayer to dispatch his Son to her and so enlighten her by his presence, so that he may speak to this same Church no longer through the mouths of the Prophets[15] but with his own mouth. Hence in the Gospel it is written of this same Bridegroom, that when he was seated on the mount and speaking lofty precepts, *Jesus opened his mouth and said . . .* [Matt 5:2]. It is as if he were saying: "He who once opened the mouths of the Prophets for the encouragement of the Church then opened his own mouth."

13. But see how, when she sighs, when she seeks him as if absent, suddenly she is aware of his presence! For the grace of our Creator has such power that when we speak about him as we seek him, we enjoy his presence. Hence it is written in the Gospel that when Cleopas and the other man were discussing him on the road, it was granted that they suddenly saw[16] him present.[17] So then, when the holy Church desires her still absent spouse to become incarnate, suddenly she is aware of his presence and adds: *For your breasts are better than wine, and the odor of your ointments surpasses all perfumes* [Song 1:1b-2a]. 'Wine' was the knowledge of the Law, the knowledge of the Prophets. But when the Lord came, since he wanted to preach his own wisdom through the flesh, he imparted it to us as if milk in

---

15. Here I read *per ora prophetarum* instead of *per prophetarum*.
16. Here I read *eum subito videre* instead of *eum videre*.
17. See Luke 24:13-35.

the breasts of his flesh. For being utterly incapable of grasping his wisdom in his divinity, we can perceive it in his Incarnation. Hence it is not pointless to praise his 'breasts.' For by lowering his preaching to our level he has effected in our hearts what the teaching of the Law utterly failed to effect. After all, the preaching of the Incarnation has nourished us more than the teaching of the Law. Therefore, let her say: *Your breasts are much better than wine* [Song 1:1b].

14. Reinforcing this point, she says: *And the odor of your ointments surpasses all perfumes* [Song 1:2a]. The 'ointments' of the Lord are his powerful deeds. The 'ointment' of the Lord would be the Holy Spirit.[18] Concerning the latter, the Prophet declared to the Lord: *God, your God, has anointed you with the oil of gladness above all others* [Ps 44:8]. He was anointed with this oil at the very moment he became incarnate. For he did not first become a human being and only afterward receive the Holy Spirit. Rather, becoming incarnate through the mediation of the Holy Spirit, he was anointed with this same oil at the very moment he was made a human being. Therefore, the 'odor of his ointment' is the fragrance of the Holy Spirit who remains upon him, even though the Holy Spirit proceeds from him.

The 'odor of his ointments' is the fragrance of the powerful deeds that he performed. The Church should inhale these perfumes because she has acquired many gifts of the Spirit, which in the house of God, which is to say in the communion of saints, give off an odor of good repute and announce the sweet scent of the Mediator to come. But *the odor of your ointments surpasses all perfumes* because the fragrance of the powerful deeds that the Bridegroom accomplished through his Incarnation is far more excellent than the figurative declarations of the Law which the Bridegroom conferred as pledges. After all, the more the Church grew in understanding, the more she merited to be enlightened by the grace of a fuller vision. Angels dispensed those perfumes of the Law, whereas the presence of the Bridegroom bestows this ointment. But since

---

18. Note the significance of difference between the singular and plural of 'ointment.'

the brightness of his presence has eclipsed the blessings of the Law, even though they were once believed to be lofty, it is right for it to be said: *The odor of your ointments surpasses all perfumes.*

The Second Interpretation of Song 1:1–2a (15–17)

Christ's Interior Presence

15. But this which we have said collectively about the whole Church, let us now understand how it applies to every soul[19] in particular. Let us bring before our eyes a certain soul who is committed to the pursuit of the gifts[20] and acquires understanding through the preaching of another. She also desires to be enlightened by divine grace so that she may one day also understand on her own. She ponders the fact that no understanding comes to her save by the words of preachers. Accordingly, she says: *Let him kiss me with the kiss of his mouth* [Song 1:1a]. "May he touch me interiorly so that I may know with understanding and no longer find enjoyment in the voices of preachers but only in the touch of his interior grace." It is as if he 'kissed' Moses 'with the kiss of his mouth' when he extended understanding to him by his pledge of the grace of intimate friendship.[21] Hence it is written: *If he were a prophet, I would speak to him in his sleep and not as with my intimate friend Moses, for I spoke to him mouth to mouth* [Num 12:6-8].[22] For to speak mouth to mouth is as it were to kiss and to touch the mind with interior understanding.

Christ's Humble Wisdom Compared to the Wisdom of the World

16. It follows: *For your breasts are better than wine* [Song 1:1b]. The 'breasts' of God, as we said earlier, are the most humble preach-

---

19. Here I read *unaquaque* instead of *unaquaeque*.
20. Presumably, Gregory means the gifts of the Holy Spirit.
21. See Exod 33:11, 17-23.
22. Lat. *os enim ad os loquor ei*, often translated "face-to-face."

ing of his Incarnation.[23] But the wisdom of the world resembles 'wine.' For it intoxicates the mind by estranging it from humble understanding. It is as if philosophers are intoxicated by a kind of 'wine' when by their worldly wisdom they go beyond the normal way of doing things. The holy Church should despise this sort of wisdom. She should pursue the most humble preaching of the Incarnation of the Lord.[24] She should prefer to savor[25] the nourishment offered by the weakness of his flesh rather than what this world extols through the pride of false sagacity, and she should say: *For your breasts are better than wine* [Song 1:1b]. That is, "The most humble preaching of your Incarnation is superior to the proud wisdom of the world." Hence it is written: *The weakness of God is stronger than man, and the foolishness of God is wiser than man* [1 Cor 1:25].[26]

17. But sometimes even the wise of this world appear to devote themselves to some of the virtues. For you notice that many have charity, observe mildness, practice exterior goodness toward all. Yet they display these virtues not to please God but men. Accordingly, they are not really virtues at all since they do not strive to please God. Nevertheless, a pleasant odor reaches people's noses when they think that these so-called virtues confer a good reputation. But if these were to be compared to the true odor of our Redeemer, they would be compared to the truly true virtues,[27] and it would be said: *The odor of your ointments surpasses all perfumes* [Song 1:2a]. That is, "The aroma of your virtues is superior to every pretence of virtue

---

23. Here I read *humillimae praedictiones Incarnationis eius* instead of *humillimae Incarnationis eius*.

24. Here I read *humillimam praedicationem dominicae Incarnationis* instead of *humillimam praedicationis dominicae Incarnationem*.

25. Here Gregory plays on *sapientia* ("wisdom") and *sapere* ("to savor"), commonly thought in antiquity to be etymologically connected.

26. Gregory's version differs slightly from the Vulgate: *The foolishness of God is stronger than men, and the weakness of God is wiser than men.*

27. Lat. *veris veris virtutibus*. The repetition of *veris* is an intensive, unless it is a corruption.

possessed by the wise of this world precisely because by its truth it transcends their concocted facades of virtue."

THE THIRD INTERPRETATION OF SONG 1:1-2A (18–20)

COMPUNCTION

18. We said above in the second interpretation that what is said applies to every soul, and so let us develop this same understanding in greater detail, insofar as we can with God's help.[28] Every soul that fears God is already under his yoke but is still distant from him because she fears. For the closer anyone comes[29] to God, the more she is relieved of the burden of fear and receives from him the grace of charity. Let us bring before our eyes the soul of any elect person who is enkindled through unceasing desire for the love of the sight of the Bridegroom. Since she cannot fully perceive him in this life, she contemplates his grandeur and feels compunction[30] on the basis of this love for him. Now this compunction, which occurs through charity, which is enkindled from desire, resembles a kiss. For as often as the soul kisses God, so often does she feel compunction in the love of him. There are many who indeed already fear the Lord and have received the ability to do good works. But they still do not kiss him because they do not in any way feel compunction through love for him.

This is well illustrated at the banquet of the Pharisee. After he welcomed the Lord into his home and cursed in his heart the woman kissing the Lord's feet, he heard: *I entered into your home, you did not give me a kiss. But this woman, from the moment she came in, has not ceased kissing my feet* [Luke 7:44-45]. In a certain sense, everyone who already gives alms, who is already devoted to good works, welcomes Christ at the banquet. He provides food for Christ when he does not cease to sustain him in his members. But if he still does not feel

---

28. Here I read *deo* instead of *domino*.
29. Here I read *prope fit* instead of *proficit*.
30. Lat. *compungitur*.

compunction through love, he has still not kissed Christ's feet. Therefore, the woman who kisses is preferred to the pastor because whoever amid desire for the Lord feels compunction in interior ardor of mind is preferred to the one who provides exterior goods.[31]

Now *she has not ceased kissing my feet* [Luke 7:45] is well said. For in the love of God it does not suffice to feel compunction once and then do nothing. Rather, once compunction happens, it ought then increase in frequency. Hence the woman is praised because 'she did not cease kissing,' which is to say because she did not in any way cease to feel compunction. Hence it is also said through the Prophet: *Establish a solemn day with great frequency*[32] *even unto the horn of the altar* [Ps 117:27]. It is 'a solemn day' for the Lord when our heart feels compunction. But a solemn day is established 'with great frequency' when the mind is constantly moved to tears out of love for him. Then it is as if we had asked him: "How long are we to do these things? How long are we to be afflicted by tribulations?" For straightaway he tells us how far we must go: *even unto the horn of the altar*. Now 'the horn of the altar' is the highest point of an interior sacrifice. When we have reached it, we no longer have any need to celebrate a solemn day for the Lord with our lamentation. So then, the soul who already desires to feel compunction through love, who already strives to contemplate the sight of her Bridegroom, let her say: *Let him kiss me with the kisses of his mouth* [Song 1:1a].

THE SUPERIORITY OF CONTEMPLATION

19. Then again, the kiss of his mouth is surely the very fullness of interior peace. Whenever we obtain it, nothing more remains for us to seek. Hence it is fittingly added: *For your breasts are better than wine* [Song 1:1b]. For 'wine' is the knowledge of God we

---

31. Here I read *exteriora sua danti is* instead of *exteriora suadenti is*.
32. Lat. *in confrequentationibus*. Though this phrase could mean either "with great throngs of people" or "with great frequency," Gregory's interpretation depends on the latter, and I translate accordingly.

receive while situated in this life. But as for the 'breasts' of the Bridegroom, we embrace them when in the present time we contemplate him in the eternal homeland through the embrace of his presence. Therefore, let her say: *Your breasts are better than wine*. It is as if she were saying: "Great indeed is the knowledge[33] of you that you have granted me in this life. Great is the wine of the knowledge[34] of you by which you intoxicate me. But 'your breasts are better than wine' because that is when we transcend, through sight and through the loftiness of contemplation, all that we presently know about you through faith."

20. *And the odor of your ointments surpasses all perfumes* [Song 1:2a]. Here in this life the holy Church possesses 'perfumes' when she is illustrious in the virtue of knowledge, in the virtue of chastity, in the virtue of mercy, in the virtue of humility, in the virtue of love. If the life of the saints did not possess an 'odor' that arose from the 'perfumes' of the virtues, Paul would not have declared: *We are the good odor of Christ in every place* [2 Cor 2:15]. But far more excellent is the 'ointment' of the contemplation of God to which we will someday be led. Far more excellent than the 'perfumes' of our virtues is the 'odor of God's ointments.' And if that which we have received is already great, far greater is that which we will receive from the contemplation of our Creator. Hence let the soul sigh and say: *The odor of your ointments surpasses all perfumes*. In other words: "Those blessings you prepare for us when we contemplate you are far more excellent than all the gifts of the virtues you have bestowed upon us in this life."

THE FIRST INTERPRETATION OF SONG 1:2BC (21–22)

THE INCARNATION OF CHRIST

21. Let us tell this Church, let us tell this soul, so loving, so ardent in the love of her Bridegroom, where she can perceive what

---

33. Lat. *scientia*.
34. Lat. *notitia*.

she so greatly desires, where she can grasp a knowledge of his divinity. But see how the Bride herself tells us where when she says: *Your name is ointment poured-out* [Song 1:2b]! 'Ointment poured-out' is the incarnate divinity. For when ointment is stored in a small bottle, there is no odor outside of it. But when it is poured out, the odor of the poured-out ointment spreads far and wide. So then, the name of God is 'ointment poured-out' because he poured himself out exteriorly from his immeasurable divinity into our nature, making himself visible from his invisible being. Now if he had not 'poured himself out,' he would in no way have made himself known to us. He 'poured himself out as ointment' when he both preserved himself as God and manifested himself as man. Paul spoke of this 'pouring-out': *Although he was in the form of God, he did not consider it robbery that he was equal to God, but he emptied himself, taking to himself the form of a slave* [Phil 2:6-7]. Paul called 'emptying' what Solomon called 'pouring-out.' Therefore, because the Lord has made himself known to the human race through the humility of the Incarnation, let it be said to him: *Your name is ointment poured-out* [Song 1:2b].

THE LOVE OF THE NEWLY BAPTIZED FOR CHRIST

22. It follows: *Therefore the young girls have loved you* [Song 1:2c]. How are we to take the 'young girls' in this passage if not as the souls of the elect renewed through baptism? For sinful conduct pertains to the old man, whereas holy conduct to the new. So then, by 'pouring himself out as ointment' he has made the 'young girls ardent in the love of him' because by renewing them he has made their souls burn with desire for him. Childhood is the stage of life that is inappropriate for love, whereas old age is the stage of life when people give up on love. A child is someone who has yet to begin the pursuit of the life of love, whereas an old man is someone who once began such a life but has given up on it. So then, neither of them burns for the Lord: either those who have yet to begin or those who once began but have now gone cold. Because of this, no mention is made of the conduct of the child and the old man,

whereas the 'young girls' are said to run, which is to say those souls in the fervor of love.

The Second Interpretation of Song 1:2bc (23)

How Angels and Human Beings Love Christ Differently

23. Yet we can understand this passage in another way. For 'youth' can refer to weakness.[35] The ages of adulthood represent the order of the angels, who are not mastered by any feebleness nor subject to any weakness. Therefore, let it be said: *Your name is ointment poured-out; therefore the young girls have loved you* [Song 1:2bc]. In other words: "Since by your Incarnation you have 'poured out' knowledge of yourself outwardly, weak souls can accordingly 'love you' in your human nature. Now those highest powers, as if the ages of adulthood, love you even there where you are not poured out because they even see you there where you remain in your divine condition. So then, even though those highest orders of angels, as if the ages of adulthood, see you as not 'poured-out,' you nonetheless 'poured yourself out' outwardly for the sake of human beings, so that 'you could be loved by the young girls,' which is to say by weak minds."

The Interpretation of Song 1:3 (24–31)

The Divided Human Will

24. It follows: *Draw me* [Song 1:3a]. Everyone drawn is led either because of incapacity or because of unwillingness when summoned. But she who says, *Draw me*, possesses something that wills, possesses something that is incapable. Human nature wants to follow God. But overcome by a habit of weakness, it is incapable of following him as it should. And so, it sees something in itself whereby it strives and something in itself which is incapable, and

---

35. "Youth" (*adulescentia*) is the age of the "young girls" (*adulescentulae*).

rightly it says: 'Draw me.' Paul saw that he was as it were willing but incapable when he said: *With my mind I serve the law of God but with my flesh I serve the law of sin* [Rom 7:25]. And: *I see another law in my members fighting against the law of my mind* [Rom 7:23]. Therefore, because there is something in us which urges us forward and something which holds us back, let us say: 'Draw me.'

THE THREE WAYS OF FOLLOWING GOD

25. *After you we shall run in the odor of your ointments* [Song 1:3b]. We 'run in the odor of God's ointments' when, catching the scent of his spiritual gifts, we long in love to see him. But note that when people follow God, sometimes they walk, sometimes they run, sometimes they run very fast. It is as if a person walks after God when he follows him tepidly. A person runs after God when he follows him fervently. A person runs after God perfectly when he follows him perseveringly. Now our heart was adamant in not following God and unwilling to walk after him, when the coming of the Lord into the world was manifested and roused human minds from their obtuse condition. Hence it is written: *His feet stood still and the earth was moved* [Hab 3:5-6]. Here reference is made to 'running,' not 'moving,' because movement does not suffice for following God unless we run with desire. But since running does not suffice unless one runs perfectly, Paul said: *So run that you may obtain* [1 Cor 9:24].

But some people,[36] by running too strenuously, will overextend themselves through indiscretion. For they are wiser than necessary and place more value on themselves than on him whom they are following, deciding for themselves what virtuous deeds they will do and disregarding the commandments of him whom they are following. So then, when 'after you' is placed before 'we run,' it is well said. For they 'run' after God who ponder his commandments, place more value on his will than on their own, and use discretion in their endeavor to reach him by means of worthy actions. Hence the Prophet, pondering and following God's will, said: *My soul has*

---

36. Here I read *sed nonnulli* instead of *et nonnulli*.

clung to you [Ps 62:9]. Hence it is said to Peter when he offered advice: *Get behind me, Satan! For you do not have the wisdom that belongs to God but that which belongs to men!* [Mark 8:33; cf. Matt 16:23]. And so, since perfect souls study God's commandments with the utmost care and presume neither to fall short of them through cold indifference nor to surpass them through ill-conceived fervor, it is well said: *After you we run in the odor of your ointments.* For 'after you we run' only when we follow his divine commandments out of love and do not surpass them out of fear.

The Church Is Like a King's House

26. *The king has brought me into his bedchamber. We shall rejoice and be glad in you* [Song 1:3cd]. The Church of God is like the house of a king. And this house has an entrance. It has a staircase. It has a banqueting hall. It has bedchambers. Everyone who has faith within the Church has already passed through the entrance of this house. For as an entrance gives access to the rest of the house, so faith is the gateway to the rest of the virtues. Everyone who has hope within the Church has already reached the staircase of this house. For hope lifts the heart such that it pursues the lofty regions and abandons the lowly. Every resident of this house who has charity walks as if in the banquet halls. For vast is charity, which extends itself[37] even to the love of enemies. Every resident of the Church who already scrutinizes God's lofty secrets, who already ponders his hidden commandments, has entered as if into the bedchamber.

Someone mentioned the entrance to this house: *Open to me the gates of holiness; and I will enter them and confess to the Lord* [Ps 117:19]. He mentioned the staircase of hope: *He has arranged staircases in his heart* [Ps 83:6].[38] Mention was made of the vast banquet halls of this house: *Your command is exceedingly vast* [Ps 118:96]. This 'vast command' refers in particular to charity. As for the bedchamber of

---

37. Here I read *extenditur* instead of *tenditur*.

38. Full citation: *The blessed man whose help is from God has arranged staircases in his heart.*

the king, he spoke of it who said: *My secret is my own* [Isa 24:16]. And on another occasion: *I have heard mysterious words which people are not permitted to utter* [2 Cor 12:4].

So then, the first point of entry into this house is the entrance of faith. The second step is the staircase of hope. The third is the vastness of charity. The fourth is the perfection of charity for the comprehension of God's secrets. Therefore, because the holy Church in her perfect members, in her holy teachers, in those already filled with and rooted in the mysteries of God, reaches as it were the lofty secrets and even penetrates them while still residing in this life, she said: *The king has brought me into his bedchamber.* For through the Prophets, through the Apostles, and through the teachers residing in this life here who have already penetrated the lofty secrets of that life there, the Church has entered the 'bedchamber of the king.'

THE NEED FOR REVERENCE AND HUMILITY IN CONTEMPLATION

27. And we must carefully examine why it does not say "into the bedchamber of the Bridegroom" but *into the bedchamber of the king* [Song 1:3c]. Now by mentioning the 'king' it wants to indicate the reverence owed to its secrets. For the more noble the bedchamber, the greater the reverence that should be shown to those things for the sake of which it is entered. Therefore, lest anyone exalt himself and fall into pride when he comes to know the secrets of God, when he scrutinizes God's hidden commandments, when he is raised up to the lofty heights of contemplation, it is said that he enters 'the bedchamber of the king.' In other words, the more a soul is brought to the knowledge of his secrets, the greater the reverence that should be shown. Accordingly, anyone who progresses, who is already exalted through grace and has reached the lofty secrets, should be mindful of himself and be all the more humbled by his very progress. Hence whenever Ezekiel was brought to the lofty heights of contemplation, he was called 'son of man.'[39]

---

39. Lat. *filius hominis*. The phrase occurs some ninety times in Ezekiel, translated by Jerome in the Vulgate with the vocative in the classical form: *fili hominis*.

It is as if it were said to him: "Be mindful of what you are. And do not exalt yourself on account of those things to which you have been raised."

Mercy and Forgiveness Are the Consolation of Those Who Cannot Contemplate God

28. But only a few people in the Church ever come to scrutinize and comprehend these lofty and hidden commandments of God. Yet when we see that strong men can attain such great wisdom that the secrets of God are contemplated in their hearts, even we little children have confidence of someday obtaining forgiveness, of someday obtaining God's grace. Hence it continues with the words of the young girls: *We shall rejoice and be glad in you* [Song 1:3d]. While the Church in those who are perfect enters the 'bedchamber of the king,' the 'young girls look forward to the hope of rejoicing' because while the strong attain the lofty heights of contemplation, the weak find hope in the forgiveness of their sins.

The Church's Preachers

29. *The king has brought me into his bedchamber. We shall rejoice and be glad in you, mindful of your breasts that surpass wine. The upright love you* [Song 1:3c-f]. The Bridegroom, who out of reverence is also called the 'king,' has 'breasts.' He has 'breasts,' holy men clinging[40] to him with their heart. Breasts are affixed to the ribcage. They draw from inward nourishment in order to nourish outwardly. So then, holy men are the Bridegroom's 'breasts' because they draw from their innermost depths and nourish outwardly. His breasts are the Apostles. His breasts are all the preachers of the Church. As we said above, there was 'wine' in the Prophets. There was 'wine' in the Law. But since the commandments given through the Apostles are better than those given through the Prophets, they are *mindful of your breasts that surpass wine*. For there can be no doubt

---

40. Here I read *adherentes* instead of *adherentium*.

that those who can fulfill the commandments of the New Testament surpass the knowledge of Law.

Humility Surpasses Knowledge

30. Yet there is another way to understand the passage: *Mindful of your breasts that surpass wine* [Song 1:3e]. There are many who indeed possess the 'wine' of wisdom but lack an appreciation for humility; *knowledge puffs them up* since *charity does not build them up* [1 Cor 8:1]. But there are many who possess the 'wine' of knowledge such that they know how to ponder the gifts of teaching, the gifts of spiritual grace. For the gifts of spiritual grace are like nipples on the chest, which tenderly sustain and nourish through hidden spiritual passageways. So then, they are 'mindful of your breasts that surpass wine' because these are the ones who know how to pursue the gifts of your grace such that they do not attribute their wisdom to themselves and do not exalt themselves on account of the wisdom they have received, and so they surpass those who have exalted and raised themselves up on account of their own wisdom. For being wise humbly is better than merely being wise; in fact, you are not really wise at all if you are not wise humbly. So then, they are 'mindful of your breasts that surpass wine' because in knowing how to ponder the gifts of spiritual grace they are superior to those who indeed possess knowledge but lack an appreciation for these gifts in their memory. So then, 'mindful of your breasts that surpass wine' is said in plain speech insofar as humility is stronger than knowledge. For 'wine' is the knowledge that makes one tipsy, whereas it is the 'mindfulness of the breasts' that makes one very drunk and brings one back to an appreciation for these gifts. Therefore, they are 'mindful of your breasts which surpass wine' because humility triumphs even over an abundance of knowledge.

Perfect Love Is without Fear

31. *The upright love you* [Song 1:3f]. It is as if she were saying: "Those who are not upright still fear." *The upright love you.* On the one hand, everyone who does good works out of fear, though

'upright' in deed, is not 'upright' in desire. For he wishes that there were nothing to fear and that he did not have to do good works. On the other hand, the one who does good works out of love is 'upright' both in deed and in desire. But the sweetness of love is hidden from those who fear. Hence it is written: *How great is the abundance of your sweetness, Lord, which you have hidden from those who fear you and have brought to fruition for those who hope in you!* [Ps 30:20].[41] For the sweetness of God is unknown to those who fear God but becomes known to those who love him. So then, whoever has endeavored to be upright through love[42] has a love[43] that is perfect, such that he does not fear the coming Judge, such that he does not tremble at reports of eternal punishments. Hence Paul, while awaiting the coming of the Judge, while seeking the rewards of eternal life, said: *God has prepared these things, not only for me but also for all who love his coming* [2 Tim 4:8]. The Judge prepares eternal rewards for those who love because everyone who knows that he does evil works fears the coming Judge, but everyone who is confident about his works seeks the coming of the Judge. So then, rewards are prepared for those who wait for God's coming and love his coming because people do not love the coming of the Judge unless they are confident about their case. And so all certainty of uprightness is a question of love, and therefore it is rightly said: *The upright love you* [Song 1:3f].

---

41. Psalm 30:20 reads: *Quam magna multitudo dulcedinis tuae, domine, quam abscondisti timentibus te, et perfectisti eam sperantibus in te. Timentibus* is meant to be understood as a dative and thus would be translated "which you have laid up for those who fear you" and therefore forms a parallel with "have brought to fruition for those who hope in you." But it is clear from what follows that Gregory takes *timentibus* as an ablative of separation. Thus, Gregory sees the two latter phrases of this verse as presenting an antithesis between those who merely fear God and those who hope in him.

42. Lat. *amor*.

43. Lat. *dilectio*.

The First Interpretation of Song 1:4-5 (32–35)

On Jewish Converts to Christianity

32. *I am black but beautiful, daughters of Jerusalem, like the tents of Kedar, like the curtains of Solomon. Do not stare at me because I am dark, for the sun has scorched me* [Song 1:4-5a]. We know that at the time of the Church's origins, when the grace of our Redeemer was preached, some from Judaea believed, whereas others did not believe. But those who believed were scorned by those who did not believe, suffered persecution, and were judged for *having departed to the way of the Gentile nations* [Matt 10:5]. Hence the Church in [the voice of] these same believers cries out against the unconverted: *I am black but beautiful, daughters of Jerusalem.* "I am indeed black in your judgment but beautiful through the enlightenment of grace." In what way black? *Like the tents of Kedar.* 'Kedar' interpreted means 'darkness.' For Kedar was the second son of Ishmael.[44] And the tents of Kedar belonged to Esau.[45] So then, in what way black? *Like the tents of Kedar* because "in your sight I am judged to resemble the Gentile nations, that is, to resemble sinners." In what way beautiful? *Like the curtains of Solomon.* It is reported that when Solomon built the temple, he draped all the utensils of the temple in finished curtains.[46] But Solomon's curtains must have been very beautiful, as they were appropriate for the tabernacle. These curtains would not have been in his tabernacle unless they were beautiful enough for the service of a king. But since 'Solomon' interpreted means 'peaceful one,' we for our part may understand him as the true Solomon. For all souls attached to God are the 'curtains of Solomon,' softening[47] and acclimatizing themselves for the service

---

44. See Gen 25:13 and 1 Chr 1:29.
45. This is not recorded in Scripture.
46. The word for "curtains" is *pelle*, which means either animal skin or the commodities made from animal skins such as blankets, tents, and curtains.
47. Lat. *macerantes*. This word literally refers to the "treatment" of animal skins, whether by "softening" or "weakening," in order to make them fit for other uses. The same word is also used by Gregory for the ascetic "chastisement" of the body.

of the King of Peace. "In your judgment I am indeed like the 'tents of Kedar' because I am judged to have departed to the way of the Gentile nations,[48] but in reality I am like the 'curtains of Solomon' because I am attached to the service of the King."

33. *Do not stare at me because I am dark, for the sun has scorched me* [Song 1:5a-b]. The group which did not believe in Christ regarded the group which believed as sinners. But let the latter group say: *Do not stare at me because I am dark, for the sun has scorched me* [Song 1:5a-b]. "It is the sun, the Lord himself, who scorched me when he came." By his own precepts he shows that they were not beautiful through the precepts of the Law. The sun scorches the one upon whom it intensely shines; similarly, when the Lord came, he scorched with his grace the one upon whom he intensely shined. For the nearer we draw to his grace, the more we recognize ourselves as sinners. Let us have a look at Paul, who came from Judaea, who was scorched by the sun: *But if we wished to be made righteous in Christ, we ourselves were also found to be sinners* [Gal 2:17]. Whoever 'finds himself to be a sinner in Christ' finds that he has been scorched by the sun.

34. But note that the group from Judaea which believed suffered persecution from the Jews who did not believe and was afflicted and beset by many troubles. Hence it follows: *The sons of my mother fought against me* [Song 1:5c]. For the sons of the synagogue who persisted in their disbelief waged a war of persecution against believers from the synagogue.

35. But when the group who came to belief from among the Jews suffered persecution, they departed to preach to the Gentile nations. They forsook Judaea and went to preach to the Gentile nations. Hence it follows: *They stationed me as a guardian in their vineyards, but I have not guarded my own vineyard* [Song 1:5de]. "For when they persecuted me, those who are in Judaea made me a guardian in the Churches. 'I have not guarded my own vineyard' because I forsook Judaea." Hence Paul says, hence the Apostles: *The*

---

48. See Matt 10:5.

word of God was sent to us, but since you have been judged unworthy of it, let it be known that we are going to the Gentile nations [Acts 13:26, 46]. It is as if he were saying: "We wanted to guard our own vineyard, but since you yourselves have rejected us, you send us to guard the vineyards of others."

THE SECOND INTERPRETATION OF SONG 1:4-5 (36–38)

ON GENTILE CONVERTS TO CHRISTIANITY

36. What we have said about the synagogue converted[49] to belief can be now said about the Church called[50] to belief: *I am black but beautiful, daughters of Jerusalem* [Song 1:4a]. The Church coming from the Gentile nations ponders the souls of believers, which she has acquired, which she calls 'the daughters of Jerusalem.' After all, 'Jerusalem' means 'vision of peace.' She ponders what she was. She ponders what she has become.[51] And she acknowledges her past faults lest she be proud, acknowledges her present conduct lest she be ungrateful, and says: *I am black but beautiful.* She is 'black' through what she deserves but beautiful through grace; black through her past conduct but beautiful through her subsequent way of life. In what way black? *Like the tents of Kedar* [Song 1:4b]. For the tents of Kedar[52] belonged to the Gentile nations; they were tents of darkness. And it was said to the Gentile nations: *You were once darkness, but now you are light in the Lord* [Eph 5:8]. In what way beautiful? *Like the curtains of Solomon* [Song 1:4c]. For we have been softened[53] through the works of penance. Flesh is mortified through the works of penance as skins are treated to make curtains for the service of a king. All those who afflict themselves through the works of penance make themselves members of Christ. So then, the members of Christ

---

49. Here I read *conversa* instead of *conversam*.
50. Here I read *vocata* instead of *vocatam*.
51. Here I read *considerat quid facta est* instead of *quid facta est*.
52. Here I read *Cedar quippe* instead of *Cedar*.
53. See n. 47 above on *macerantes*.

afflicted through the works of penance are 'the curtains of Solomon' because they become mortified flesh.

37. But note that *there were in Judaea* [Acts 11:1] some believers who judged the Gentiles unworthy of coming to belief. Hence they criticized Peter because he accepted Cornelius.[54] Hence she adds in [the voice of] the Church of the Gentile nations: *Do not stare at me because I am dark* [Song 1:5a]. "Do not disdain my Gentile disbelief. Do not disdain my former sins. Do not focus on what I was." Why? *Because the sun has scorched me* [Song 1:5b]. The sun scorches the one on whom it narrowly concentrates its rays.[55] When God delivers a severe judgment, it is as if he intensely pours forth a concentration of his rays. And he scorches when he shines intensely because it is when he concentrates his rays in a penetrating way that he judges with severity. Now the sun retracts its rays as it were when God considers our works with mercy. It is as if God pours forth his power in a concentrated way when he ponders our works with severity. Therefore, let the Church say: "I am dark for this reason, I am a sinner for this reason: because the sun has scorched me. For when my Creator forsook me, I slid into error."

38. But O! you, so afflicted, so deprived, what did you do to deserve this? What did you gain from this gift? *The sons of my mother fought against me* [Song 1:5c]. The 'sons of the mother' are the Apostles. For the mother of all is the Jerusalem above.[56] They 'fought against' the Church when bringing her from disbelief to belief they stabbed her with their preaching as if with lances. Hence Paul spoke like a fighter: *We destroy speculative arguments and every lofty thing raising itself up in pride against the knowledge of God* [2 Cor 10:4-5]. Because he destroyed the 'lofty thing,' he surely is a fighter. And so, those fighters, those sons of mother Jerusalem, waged war

---

54. See Acts 10:1–11:18.

55. This sentence and the following are difficult to translate because of Gregory's wordplay with *districtius*, *districte* ("with severity, severely"), *districtus* ("severe"), and *districtio* ("a concentration" of the sun's rays).

56. See Gal 4:26.

against the Church to bring her from error and establish her in righteousness.

The sons of my mother fought against me. And what did these fighters do? *They stationed me as a guardian in their vineyards* [Song 1:5d]. The 'vineyards' of the Church are the virtues which bear fruit. "For when they fight against the vices in me, it is as if they extricate me from my evils.[57] They bestowed upon me an abundance of fruit and zeal for the virtues. 'They made me a guardian in their vineyards' so that I could bring forth[58] an abundance of fruit." After being extricated, let her say of herself in particular: *I have not guarded my own vineyard* [Song 1:5e]. The Church's 'vineyard' is the ancient habit of error. When she was stationed as a guardian of the virtues, she forsook that vineyard, the ancient habit of her error.

THE THIRD INTERPRETATION OF SONG 1:4-5 (39–40)

PROPER SELF-DISCLOSURE

39. We have spoken about the synagogue that comes to belief. We have spoken about the converted Gentile nation. Let us now speak about the whole Church collectively and about what ought to be understood for each soul in particular. Bad students are in the habit of pondering not what their teachers are but what they were. But good teachers both acknowledge what they were and communicate what they are. Thus they neither conceal that they are sinners nor again deny the gifts given to them as if ungrateful. Therefore, let the Church say in [the voice of] them: *I am black but beautiful* [Song 1:4a]. "I am black on my own but beautiful through the gift given to me; black due to my past but beautiful because of what I have become for the future." In what way black? In what way beautiful? Black *like the tents of Kedar*, beautiful *like the curtains of Solomon* [Song 1:4bc]. And it is not right to judge someone based upon past conduct and to place more weight on what she was

---

57. Here I read *malis meis* instead of *mala mea*.
58. Here I read *afferem* instead of *afferent*.

rather than what she is. Hence she adds: *Do not stare at me because I am dark, for the sun has scorched me* [Song 1:5ab]. Sometimes in Sacred Scripture the sun represents the excessive heat of earthly desires. So then, why is she dark? "'For the sun has scorched me' and I have been scorched by the ardor of earthly love in the eyes of the Bridegroom, which is to say I have become ugly in the eyes of the King."

THE STRUGGLE WITH OUR BROTHERS, THE FALLEN ANGELS

40. *The sons of my mother fought against me* [Song 1:5c]. In the whole of creation, there are two creatures endowed with reason, the human and the angelic. The angel fell and seduced the man. Now the mother of every creature is the kindness and power of God. So then, because both we and the angels are endowed with reason, it is as if we possess a kind of brotherly association. So the angels have been created by the same power as we have been. And yet after they fell, the angels wage war against us every day. Because of this, let her say: *The sons of my mother fought against me* [Song 1:5c]. Note that when these rational spirits fight, these spirits who are the 'sons of the mother,' when they fight against the soul, they entangle her in earthly affairs, plunge her into worldly concerns, addict her to transitory goods. Hence she adds: *They stationed me as a guardian in their vineyards; I have not guarded my own vineyard* [Song 1:5de]. Now the 'vineyards' are earthly concerns. It is as if she were saying: "They stationed me as a guardian in the midst of earthly concerns." And why? "I have failed to keep guard over my own 'vineyard,' which is to say my soul, my conduct, my mind. For while I was engrossed exteriorly in concern for earthly matters, I dropped my interior guard." Many judge themselves on the basis of what is associated with them, not what they are. High-ranking positions are associated with them. Exterior ministries are associated with them. And when they guard what has been associated with them, they fail to guard themselves. Therefore let her say: *They stationed me as a guardian in the vineyards; I have not guarded my own vineyard* [Song 1:5de]. In other words: "When I devoted myself to

exterior guarding in the concerns of the world, my solicitude for interior guarding disappeared."

THE INTERPRETATION OF SONG 1:6 (41–43)

WHERE THE REDEEMER IS FOUND INTERIORLY

41. Once returned to the grace of her Creator, see how the soul now loves him, now seeks where she may find her Redeemer! Hence it follows: *Show me, you whom my soul loves, where you pasture, where you lie down at midday* [Song 1:6a]. At midday the sun is hotter. Everyone who is fervent in belief is fervent in the love of desire. In the heart of such people the Bridegroom, who is called a *young hart* below [Song 2:19], 'pastures' on the green grass of the virtues. In the heart of such people he 'lies down at midday,' in the burning fervor of charity. *Show me, you whom my soul loves, where you pasture, where you lie down at midday* [Song 1:6a].

HERETICAL TEACHERS ONLY APPEAR TO BE THE COMPANIONS OF GOD

42. "Why do you seek thus where he pastures, where he lies down?" She replies with the reason for her inquiry: *Lest I begin to wander after the flocks of your companions* [Song 1:6b]. God's 'companions' are his friends and family members, as are all who lead a good life. But many appear to be his companions but are not his companions. For many teachers who promoted wicked doctrine really seemed to be his companions but were discovered to be his enemies. While they were still teachers, Arius, Sabellius, and Montanus seemed to be his companions. But when they were carefully examined, they were unmasked as his enemies.[59] And it often happens that believing souls, who cling to the word of God, who love in their teachers what enables them to make progress, do not know how to be wary of what wicked teachers say and falter

---

59. Here Gregory lists the most infamous heretics of the fourth, third, and second centuries, respectively.

because of their teaching. How many people believed because of the companions but when they followed them went astray through the 'flocks' of the companions! And so she says: *Show me where you pasture, where you lie down at midday, lest I begin to wander after the flocks of your companions* [Song 1:6ab]. It is as if she were saying: "Show me in whose hearts you truly repose 'lest I begin to wander after the flocks of those who seem to be your companions,' which is to say those who are regarded as your family members but are not." All priests, all teachers are companions of God insofar as outward appearance is concerned. But insofar as conduct is concerned, many are not his companions but his adversaries.

Catholic Teachers Leading Bad Lives Are Not the Companions of God

43. But what we have said about heretical teachers can be said about Catholics who do not live a good life. For many little children in the Church who believe strive to lead a good life. They want to have upright conduct. They ponder the conduct of the priests who preside over them. And when priests themselves do not lead a good life, when those who preside do not live in an upright manner, those who follow them will slip into error. Hence the Church as if in [the voice of] these same little children who believe says: *Show me, you whom my soul loves, where you pasture, where you lie down at midday* [Song 1:6ab]. That is to say:[60] "Show me the conduct of those who truly serve you, that I may know where you 'pasture' on the green grass of the virtues, that I may know where you 'lie down at midday,' which is to say where you repose in the burning fervor of charity. Otherwise when I watch the 'flocks of your companions' I will begin to wander, not knowing on whose words and teachings I can depend." Now every student, every weak person, must carefully ponder whose words he should trust, whose teaching he should put into practice, whose examples he should follow.

---

60. Here I insert *Id est*.

The Interpretation of Song 1:7 (44)

The Consequences of Lack of Self-Knowledge

44. And note the words of the Bridegroom when he replies to the Bride: *If you do not know yourself, O beautiful among women, set out and follow the tracks of the flocks, and pasture your young goats near the tents of the shepherds* [Song 1:7]. Every soul should care for nothing more than to know herself. For whoever knows herself recognizes that she has been made in the image of God. If she is made in the image of God, then she should not behave like beasts, squandering herself either in self-indulgence or in the pursuit of present goods. It is said of this ignorance elsewhere: *When man is held in honor, he lacks understanding; he is compared to foolish beasts and becomes like them* [Ps 48:13]. The 'tracks of the flocks' are the activities of the crowds: the more we engage in such activities, the more they hamper, the more they misguide.

So then, let it be said to the Church: *If you do not know yourself, O beautiful among women, set out and follow the tracks of the flocks and pasture your young goats near the tents of the shepherds* [Song 1:7]. "O you who were filthy through ignorance have through faith become beautiful among the souls of others!" This is clearly said to the Church of the elect. "'If you do not know yourself,' that is, if you do not know that you have been made in my image, then 'set out,' that is, go forth.[61] But if you do not realize by whom you have been made, then 'set out and follow,' that is, hasten after 'the tracks of the flocks.' Do not follow examples I have given you, but the examples of the crowds."

Pasture your young goats near the tents of the shepherds. Our 'young goats' are the stirrings of carnal desire. Our young goats are illicit temptations. "'Follow the tracks of the flocks,' that is, depart, follow the examples of the crowds. 'And pasture your young goats,' that is, indulge your stirrings of carnal desire. No longer nourish your spiritual thoughts but your stirrings of carnal desire. 'Go near the

---

61. Here I read *egredere id est foras exi* instead of *egredere id est exi*.

tents of the shepherds.' If you were pasturing lambs, you would have pastured them in the tents of shepherds, that is, in the teachings of the masters, in the teachings of the Apostles, in the teachings of the Prophets. But if you are pasturing young goats, pasture them 'near the tents of the shepherds,' so that you will be called a Christian by belief and not by works. For you will be viewed as within [the Church] through your belief but as not within through your works."

Look how you have chided her! Look how you have rebuked her! Why aren't you saying that you have already worked in her out of kindness? Speak plainly!

THE INTERPRETATION OF SONG 1:8 (45–46)

PREDESTINATION

45. For it follows: *I have associated you, my sweetheart, with my cavalry while you were in the chariots of Pharaoh* [Song 1:8].[62] All enslaved to self-indulgence, pride, greed, envy, falsehood are still under the yoke of Pharaoh's chariot. They are like horses under the yoke of his chariot, which is to say under the control of the devil. But everyone who is fervent in humility, in chastity, in teaching, in charity has already become a horse of our Creator, is already hitched to the chariot of God, already has God as his charioteer. Hence the Lord said to the man whose conductor he already was: *It is hard for you to kick against the goad* [Acts 26:14]. It is as if he were saying: "You are my horse. You can no longer kick against me. I am now your conductor." These horses are mentioned elsewhere: *You have sent your horses into the sea, throwing the many waters into confusion* [Hab 3:15]. And so, God has chariots. He is the conductor of holy souls and travels around everywhere by means of holy souls.

---

62. Lat. *Equitatui meo in curribus pharaonis adsimilavi te, amica mea.* Gregory seems to interpret the preposition *in* in a temporal sense ("while in"), whereas it merely denotes a physical position ("in"). I have reflected this interpretation of Gregory in the translation.

Hence it is written: *The chariots of God are ten-thousand, many thousands of those rejoicing* [Ps 67:18]. Pharaoh has chariots. But his chariots were submerged in the Red Sea[63] insofar as many wicked people have been transformed in baptism. So then, let the Bridegroom say: *I have associated you, my sweetheart, with my cavalry while you were in the chariots of Pharaoh* [Song 1:8]. In other words: "While you were still in the chariots of Pharaoh, while you were still enslaved to demonic works, I associated you with my cavalry. For I consider what I will have accomplished in you through predestination. And so I have placed you among my horses." For God sees that many are still servants of self-indulgence and greed, and yet by a secret judgment considers what he has already worked in them. For God has horses but he sees that many are still the horses of Pharaoh.

46. And since God knows by a hidden judgment who will be changed for the better by a hidden predestination, he already considers them to be like his own horses. For he sees that he will lead to his own chariot those who were once slaves in Pharaoh's chariot. At this point let us ponder his hidden judgments. For many appear to be horses of God on account of their preaching, wisdom, chastity, generosity, longsuffering. Yet by a hidden judgment of God they are associated with the horses of Pharaoh. And many appear to be horses of Pharaoh on account of their greed, pride, envy, self-indulgence. And yet by a hidden judgment of God they are associated with the horses of God. For God both sees those who will turn from good to evil and sees those who will return from evil to good. So then, in his severity many who appear to be God's horses are actually Pharaoh's horses because of the reprobate conduct which will ensue for them; likewise, in his pity many who appear to be Pharaoh's horses are actually his elect because of the holy conduct which they will observe in the end and are thus associated with God's horses. Hence the Bridegroom encourages the Bride and says: *I have associated you, my sweetheart, with my cavalry while you were in the chariots of*

---

63. See Exod 14:28.

Pharaoh [Song 1:8]. In other words: "You were still enslaved, hitched to the chariots of Pharaoh. You were running under the yoke of your vices. But I consider what I accomplished in you through predestination. I have associated you with my cavalry, which is to say I consider you to be like my elect."

+

Here it ends.[64]

---

64. Lat. *explicit*. This is the most primitive scribal *explicit* which is found in mss. α^2, β^1, δ^2; other more developed *explicit*s read: "Here ends the second sermon taken from the notary's transcription" (α^{1*3}); "Here ends the second homily" (β^2, δ^5); "Here ends the exposition on the Songs of Songs by Blessed Gregory, Pope" (β^5); and "Here ends the book called on the Songs of Songs by Gregory, Pope of the City of Rome" (δ^6).

EXCERPTS FROM THE WORKS OF GREGORY THE GREAT ON THE SONG OF SONGS

Compiled by Paterius and Bede

Introduction

There is no critical edition of the *Liber testimonium* of Paterius. Therefore, I have based my translation on the defective Maurist edition of 1705[1] that was reprinted by Migne in 1849.[2] I have also utilized the corrections to this edition that were suggested by Raymond Étaix in his study of the manuscript tradition.[3] I have omitted the phrase *adiunctum est* that the Maurists inserted before the scriptural citation in their edition, as André Wilmart has noted that it is not found in the manuscripts.[4] The situation for Bede's *Commentary on the Song of Songs* is much better. My translation is based on the critical edition established for *Corpus Christianorum Series Latina* by Dom David Hurst, OSB, in 1983.[5] I have emended both these editions in a number of cases. These emendations, as well as other significant divergences between the excerpters and Gregory, are listed and explained in appendix 4.

1. *Sancti Gregorii Papae I cognomento Magni Opera omnia*, Édition des Bénédictins de Saint-Maur, t. IV (Paris, 1705), 2ᵉ part, cols. 1–310.
2. PL 79:683–916. In his "Le recueil grégorien de Paterius et les fragments wisigothiques de Paris." *Revue Bénédictine* 39 (1927): 81–104, André Wilmart determined that only the excerpts on the first thirteen biblical books (Gen, Exod, Lev, Num, Deut, Judg, 1–2 Sam, 1–2 Kgs, Pss, Prov, and Song) at PL 79:683–916 were authentic to Paterius.
3. Raymond Étaix, "Le *Liber testimonium* de Paterius," *Revue des sciences religieuses* 32 (1958): 66–78. The corrections that pertain to the Song of Songs can be found on pp. 74–75.
4. Wilmart, "Le recueil grégorien de Paterius," 90.
5. D. Hurst and J. E. Hudson, eds., *Bedae Venerabilis Opera. Pars II, Opera exegetica. 2B: in Tobiam, in Proverbia, in Cantica Canticorum, in Habacuc*, CCSL 119B (Turnhout: Brepols, 1983), 165–375.

There is much overlap in the excerpts compiled by Paterius and Bede. Rather than producing two separate translations with much repetition, it was thought best to present a single translation of Gregory's comments on the Song of Songs as compiled by both authors. Both excerpters for the most part simply cite blocks of text from their source, though not always the same lines. Accordingly, the "dimensions" of their respective excerpts are indicated in each case. The signal within curly brackets { } indicates to whose excerpt the following text belongs. For example, {**P10**} indicates that the following part of the excerpt is drawn from Paterius and that it is the tenth of his collection; {**B9**} that what follows is drawn from Bede and that it is the ninth excerpt from his collection. In cases of overlap, annotations such as {**P4/B2**} are used. See appendix 2 for a table that lists how Paterius's and Bede's excerpts correspond to Gregory's original text. The translation of these excerpts is preceded by Bede's preface to his collection.

Bede's Preface to *Commentary on the Song of Songs* VI

In the Exposition on the Song of Songs, which we have expounded in five books (now the first volume of this work was written particularly against Julian[6] in order to defend the grace of God which he had attacked; for which reason, when grace abandoned him, he perished), we followed in the footsteps of the fathers, with the result that we have in the meantime left untouched the works of our Pope and Father Gregory, beloved by God and men. I suppose that readers would be happier if we could bring together all the discussions scattered throughout his works in which he interprets the Song of Songs, since he spoke abundantly on it and said many things, and collect them into a single volume. It is this that we now plan to do, with the Lord's help. Therefore, we have composed a sixth[7] book on the Song of Songs. It is a collection of texts made through our very own efforts, but one which brings together the words and thought of Blessed Gregory so that if there should perhaps be anyone who judges that there is good reason to scorn our work, he may have ready access to those statements of Gregory that ought to be read, which all agree are not to be scorned in any way. But if someone should be seized by love and also read what we have written, then it would be as if a great architect were placing a golden roof on our insignificant marble buildings. I have heard, moreover, that Paterius, a disciple of the same blessed Pope Gregory, collected Gregory's interpretations of all the Holy Scriptures from all the parts of his works and gathered them in order into a single volume. If I should have had this work at hand, I would have accomplished the task I set for myself far more easily and more perfectly. But since I have not yet merited to see this work, I myself have tried to imitate it on my own to the best of my ability, with the Lord's help.

---

6. Julian of Eclanum (ca. 386–454), a major opponent of Augustine in the "Pelagian" controversy.

7. The text says *septimus* (*Cant.* 6, 10–11 [CCSL 119B:359]). See pp. 52–53 of the introduction.

Translation of the Compilations of Paterius and Bede

Song 1:1a. *Let him kiss me with the kiss of his mouth!*

From the Exposition on Blessed Job, Book 14[8]—**{B2}** When Matthew observed the Lord giving commandments on the mount, he said: *Opening his own mouth, he said* . . . [Matt 5:2]. It is as if he were saying in plain speech: "Then he who had earlier opened the mouths of the Prophets opened his own mouth." For the same reason the Bride who desired his presence said of him: *Let him kiss me with the kiss of his mouth!* For **{P1.1/B2}** as many commandments the holy Church learned from his preaching, so many 'kisses of his mouth,' as it were, did she receive. **{P1.2}** She who readies herself through love to obey her Creator is right to desire his 'kiss.'[9]

From the Exposition on Blessed Job, Book 27—**{B1.1}** The Only-Begotten Son can be designated as the "Mouth" of God. Just as he is spoken of as the "Arm" of God because the Father accomplishes all things through him (about this Arm the Prophet says: *To whom is the Lord's Arm revealed?* [Isa 53:1]; and John the Evangelist says: *All things were made through him* [John 1:3]), so too may he be spoken of as the "Mouth." **{B1.2}** It is as if "Word" were being said in plain speech when the term "Mouth" is used, just as we are accustomed to say "tongue" for "language." For when we use the expression "the Greek or Latin tongue," we mean "the Latin or Greek language."[10] Therefore, we are right to take the

---

8. Formulae introducing the excerpts are found in both Paterius and Bede. The titles used for Gregory's works vary both within each excerpter and between them. Accordingly, standardized references have been adopted. Errors have been tacitly corrected.

9. P1.2 is actually excerpted from the *H.Ev.* 33, though Paterius adds it to P1.1, from *Mor.* 14; see appendix 2.

10. Gregory's clever point is lost in translation. Gregory justifies saying that the term "mouth" is equivalent to saying "Word" (*verbum*) by appeal to the custom

"Mouth" of the Lord as his Son, **{B1.3}** through which he speaks all things to us. **{B1.4}** The Prophet speaks in this way: *For the Mouth of the Lord has spoken this* [Isa 1:20; 58:14]. **{B1.5}** The Bride too speaks to him in this way in the Song of Songs: *Let him kiss me with the kiss of his mouth.* It is as if she were saying in plain speech: "Let him touch me with the sweetness of the presence of his Only-Begotten Son, my Redeemer."

Song 1:1b. *Your breasts are better than wine.*

From the Exposition on Blessed Job, Book 30—**{B3}** Teachers are the 'breasts,' which are connected to the hidden part of the chest and give milk to drink, because they cling to hidden matters in the loftiest contemplation and nourish us with their perceptive preaching.[11]

Song 1:2c. *The young girls have loved you.*

From the Exposition on Blessed Job, Book 24—**{B4/P2}** Sacred Scripture is frequently accustomed to put "youth" for "newness of life." Hence it is said to the approaching Bridegroom: *The young girls have loved you,* which is to say the souls of the elect, renewed by the grace of baptism, who do not succumb to the practices of their former ways but are adorned with the way of life that belongs to *the new man* [Eph 4:24].

Song 1:4a. *I am black but beautiful.*

From the Exposition on Blessed Job, Book 18—**{B5}** Preachers never pride themselves on the true light of their righteousness but through the grace of humility acknowledge in themselves the blackness of sin. Hence it is also said by the Church of the elect: *I am black but beautiful.* And John said: *If we were to say that we have no sin, we are deceiving ourselves* [1 John 1:8].

---

of saying "tongue" for "language" (*verba*). Even in everyday language, the organs of speech have a transferred sense by which they refer to the words or language they produce.

11. See P29.

Song 1:5d–e. *They placed me as a guardian in their vineyards; I have not guarded my own vineyard.*

From the Exposition of the Gospels, Homily 17—**{B6}** The holy Church says these words about her weak members. **{P3/B6}** The 'vineyards' are our activities that we cultivate by our practice of daily labor. We are 'placed as guardians in their vineyards' but 'do not guard our own vineyard' because when we entangle ourselves in external activities, we neglect the ministry of our own activity.[12]

Song 1:6a. *Show me, you whom my soul loves, where you pasture, where you lie down at midday.*

From the Exposition on Blessed Job, Book 30—**{P5/B7}** The Lord 'pastures himself' when he finds delight in our good deeds. But he 'lies down at midday' when turning from the hearts of the reprobate, which burn with carnal desires, he finds the cool refreshment of good thought in the hearts of his elect.

Song 1:7. *If you do not know yourself, O beautiful among women, set out and follow the tracks of the flocks and pasture your young goats.*

From the Exposition on Blessed Job, Book 30—**{P6/B8}** She who is 'beautiful among women' knows herself when every elect soul, even if placed among sinners, remembers that she was created in the image and likeness of her Creator and lives in a manner befitting this status of likeness that she has perceived. If she 'does not know herself,' she 'sets out' because, being exiled from the secret depths of her heart, she is dissipated by external objects of desire. But when she 'sets out,' she 'follows the tracks of the flocks' because clearly by forsaking her interior life she is brought to the wide way[13] and follows the examples of the masses. She no longer 'pastures' lambs but 'goats' because she makes no effort to nourish the harmless thoughts of the mind but encourages the wicked stirrings of the flesh.

---

12. That is, preaching.
13. See Matt 7:13.

Song 1:11. *While the king was on his couch, my nard gave its odor.*

From the Exposition on Blessed Job, Book 35—**{B9}** The virtues of those making progress are in a certain sense fragrant with a sweet odor when other people come to know them. Paul spoke in this way: *We are the good odor of Christ for God* [2 Cor 2:15]. Similarly, the holy Church, being fragrant with a kind of sweet odor in her elect, spoke in this way in the Song of Songs, saying: *While the king was on his couch, my nard gave its odor.* **{P7/B9}** It is as if she were saying in plain speech: "As long as the king is hidden from my sight, secluded by himself in his heavenly repose, the conduct of the elect is occupied with giving forth the wonderful odors of the virtues. Hence even though it still does not see him whom it seeks, it may burn all the more ardently with desire." And so 'nard gives off its odor while the king is settled upon his couch' because the virtue of the saints in the Church supplies us with the pleasantness of great sweetness while the Lord is at rest in his blessedness.

Song 2:5a. *Bolster me with flowers, surround me with apples, for I grow faint with love.*

From the Exposition on Ezekiel, Homily 3 in Book 2—**{B10.1}** She who passionately loves her Bridegroom ordinarily gains a single consolation from the delay of the present life, if throughout her separation from the sight of him the souls of others make progress by her word and thereby are inflamed with the firebrands of love for the heavenly Bridegroom. **{B10.2}** Hence the Bride says in the Song: *Bolster me with flowers, surround me with apples, for I grow faint with love.* **{P8/B10.2}** For what are 'flowers,' if not souls who are already beginning to do good work and are redolent with heavenly desire? What are the 'apples' from the 'flowers,' if not the perfect minds of those already good who attain the fruit of good work from the moment they chose a holy way of life? So then, she who 'grows faint with love' seeks to be 'bolstered with flowers' and 'surrounded with apples,' because, even though she is still not permitted to see him whom she desires, she gains great consolation by finding joy in the progress of others. Therefore, a soul who has 'grown faint with holy love' is 'surrounded with flowers and apples,' so that she may find rest in the good work of her neighbor when she is still unable to contemplate the face of God.

Song 2:5b (LXX). *I have been wounded by love.*

From the Exposition on Blessed Job, Book 6—**{P9/B11}** The soul that is sickly and lies prostrate in the blind security of this exile has neither seen God nor sought to see him.[14] But when she is struck by the darts of his love, she is 'wounded' in her innermost recesses with tender devotion, burns with desire for contemplation, and marvelously is restored to life through her wound, though once she lay dead in health. She yearns, she pants, and she desires now to see him whom she fled. Thus by being struck she recovers her health, recalled to the secure state of inward repose by the overturning of her self-love. **{P9}** But when the wounded mind begins to pant for God, when she despises all that is attractive in this world and thereby stretches to her homeland above through desire, whatever she used to consider pleasing and attractive in the world is straightaway turned into source of temptation for her. For those who had a fond affection for her when she was a sinner cruelly assault her when she lives uprightly. And the soul that is upright in God endures attacks from her very own flesh in which she formerly groveled with delight, enslaved to her vices. Previous pleasures return to the memory and afflict the mind with an oppressive struggle as it opposes them. But by being exhausted in toil that is transitory, we are freed from sorrow that is everlasting.

Song 2:6. *His left hand is under my head and his right hand will embrace me.*

From the Book on Pastoral Rule, Chapter 50 in Book 3—**{P10/B12}** In a certain sense, she[15] has put the 'left hand' of God,

---

14. Instead of Gregory's *nec videre requirebat*, "nor sought to see him," Paterius has *nec videri requirebat a Domino*, "nor has she sought to be seen by the Lord." See appendix 4, note 1P.

15. Bede inserts *ecclesia*, "the church," as the subject of the verb "has put." See appendix 4, note 1B.

which is to say the prosperity of the present life, 'under her head,' and pushes it with the intentness of the highest love. But the 'right hand' of God embraces her because in her total commitment she is kept safe under his eternal beatitude. {B12} Again, for this reason it is written: *With your right hand, Lord, you have shattered the enemies* [Exod 15:6]. For God's enemies, even though they thrive in his left hand, are smashed by his right hand, because the present life is usually favorable to the wicked but the coming of eternal beatitude dooms them.

Song 2:8. *Behold! He comes leaping upon the mountains, springing across the hills.*

From the Exposition on the Gospels, Homily 29—{P11.1} Considering his great works to be like lofty peaks, she said: *Behold! He comes leaping upon the mountains.* {P11.2/B13} For by coming for our redemption the Lord performed, if I may put it so, a certain number of leaps. {B13} Dear brothers, do you want to learn what these leaps of his were? {P11.2/B13} From heaven he came into the womb. From the womb he came into the manger. From the manger he came onto the cross. From the cross he came into the tomb. From the tomb he returned to heaven. Behold! Truth manifested in the flesh performed for our benefit a certain number of leaps so as to make us run after him. {B13} *He exulted like a giant to run his course* [Ps 18:6] so that we might say to him from our heart: *Draw me! After you we shall run in the odor of your ointments* [Song 1:3].

Song 2:9b. *Lo! He stands behind our wall, looking through the windows, peering through the lattices.*

From the Exposition on Ezekiel, Homily 1 in Book 2—{B14} In the voice of the Bride the holy Church plainly desires to see him in the present time, saying: *Lo! He stands behind our wall.* {P12/B14} For he who displayed to human eyes that which he assumed from mortal nature,[16] and remained invisible in himself, 'stood' as if 'behind

---

16. Bede mistakenly omits *natura*; see appendix 4, note 2B.

a wall' for those seeking to see him in the open because he did not allow himself to be seen with his majesty manifest. Now he 'stood' as if 'behind a wall' when he displayed the nature of the humanity that he assumed and kept the nature of his divinity hidden from human eyes. Hence it is added there: *Looking through the windows, peering through the lattices.* For anyone who 'looks through windows and lattices' is neither entirely seen nor entirely unseen.[17] Thus, thus our[18] Redeemer came before the eyes of doubters surely for the following reasons: if he had performed miracles without suffering as a man, he would have appeared to them[19] exclusively as God. Then again, if he had experienced human suffering without accomplishing anything as God, they would have considered him a mere man. But since he both accomplished divine acts and experienced human suffering, it is as if he 'peered' at human beings 'through windows and lattices.' For he both manifested himself as God through his miracles and hid that he was God through his sufferings. He was perceived as a man on account of his sufferings and yet was recognized as superior to a man on account of his miracles.

Song 2:10-12. *Arise, make haste, my love, my beautiful one, and come! For now the winter is past, the rains are over and gone.*

From the Exposition on Blessed Job, Book 27—**{B15}** Holy preaching will cease when the present life ends, which is to say rains will cease when winter ends. Hence the soul that is departing from this life and hastening to the regions of eternal summer rightly hears the voice of the Bridegroom persuading her say: *Arise, make haste, my love, my beautiful one, and come! For now the winter is past, the rains are over and gone.* After all, **{P13/B15}** when 'winter is past,

---

17. Instead of Gregory's *nec totus videtur, nec totus non videtur*, "neither entirely seen nor entirely unseen," Paterius has *nec totus latet nec totus videtur*, "neither entirely hidden nor entirely seen." Paterius also omits the second *sic*, "thus," at the beginning of the next sentence. See appendix 4, note 2P.

18. Bede mistakenly omits the *noster* found in Gregory; see appendix 4, note 3B.

19. Bede mistakenly reads *eius*, "of him," instead of Gregory's *eis*, "to them." See appendix 4, note 4B.

the rains are gone' because when the present life is over, in which the numbing cold of the corruptible flesh holds us back in a cloud of ignorance, every ministry of preaching ceases. For at that time we will see more clearly with our own eyes that which we now hear somewhat obscurely through the voices of the saints.

From the Exposition on Ezekiel, Homily 4 in Book 2—{**B16**} Whether she is the holy Church or any elect soul, she is the 'love' of the heavenly Bridegroom on account of her love, his 'dove' on account of her spirit, and his 'beautiful one' on account of the beauty of her conduct. When she is raised from the corruption of the flesh, do not doubt that 'now the winter is past' for her because the numbing cold of the present life departs. Furthermore, 'the rains are over and gone' because when she is raised to the contemplation of Almighty God in his own essence, there is no further need for the rain of preaching to drench her. For she will see more fully what she could hardly hear at all. At that time 'flowers will appear in the land' because when a soul begins to receive a kind of initial foretaste of the pleasantness of eternal beatitude, it is as if the soul is already sniffing fragrances among flowers as she departs. For after she has quit this life, she will have fruit in greater abundance. This is why it is added in that place: *The time for pruning has come* [Song 2:12]. When someone is pruning, he cuts away the barren branches in order that the vigorous ones may bear fruit in greater abundance. And so, 'the time for our pruning comes' when we forsake the unfruitful and harmful corruption of the flesh so as to be able to attain the fruit of the soul.

Song 3:1-4. *In my little bed night by night I sought him whom my soul loves; I sought him but I did not find him. I will arise and scour the whole city; in the streets and the squares I will seek him whom my soul loves. I sought him but I did not find him. The watchmen who guard the city found me. Have you seen him whom my soul loves? When I had passed by them a little ways, I found him whom my soul loves.*

From the Exposition on the Gospels, Homily 25—{**P15/B17**} We seek the beloved 'in the little bed' when we sigh with desire for our Redeemer during the brief respite of the present life. We seek 'night by night' because even though our mind already watches for him, yet our eye is still darkened. But when she does not find her beloved, 'she arises and scours the city,' which is to say she uses her mind to travel about the holy Church of the elect on a quest. 'She seeks him in the streets and the squares,' which is to say she looks at those strolling in narrow and wide places, seeking if any trace of him can be found in them. For even among those who lead a worldly life, there are some who display a modicum of virtue in their actions that is worth imitating. As we search, 'the watchmen who guard the city' find us because the holy fathers, who are the guardians of the Church's stability, run to meet our good efforts in order to teach us by their deeds, their words, or their writings. When we 'have passed by them a little ways,' we find him whom we love because our Redeemer, even though he lived in humility as a human being among human beings, was yet above human beings on account of his divinity. Therefore, when the watchmen are passed by, the beloved is found because when we come to consider the Prophets and the Apostles as inferior to him, we realize that he who is God by nature is superior to human beings. Therefore, the Bridegroom when not found is first sought so that later when found he may be held more closely.

From the Exposition on Ezekiel, Homily 7 in Book 2—{B19} Here is what the Bride in the Song of Songs says when she is anxious with holy desires: *In my little bed night by night I sought him whom my soul loves; I sought him but I did not find him.* {P17/B19} For she seeks the beloved 'in the little bed' when the soul, in her eagerly sought leisure and repose, already yearns to see the Lord, already desires to depart to him, already[20] longs to be free of the darkness of the present life. But 'she seeks him and does not find him' because, although she desires with great love, she is still not permitted to see him whom she loves.

From the Exposition on Blessed Job, Book 5—{P18} The Bridegroom hides himself when sought so that upon not being found he may be sought all the more ardently. The Bride who seeks

---

20. Bede omits the *iam*, "already," found in Gregory; see appendix 4, note 5B.

him is kept at a distance lest she find him, in order that she may be rendered more receptive by the delay and thereby one day find a thousandfold what she sought.

From the Exposition on Blessed Job, Book 18—**{P19}** Whom ought we take as 'the watchmen who guard the city,' if not the earlier fathers and prophets who devoted themselves to watching by the words of holy preaching so as to guard us? **{P19/B18}** But when the Church sought her Redeemer, she was not willing to set her hope on those same ancient preachers, saying: *When I had passed by them a little ways, I found him whom my soul loves.* After all, she would not have been able to find him unless she had been willing to pass them by. **{P19}** The unbelievers entrusted themselves to these same sentries since they believed that Christ the Son of God was one of them. So then, by means of the words and faith of Peter the holy Church passed by the watchmen whom she found, since she refused to believe that the Lord of the Prophets was one of the Prophets.

From the Exposition on Blessed Job, Book 27—**{P20}** *When I had passed by them a little ways, I found him whom my soul loves* because the mind eager for the sight of him cannot find him who is above humanity, unless she 'passes by' the high esteem of the Prophets, the loftiness of the Patriarchs, and the stature of all people. So then, 'to pass by the watchmen' means to consider even those whom the soul admires as of less value when compared to him. And he who was sought is then beheld, if he is believed to be a human being and yet at the same time beyond the stature of human beings.

Song 3:6. *Who is this coming up through the desert like a column of smoke arising from incense made of myrrh and frankincense and all the fragrant powders of the perfumer?*

From the Exposition on Blessed Job, Book 1—**{P21}** The holy Church is 'coming up like a column of smoke arising from incense' because she makes progress each day in the uprightness of internal 'incense'[21] on account of the virtues of her conduct. Nor does she

---

21. I.e., interior virtue.

become dissipated in scattered thoughts, but confines herself within the hidden recesses of her heart by means of the rod of severity.[22] As long as she never ceases to ponder and consider anew what she does, she indeed has 'myrrh and frankincense' in her deeds but 'powder' in her thoughts.

From the Exposition on Ezekiel, Homily 10 in Book 2—{B20} The holy Church of the elect, when with ardent love she raises herself from this world amid holy prayers, 'is coming up through the desert,' which she leaves behind. But it adds how she comes up: *like a column of smoke arising from incense.* Smoke is produced by incense, as is said through the Psalmist: *Let my prayer arise in your presence like incense* [Ps 140:2]. Smoke ordinarily provokes tears. And so, the 'smoke arising from incense' is the compunction of prayer produced by the virtues of love. Yet this prayer is called 'a column of smoke' because, when it asks only for heavenly goods, it soars upward so directly that it never turns back to seek earthly and temporal goods.[23] And note that it is not called a "rod" but a 'column' because sometimes in the ardor of compunction the force of love is of such subtlety[24] that not even the soul itself, which when enlightened merits to possess it, can comprehend it. Furthermore, 'made of myrrh and frankincense' is well said. For the Law prescribes that frankincense be burned in sacrifice to the Lord but that dead bodies be embalmed with myrrh to prevent corruption by worms. Therefore, a sacrifice of myrrh and frankincense is offered by those who afflict their flesh lest they be dominated by the vices of corruption, who burn the pleasing offering of their love in the presence of the Lord,[25] and who present themselves to God

---

22. Here, Gregory plays on "column" (*virgula*) and "rod" (*virga*).

23. At this point Bede adds *pro terreno studio*, "in an earthly pursuit." On the significance of this addition, see appendix 4, note 6B.

24. Bede reads *simplicitatis*, "simplicity," instead of Gregory's *subtilitatis*, "subtlety." See appendix 4, note 7B.

25. Here, Bede adds the parenthetical: *murram itaque quia se cruciant et cruciando a vitiis conservant, tus vero quia Dei visionem diligunt ad quam pervenire medullitus inardescunt*, "myrrh because they crucify themselves and by crucifying themselves

amid holy virtues. This is why it is added in that place: *And all the fragrant powders of the perfumer.* The fragrant powder of the perfumer is the virtue of the one who acts well. And note that the virtues of those who act well are not called "paints" but 'fragrant powders.' For when we do any good work, we are offering paints. But when we reconsider the very good works that we do, and on the basis of this reconsideration determine whether there is anything evil in them, and submit to this judgment, in a certain sense we make powder from paints. Thus we burn our prayer to the Lord more subtly through discretion and love.

Song 3:7. *Lo! Sixty of the most valiant men of Israel surrounded the little bed of Solomon.*

From the Exposition on Blessed Job, Book 7—{**B21.1**} The strength of the righteous is to conquer their flesh, to thwart self-will, to annihilate the delight of the present life, to love the harshness of this world for the sake of eternal rewards, to scorn the charms of good fortune, to overcome the dread of adversity in their heart. {**B21.2**} Therefore, *sixty of the most valiant men of Israel surrounded the little bed of Solomon* {**B21.3**} because all the saints contemplate interior repose without any lessening of their desire.[26]

Song 3:8a. *All are holding swords and they are very skilled in warfare.*

From the Exposition on Blessed Job, Book 19—{**P22/B22**} What the 'sword' represents in the Divine Scripture, Paul laid open when he said: *And the sword of the Spirit, which is the Word of God* [Eph 6:17]. Now Solomon did not say, "All have swords," but: *All are holding swords*, clearly because is it wonderful not only to know the Word of God but also to do it. After all, a sword is had but not held when someone knows the divine speech but makes no effort

---

they keep themselves from vices, but frankincense because they love the vision of God, which in the depths of their heart they long to attain." On the significance of this addition, see appendix 4, note 8B.

26. Instead of Gregory's *ulla debilitate desiderii*, "without any lessening of their desire," Bede has *ulla dubietate desiderii*, "without any wavering in their desire." See appendix 4, note 9B.

to live according to it. And a man can no longer be skilled in warfare if he does not train with the spiritual sword he has. For he is altogether unequal to the task of resisting temptations **{P22}** if by living a bad life he puts off holding this sword of the Word of God.

Song 3:8b. *Everyone's blade is upon his thigh on account of nocturnal fears.*

From the Exposition on Blessed Job, Book 20—**{P23/B23}** 'Nocturnal fears' are the hidden snares of temptation. But a 'blade is upon the thigh' when vigilant guarding subdues the enticements of flesh. So then, lest 'nocturnal fear,' which is to say hidden and sudden temptation, catch us unawares, the 'blade' of guarding 'placed upon our thigh' must always subjugate it. For even though holy people are so confident in their hope, they nevertheless always look upon temptation with mistrust. After all, to them it is said: *Serve the Lord with fear and rejoice in him with trembling* [Ps 2:11], **{B23}** meaning that rejoicing is born of their hope and trembling of their mistrust.

From the Book on Pastoral Rule, Chapter 56 in Book 3—**{B24}** A 'blade is placed upon the thigh' when a wicked suggestion of the flesh is subjugated by the sharp edge of holy preaching. But the term 'night' refers to the blindness that characterizes our enfeebled state. For we do not see the forces of opposition that threaten us at night. Therefore, *everyone's blade is on his thigh on account of nocturnal fears* because it is clear that holy people, while they dread the dangers they do not see, are always prepared to ward off an attack.

Song 3:9-10. *King Solomon made himself a palanquin from the wood of Lebanon. He made its posts of silver, its seat of gold, its ladder of purple, and he covered the insides with love on account of the daughters of Jerusalem.*

From the Exposition on Ezekiel, Homily 3 in Book 2— **{P24.1/B25.1}** Now we ought not believe about Solomon, a king of such greatness, who abounded in such immeasurable riches that the weight of his gold could not be estimated and in whose days silver was worthless,[27] that *he made himself a palanquin from wood.*

---

27. See 1 Kgs 10:21.

Rather, it is Solomon, namely our king and our peacemaker, who *made himself a palanquin from the wood of Lebanon.* For the cedar wood of Lebanon is most imperishable. And so, the palanquin of our king is the holy Church, which was built from our strong forefathers, which is to say from imperishable minds. She is rightly called a 'palanquin' because each day she transports souls to the eternal banquet of her Creator.

The 'posts' of this palanquin were made 'of silver' because the preachers of the holy Church shine with the splendor of eloquent speech. But there is a 'seat of gold' in addition to the 'posts of silver' because when the luminous words of holy preachers are heard, the minds of those who hear them discover the brightness of inner clarity, in which they may recline. For when they hear these clear and plain words they find rest in the clarity that has come to their heart. So then,[28] its[29] 'posts' are 'of silver' and its 'seat' was made 'of gold' because the splendor of speech enables the discovery of restful clarity in the soul. For this interior brightness illumines her mind in the present time so that by means of attention she may find rest in that place where the grace of preaching is not required.

{P24.2/B25.2} But in addition to this revelation of interior clarity, the quality of the ladder is described by an additional statement made about the same palanquin: *its ladder of purple.* Since real purple is achieved by dyeing with blood, it is not unjust to view it as representing the color of blood. And so, since the greatest multitude of the faithful at the beginning of the Church in its infancy attained the kingdom through the blood of martyrdom, our king made a 'ladder of purple' in his palanquin because one attains the clarity seen within through the trial of blood.

So then, what are we to do, miserable as we are and bereft of all strength? Look, we cannot be 'posts' in this palanquin because neither the strength needed for working nor the splendor of

---

28. At this point both Paterius and Bede omit Gregory's *ergo*, "so then." See appendix 4, notes 3P and 10B.

29. Bede omits Gregory's *eius*, "its." See appendix 4, note 11B.

preaching shines in us. We do not possess a 'seat of gold' because, as is fitting, we still do not perceive the rest of interior clarity through spiritual understanding. We are not a 'ladder of purple' because we are unable to shed blood for our Redeemer.[30] So then, what is to be done about us? What hope will there be if no one attains the kingdom except the one who is endowed with the most excellent virtues?

But there is also consolation for us. Let us love God as much as we can, let us love our neighbor, and at the same time too let us strive for the palanquin of God, because as it is written in that same place: *he covered the insides with love*. Have love, and without a doubt you will reach that place where the 'post of silver' is set and the 'ladder of purple' is kept. Yet that this is said on account of our weakness is clearly shown when it is added further on in the same place: *on account of the daughters of Jerusalem*. Since the word of God does not say "sons" but 'daughters,' what else has been signified by the female sex other than the weak parts of our minds?

{P24.2} Therefore, because in this passage[31] it is said that in the midst of the 'posts of silver,' the 'seat of gold,' and the 'ladder of purple' there is love 'on account of the daughters of Jerusalem,' this is designated here[32] by *the five cubits between the rooms* [Ezek 40:7]. For even those who lack the strength for the virtues, if they do not fail to do the good that they can do with love, then they are not strangers to the edifice of God.

Song 4:1. *How beautiful you are, my love, how beautiful! Your eyes are dovelike, aside from what is veiled within.*

From the Exposition on Blessed Job, Book 9—{B26} He describes her as 'beautiful,' then repeats himself, calling her 'beautiful' a second time. For she possesses one sort of beauty, the beauty of

---

30. Bede (or a copyist) omits the beginning of this paragraph up to this point; see appendix 4, note 12B.

31. I.e., Song 3:9-10.

32. I.e., in Ezek 40:7. Paterius retains this line of the excerpt though it makes little sense outside of its context in *H.Ez*.

conduct, whereby she is recognized in the present time, and another sort of beauty, the beauty of rewards, whereby she will later be lifted up through the sight of her Creator. Because all her elect members do everything with simplicity, her eyes are called 'dove-like.' They shine with great splendor because they sparkle with the miracles that she sees. But as great as every miracle is because it can be seen, an interior miracle is more wonderful because it cannot be seen in the present time. Regarding this it is appropriately added in that place: *aside from what is veiled within*. For the glory of an observable work is great, but the glory of a hidden reward is far beyond comparison.[33]

Song 4:2. *Your teeth are like a flock of shorn sheep coming up from a washing.*

From the Exposition on Blessed Job, Book 33—**{B27.1}** We take the holy Church's 'teeth' as those who masticate the toughness of sinners with their preaching. **{P25/B27.2}** It is not unreasonable to compare them to 'shorn' and 'washed' sheep. For by adopting an irreproachable manner of life in the baptismal bath they have put aside the raggedy fleece of their previous way of life.

Song 4:3. *Your lips are like a scarlet headband, my Bride, and your words are sweet.*

From the Exposition on Blessed Job, Book 2—**{P26/B28}** A headband binds the hairs of the head. Therefore, the Bride's 'lips' are like a 'headband' because the exhortations of the holy Church bind together all wandering thoughts in the minds of those who listen. It keeps them from running riot, being scattered by forbidden thoughts, and, once scattered, troubling the eyes of the heart. And so it enables them to gather themselves together, as it were, into a single purpose as long as the headband of holy preaching binds them. How good is it too that the headband is called 'scarlet'! For the preaching of the saints burns only with the ardor of love.

---

33. Bede reads *retributionis*, "retribution," instead of Gregory's *remunerationis*, "reward." See appendix 4, note 13B.

{P26} But what is meant by the head, if not that which is the principle of each and every action, the mind itself? This is reminiscent of something said elsewhere: *And let not oil be lacking from your head* [Eccl 9:8]. Now oil on the head means love in the mind, and oil is not lacking from the head when love has not departed from the mind.

Song 4:4. *Your neck is like the tower of David, built with its own bulwarks; a thousand bucklers hang upon it, every one of them the armament of valiant men.*

From the Exposition on Ezekiel, Homily 3 in Book 2—
{B29.1} In the neck one finds the throat, and in the throat one finds the voice. So then, what is meant by the 'neck' of the holy Church, if not the Sacred Words? When it is mentioned that *a thousand bucklers hang upon it*, this number of perfection indicates the number of totality because the Sacred Word contains our total defense. For that is where we find the precepts of God, that is where we find the examples of the righteous. **{B29.2}** Therefore, 'upon the neck of the Church,' which is to say in the preaching of the Sacred Word (said to be 'like the tower of David' because of its strong position and height), 'a thousand bucklers hang' because there all the precepts are also defenses for our heart. **{B29.3}** And so do we hasten to be 'valiant' against the powers of the air? We find the 'armament' of our mind in this 'tower' and from it we take the precepts of our Creator and the examples of our predecessors by which we become invincibly armed against our adversaries.

{B29.4} And note that the tower is said to have been *built with its own bulwarks*. Now bulwarks perform the same function as bucklers do, since both protect the one who fights. But there is a difference between them: while we can move bucklers at will to protect ourselves, we can defend ourselves with a bulwark but without being able to move it. A buckler is clutched in the hand, but a bulwark is not. So then, what is the difference between a bulwark and a buckler, if not the fact that in the Sacred Word we both read the miracles of the fathers who have gone before us and hear the virtues of their good works? **{B29.5}** And so, their miracles testify that they proclaimed the truth about the Lord, since they would not have been able to do such things through him unless they were telling the truth about him. And their activities testify to how devoted, how humble, how kind they were. {**B29.6**} So then, what are their miracles, if not our bulwarks? For they can protect us, and yet we do not hold them in our hand as things within our power to choose, seeing that we cannot do such things. But we do have a buckler in our hand and it defends us because the virtue of patience and the virtue of mercy, so long as grace precedes, are within our power to choose, and they protect from the danger of adversity.

Song 4:5-6. *Your two breasts are like two fawns of a roe deer, twins, who feed on the lilies until the day breaks and the shadows recede.*

From the Exposition on Blessed Job, Book 24—{**P27/B30**} What are the 'two breasts' of the Bride, if not the two peoples coming from the Jews and from the Gentiles, who are implanted in the body of the holy Church through their efforts to attain wisdom in the hidden depths of their heart? Accordingly, those elected from these peoples are compared to the 'fawns of a roe deer' because through their humility they have come to understand that they are truly insignificant and sinful. But if they encounter any hurdles of temporal encumbrance, running by love they surmount them and making leaps of contemplation[34] they ascend to heavenly realities.

In order to do these things they[35] reflect on the examples of the saints who have preceded them. This is why reference is made to the fact that they *feed on the lilies*. For what is indicated by lilies, if not the conduct of those who can truly say: *We are the good odor of Christ for God* [2 Cor 2:15]? So then, the elect, in order to gain

---

34. Paterius mistakenly has *contemplationum*, "of contemplations," instead of Gregory's *contemplationis*, "of contemplation." See appendix 4, note 4P.

35. Paterius reads *Quia ut haec agant*, "Since in order to do these things they," instead of Gregory's *Qui ut haec agant*, "In order to do these things they." See appendix 4, note 5P.

the strength to follow them to the highest regions, completely satisfy themselves by reflecting upon the fragrant and pure conduct of the righteous. Even in the present time they thirst to see God. In the present time they burn with the fires of love that they may be completely satisfied by the contemplation of him. But since they are still incapable of doing so while placed in this life, they feed in the meantime on the examples of the fathers who have preceded them.

Hence that passage fittingly gave a limit to the time for their 'feeding on the lilies,' when it is said: *Until the day breaks and the shadows recede.* For we need to be nourished with the examples of the righteous for only so long, until we pass beyond the shadows of our present mortality when that eternal day breaks. After all, when the shadow of this transitory time has receded and this mortal state has passed away, since we behold the inner light of day itself, we no longer seek to be kindled with love for it through the examples of others. But as it is now, since we are still unable to gaze upon it, we especially need to be aroused by reflecting on the actions of those who have pursued it perfectly.

{P27} So then, let us gaze upon the beautifulness of the alacrity of those who pursue it, and let us notice the disgracefulness of the sloth of the lazy. For as soon as we reflect on the deeds of those who live good lives, we pass judgment on ourselves in our profound embarrassment. Soon feelings of shame assail our mind, soon a rightfully harsh accusation is levied upon us, and we are even sorely displeased with our disgraceful behavior, which perhaps we still find pleasurable.

Song 4:8. *You shall be crowned from the summit of Amana, from the peak of Senir and Hermon, from the dens of lions.*

From the Exposition on Blessed Job, Book 17—**{P28/B31}** What else could the word 'lions' designate[36] other than the demons who rage against us with wrath of the most savage sort of cruelty?

---

36. Paterius mistakenly reads *signantur*, "signify," instead of Gregory's *designantur*, "designate." See appendix 4, note 6P.

And because sinners are called to faith, whose hearts were once[37] 'dens of lions,' when they confess their belief in the Lord's victory over death, it is as if he is 'crowned from the dens of lions.' After all, the reward for victory is a crown. Therefore, the faithful offer a crown to the Lord as often as they confess that he is victorious over death through his resurrection.

Song 4:10. *Your breasts are better than wine.*

From the Exposition on Blessed Job, Book 30—{**P29**} Preachers are the 'breasts,' which are connected to the hidden part of the chest and give milk to drink, because they cling to hidden matters in the loftiest contemplation and nourish us with their perceptive preaching.[38]

Song 4:11. *Honey and milk are under your tongue.*

From the Exposition on Blessed Job, Book 15—{**B32**} When most of the righteous see any persons living wicked lives, who deserve to be chastised with harsh rebukes, they put sternness on the tongue. But 'under the tongue' they conceal the gentleness of their mind. This is why it is said to the holy Church in the voice of the Bridegroom: *Honey and milk are under your tongue.* {**P30/B32**} For they prefer not to disclose the sweetness of their mind to the weak, but when they speak they chastise them with a degree of sternness. And yet amid their harsh words they sprinkle droplets of sweetness, on the sly as it were. It is people such as these who do not have sweetness on the tongue but rather 'under the tongue.' For amid the harsh words which they utter, they also give out some that are consoling and sweet whereby the mind of a distressed person can be restored on account of their gentleness. {**P30**} Similarly, because some of the wicked do not have evil on the tongue but rather 'under the tongue,' they make a pretence of sweetness in their words but formulate wicked plans in their thoughts.

---

37. Paterius mistakenly omits Gregory's *quondam*, "once." See appendix 4, note 7P.
38. See B3.

Song 4:13. *Your shoots are a garden of pomegranates.*

From the Book on Pastoral Rule, Chapter 15 in Book 2—{**B33**} What is designated by 'pomegranates,' if not the unity of the faith? For just as in a pomegranate many seeds that are inside are protected by a single outer rind, so too does the unity of the faith shelter the countless people of the holy Church, who though diverse in merit are held together within it.

Song 4:16. *Arise, north wind, and come, south wind, blow through my garden and let its sweet scents spread around.*

From the Exposition on Blessed Job, Book 9—{**P31**} What is designated by the phrase 'south wind,' if not the fervor of the Holy Spirit? When anyone is filled with him, love for the spiritual homeland is enkindled in her. This is why in the Song of Songs it is said in the voice of the Bridegroom: *Arise, north wind, and come, south wind, blow through my garden and let its sweet scents spread around.* For 'the south wind comes' and 'the north wind arises and departs,' when the ancient enemy, who chills the mind with lethargic numbness, is expelled by the arrival of the Holy Spirit and betakes himself away. But 'the south wind blows through the garden' of the Bridegroom to 'spread its sweet scents around' because surely when the Spirit of truth fills the holy Church with the virtues that are his very own gifts, he spreads far and wide from her the odors of good works. Therefore, *the chambers of the south wind* [Job 9:9] are those hidden orders of angels and the unfathomable depths of the heavenly homeland, which are filled with the warmth of the Holy Spirit. After all, that is where the souls of the saints go, both at the present time when they are divested of their bodies and hereafter when they are restored to their bodies, and like stars they lay hidden in remote realms. There day after day, it is as if the fire of the sun were burning intensely at high noon because the brightness of the Creator, which at the present time is obscured by the darkness of our mortality, is more clearly seen. And it is as if a ray of that orb raised itself to higher regions because truth enlightens us through and through from its own resources. There the light of interior contemplation is observed without the intervening shadow of mutability. There the warmth of the supreme light is seen without being obscured by the body. There the invisible choirs of angels glitter like stars in remote realms, which cannot be seen by human beings at the present time, because they are deeply bathed in the flame of the true light.

From the Exposition on Blessed Job, Book 27—{B34} The 'south wind'—a wind that is certainly warm—is not an unsuitable designation for the Holy Spirit. For when anyone is touched by him, she is freed from the lethargic numbness of her evil ways. Hence it is well said in the Song of Songs: *Arise, north wind, and come, south wind, blow through my garden and let its sweet scents spread around.* For the 'north wind' is ordered to 'arise,' undoubtedly in order that the hostile spirit, who chills the hearts of mortals, may take flight. The 'south wind comes and blows through the garden' in order that 'its sweet scents spread around' because when human minds are filled by the coming of the Holy Spirit, soon after this their reputation for virtues is scattered abroad. Hence the tongue of the saints, like 'a garden through which the south wind blows,' may justly say in the present time: *We are the good odor of Christ for God* [2 Cor 2:15].

Song 5:2. *I sleep but my heart is awake.*

From the Exposition on Ezekiel, Homily 2 in Book 2—{B35} Exceedingly lovely is the sweetness of the contemplative life, which carries the soul above herself, discloses heavenly secrets, shows that earthly goods are to be scorned, reveals spiritual truths to the eyes of the mind, and hides corporeal objects. So the Church speaks well when she says in the Song of Songs: *I sleep but my heart is awake.* {P32/B35} For she sleeps with a 'heart' that 'is awake' because[39] on account of her interior progress in contemplation she is undisturbed by disturbing exterior works. {P32} But note that, amid these things, as long as life continues in this mortal flesh, no one progresses in the virtue of contemplation so much so that in the present time the eyes of the mind can be fixed on the uncircumscribed ray of light itself. For in the present time there is no vision

---

39. Bede mistakenly reads *qui*, "which," instead of Gregory's *quia*, "because." See appendix 4, note 14B.

of Almighty God in his brightness, but the soul glimpses something short of it whereby she is revived and advances further. But in the hereafter she attains to the glory of the vision of God.

From the Exposition on Blessed Job, Book 23— **{P33/B36}** As if she were saying: "While I give my exterior senses rest from the worries of this life, I have a more lively comprehension of interior realities since my mind is free. 'I sleep' exteriorly, but 'my heart is awake' interiorly because while I have no perception, as it were,[40] of exterior objects, I have a keen comprehension of interior realities."

Song 5:4. *My beloved put his hand through the opening, and my insides trembled at his touch.*

From the Exposition on Ezekiel, Homily 7 in Book 2—**{P34/B37}** Surely 'the beloved puts his hand through the opening' when the Lord by his own power moves our soul to a refined understanding. And 'the insides tremble at his touch' because our weakness, on account of being touched by an understanding of heavenly joy, is thrown into confusion by our own ecstasy. And panic seizes her mind in her rejoicing[41] because in the present time she experiences a bit of the heavenly joy that she loves and yet[42] she dreads not retaining what she experiences so fleetingly. **{P34}** Therefore, what are they to do, all who have an appreciation for the joys of the heavenly homeland, if not to direct their feet along the path of a more perfect life?

---

40. Bede reads *suasi*, which is ungrammatical, instead of Gregory's *quasi*, "as it were." See appendix 4, note 15B.

41. While Gregory's text reads *in laetitia*, "in her rejoicing," Paterius has *cum laetitia*, "with her rejoicing." In addition, Bede has *ac laetitia*, which would alter the translation as follows: "And panic, as well as rejoicing, seizes her mind." See appendix 4, notes 8P and 16B.

42. While Gregory's text reads *quia iam sentit quod de caelesti gaudio diligat, et adhuc*, Paterius has *et si* in place of *quia* and omits *et*. Paterius's reading would alter the translation thus: "And panic seizes her mind in her rejoicing; even though at the present time she experiences a bit of the heavenly joy that she loves, yet she dreads not laying hold of what she experiences so fleetingly." See appendix 4, note 9P.

Song 5:6. *My soul was melted when my beloved spoke.*

From the Exposition on Blessed Job, Book 4—**{P34B}** There can be no doubt that when the mind is touched by the breath of secret speaking, she loses the seat of her own strength and 'is melted' by the very desire that consumes her. And then she discovers that she is inherently weak, which enables her to realize that beyond herself there is a strength which deigns to come down.

From the Exposition on the Gospels, Homily 25—**{B38}** The mind of the person who does not seek the sight of her Creator is very hard because she persists in a frozen state on account of herself. But if in the present time she starts to burn with the desire to follow him whom she loves, 'melted' by the fire of love, she runs. She becomes eager with desire. She reviles all worldly things that used to bring her pleasure. Nothing except her Creator pleases her. What first delighted her soul afterward becomes grievously burdensome. Nothing consoles her grief as long as she has still not looked upon him whom she desires. Her mind sorrows. Light itself is wearisome. Scorching fire burns away the rust of sin in her mind. The soul is enflamed like gold because gold loses its luster through use but regains its brightness through fire.

Song 5:7. *The sentries who patrol the city found me. They beat me. They wounded me. The sentries of the walls took my cloak from me.*

From the Exposition on Blessed Job, Book 27—**{B39}** 'The watchmen find the Bride as she searches for him, and wound her, and take away her cloak' because **{P35/B39}** when dutiful teachers find that any soul is already seeking the sight of her Redeemer, they 'wound her' with the darts of heavenly love through the word of preaching. And if she still possesses any covering of her old way of life, they 'take it away' so that the more she is stripped of the burden of this world, the more quickly she may find him whom she seeks.

Song 5:11. *His head is the finest gold.*

From the Exposition on Blessed Job, Book 34—**{P36/B40}** *The head of Christ is God* [1 Cor 11:3] but there is no metal more resplendent than gold. Hence the Bridegroom's head is called 'gold' because his humanity rules over us on account of the brightness of his divinity.

Song 6:3. *You are beautiful, my love, charming and lovely as Jerusalem, terrifying as an army's front poised for battle.*

From the Exposition on Ezekiel, Homily 8 in Book 1—{**P37/ B41**} The interpretation of the name 'Jerusalem' is "vision of peace," which represents the heavenly homeland. So then, the holy Church is called 'charming and lovely as Jerusalem' because her conduct and desire[43] are being compared to the vision of inner peace. Hence insofar as she loves her Creator and yearns to see the face of him about whom it is written, *He upon whom the angels desire to look* [1 Pet 1:12], she is said to be like the angels on account of these very desires of her love. She becomes pleasing to God to the extent that[44] she makes an effort to become terrifying to wicked spirits.

Another comparison shows just how terrifying she is: *like an army's front poised for battle.* Why do the enemies of the holy Church fear her as if she were 'an army's front'? Now this comparison does not lack great insight and so we must examine it in detail. For we know and it is undisputed that an army's front appears terrifying to enemies when it is drawn up so tightly and packed together so closely that no gaps can be seen anywhere. For if it is deployed such that there is an empty space through which the enemy could enter, it would certainly no longer be terrifying to its enemies. Therefore, when we form the line for spiritual battle against wicked spirits, it is of the utmost importance that we always be united to one another and joined closely together through charity and[45] never found separated from one another through discord. For even though we may do good works, if charity is lacking, the evil of

---

43. Bede mistakenly reads *eius vitae desiderium*, "her desire for life," instead of Gregory's *eius vita et desiderium*, "her conduct and desire." See appendix 4, note 17B.

44. Paterius mistakenly reads *quantum* instead of Gregory's *quanto* (the meaning is the same). See appendix 4, note 10P.

45. Bede reads *ut*, "so as to be" instead of Gregory's *et*, "and." See appendix 4, note 18B.

discord opens a gap in the battle-line through which the enemy can enter and smite us.

{**P37**} The ancient enemy does not fear our self-control if it is without charity because he is not oppressed by flesh such that he destroys himself through self-indulgence. He does not fear our abstinence because he who[46] is not urged by the needs of the body does not eat food. He does not fear it when we donate our earthly goods if we do so without charity because he has no need for the benefits of riches. But he very much fears the true charity in us, which is to say the humble love that we mutually extend to one another. And he greatly begrudges our concord because we ourselves retain on earth what he himself, choosing not to retain it, lost in heaven. Therefore, *terrifying as an army's front poised for battle* is well said because the wicked spirits tremble with fear at the multitude of the elect insofar as they observe them united and assembled against themselves through the concord of charity.

Song 6:6. *Like the skin of a pomegranate are your cheeks, apart from what you hide.*

From the Commentary on Ezekiel, Homily 4 in Book 2—
{**P38/B42**} The 'cheeks' of the holy Church are the spiritual fathers, who at the present time glow in her with marvelous deeds and in a certain sense give a venerable appearance to her face. For when we see many perform wonders, prophesy future events, perfectly forsake the world, and ardently burn with heavenly desires, the holy Church's[47] cheeks blush 'like the skin of a pomegranate.' But what is all this that we admire in comparison to that reality of which it is written: *What eye has not seen, nor ear heard, nor entered into the heart of man, which God has prepared for those who love him* [1 Cor 2:9]? Therefore, when he admired the cheeks of the Church, it is good that he added: *apart from what you hide*. It is as if he were saying in

---

46. Paterius mistakenly reads *quia*, "because he," instead of Gregory's *qui*, "who." See appendix 4, note 11P.

47. Paterius mistakenly omits Gregory's *ecclesiae*, "Church's." See appendix 4, note 12P.

plain speech: "Indeed, those things in you which are not hidden are great, but those which are hidden are utterly inexpressible."

Song 6:9. *Who is this coming forth, rising like the dawn?*

From the Exposition on Blessed Job, Book 4—{**P39**} The Church of the elect is 'rising like the dawn' since she has left the darkness of her former wickedness and turned herself to the radiance of new light. So then, in that light which is manifested at the coming of the strict Judge, the body of our enemy when condemned will not see the break of the rising dawn. For when the strict Judge comes for retribution, each wicked person, being oppressed by the blackness of his own deserts, is kept from knowing the wondrous splendor with which the holy Church rises to the interior light of the heart. At that time the mind of the elect is transported on high such that she is illumined with the rays of Divinity, and she is bathed in the light of his countenance to the extent that she is lifted above herself in the refulgence of grace. At that time the holy Church becomes a full dawn since she has wholly parted with the darkness of her mortality and ignorance. So then, at the judgment she is still dawn but in the kingdom she is day. For though she already begins to behold the light at the judgment when bodies are resurrected, yet she attains a fuller vision of it in the kingdom. And so, the break of dawn is the beginning of the Church in splendor, which the reprobate cannot see. For oppressed by the weight of their evils, they are dragged from the sight of the strict Judge into darkness.

From the Exposition on Blessed Job, Book 29—{**P40/B43**} The holy Church as she pursues the rewards of the heavenly life is called the 'dawn' because when she leaves the darkness of sin she shines with the light of righteousness. Yet we have here something quite profound which ought to be pondered by considering the characteristics of the daybreak or dawn. Now the dawn or daybreak announces that the night is past, but does not yet put forward the full brightness of day. Rather, while it dispels the night and takes on the day, it keeps the light intermingled with the darkness. And so, what are all of us who follow the truth in this life, if not the dawn or daybreak? For in the present time we both do some things which belong to the light, and yet are not free from the rest of the other things which still belong to the darkness.

Song 7:4. *Your nose is like the tower which is in Lebanon.*

From the Exposition on Blessed Job, Book 31—{**B44**} We use our nose to distinguish between pleasant scents and foul odors. {**P41/B44**} And what is meant by the Church's 'nose,' if not the farseeing discernment of the saints? Now a watchtower is placed on high so that the approaching enemy may be spotted from afar. So then, the Church's 'nose' is rightly said to be 'like the tower in Lebanon' because as long as the farseeing discernment of the saints placed on high carefully monitors all possible places, it catches sight of sin before its arrival. And so, the greater the vigilance in detecting sin before its arrival, the greater the strength to avoid it.

From the Exposition on Ezekiel, Homily 11 in Book 1—{**B45**} To preserve the truth of preaching, a loftiness of conduct must be maintained. Hence in the Song of Songs it is rightly said to the holy Church in the voice of the Bridegroom: *Your nose is like the tower of Lebanon.* What kind of praise is it, my brothers, for the Bride's nose to be compared to a tower? Seeing that we always use our nose to distinguish between pleasant scents and foul odors, {**P42/B45**} what is meant by the nose, if not the discernment of the watchmen? Surely the nose is said to be 'like the tower of Lebanon' because clearly the discernment of superiors ought always be fortified with careful attention and be established on loftiness of conduct, which is to say they ought not lie in the valley of feeble effort. For as a tower is placed on a mountain to spot enemies coming from afar, so too ought the conduct of a preacher always remain fixed on high. Thus like a nose he may distinguish between the foul odors of vices and the pleasing scents of virtues, perceive from afar the onslaughts of malicious spirits, and through his providence safely return the souls entrusted to him.

Song 7:12. *Let us get up early to go to the vineyards. Let us see whether the vine has budded, whether the buds are ready to produce fruits.*

From the Exposition on Blessed Job, Book 12—{**P43/B46**} Vines have 'budded' when the minds of the faithful plan good works. But they do not 'produce fruits' if they falter in carrying out their plans when overcome by certain erring practices. We ought then not look to see if the vines have budded but if the buds are strong for producing fruits. For there is nothing to admire if someone begins good works, but there is much to admire if someone persists in a good work with the right intention.

Song 8:5. *Who is this ascending from the desert overflowing with an abundance of delights?*

From the Exposition on Blessed Job, Book 16—**{B47}** Surely if the holy Church were not 'overflowing with an abundance of delights,' which is to say with the words of God, she could not 'ascend from the desert' of the present life to the regions above. So then, she is 'overflowing with an abundance of delights' and 'ascending' because when she is nourished by mystical understandings she is lifted up daily in the contemplation of heavenly things.

Song 8:5 (LXX). *Who is this who ascends made white?*

From the Exposition on Blessed Job, Book 18—**{P44/B48}** The holy Church does not have the heavenly life by nature but when the Spirit comes upon her she is adorned with the beautifulness of gifts. For this reason she is described not as "white" but as 'made white.'

Song 8:6a. *Set me as a seal upon your heart.*

From the Exposition on Blessed Job, Book 29—**{P45/B49}** Now a seal is set on things so that they may not be violated by any audacity of plunderers. So then, the Bridegroom is 'set as[48] a seal on our heart' when the mystery of faith in him is impressed upon us for the safe keeping of our thoughts. Hence when that faithless servant, namely our adversary, observes our hearts sealed by faith,[49] he does not have the audacity to break into them with temptation.

---

48. Bede adds an *ut* not found in Gregory, though it does not change the translation; see appendix 4, note 19B.

49. Both Paterius and Bede have corrupt versions of Gregory's *signata fide corda*, "hearts sealed by faith." See appendix 4, notes 13P and 20B.

Song 8:6b. *Strong as death is love.*

In the Exposition on the Gospels, Homily 11—{**P46/B50**} As death destroys the body, so love of eternal life makes one dead to the love of corporeal things. For whomever it utterly consumes becomes impervious to outward earthly desires.

Song 8:8. *Our sister is little and she has no breasts.*

From the Exposition on Blessed Job, Book 19—{**B51**} As the age of each individual person is described, so that of the holy Church. For she was 'little' when fresh from birth she could not preach the word of life. Hence it is said about her, *Our sister is little and she has no breasts*, because surely {**P47/B51**} before the holy Church made progress by growth in virtue, she could not offer the 'breasts' of preaching to each of her weak listeners. But the Church is called "adult" when, being wedded to the Word of God and filled with the Holy Spirit, she conceives children through the ministry of preaching, enters into labor with them by exhortation, and gives birth to them by effecting conversion. {**B51**} Concerning this age of hers it is said to the Lord: *The young girls have loved you* [Song 1:2]. For all the churches which constitute the one Catholic Church are called 'young girls.' They are at present not aged through sin but youthful through grace, not barren on account of old age but suited for spiritual fecundity on account of the youthful age of their mind.

Song 8:13. *You who dwell in gardens, the friends are listening: make me hear your voice.*

From the Exposition on Ezekiel, Homily 2 in Book 2—{**B52**} 'In gardens' the holy Church, {**P48/B52**} 'in gardens' every individual soul 'dwells' who in the present time is filled with the greenness of hope and good works. For hope in this age is barren because all things loved here hastily wither away. And so Peter the Apostle urges us to hasten *to an inheritance that never perishes, never spoils, and never withers away* [1 Pet 1:4]. So then, she who already 'dwells in gardens' must 'make' her Bridegroom 'hear her voice,' which is to say she must sing the song of good preaching in which he whom she desires will delight, because[50] 'the friends are listening,' namely all the elect who in order to return to life again in the heavenly homeland desire to hear the words of life.

Song 8:14. *Escape, my beloved, escape!*

From the Exposition on Blessed Job, Book 17—{**P49/B53**} We say "it escapes me" as often as what we want to remember does not come to mind. We say "it escapes me" when we do not retain in our memory what we want to remember.[51] So the holy Church, after narrating the Lord's death, resurrection, and ascension, cries out to him, filled with a prophetic spirit: *Escape, my beloved, escape!* It is as if she were saying: "You who were made comprehensible to us by the flesh, transcend the grasp of our senses by your divinity and remain incomprehensible to us in your very own self!"

---

50. Bede omits this *quia*, "because." See appendix 4, note 21B.

51. Paterius mistakenly abbreviates these two sentences to "We say 'it escapes me' as often as what we want to remember we do not retain in our memory." See appendix 4, note 14P.

WILLIAM OF SAINT THIERRY'S

Excerpts from the Books of Blessed Gregory on the Song of Songs

INTRODUCTION

The first modern edition of William of Saint Thierry's *Excerpts from the Books of Blessed Gregory on the Song of Songs* was published at Leiden in 1692.[1] This edition was based on the autograph of the text from the Abbey of Signy, where William lived as a monk from 1135 until his death in 1148. Unfortunately, this manuscript has since been lost. The Leiden text was reprinted in 1781 by André Galland and then in 1855 by J.-P. Migne.[2] While this edition and its reprints are not critical editions, they remain nonetheless extremely valuable because they witness to the lost autograph of Signy. I will designate this lost manuscript as S.

The critical edition of William of Saint Thierry's *Excerpts from the Books of Blessed Gregory on the Song of Songs* was established for *Corpus Christianorum Continuatio Mediaevalis* by Paul Verdeyen in 1997.[3] Though there are eight extant manuscripts of this florilegium, Verdeyen used the best four for his edition. He then classified these four into two families, one representing the Benedictine manuscript tradition and the other the Carthusian manuscript tradition. Three manuscripts represent the Benedictine tradition: (1) Reims,

---

1. *GUILLELMI abbatis primum Sancti Theodorici Remensis ac postea Signiacensis monachi ordinis cisterciensis Commentarius in Cantica canticorum. Ex MS codice autographo abbatiae Signiaci* (Lugduni Batauorum: P. van der Meersche, 1692). This edition does not list the editor, but some scholars have claimed that it was Casimir Oudin. For the following review of the mss. and editions I am indebted to Paul Verdeyen et al., *Guillelmi a Sancto Theodorico Expositio super Cantica canticorum, Brevis commentatio, Excerpta de libris beati Ambrosii et Gregorii super Cantica canticorum*, CCCM 87 (Turnhout: Brepols, 1997), 387–92.

2. André Galland, *Bibliotheca veterum Patrum et antiquorum Scriptorum ecclesiasticorum* (Venice, 1781), Tome 14, 394f.; PL 180:441–74.

3. Verdeyen et al., *Guillelmi a Sancto Theodorico*, 387–444.

Bibliothèque municipale, ms. 142, thirteenth century, originally from the Abbey of Saint Thierry [=R]; (2) Valenciennes, Bibliothèque municipale, ms. 50, twelfth century, originally from the Abbey of Saint-Amand [=V]; and (3) Dendermonde, Abbaye Saint-Pierre et Saint-Paul, ms. 19, twelfth century [=A]. Note that the first two manuscripts are from Saint Thierry and Saint-Amand, the latter of whose prior, Hellinus, succeeded William as abbot of Saint Thierry. From this, Verdeyen concludes "that William probably made the two florilegia during his abbacy (between 1121 and 1135) and that his successor had them copied for his original monastery."[4] Hence we possess manuscripts not far removed from William's lost autograph (S). The Carthusian tradition is represented only by Darmstadt, Hessische Landes- und Hochschulbibliothek, ms. 21, fourteenth century, originally from the Charterhouse of Saint-Barbe in Cologne [=D].[5] While the manuscript that William sent to the Carthusian monks of Mont-Dieu is lost, it is likely that D was copied from it.

Verdeyen used R as the basis for his edition, correcting it where necessary by A, V, and D, as well as by Gregory's own works. A is the second most important manuscript since either its copyist or corrector (the latter designated as A^c) compared R with the works of Gregory, and it thus constitutes a corrected text. The use of the text of the Carthusian tradition represented by D for establishing original readings must proceed with caution since its text is an expanded version of the text found in A, R, and V. Numerous minor alterations (both additions and omissions) and six major additions have been made to the text: five of these major additions are taken from the *Moralia* (see W13, W15, W21, W25, and W26) and the other from Augustine (see W16). Furthermore, the text of *Excerpta* 3, 141–156 in D is completely reworked (W25). Therefore, it seems that D is a revised version of the text, but not one made by William. There are two

---

4. Verdeyen et al., *Guillelmi a Sancto Theodorico*, 387.

5. The four mss. of this text not used for this edition are: (1) Cambridge, Gonville and Caius College, ms. 239; (2) Heiligenkreuz, ms. 253; (3) München, Clm. 15912; and (4) Wien, Nat. Bibl. ms. 2164.

reasons for not attributing the revision to William. First, William's vast knowledge of the fathers of the Church would seem to preclude his mistakenly inserting an Augustinian text into his Gregorian florilegium. Second, it makes little sense to attribute the rearrangement of *Excerpta* 3, 141–156 to William when the original version was already a careful pastiche of Gregorian texts. Hence, some unknown Carthusian monk is probably responsible for the revised version.

I have based my translation on Verdeyen's edition, though not without minor disagreement. I depart from Verdeyen's text in twenty-six instances. In four of these departures I have preferred the readings of S, an important witness which Verdeyen did not utilize in his edition. Twice I preferred the reading of S over against all other manuscript support, and twice when the reading of S was supported by other manuscripts. I have also identified twenty-two primitive errors in William's text based on a comparison with the original Gregorian texts. Some of these are corruptions, others accidental omissions. These twenty-six departures from Verdeyen are reflected in the translation and footnoted in each case. The emendations employed in my translation of William's excerpts are listed and discussed in appendix 5.

Finally, I have divided each of William's excerpts into verses. Each verse is marked by superscript italic numeral. See appendix 2 for a table that lists how each of William's verses corresponds to Gregory's original text.

EXCERPTS FROM THE BOOKS OF BLESSED GREGORY ON THE SONG OF SONGS[6]

CHAPTER ONE

Song 1:1a. *Let him kiss me with the kiss of his mouth!*

W1. [1]The Only-Begotten Son can be designated as the "Mouth" of God. Just as he is spoken of as the "Arm" of God since the Father accomplishes all things through him (about this Arm the Prophet says: *To whom is the Lord's Arm revealed?* [Isa 53:1]; and John the Evangelist says: *All things were made through him* [John 1:3]), so too may he be spoken of as the "Mouth" [2]through which the Father speaks all things to us. [3]The Prophet speaks in this way: *For the Mouth of the Lord has spoken this* [Isa 1:20; 58:14]. [4]It is as if "Word" were being said in plain speech when the term "Mouth" is used, just as we are accustomed to say "tongue" for "language." For when we use the expression "the Greek or Latin tongue," we mean "the Latin or Greek language."[7] Therefore, we are right to take the "Mouth" of the Lord as his Son. Thus the Bride prays to the Father of the Bridegroom and says: *Let him kiss me with the kiss of his mouth.* It is as if she were saying: "Let him touch me with the sweetness of the presence of his Only-Begotten Son, my Redeemer."

---

6. This is the *titulus* of ms. R.

7. Gregory's clever point is lost in translation. Gregory justifies saying that the term "Mouth" is equivalent to saying "Word" (*verbum*) by appeal to the custom of saying "tongue" for "language" (*verba*). Even in everyday language, the organs of speech have a transferred sense by which they refer to the words or language they produce.

W2. *¹*It is as if he were saying in plain speech: "Let him, who before his Incarnation gave me so many commandments to do through the mouths of the Prophets, come to me in the flesh and speak with his own mouth." ²After all, as many commandments the holy Church learned from his preaching, so many 'kisses of his mouth,' as it were, did she receive. ³So when Matthew observed the Lord giving commandments on the mount, he said: *Opening his own mouth, he said* [Matt 5:2]. It is as if he were saying in plain speech: "Then he who had earlier opened the mouths of the Prophets opened his own mouth to give commandments."

W3. *¹*Concerning the sinful woman who did not cease kissing the Lord's feet (onto which she poured her tears and which she wiped with her hair), ²the Lord said to the indignant Pharisee: *You have not given me a kiss, yet this woman has not ceased kissing my feet since I entered* [Luke 7:45]. A kiss is a sign of love. ³But his 'feet' are to be understood as the very mystery of the Lord's Incarnation, through which divinity touched the earth. For he assumed flesh: *The Word became flesh and dwelt among us* [John 1:14]. ⁴But whom does the Pharisee presuming on his false righteousness represent, if not the Jewish people? Who is represented by the woman who was a sinner but came to the Lord's feet and wept, if not the converted Gentile nation? ⁵On the one hand, that faithless people did not give a kiss to God because they chose not to love with charity him whom they served with fear. On the other hand, after the Gentile nation was called, they have not ceased to kiss the 'feet' of their Redeemer because they sigh with unceasing love for him ⁶and love the mystery of his Incarnation with all their heart. ⁷Since they ready themselves through love to obey their Creator, they are right to desire his 'kiss,' saying: *Let him kiss me with the kiss of his mouth.*

Song 1:1b. *Your breasts are better than wine.*

W4. The 'breasts' of the Bridegroom are his holy preachers. Now breasts are connected to the hidden part of the chest and give us milk to drink. Holy preachers are 'breasts' because they cling to hidden matters in the loftiest contemplation and nourish us with their perceptive preaching.

Song 1:2c. *The young girls have loved you.*

W5. ¹Sacred Scripture is frequently accustomed to put "youth" for "newness of life." ²All the churches, you see, which constitute the one Catholic Church are called "young girls." At present, they are not enfeebled by sin but renewed by grace; not barren by old age but ready for spiritual fruitfulness by the age of their mind. ³Hence it is said to the approaching Bridegroom: *The young girls have loved you*,[8] which is to say the souls of the elect, renewed by the grace of baptism, who do not succumb to the practices of their former ways but are adorned with the way of life that belongs to *the new man* [Eph 4:24].

Song 1:3b. *We shall run in the odor of your ointments.*[9]

W6. ¹It is the Bride desiring the Bridegroom who said this.[10] ²In Sacred Scripture, 'the odors of ointments' usually indicate a reputation for virtue. ³Hence the Apostle Paul, knowing that he was fragrant with the renown of the virtues, said: *We are the good odor of Christ for God* [2 Cor 2:15].

Song 1:4a. *I am black but beautiful.*

W7. ¹The more we prize ourselves, the more God despises us; the more we despise ourselves for God's sake, the more God prizes us. For *he looks on the lowly and recognizes the haughty from afar* [Ps 137:6]. ²For the righteous never pride themselves on the light of their righteousness but through the grace of humility acknowledge in themselves the blackness of sin. ³Hence John said: *If we were to say that we have no sin, we are deceiving ourselves* [1 John 1:8].

Song 1:5de. *They placed me as a guardian in their vineyards; I have not guarded my own vineyard.*

W8. There is something in the conduct of pastors, dear brothers, that causes me intense suffering. What I am saying here is

---

8. The Carthusian version (ms. D) omits: "Hence it is said to the approaching Bridegroom."

9. For Song 1:3b the Vulgate reads: *After you we shall run.*

10. The Carthusian version (ms. D) omits this sentence.

consistent with earlier statements of mine. But lest this charge of mine seems perhaps hurtful to anyone, I accuse myself equally. We have become bogged down in the business of exterior affairs. We undertake one thing out of a sense of honor, another thing out of a sense of duty to take action. We abandon the ministry of preaching, and in my opinion, we are called bishops in a way that makes us worthy of blame: we retain the prestige of the name but not its virtue. Those entrusted to us abandon God, and we keep silent. They lay low in depravities, and we do not extend the hand of correction. They perish daily through many wicked deeds, and in our negligence we observe them wending their way toward hell. But when will we, who neglect our own lives, be able to correct another's life? Being engrossed in secular cares, the more our interior life slips away, the more enthusiastic we appear for exterior affairs. For the soul becomes calloused to heavenly desire through its engagement with earthly cares. When the soul is made calloused in this very engagement through its worldly activity, it cannot be softened for what pertains to the love of God. So the holy Church was right to say of her weak members: *They placed me as a guardian in their vineyards; I have not guarded my own vineyard.*[11] For the 'vineyards' are our activities, and we cultivate them by engaging in daily labor. But 'placed as guardians in their vineyards, we do not guard our own vineyard.' For when we become entangled in exterior activities, we neglect the ministry of our own activity.[12]

Song 1:6a. *Show me, you whom my soul loves, where you pasture, where you lie down at midday.*

W9. ¹The Lord 'pastures himself' when he finds delight in our good deeds. But he 'lies down at midday' when turning from the hearts of the reprobate, which burn with carnal desires, he finds the cool refreshment of good thought in the hearts of his elect. ²After all, it is hottest at midday, and the Lord seeks a shady place not affected by the fiery heat. So the Lord finds rest in those hearts

---

11. The Carthusian version (ms. D) omits the entire paragraph until this point.
12. That is, preaching.

which do not burn with love for this present age, which are not ablaze with carnal desires, which have not become dry from being scorched by the anxiety brought on by their craving for this world. Hence it is said to Mary: *The Holy Spirit shall come upon you, and the power of the Most High will overshadow you* [Luke 1:35]. So the Lord 'seeks shady places at midday to pasture himself,' because he pastures himself in minds not ablaze with bodily desires on account of their appreciation for the grace of temperance. And so, Mary, the sinner who repented, pastured the Lord interiorly more than the Pharisee pastured him exteriorly because our Redeemer fled from the heat of the carnal to her mind, to which the shade of repentance brought temperance after the fire of her vices.

Song 1:7. *If you do not know yourself, O beautiful among women, set out and follow the tracks of the flocks and pasture your young goats.*

W10. ¹All the elect carefully reflect upon by whom and in what they have been created. After a proper consideration of the image they have received, they disdain to follow the vulgar herd. This is why ²the Bridegroom addresses his Bride: *If you do not know yourself, O beautiful among women,*[13] which is to say: "if when living a good life you do not know the honor that you have received in virtue of being created in the likeness of God, then depart from the sight of the contemplation of me and imitate the conduct of the ignorant masses." ³For the word 'flocks' designates the ignorant masses. ⁴Now she who is 'beautiful among women' knows herself when every elect soul, even if placed among sinners, remembers that she was created in the image and likeness of her Creator and lives in a manner befitting this status of likeness that she has perceived. If she 'does not know herself,' she 'sets out' because, being exiled from the secret depths of her heart, she is dissipated by external objects of desire. But when she 'sets out,' she 'follows the tracks of the flocks' because clearly by forsaking her interior life

---

13. The context seems to require the rest of the verse: *set out and follow the tracks of the flocks and pasture your young goats.*

she is brought to the wide way[14] and follows the examples of the masses. She no longer 'pastures' lambs but 'goats' because she makes no effort to nourish the harmless thoughts of the mind but encourages the wicked stirrings of the flesh.

Song 1:11. *While the king was on his couch, my nard gave its odor.*

W11. [1]It is as if [2]the holy Church, being fragrant with a kind of sweet odor in her elect, [3]were saying in plain speech: "As long as the king is hidden from my sight, secluded by himself in his heavenly repose, the conduct of the elect is occupied with giving forth the wonderful odors of the virtues. Hence even though it still does not see him whom it seeks, it may burn all the more ardently with desire." And so 'nard gives off its odor while the king is settled upon his couch' because the virtue of the saints in the Church supplies us with the pleasantness of great sweetness while the Lord is at rest in his blessedness. [4]For the virtues of the elect making progress are in a certain sense fragrant with a sweet odor when other people come to know them. Paul spoke in this way: *We are the good odor of Christ for God* [2 Cor 2:15].[15]

CHAPTER TWO

Song 2:2. *As a lily among thorns, so is my love among the daughters.*

W12. [1]In the holy Church there cannot be bad people without the good, and good people without the bad. [2]For as long as we live here below, we must walk the path of this present age intermingled. But we are distinguished when we reach the next life. Now the good are never alone except in heaven and the bad are never alone except in hell. But just as this life, which lies between heaven and hell, is accessible to all, so too it admits citizens from both regions alike. Though the holy Church now receives them both indiscriminately, afterward she will make distinctions between them as they exit from this life. And so, if you are good, for as long as you abide in this life, calmly bear with the bad. For anyone who does not

---

14. See Matt 7:13.
15. The Carthusian version (ms. D) omits the entirety of W11.4.

bear with the bad through a lack of forbearance testifies against himself that he is not good. The one whom a Cain does not vex with wickedness refuses to be an Abel. Just as on threshing floors grains are pressed under the chaff, so too do flowers rise among thorns and a fragrant rose grows when a thorn pricks it.

Now the first man had two sons: one of these was elect, the other was reprobate. Noah's ark held three of his sons: while two were steadfast in their humility, one was quick to mock his father. Abraham had two sons: one was innocent but the other was the persecutor of his brother. Isaac had two sons: one served in humility but the other was reprobate even before he was born. Jacob had twelve sons: one of them was sold on account of his innocence but the others sold their brother on account of their wickedness. Twelve Apostles were elected but one of them became involved with the reprobate in order to put the others to the test, persecuting them lest they remain untested. There were seven deacons ordained by the Apostles: six were steadfast in correct faith but one arose as an originator of error.[16]

[3]And so, dear brothers, reflect upon these past times and strengthen yourselves to bear with mean people. For if we are the sons of the elect, their examples teach us how we ought to progress. After all, none of them was good if he refused to bear with the bad. [4]It is not very praiseworthy if someone is good with the good, but rather if someone is good with the bad. Just as not being good among the bad is a serious fault, so too does being good even among the bad deserve boundless commendation. [5]Thus blessed Job claimed about himself: *I was a brother of dragons and a companion of ostriches* [Job 30:29]. [6]Peter exalted Lot with great praises for the same reason, because he found him good among the reprobate: *And he rescued the righteous Lot who was oppressed by sacrilegious men's lawless way of life. For Lot was righteous in his sight and hearing, dwelling*

---

16. Here Gregory alludes to the ancient tradition of ascribing the heresy of the Nicolaitans mentioned in Revelation (Rev 2:6, 15) to Nicolaus of Antioch, one of the first seven deacons (Acts 6:5).

among those who from day to day tortured that righteous man's soul with unrighteous works [2 Pet 2:7-8]. Surely, he could not have been tortured unless he both heard and witnessed the wicked deeds of his neighbors. And yet he is called 'righteous in his sight and hearing' because when the ears and eyes of the righteous man perceived the conduct of the iniquitous, he did not delight in it but rather bore it. ⁷Thus the blessed Job is also reported to have lived in a land of Gentiles among iniquitous people, ⁸so that the excellence of his virtue could be portrayed; ⁹and so that he could be praised for having been good among the bad ¹⁰and for having grown (according to the Bridegroom's commendation) *as a lily among thorns*. ¹¹Hence Paul both praised and strengthened the conduct of the disciples when he said: *in the midst of a wicked and perverse people, among whom you shine like lamps in the world* [Phil 2:15].

¹²Listen carefully, dear brothers! Now that we have gone through just about every example, we realize that no one is good unless he is put to the test by the wickedness of the bad. ¹³Yet we complain: "Why aren't all who live with us good?" For we are unwilling to bear the misdeeds of our neighbors. We think that everyone should already be a saint when we do not want to bear anything from our neighbors. But the situation is clear: as long as we refuse to bear with the bad, we ourselves still possess far less goodness. For someone is not entirely good unless he can be good even with the bad. ¹⁴If I may put it so, the iron sword of our soul does not become razor-sharp unless the file of another's wickedness grinds it.

¹⁵When we grumble frequently about the conduct of our neighbors, attempt to relocate, and try to find a quiet place for a life of greater seclusion, clearly we are ignorant of the fact that if the Spirit is lacking, no place will be of help to us. Though Lot was holy in Sodom, he sinned on the mountain. That places do not protect the mind is proved by the fact that the very first parent of the human race fell in paradise. ¹⁶If a place had been able to save, Satan would not have fallen from heaven. So when the Psalmist observed people being tempted everywhere in this world, he sought

a place to which he might flee, but could not find one that was safe without God. Because of this he even begged God to become for him the place that he was seeking: *Be for me a protecting God and a safe place, that you might save me* [Ps 30:3]. Therefore, neighbors are to be borne with everywhere because he whom a Cain does not vex with wickedness cannot become an Abel.

But there is one reason for shunning the company of the bad. If perhaps the bad are incorrigible, they are to be shunned lest they seduce others to imitate themselves. When they cannot be changed from their wickedness, they are to be shunned lest they mislead those associated with them. This is why Paul said: *Crooked speech corrupts good habits* [1 Cor 15:33]. And Solomon said: *Do not be a friend to an irritable man nor walk with a man liable to rage lest you inadvertently learn his ways and take a stumbling block to your soul* [Prov 22:24-25]. And so, just as perfect men ought not flee their wicked neighbors because they often induce them to uprightness and are themselves never induced to wickedness, so too the weak ought to turn from the company of the bad lest they are enticed to imitate the misdeeds they frequently see and cannot correct. So then, each day we take the words of our neighbors into our mind by hearing, in the manner that we draw air into the body by inhaling and exhaling. And just as the continual breathing of bad air infects the body, so too the continual hearing of wicked speech infects the soul of the weak, so that it languishes from delight in wicked works and unceasing evil conversation. [17]So then, a sinner plus wickedness is joined to the righteous and perfect man, as in a furnace dross plus fire is united to gold, so that wherever the dross burns the gold is refined. Therefore, they are truly good who can persevere in goodness even among the bad.

Song 2:3. *I sat under the shadow of him whom I had desired.*

W13. [1]"Overshadowing' is sometimes used in the Sacred Word for the Incarnation of the Lord or the relief of the mind from the heat of carnal thoughts. Hence the term 'shadow' implies this relief of the heart through heavenly protection, [2]as the Psalmist said: *Protect me under the shadow of your wings* [Ps 16:8]. And so, the Bride, having awaited the coming of the Bridegroom, makes this announcement: *I sat under the shadow of him whom I had desired.* ³Here 'shadow' expresses the relief of the heart through heavenly protection. ⁴It is as if the Bride were saying: "I rested under the protection of his coming from the heat of carnal desires." ⁵That the term 'overshadowing' could signify Incarnation of the Lord without destroying the veracity of the narrative is proved by the message of the angel, who says to the blessed Mary:[17] *The power of the Most High shall overshadow you* [Luke 1:35]. Now a shadow is caused in no other way than by a light and a body. Accordingly, the power of the Most High overshadowed her because the incorporeal Light took[18] a body within her womb. Because of this overshadowing she received in herself every relief of mind.

Song 2:5a. *Bolster me with flowers, surround me with apples, for I grow faint with love.*

W14. The mind that passionately loves her Bridegroom ordinarily gains a single consolation from the delay of the present life, if throughout her separation from the sight of him the souls of others make progress by her word and thereby are inflamed with the firebrands of love for the heavenly Bridegroom. She mourns[19] because she realizes that she is separated. Everything she sees makes her sad because she still does not see him whom she longs to see. But when a fervent soul is separated, it is, as I said, no small consolation if she gathers together many people. In consequence of this, him whom she wanted to see sooner all by herself she will see later in the company of many others. Hence here the Bride says: *Bolster me with flowers, surround me with apples, for I grow faint with love.* For what are 'flowers,' if not souls who are already beginning to do good work and are redolent with heavenly desire? What are the 'apples' from the 'flowers,' if not the perfect minds of those

---

17. The Carthusian version (ms. D) replaces the sentence up to this point with: "On account of this cooling of mind given from heaven, it is said to Mary."
18. Here I read *sumpsit* instead of *assumpsit*; see appendix 5, note 1.
19. Here I read *maeret* instead of *merito*; see appendix 5, note 2.

already good who attain the fruit of good work from the moment they chose a holy way of life? So then, she who 'grows faint with love' seeks to be 'bolstered with flowers' and 'surrounded with apples,' because, even though she is still not permitted to see him whom she desires, she gains great consolation by finding joy in the progress of others. Therefore, a soul who has 'grown faint with holy love' is 'surrounded with flowers and apples' so that she may find rest in the good work of her neighbor when she is still unable to contemplate the face of God.

Let us ponder, if you please, what sort of mind Paul had. He said: *For me to live is Christ and to die is gain* [Phil 1:21]. If he thought that his life was Christ alone and to die was gain, the love with which he joined himself to Almighty God must have been very great. Thus he repeats himself: *I have a desire to be dissolved and to be with Christ, which is far better* [Phil 1:23]. But let us now consider the love with which he who desired to be dissolved grows faint. Because he realizes that for the present he is separated, doesn't he seek to be 'surrounded with flowers'? It is clear that he does seek this, for it follows: *But to stay in the flesh is necessary for your sake* [Phil 1:24]. And he says to his disciples who are making progress: *For what is our hope or joy or crown of glory? Is it not you before our Lord Jesus Christ?* [1 Thess 2:19].

Song 2:5b (LXX). *I have been wounded by love.*

W15. ¹In two ways Almighty God wounds those whom he is concerned to restore to health. Sometimes ²he whips them outwardly on the flesh in order to cure the poison of sins.[20] Sometimes,

---

20. Here I read *ut virus delictorum curet* instead of *ut intus delictorum vulnera curet*; see appendix 5, note 3. At this point, the Carthusian version (ms. D) contains a fuller citation of *Mor.* 6.25 [42], 2–26 (CCSL 143:314–15): "Sometimes he strikes the flesh and softens the hardness of the mind through fear of him. Therefore, by wounding he recalls to health when he afflicts his elect outwardly so that they may live inwardly. Thus it is said through Moses: *I will kill and I will make alive; I will strike and I will heal* [Deut 32:39]. For he kills in order to make alive, he strikes in order heal, in that he applies wounds outwardly in order to cure the wounds of sins inwardly."

even if the outward blows seem to have stopped, he inflicts wounds inwardly because[21] he strikes the hardness of our mind with desire for him. Yet by striking he heals because, when we have been pierced by the spear of fear of him, he recalls us to an upright frame of mind. For our hearts are sickly when stricken with no love for God, when unmindful of the woefulness of our pilgrimage, when apathetic with hardly any feeling at all toward the weakness of our neighbor. But they are wounded that they may be healed because God strikes unfeeling minds with the darts of love for him and soon makes them full of feeling through the burning heat of charity. Hence here the Bride says: *I have been wounded by love*. For the soul that is sickly and in the state of this exile lies prostrate in blind security[22] has neither seen God nor sought to see him. But when she is struck by the darts of his love, she is 'wounded' in her innermost recesses with tender devotion, burns with desire for contemplation, and marvelously is restored to life through her wound, though once she lay dead in health. She yearns, she pants, and she desires to see him whom she fled.

³She burns with desire for him. At present she yearns for nothing that is in the world, considers the length of the present life as punishment, hastens to depart and to find rest with a loving embrace in the vision of the heavenly Bridegroom. And so, a mind that is already in this state receives no consolation from the present life but in the very depths of her being sighs, burns, is anxious for him whom she loves.[23] The very health of her body becomes of little worth because she is pierced by the wound of love.[24] ⁴Yet sickly is the heart which does not know the pain of this wound. But when she has already started to long for heavenly desire and to feel the wound of love, the soul which was once sick from health becomes healthier from a wound. ⁵Thus by being struck she recov-

---

21. Here I read *quia* instead of *qui*; see appendix 5, note 4.

22. For textual comments on this line, see appendix 5, note 27.

23. The Carthusian version (ms. D) omits: "but in the very depths of her being sighs, burns, is anxious for him whom she loves."

24. For textual comments on this line, see appendix 5, note 28.

ers her health, recalled to the secure state of inward repose by the overturning of her self-love.

⁶Anyone who has been able to reach for the truth burns with this love and desire. For this reason David said: *My soul has thirsted for the strong living God; when shall I come and appear before the face of God?* [Ps 41:3]. He warns us for the same reason: *Always seek his face* [Ps 104:4]. For the same reason Isaiah the Prophet said: *My soul desired you in the night but in the morning I shall keep watch for you deep within my heart with my spirit* [Isa 26:9]. And so, for the same reason the holy Church says to him: *I have been wounded by love* [Song 2:5]. Bearing in her heart the wound of love caused by the heat of desire for him, she is right to reach for health from the vision of the Physician.

Song 2:6. *His left hand is under my head and his right hand will embrace me.*

W16. ¹Let the things that support us outwardly be of service in such a way that they do not deflect the soul from the pursuit of heavenly love. Let the things that assist us in our exile not assuage the sorrow of our interior pilgrimage. We should not rejoice as if we are made fortunate by transitory things since we understand how miserable we are for as long as we are separated from eternal realities. Thus here the Church says in the voice of the elect: *His left hand is under my head and his right hand will embrace me.* ²For what is meant by the 'left hand,' if not the present life? What is signified by the 'right hand,' if not everlasting life?[25] ³In a certain sense, she has put the 'left hand' of God, which is to say the prosperity of the present life, 'under her head,' and pushes it with the intentness of the highest love. But the 'right hand' of God embraces her because in her total commitment she is kept safe under his eternal beatitude. Thus it is said

---

25. At this point the Carthusian version (ms. D) inserts a citation from Augustine: "The Bride is speaking about the Bridegroom, the Church is speaking about Christ in an embrace of piety and love. For what does she say before? What does it mean when his right hand is above her and his left hand beneath her? It means that when the Bridegroom embraces the Bride, he puts his left hand beneath her to comfort her, and his right hand above her to protect her" (*Enarr. in Ps.* 120.9, 3–8).

through Solomon: *Length of days is in his right hand, but in his left hand are riches and glory* [Prov 3:16]. He teaches how 'riches and glory' should be held; he recorded that they are placed in the 'left hand.' Thus the Psalmist said: *Save me by your right hand* [Ps 59:7]. Now he did not say "by your hand" but 'by your right hand,' clearly so that he could make it known by mentioning the right hand that he seeks eternal salvation. Again, for this reason it is written: *With your right hand, Lord, you have shattered the enemies* [Exod 15:6]. For God's enemies, even though they thrive in his left hand, are smashed by his right hand, because the present life is usually favorable to the wicked but the coming of eternal beatitude dooms them.

Song 2:8. *Behold! He comes leaping upon the mountains, springing across the hills.*

W17. By coming for our redemption the Lord performed, if I may put it so, a certain number of leaps. Dear brothers, do you want to learn what these leaps of his were? From heaven he came into the womb. From the womb he came into the manger. From the manger he came onto the cross. From the cross he came into the tomb. From the tomb he returned to heaven. Behold! Truth manifested in the flesh performed for our benefit a certain number of leaps so as to make us run after him. *He exulted like a giant to run his course* [Ps 18:6] so that we might say to him from our heart: *Draw me! After you we shall run in the odor of your ointments* [Song 1:3]. And so, dear brothers, it is fitting that we follow him with our heart to where we believe he ascended with his body.

Song 2:9a. *My beloved is like a roe and the young hart of deer.*

W18. ¹The Lord is called 'the young hart of a deer' because of the flesh that he assumed as the son of the ancient fathers. ²Thus the Apostle: *Whose are the fathers, from whom Christ came according to the flesh, who is above all things God blessed forever* [Rom 9:5].

Song 2:9b. *Lo! He stands behind our wall, looking through the windows, peering through the lattices.*

W19. ¹When our Redeemer became incarnate for our sake out of mercy, he 'stood' before human eyes as if 'behind a wall' because he made himself visible through his humanity and kept himself invisible in his divinity. Hence the Jews, who had awaited him because of the promise of the Prophets, were disturbed on account of the confused nature of their mistaken beliefs. For they saw as mortal him whom they had believed would come for their rescue. ²When they saw his miracles, they were drawn to believe; then again, when they pondered his sufferings, they refused to believe that he whom they saw mortal in the flesh was the Lord. Hence it came to pass that they hesitated to recognize him. For they saw him hungry, thirsty, eating, drinking, tired, sleeping, and inferred that he was a mere man. They saw him reviving the dead, cleansing lepers, giving light to the blind, casting out demons, and deduced that he was superior to men. Yet his humanity obscured [the significance of] his miracles, which they pondered in their heart.

Thus the holy Church in the voice of the Bride[26] ³plainly desires to see his form in his divinity, though not capable of it, because the humanity he assumed has hidden from her eyes the form of his eternity which she has longed to behold. In her sorrow here she says: *Lo! He stands behind our wall.* It is as if she were saying in plain speech: "For my part, I now desire to see him in the form of his divinity, but the wall of the flesh he assumed still prevents me from seeing him."

⁴For he who displayed to human eyes that which he assumed from mortal nature, and remained invisible in himself, 'stood' as if 'behind a wall' for those seeking to see him in the open because he did not allow himself to be seen with his majesty manifest. Now he 'stood' as if 'behind a wall' when he displayed the nature of the humanity that he assumed and kept the nature of his divinity hidden from human eyes. Hence it is added: *Looking through the windows, peering through the lattices.* For anyone who 'looks through windows and lattices' is neither entirely seen nor entirely unseen. Thus our Redeemer came before the eyes of doubters surely for the following

---

26. Here the text reads *sponsi*, but should read *sponsae*; see appendix 5, note 29.

reasons: if he had performed miracles without suffering as a man, he would have appeared to them exclusively as God. Then again, if he had experienced human suffering without accomplishing anything as God, they would have considered him a mere man. But since he both accomplished divine acts and experienced human suffering, it is as if he 'peered' at human beings 'through windows and lattices.' For he both manifested himself as God through his miracles and hid that he was God through his sufferings. He was perceived as a man on account of his sufferings and yet was recognized as superior to a man on account of his miracles.

Song 2:10-12. *Arise, make haste, my love, my dove, my beautiful one, and come! For now the winter is past, the rains are over and gone, flowers have appeared in the land, the time for pruning has come.*

W20. [1]The present life is indeed 'winter,' in which, despite hope even now guiding us to the things above, nonetheless the numbing cold of our mortality still holds us back. For it is written: *The body that is corrupt weighs down the soul and the earthly dwelling presses down on the mind pondering many things* [Wis 9:15]. In addition, there are 'rains' during winter, which are surely the preachings of ecclesiastical rulers. With regard to these rains, it is of course said through Moses: *Await what I say like falling rain, and let my words come down like dew* [Deut 32:2]. These rains are indeed appropriate for winter but will cease in summer because at present when the heavenly life is hidden from the eyes of the carnal, we need to be doused by the preachings of the saints. But when the heat[27] of eternal judgment has reached its peak, no one will then regard the words of preachers as necessary.

[2]Holy preaching will cease when the present life ends, which is to say rains will cease when winter ends. Hence the holy Church, or the soul that is departing from this life, hastening to the regions of eternal summer, [3]and awaiting the day of true light as the season of spring, rightly hears the voice of the Bridegroom persuading her say: [4]*Arise, make haste, my love, my dove, my beautiful one, and come,*

---

27. Here Gregory plays on "heat" (*aestus*) and "summer" (*aestas*).

for now the winter is past and the rains are over and gone. ⁵Whether she is the holy Church or any elect soul, she is the 'love' of the heavenly Bridegroom on account of her love, his 'dove' on account of her spirit, his 'beautiful one' on account of her conduct. When she is raised from the corruption of the flesh, do not doubt that 'now the winter is past' for her because the numbing cold of the present life departs. Furthermore, 'the rains are over and gone' because when she is raised to the contemplation of Almighty God in his own essence, there is no further need of the rain of preaching to drench her. ⁶After all, when 'winter is past, the rains are gone' because when the present life is over, in which the numbing cold of the corruptible flesh holds us back in a cloud of ignorance, every ministry of preaching ceases. For at that time we will see more clearly with our own eyes that which we now hear somewhat obscurely through the voices of the saints. ⁷At that time 'flowers will appear in the land' because when a soul begins to receive a kind of initial foretaste of the pleasantness of eternal beatitude, it is as if the soul is already sniffing fragrances among flowers as she departs. For after she has quit this life, she will have fruit in greater abundance. This is why it is added: *The time for pruning has come.* When someone is pruning, he cuts away the barren branches in order that the vigorous ones may bear fruit in greater abundance. And so, 'the time for our pruning comes' when we forsake the unfruitful and harmful[28] corruption of the flesh so as to be able to attain the fruit of the soul. This fruit will be as abundant as possible for us: the vision of the one God.

CHAPTER THREE

Song 3:1-4. *In my little bed night by night I sought him whom my soul loves; I sought him but I did not find him. I will arise and scour the whole city; among the streets and the squares I will seek him whom my soul loves. I sought him but I did not find him. The watchmen who guard the city*

---

28. Here I read *ac noxiam* instead of *hanc nos iam*; see appendix 5, note 5.

found me. Have you seen him whom my soul loves? When I had passed by them a little ways, I found him whom my soul loves.

W21. ¹The Bride says these lines in the guise of every soul, energized by holy desires and urged by hidden goads of holy love. ²We ought to know that in the Sacred Word a "bed," a "chamber," or a "mattress" is usually understood as the secret depth of the heart. ³And so, the beloved is sought 'in the little bed' and 'night by night' because the invisible Creator appears in the chamber of the heart (though any kind of corporeal seeing is precluded), ⁴because he is desired in anguish of spirit within the secret chambers of the heart.

⁵We seek the beloved 'in the little bed' when we sigh with desire for our Redeemer during the brief respite of the present life. We seek 'night by night' because even though our mind already watches for him, yet our eye is still darkened. ⁶Nonetheless, the Bride 'does not find him' when she seeks because every elect soul already ⁷yearns to see the Lord, already desires to depart to him, already longs to be free of the darkness of the present life. ⁸Although she desires with great love, she is still not permitted to see him whom she loves, ⁹so that the deferred love may profit from its very deferment and what seems as if denied may intensify through ardent desire, ¹⁰so that deferred desires may intensify and as they intensify take possession of what they will have found. ¹¹Therefore, the Bridegroom when not found is first sought so that later when found he may be held more closely. For holy desires intensify when deferred; but if they fade when deferred, they were not desires.²⁹

¹²The Bridegroom hides himself when sought so that upon not being found he may be sought all the more ardently. The Bride who seeks him is kept at a distance lest she find him, in order that she may be rendered more receptive by the delay and thereby one

---

29. The passage "Although she desires with great love . . . they were not desires" (vv. 8-11) is replaced in the Carthusian version (ms. D) with: "But the sight of him is still denied to her who longs so as to intensify the desire of the lover. It is as if water is taken away in thirst, causing the heat of her thirst to increase: the longer she desires it when thirsty, the more avidly she takes it when given" (*Mor.* 27.2 [4], 33–37 [CCSL 143:1332–33]). See W39.

day find a thousandfold what she sought. *¹³*But when she does not find her beloved, 'she arises and scours the city,' which is to say she uses her mind to travel about the holy Church of the elect on a quest. 'She seeks him among the streets and the squares,' which is to say she looks at those strolling in narrow and wide places, seeking if any trace of him can be found in them. For even among those who lead a worldly life, there are some who display a modicum of virtue in their actions that is worth imitating. *¹⁴*And so, the Bride first seeks her beloved but finds nothing. *¹⁵*Failing to find him, she then redoubles her efforts, saying: *I sought him but I did not find him.* But since finding is not long delayed if the quest does not falter, she adds: *The watchmen who guard the city found me.*

*¹⁶*Whom ought we take as 'the watchmen who guard the city,' if not the holy fathers and prophets and teachers who devoted themselves to watching by the words of holy preaching so as to guard us? *¹⁷*Therefore, every soul seeking the sight of her Redeemer *¹⁸*is found by the holy fathers and attentive teachers who are the guardians of the Church's stability because they run to meet her good efforts in order to teach her by their deeds,[30] their words, or their writings. *¹⁹*But when the Church sought her Redeemer, she was not willing to set her hope on those same fathers and teachers, saying: *When I had passed by them a little ways, I found him whom my soul loves.* After all, she would not have been able to find him unless she had been willing to pass them by. The unbelievers entrusted themselves to these same sentries since they believed that Christ the Son of God was one of them. But by means of the words and faith of Peter the holy Church passed by the watchmen whom she found, since she refused to believe that the Lord of the Prophets was one of the Prophets.

*²⁰*So then, the mind eager for the sight of him cannot find him who is above humanity, unless she 'passes by' the high esteem of the Prophets, the loftiness of the Patriarchs, and the stature of the Apostles, teachers, and all people. *²¹*For our Redeemer, even though

---

30. Here I read *suo* instead of *solo*; see appendix 5, note 6.

he lived in humility as a human being among human beings, was yet above human beings on account of his divinity. [22]So then, 'to pass by the watchmen' means to consider even those whom the soul admires as of less value when compared to him [23]and to be unwilling to set her hope on them. [24]Therefore, when the watchmen are passed by, the beloved is found because when we come to consider the Prophets, Apostles, and teachers as inferior to him, we realize that he who is God by nature is superior to human beings, [25]if he is believed to be a human being and yet at the same time beyond the stature of human beings.

Song 3:6. *Who is this coming up through the desert like a column of smoke arising from incense made of myrrh and frankincense and all the fragrant powders of the perfumer?*

W22. [1]Here the virtue of the Bride is praised in the voice of Bridegroom. The holy Church of the elect, when with ardent love she raises herself from this world amid holy prayers, 'is coming up through the desert,' which she leaves behind. But it adds how she comes up: *like a column of smoke arising from incense*. Smoke is produced by incense, and it is said through the Psalmist: *Let my prayer arise in your presence like incense* [Ps 140:2]. Smoke ordinarily provokes tears. And so, the 'smoke arising from incense' is the compunction of prayer that is produced by the virtues of love. Yet this prayer is called 'a column of smoke' because, when it asks only for heavenly goods, it soars upward so directly[31] that it never turns back to seek earthly and temporal goods. [2]The holy Church is 'coming up like a column of smoke arising from incense' because she makes progress each day in the uprightness of internal 'incense'[32] on account of the virtues of her conduct. Nor does she become dissipated in scattered thoughts, but she confines herself within the hidden recesses of her heart by means of the rod of severity.[33]

---

31. Here I read *sic recta* instead of *erecta*; see appendix 5, note 7.
32. I.e., interior virtue.
33. Here Gregory plays on "column" (*virgula*) and "rod" (*virga*).

³And note that prayer is not called a "rod" but a 'column' because sometimes in the ardor of compunction the force of love is of such subtlety that not even the soul itself, which when enlightened merits to possess it, can comprehend it. Furthermore, *made of myrrh and frankincense* is well said. For the Law prescribes that frankincense be burned in sacrifice to the Lord but that dead bodies be embalmed with myrrh to prevent corruption by worms. Therefore, a sacrifice of myrrh and frankincense is offered by those who afflict their flesh lest they be dominated by the vices of corruption, who burn the pleasing offering of their love in the presence of the Lord, and who present themselves to God amid holy virtues. This is why it is added in that place: *And all the fragrant powders of the perfumer.* The fragrant powder of the perfumer is the virtue of one who acts well. And note that the virtues of those who act well are not called "paints" but 'fragrant powders.'³⁴ For when we do any good work, we are offering paints. But when we reconsider the very good works that we do, and on the basis of this reconsideration determine whether there is anything evil in them, and submit to this judgment, in a certain sense we make powder from paints. Thus we burn our prayer more subtly through discretion and love.

⁴And so, as long as we never cease to ponder and consider anew what we do, we indeed have 'myrrh and frankincense' in our deeds but 'powder' in our thoughts. ⁵Therefore, dearly beloved, let us seek nothing earthly, nothing transitory through tears of compunction. Let him alone who made all things suffice for us. Let us pass beyond all things through desire, that we may focus our mind upon the One. Ignited no longer by the fear of punishment nor the remembrance of our offenses, but by the flames of love, let us burn in tears with the odor of virtues.

Song 3:7. *Lo! Sixty of the most valiant men of Israel surrounded the little bed of Solomon.*

W23. ¹All the saints contemplate interior repose without any lessening of their desire. ²It is said to them through the Psalmist:

---

34. Here I read *pulveres* instead of *pulvis*; see appendix 5, note 8.

Be strong, and let your heart take courage, all you who hope in the Lord! [Ps 30:25]. ³For the strength of the righteous is to conquer their flesh, to thwart self-will, to annihilate the delight of the present life, to love the harshness of this world for the sake of eternal rewards, to scorn the charms of good fortune, to overcome the dread of adversity in their heart, ⁴to concern themselves with perils of the world needing toleration for the world's sake in order to be lessened, to gaze upon their own end, to mark how transitory the present life is, and for these reasons to refuse to undergo outward toils, whose delight they conquer inwardly.

Song 3:8a. *All are holding swords and they are very skilled in warfare.*

W24. ¹What the 'sword' represents in the Divine Scripture, Paul laid open when he said: *And the sword of the Spirit, which is the Word of God* [Eph 6:17]. ²When Solomon described the valiant men as warriors in the spiritual battle, ³he did not say: "All have swords," but: *All are holding swords,* clearly because is it wonderful not only to know the Word of God, but also to do it. After all, a sword is had but not held when someone knows the divine speech but makes no effort to live according to it. And a man can no longer be skilled in warfare if he does not train with the spiritual sword he has. For he is altogether unequal to the task of resisting temptations if by living a bad life he puts off holding this sword of the Word of God.

Song 3:8b. *Everyone's blade is upon his thigh on account of nocturnal fears.*

W25. ¹This verse speaks of the valiant warriors of the heavenly homeland. ²A 'blade is placed upon the thigh' when a wicked suggestion of the flesh is subjugated by the sharp edge of holy preaching. ³A 'blade is upon the thigh' when vigilant guarding subdues the enticements of the flesh. ⁴But 'nocturnal fears' are the hidden snares of temptation. ⁵After all, the term 'night' refers to the blindness that characterizes our enfeebled state. For we cannot see the forces of opposition that threaten us at night. Therefore, *everyone's blade is on his thigh on account of nocturnal fears* because it is clear that holy people, while they dread the dangers they do not see, are always prepared to ward off an attack.³⁵ ⁶For even though holy people are so confident in their hope, they nevertheless always look upon temptation with mistrust. After all, to them it is said: *Serve the Lord with fear and rejoice in him with trembling* [Ps 2:11], meaning that rejoicing is born of hope and trembling of their mistrust. ⁷Therefore, lest 'nocturnal fear,' which is to say sudden and hidden temptation, catch us unawares, the 'blade' of guarding 'placed upon our thigh' must always subdue it.³⁶

Song 3:9-10. *King Solomon made himself a palanquin from the wood of Lebanon. He made its posts of silver, its seat of gold, its ladder of purple, and he covered the insides with love on account of the daughters of Jerusalem.*

W26. Now we ought not believe about Solomon, a king of such greatness, who abounded in such immeasurable riches that the weight of his gold could not be estimated and in whose days silver was worthless,³⁷ that *he made himself a palanquin from wood*, as

---

35. For textual comments on this line, see appendix 5, note 30.
36. In the Carthusian version (ms. D), this paragraph is replaced by: "Now 'nocturnal fears' are the hidden snares of temptation. But a 'blade is upon the thigh' when vigilant guarding subdues the enticements of flesh. So then, lest 'nocturnal fear,' which is to say hidden and sudden temptation, catch us unawares, the 'blade' of guarding 'placed upon our thigh' must always subjugate it. For even though holy people are so confident in their hope, they nevertheless always look upon temptation with mistrust. After all, to them it is said: *Serve the Lord with fear and rejoice in him with trembling* [Ps 2:11], meaning that rejoicing is born of their hope and trembling of their mistrust. Likewise: *Everyone's blade is on his thigh on account of nocturnal fears* [Song 3:9]. A 'blade is placed upon the thigh' when a wicked suggestion of the flesh is subjugated by the sharp edge of holy preaching. But the term 'night' refers to the blindness that characterizes our enfeebled state. For we do not see the forces of opposition that threaten us at night. Therefore, *everyone's blade is on his thigh on account of nocturnal fears* because it is clear that holy people, while they dread the dangers they do not see, are always prepared to ward off an attack." The translation of the final sentence assumes the emendation outlined in the previous footnote. The arrangement of the Carthusian version of the passage here merely consists of *Mor.* 20.3 [8], 79–87 (CCSL 143:1007–8) followed by *Reg. past.* 3.32, 49–58 (SChr 382:492–94), which are the two excerpts from Bede in order (B23–24). In the original version of his florilegium, William has interspliced these two excerpts.
37. See 1 Kgs 10:21.

the Bride says here. Rather, it is Solomon, namely our king and our peacemaker, who *made himself a palanquin from the wood of Lebanon*. For the cedar wood of Lebanon is most imperishable. And so, the palanquin of our king is the holy Church, which was built from our strong forefathers, which is to say from imperishable minds. She is rightly called a 'palanquin' because each day she transports souls to the eternal banquet of her Creator.

The 'posts' of this palanquin were made 'of silver' because the preachers of the holy Church shine with the splendor of eloquent speech.[38] But there is a 'seat of gold' in addition to the 'post of silver' because when the luminous words of holy preachers are heard, the minds of those who hear them discover the brightness of inner clarity, in which they may recline. For when they hear these clear and plain words[39] they find rest in the clarity that has come to their heart. So then, its 'posts' are 'of silver' and its 'seat' was made 'of gold' because the splendor of speech enables the discovery of restful clarity in the soul. For this interior brightness illumines her mind in the present time so that by means of attention she may find rest in that place where the grace of preaching is not required. Indeed it is written of the same holy Church: *The wings of a dove are covered with silver and its rump with the appearance of gold* [Ps 67:14]. For here filled with the spirit of mildness, she like the dove has wings covered with silver and on her rump the appearance of gold because here she endows her preachers with the splendor of speech but in a later age[40] shows in herself the brightness of clarity.

---

38. At that point the Carthusian version (ms. D) adds: "By 'silver' we understand the brightness of holy and eloquent speaking, but 'gold' usually indicates the brightness of conduct or of wisdom" (*Mor.* 18.16 [24], 4 [CCSL 143:900] combined with *Mor.* 18.26 [39], 2–4 [CCSL 143:910]).

39. Here I read *quod luculente et aperte audiunt* instead of *quod occulta aperte audiunt*; see appendix 5, note 9.

40. Gregory's wordplay here is untranslatable. In the exegesis of Ps 67:14, "in a later age" (*in posteriori saeculo*) actually corresponds to "rump" (*posteriora dorsi*), which literally translated would read: "the hinder parts of the back."

But in addition to this revelation of interior clarity, the quality of the ladder is described by an additional statement made about the same palanquin: *its ladder of purple*. Since real purple is achieved by dyeing with blood, it is not unjust to view it as representing the color of blood. And so, since the greatest multitude of the faithful at the beginning of the Church in its infancy attained the kingdom through the blood of martyrdom, our king made a 'ladder of purple' in his palanquin because one attains the clarity seen within through the trial of blood.

So then, what are we to do, miserable as we are and bereft of all strength? Look, we cannot be 'posts' in this palanquin because neither the strength needed for working nor the splendor of preaching shines in us. We do not possess a 'seat of gold' because, as is fitting, we still do not perceive the rest of interior clarity through spiritual understanding. We are not a 'ladder of purple' because we are unable to shed blood for our Redeemer. So then, what is to be done about us? What hope will there be if no one attains the kingdom except the one who is endowed with the most excellent virtues?

But there is also consolation for us. Let us love God as much as we can, let us love our neighbor, and at the same time too let us strive for the palanquin of God, because as it is written in that same place: *he covered the insides with love*. Have love, and without a doubt you will reach that place where the 'post of silver' is set and the 'ladder of purple' is kept. Yet that this is said on account of our weakness is clearly shown when it is added further on in the same place: *on account of the daughters of Jerusalem*. Since the word of God does not say "sons" but 'daughters,' what else has been signified by the female sex other than the weak parts of our minds? Therefore, in this passage it is said that in the midst of the 'posts of silver,' the 'seat of gold,' and the 'ladder of purple,' there is love 'on account of the daughters of Jerusalem.' For even those who lack the strength for the virtues, if they do not fail to do the good that they can do with love, then they are not strangers to the 'palanquin' of God.

Chapter Four

Song 4:1. *How beautiful you are, my love, how beautiful! Your eyes are dovelike, aside from what is veiled within.*

W27. ¹He describes her as 'beautiful,' then repeats himself, calling her 'beautiful' a second time. For she possesses one sort of beauty, the beauty of conduct, whereby she is recognized in the present time, and another sort of beauty, the beauty of the rewards, whereby she will later be lifted up through the sight of her Creator. Because all her elect members do everything with simplicity, her eyes are called 'dovelike.' They shine with great splendor because they sparkle with the miracles that she sees. But as great as every miracle is because it can be seen, an interior miracle is more wonderful because it cannot be seen in the present time. Regarding this it is appropriately[41] added in that place: *aside from what is veiled within*. For the glory of an observable work is great, but the glory of a hidden reward is far beyond comparison. ²All that is seen by divine providence in the face of heaven, as it were, is beautiful; but that attained without being seen is incomparably far more beautiful.

Song 4:2. *Your teeth are like a flock of shorn sheep coming up from a washing.*

W28. ¹We take the holy Church's 'teeth' as the holy preachers who masticate the toughness of sinners with their preaching. ²It is not unreasonable to compare them to 'shorn' and 'washed' sheep. For by adopting an irreproachable manner of life in the baptismal bath they have put aside the raggedly fleece of their previous way of life.

Song 4:3. *Your lips are like a scarlet headband, my Bride, and your words are sweet.*

W29. ¹A headband binds the hairs of the head. ²But what is meant by hairs, if not the soul's racing thoughts? ³Therefore, the Bride's 'lips' are like a 'headband' because the exhortations of the holy Church bind together all wandering thoughts in the minds

---

41. Here I read *apte* instead of *aperte*; see appendix 5, note 10.

of those who listen. It keeps them from running riot, being scattered by forbidden thoughts, and, once scattered, troubling the eyes of the heart. And so it enables them to gather themselves together, as it were, into a single purpose as long as the headband of holy preaching binds them. How good is it too that the headband is called 'scarlet'! For the preaching of the saints burns only with the ardor of love.

Song 4:4. *Your neck is like the tower of David, built with its own bulwarks; a thousand bucklers hang upon it, every one of them the armament of valiant men.*

W30. *¹*In the neck one finds the throat, and in the throat one finds the voice. So then, what is meant by the 'neck' of the Bride to whom the Bridegroom speaks these words, if not the Sacred Words of the holy Church? When it is mentioned that *a thousand bucklers hang upon it*, this number of perfection indicates the number of totality because the Sacred Word contains our total defense. For that is where we find the precepts of God, that is where we find the examples of the righteous.

If the soul has grown cold in desire for her Creator, let her hear what is said: *Love the Lord your God with all your mind and with all your strength* [Matt 22:37]. Perhaps she has fallen into hatred for her neighbor? Let her hear what is said: *Love your neighbor as yourself* [Matt 22:39]. Does she covet another's goods? Let her hear what is written there: *Do not covet your neighbor's goods* [Exod 20:17]. Is the mind stirred to anger by an injury inflicted by the word or deed of a neighbor? Let her hear what is said: *Do not seek revenge nor remember the injury of your fellow citizens* [Lev 19:18]. Does the mind troubled by evils seethe with the craving of the flesh? Lest the eye follow the mind, let her hear what was said a little before:[42] *Whoever looks at a woman in order to crave her has already committed fornication with her in his heart* [Matt 5:28].

---

42. Curiously, William did not excise the phrase "what was said a little before," a reference Gregory originally made to *H.Ez.* 2.1 [10], which is not included in the present excerpt.

Perhaps there is someone who decides to give his soul over to hatred of an enemy? Let him hear what is written there: *Love your enemies and do good to those who hate you* [Matt 5:44]. Perhaps one who already does not plunder another's goods still keeps his own goods in a way contrary to divine law? Let him hear what is said there: *Sell what you possess and give alms* [Luke 12:33]. Does the soul of a feeble person desire to enjoy God and this world at the same time? Let her hear what is written there: *No one can serve two masters* [Matt 6:24]. Does another keep possessions not to make necessary payments but to satisfy the desires of the will? Let him hear what is said there: *Whoever does not renounce all he possesses cannot be my disciple* [Luke 14:33]. While some abandon everything, many renounce while possessing, in that they keep their possessions for use in such a way that they do not fall prey to them out of desire.[43] Does someone seek indolence and dodge undertaking labor for the Lord even when capable? Let him hear what is written there: *Whoever does not gather with me scatters* [Luke 11:23]. Therefore, 'upon the neck of the Church,' which is to say in the preaching of the Sacred Word (said to be 'like the tower of David' because of its strong position and height), 'a thousand bucklers hang' because there all the precepts are also defenses for our heart.

And so, do we hasten to abide in humility so as to preserve our innocence, even if injured by a neighbor? Let Abel come before our eyes. It is written that he was murdered by his brother but we do not read that he struggled against him.[44] Is purity of mind chosen even within the bond of marriage? Enoch ought to be imitated. Though a married man, *he walked with God* [Gen 5:24] and *was not found because God took him* [Heb 11:5]. Do we hasten to prefer God's precepts to what benefits us in the present? Let Noah come before our eyes. Abandoning his domestic responsibilities at the bidding of the Almighty Lord, he lived for one hundred years engaged in

---

43. After this sentence, ms. A adds: "Let them listen to what is said: *Let him who wants to come after me deny himself*" (Matt 16:24; Luke 9:23).

44. See Gen 4:8.

the building of the ark.[45] Do we make every effort to submit to the virtue of obedience? We ought to observe Abraham. Leaving behind home, kinsfolk, and country, *he was obedient in going out to a place which he was to receive as an inheritance; he went out, ignorant of where he was going* [Heb 11:8]. He was prepared for the sake of an eternal inheritance to kill the beloved heir whom he had received. And since he did not hesitate to offer his only son to God, he received a whole multitude of peoples for his descendants.[46] Is simplicity of conduct pleasing? Let Isaac come before our mind. The tranquility of his conduct made him beautiful in the eyes of Almighty God. Is fortitude in labor sought in order to obtain it? Let Jacob be recalled to your memory. After learning how to serve a human being with fortitude,[47] he was led to it as a virtue, such that the angel who wrestled him could not prevail over him.[48]

Do we try to conquer the enticements of the flesh? Let Joseph return to your memory. He was zealous to guard chastity of the flesh[49] even to the point of endangering his life.[50] Since he had good knowledge regarding the rule of his own members, it thus came to pass that he was also entrusted with the rule of all Egypt. Do we seek to be meek? Let us bring Moses before our eyes. Even though he ruled six hundred thousand armed men (not counting women and children), he is described as having been *the meekest of all men who dwelt upon the face of the earth* [Num 12:3]. Are we enkindled by zeal for uprightness against vices? Let Phineas be brought before your eyes. By running his sword through the pair having sexual intercourse, he brought chastity back to the people and by his own wrath calmed the wrath of God.[51] Do we seek amid uncertainties

---

45. See Gen 6:13f.
46. See Gen 22:16-17; Heb 11:17-18.
47. See Gen 29:20; 29:25; 30:29.
48. See Gen 32:25.
49. At this point, ms. A adds: "when his Lady tempted him," which is original to Gregory's text at *H.Ez.* 2.3 [21], 510 (CCSL 142:252).
50. See Gen 39:12-20.
51. See Num 25:7-11.

to presume on hope in Almighty God? Let us recall Joshua to our memory. When he engaged in uncertain battles with a confident mind, he came through to victory without any uncertainty.

Do we already yearn to break free from meanness of mind, to enlarge the soul in kindness? Let Samuel enter into thought. Although rebuffed by the people with regard to the kingship, when the same people begged him to pour out prayers for them to the Lord, he answered: *Far be it from me that I should sin against the Lord such that I would cease to pray for you!* [1 Sam 12:23]. For the holy man believed he would have committed a sin if he had not returned the kindness of grace by praying for those whom he had endured as adversaries even to the point of being rebuffed. Again, when at the bidding of the Lord he was sent to anoint David as king, he replied: *How can I go? Saul will find me and kill me!* [1 Sam 16:2]. And yet when he learned that God was angered at the same Saul, he agonized over it with such mourning that the Lord said to him in person: *How long will you mourn for Saul, seeing that I have rejected him?* [1 Sam 16:1]. So then, let us ponder how great an ardor of charity inflamed the soul of him who wept even for the man by whom he feared being killed. But are we willing to look out for the one whom we fear? We ought to ponder this with an attentive mind so that, if perhaps we were to find the opportunity, we ourselves will not repay the one whom we fear evil for evil. Therefore, let David return to the memory. He found himself in pursuit of the king so that he could kill him, and yet when placed within striking distance he chose the good he ought to have done but not the evil the king deserved to suffer, saying: *Far be it from me that I should stretch out my hand against the Lord's anointed!* [1 Sam 26:11]. And when the same Saul was later destroyed by his enemies, David wept for the murdered man whom while alive he had endured as a persecutor.

Do we decide to speak candidly to those powerful in the world when they are in error? Let the authority of John be directed to your soul. When he censured Herod's wickedness, he was not afraid of being killed for the uprightness of his message. And since *Christ is the Truth* [1 John 5:6],[52] he therefore laid down his life for Christ since he laid it down for the truth. Do we hasten right now to lay down our flesh in death for God? Let Peter come to mind. He rejoiced in the midst of scourgings, when beaten withstood princes, despised his own life for the sake of Life. Are we resolved to scorn adversity with a longing for death? Let Paul be brought before your eyes. Ready not only to be fettered but also to die for Christ,[53] he does not make his own life more valuable than Christ. Do we seek to have our heart kindled with the fire of charity? Let us ponder the words of John. Everything he said burned with the fire of charity. Therefore, because we find in the voice of the Sacred Word the means of fortifying any virtue we seek, *a thousand bucklers hang upon it, every one of them the armament of valiant men.*

Now if we want to fight against spiritual wickedness, we should look for defensive weapons in the 'neck' of the Church that was built for us 'like the tower of David,' which is to say in the Divine Words. Thus from the discerning use of the precepts we gain powerful aid against vices. Look, do we hasten to be 'valiant' against the powers of the air? We find the 'armament' of our mind in this 'tower' and from it we take the precepts of our Creator and the examples of our predecessors by which we become invincibly armed against our adversaries. For when you seek to acquire any virtue and see it already fulfilled somewhere by the fathers, there you find the 'armament' by means of which you can defend yourself against spiritual onslaughts. After all, *bucklers hang upon it.* If anyone seeks to fight, let him take up that virtue and defend his heart with it, and let him launch javelins of words.

And note that the tower is said to have been *built with its own bulwarks.* Now bulwarks perform the same function as bucklers do, since both protect the one who fights. But there is a difference

---

52. Note that only the Vulgate of 1 John 5:6 reads: "Christ is the Truth." The standard Greek text reads: "the Spirit is Truth." If Gregory was not alluding to the Vulgate of 1 John 5:6 here, he many have been thinking of John 14:6.

53. See Acts 21:13.

between them: while we can move bucklers at will to protect ourselves, we can defend ourselves with a bulwark but without being able to move it. A buckler is clutched in the hand, but a bulwark is not. So then, what is the difference between a bulwark and a buckler, if not the fact that in the Sacred Word we both read the miracles of the fathers who have gone before us and hear the virtues of their good works? For we learn there that one could divide the sea,[54] another stop the sun,[55] another revive a dead person,[56] another raise up a paralytic by a word,[57] another heal the sick with his shadow,[58] another break the fevers of the infirm with his apron.[59] Yet all these were meek with the forbearance of patience and fervent with the zeal of uprightness, rich in preaching the word and at the same time abundant in mercy. And so, their miracles testify that they proclaimed the truth about the Lord, since they would not have been able to do such things through him unless they were telling the truth about him. And their activities testify to how devoted, how humble, how kind they were. Thus if our faith, which we conceived from their preaching, is put to the test, we will reflect upon the miracles of those who preach, and the faith which we received from them will be strengthened. So then, what are their miracles, if not our bulwarks? For they can protect us, and yet we do not hold them in our hand as things within our power to choose, seeing that we cannot do such things. But we do have a buckler in our hand and it defends us because the virtue of patience and the virtue of mercy, so long as grace precedes, are within our power to choose, and they protect from the danger of adversity. And so, our tower is 'built with its own bulwarks,' on which 'a thousand bucklers hang,' because the Sacred Scriptures enable us both to hide from the javelin of adversity under the

---

54. See Exod 12:21-29.
55. See Josh 10:12-14.
56. See 1 Kgs 17:17-24; 2 Kgs 4:18-37.
57. See Acts 9:32-34.
58. See Acts 5:15.
59. See Acts 19:12.

miracles of the fathers and to hold in our hand things we can do to safeguard a holy way of life.

²Therefore, dear brothers, do not scorn the writings of our Redeemer which have been sent to us. It is very remarkable that through them a soul can be restored to warmth lest she grow numb through the cold of iniquity. When we learn in them that our righteous forebears acted valiantly and we ourselves are equipped with strength for good works, the soul of the reader is kindled by the flame of holy examples. She sees their valiant deeds and she gets very annoyed with herself for not imitating such acts.

Song 4:5-6. *Your two breasts are like two fawns of a roe deer, twins, who feed on the lilies until the day breaks and the shadows recede.*

W31. ¹We must always, dear brothers, reflect on the conduct of the righteous so that we can gain subtle insight into our own. ²All the elect never stop doing this. For they study the conduct of their betters and modify the aspects of their way of life that fall short. ³What are the 'two breasts' of the Bride to whom the Bridegroom is speaking, if not the two peoples coming from the Jews and from the Gentiles, who are implanted in the body of the holy Church through their efforts to attain wisdom in the hidden depths of their heart? Accordingly, those elected from these peoples are compared to the 'fawns of a roe deer' because through their humility they have come to understand that they are truly insignificant and sinful. But if they encounter the hurdles of temporal encumbrance, running by love they surmount them and making leaps of contemplation they ascend to heavenly realities.

In order to do these things they reflect on the examples of the saints who have preceded them. This is why reference is made to the fact that they *feed on the lilies*. For what is indicated by 'lilies,' if not the conduct of those who can truly say: *We are the good odor of Christ for God* [2 Cor 2:15]? So then, the elect, in order to gain the strength to follow them to the highest regions, completely satisfy themselves by reflecting upon the fragrant and pure conduct of the righteous. Even in the present time they thirst to see God. In the present time they burn with the fires of love that they may be completely satisfied by the contemplation of him. But since they are still incapable of doing so while placed in this life, they feed in the meantime on the examples of the fathers who have preceded them.[60]

Hence that passage fittingly gave a limit to the time for their 'feeding on the lilies,' when it is said: *Until the day breaks and the shadows recede.* For we need to be nourished with the examples of the righteous for only so long, until we pass beyond the shadows of our present mortality when that eternal day breaks. After all, when the shadow of this transitory time has receded and this mortal state has passed away, since we behold the inner light of day itself, we no longer seek to be kindled with love for it through the examples of others. But as it is now, since we are still unable to gaze upon it, we especially need to be aroused by reflecting on the actions of those who have pursued it perfectly.

So then, let us gaze upon the beautifulness of the alacrity of those who pursue it, and let us notice the disgracefulness of the sloth of the lazy. For as soon as we reflect on the deeds of those who live good lives, we pass judgment on ourselves in our profound embarrassment. Soon feelings of shame assail our mind, soon a rightfully harsh accusation is levied upon us, and we are even sorely displeased with our disgraceful behavior, which perhaps we still find pleasurable. [4]And so, those who desire to be raised to the highest regions must always pay close attention to the progress of their betters, that they may judge the defects in themselves with greater severity in proportion to the greater profundity with which they see in them what they admire.

Song 4:8. *You shall be crowned from the summit of Amana, from the peak of Senir and Hermon, from the dens of lions.*

W32. [1]The approaching Bridegroom is told that he 'shall be crowned from the dens of lions.'[61] What else could the word 'lions' designate other than the demons who rage against us with wrath

---

60. For textual comments on this line, see appendix 5, note 31.
61. The Carthusian version (ms. D) omits this sentence.

of the most savage sort? ²But the 'dens' of demons were the hearts of the iniquitous.⁶² Since the demons seduced them to their own wickedness, it is as if the iniquitous rested in that place where demons dwell. But *by the midwifery of the Lord's hand* [Job 26:13] the lions are driven out of their own dens because, when divine grace heals us, the one who had possessed us, the ancient enemy, is cast out of us, as incarnate Truth says: *Now shall the prince of this world be cast out* [John 12:31].⁶³ ³And because sinners are called to faith, whose hearts were once 'dens of lions,' when they confess their belief in the Lord's victory over death, it is as if he is 'crowned from the dens of lions.' After all, the reward for victory is a crown. Therefore, the faithful offer a crown to the Lord as often as they confess that he is victorious over death through his resurrection.

Song 4:11. *Honey and milk are under your tongue.*

W33. ¹When most of the righteous see any persons living wicked lives, who deserve to be chastised with harsh rebukes, they put sternness on their tongues. But 'under the tongue' they conceal the gentleness of their mind. ²For they prefer not to disclose the sweetness of their mind to the weak, but when they speak they chastise them with a certain degree of sternness. And yet among their harsh words they sprinkle droplets of sweetness, on the sly as it were. It is people such as these who do not have sweetness on the tongue but rather 'under the tongue.' For among the harsh words which they utter, they also give out some that are consoling and sweet whereby the mind of a distressed person can be restored on account of their gentleness. Similarly, because some of the wicked and hypocritical do not have evil on the tongue but rather 'under the tongue,' they make a pretence of sweetness in their words but formulate wicked plans in their thoughts.

---

62. The Carthusian versions (ms. D) reads: "the hearts of the proud and iniquitous."

63. The Carthusian version (ms. D) omits: "as incarnate Truth says: *Now shall the prince of this world be cast out.*"

Song 4:16. *Arise, north wind, and come, south wind, blow through my garden and let its sweet scents spread around.*

W34. ¹In light of the fact that the 'north wind' chills with cold, the word 'north' is not an inappropriate designation for the lethargic numbness caused by the evil spirit.[64] Isaiah the Prophet testifies to this, declaring that the devil said he would sit *on the slopes of the north* [Isa 14:13]. ²He sits 'on the slopes of the north' because he possesses the cold minds of human beings. ³But the 'south wind'—a wind that is certainly warm—is not an unsuitable designation for the fervor of the Holy Spirit. For when anyone is touched by him, she is freed from the lethargic numbness of her evil ways. ⁴And when anyone is filled with him, love for the spiritual homeland is enkindled in her.

⁵And so, in the voice of the Bridegroom the 'north wind' is ordered to 'arise,' undoubtedly in order that the hostile spirit, who chills the hearts of mortals, may take flight. ⁶When at God's bidding the cold spirit recedes, the warm spirit takes up residence in the mind of the faithful and 'blows through the garden' of God, which is to say the holy Church, ⁷in order to 'spread its sweet scents around.' For surely when the Spirit of truth fills the holy Church with the virtues that are his very own gifts, he spreads far and wide from her the odors of good works. ⁸Thus reports of her virtues flow out like 'sweet scents' enabling them to become known to many people. Indeed, after the departure of the 'north wind,' which is to say the evil spirit, the Holy Spirit fills the mind like the 'south wind.' By blowing with his warmth, the 'sweet scents' of the virtues at once flow from the hearts of the faithful. ⁹And soon after this their reputation for virtues is scattered abroad. Hence the tongue of the saints, like 'a garden through which the south wind blows,' may justly say in the present time: *We are the good odor of Christ for God* [2 Cor 2:15].

---

64. The Latin *spiritus*, here translated as "spirit," also means "wind." In his interpretation of Song 4:16, Gregory plays on both senses of this word.

Chapter Five

Song 5:2. *I sleep but my heart is awake.*

W35. ¹In Sacred Scripture, the figurative use of 'sleep' or 'slumber' can be understood in three ways. Sometimes 'sleep' expresses the death of the flesh, sometimes the numbness of indifference, but sometimes the calmness of life that ensues when earthly desires are trod underfoot. The word 'sleep' or 'slumber' suggests the death of the flesh, as when Paul says: *Now we do not want you to be ignorant, brothers, concerning those who are asleep* [1 Thess 4:13]. And a little after: *Even so, through Jesus God will bring with him those who are asleep* [1 Thess 4:14]. Again, 'sleep' designates the numbness of indifference, as when it is said by the same Paul: *It is now the hour to rise from sleep* [Rom 13:11]. And again: *Wake up, you who are righteous, and do not sin* [1 Cor 15:34]. 'Sleep' also signifies the calmness of life that ensues when desires of the flesh are trod underfoot, as when the following is said in the voice of the Bride: *I sleep but my heart is awake* [Song 5:2], ²as if she were saying: "While I give my exterior senses rest from the worries of this life, I have a more lively comprehension of interior realities since my mind is free. 'I sleep' exteriorly, but 'my heart is awake' interiorly because while I have no perception, as it were, of exterior objects, I have a keen comprehension of interior realities." ³Indeed, the more the holy mind withholds herself from the clamor of temporal yearning, the more truly she attains knowledge of interior realities; and the more eagerly she is awake to inward concerns, the more she screens herself from outward disturbance. ⁴And so, she sleeps with a 'heart' that is 'awake' because[65] on account of her interior progress in contemplation she is undisturbed by disturbing exterior works. ⁵Whoever seeks to do the things which are of this world is, so to speak, 'awake.' But whoever in their quest for interior calm eschews the clamor of this life 'sleeps.'

---

65. Here I read *quia* instead of *qui*; see appendix 5, note 11.

Song 5:4. *My beloved put his hand through the opening, and my insides trembled at his touch.*

W36. ¹Great is the mercy of our Creator. ²For the entrance into the heavenly kingdom is opened equally to both the Jewish and Gentile peoples, and the righteous and the sinners, but only after converted from their sins. ³The joys of the heavenly kingdom are opened not only[66] to those who remain in innocence but also to condemned sinners when they repent of their sins. Thus they come to appreciate the inexpressible mysteries of the heavenly kingdom, and by appreciating them thirst for them, by thirsting for them run after them, by running after them attain them. He appreciated these mysteries of interior joy who said: *My soul has thirsted for the living God. When shall I enter and appear before the face of God?* [Ps 41:3]. The preacher to the Gentiles longed for the entrance to the heavenly kingdom when he said: *My desire is to depart and to be with Christ* [Phil 1:23]. The Bride appreciated these mysteries of hidden ecstasy when she said here: *My beloved put his hand through the opening, and my insides trembled at his touch* [Song 5:4]. Surely 'the beloved puts his hand through the opening' when the Lord by his own power moves our souls to a refined understanding. And 'the insides greatly tremble at his touch' because our weakness, on account of being touched by an understanding of heavenly joy, is thrown into confusion by our own ecstasy. And panic seizes her mind in her rejoicing because in the present time she experiences a bit of the heavenly joy that she loves and yet she dreads not retaining what she experiences so fleetingly. Therefore, what are they to do, all who have an appreciation of the joys of the heavenly homeland, if not to direct their feet along the path of a more perfect life?

Song 5:5. *My hands dripped with myrrh, my fingers full of the finest myrrh.*

W37. ¹The holy Church says this about her laborers who fight even unto death on behalf of God. ²For 'myrrh' is a figure for the mortification of our flesh. ³The Evangelist writes with regard to the Magi who came from the East to Bethlehem to adore the Lord:

---

66. Here I read *solum his* instead of *solis*; see appendix 5, note 12.

And after they opened their treasures, they offered the Lord gold, frankincense, and myrrh [Matt 2:11]. ⁴We too offer him myrrh if we mortify the vices of our flesh through self-restraint. For, as we said, myrrh keeps dead flesh from putrefying. The putrefaction of dead flesh is the enslavement of this mortal body to the dissipation caused by self-indulgence, as is said through the Prophet about certain people: *The beasts have putrefied in their own dung* [Joel 1:17]. For 'beasts putrefying in their own dung' are carnal persons ending their life in the stench of self-indulgence. Therefore, we offer myrrh to God when we use the seasoning of self-control to keep this mortal body free from the putrefaction of self-indulgence.

Song 5:6. *My soul was melted when my beloved spoke.*

W38. ¹The mind of the person who does not seek the sight of her Creator is very hard because she persists in a frozen state on account of herself. But ²when she is touched by the breath of secret speaking, she loses the seat of her own strength and 'is melted' by the very desire that consumes her. ³And if in the present time she starts to burn with the desire to follow him whom she loves, 'melted' by the fire of her love, she runs. ⁴And the more her zeal for the world cools, the more ardently love for God rises within her. ⁵She becomes eager with desire. She reviles all worldly things that used to bring her pleasure. Nothing except her Creator pleases her. What first delighted her soul afterward becomes grievously burdensome. Nothing consoles her grief as long as she has still not looked upon him whom she desires. Her mind sorrows. Light itself is wearisome. Scorching fire burns away the rust of sin in her mind. The soul is enflamed like gold because gold loses its luster through use but regains its brightness through fire.

Song 5:7. *I sought but did not find him; I called but he gave me no answer. The sentries who patrol the city found me. They beat me. They wounded me. The sentries of the walls took my cloak from me.*

W39. The Bride 'does not find him' when she seeks because every elect soul already burns with the firebrands of love for him but still is denied the sight of him who is sought, so as to intensify the desire of the lover. It is as if water is taken away in thirst, causing the heat of her thirst to increase: the longer she desires it when thirsty, the more avidly she takes it when given.[67] 'The watchmen find her as she searches for him, and wound her, and take away her cloak' because when dutiful teachers find that any soul is already seeking the sight of her Redeemer, they 'wound her' with the darts of heavenly love through the word of preaching. And if she still possesses any covering of her old way of life, they 'take it away' so that the more she is stripped of the burden of this world, the more quickly she may find him whom she seeks.

Song 5:11. *His head is the finest gold.*

W40. [1]By the term 'gold' is designated the very innermost brightness of divinity when the Bride describes the sight of the Bridegroom. [2]*The head of Christ is God* [1 Cor 11:3] but there is no metal more resplendent than gold. Hence the Bridegroom's head is called 'gold' because his humanity rules over us on account of the brightness of his divinity.

CHAPTER SIX

Song 6:3. *You are beautiful, my love, charming and lovely as Jerusalem, terrifying as an army's front poised for battle.*

W41. [1]The holy catholic Church is described in the guise of a beloved woman. [2]The interpretation of the name 'Jerusalem' is "vision of peace," which represents the heavenly homeland. So then, the holy Church is 'charming and lovely as Jerusalem' because her conduct and desire are being compared to the vision of inner peace. Hence insofar as she loves her Creator and yearns to see the face of him about whom it is written, *He upon whom the angels desire to look* [1 Pet 1:12], she is said to be like the angels on account of her very desires of her love. She becomes pleasing to God to the extent that[68] she makes an effort to become terrifying to wicked spirits.

---

67. The text ". . . but still is denied . . . she takes it when given" was employed in the Carthusian version (ms. D) of W21; see n. 29 above.

68. Here I read *quanto* instead of *quantum*; see appendix 5, note 13.

Another comparison shows just how terrifying she is: *like an army's front poised for battle.* Why do the enemies of the holy Church fear her as if she were 'an army's front'? Now this comparison does not lack great insight and so we must examine it in detail. For we know and it is undisputed that an army's front appears terrifying to enemies when it is drawn up so tightly and packed together so closely that no gaps can be seen anywhere. For if it is deployed such that there is an empty space through which the enemy could enter, it would certainly no longer be terrifying to its enemies. Therefore, when we form the line for spiritual battle against wicked spirits, it is of the utmost importance that we always be united to one another and joined closely together through charity and never found separated from one another through discord. For even though we may do good works, if charity is lacking, the evil of discord[69] opens a gap in the battle line through which the enemy can enter and smite us.

The ancient enemy does not fear our self-control if it is without charity because he is not oppressed by flesh such that he destroys himself through self-indulgence. He does not fear our abstinence because he who is not urged by the needs of the body does not eat food. He does not fear it when we donate our earthly goods if we do so without charity because he has no need for the benefits of riches. But he very much fears the true charity in us, which is to say the humble love that we mutually extend to one another. And he greatly begrudges our concord because we ourselves retain on earth what he himself, choosing not to retain it, lost in heaven. Therefore, *terrifying as an army's front poised for battle* is well said because the wicked spirits tremble with fear at the multitude of the elect insofar as they observe them united and assembled together against them through the concord of charity.

The greatness of the virtue of concord is shown by the fact that when the remaining virtues are without it, they are revealed to be non-virtues. For example, great is the virtue of abstinence.

---

69. Here I read *per* instead of *par*; see appendix 5, note 14.

But if anyone were to abstain from food in such a way that he condemns others for eating food and even denounces the foods which God created for the faithful to consume with thanksgiving, what has the virtue of abstinence become for him if not a snare of sin? Thus the Psalmist indicated that abstinence cannot exist without concord: *Praise him with timbrel and choir* [Ps 150:4]. For the dry membrane[70] on a timbrel produces a sound but the voices in a choir sing with concord. So what is meant by the 'timbrel' if not abstinence? By the 'choir' if not the concord of charity? Accordingly whoever observes abstinence so as to abandon concord does indeed 'praise with timbrel' but does not 'praise with choir.' In addition, there are some who in their eagerness to be wiser than necessary recoil from peace with their neighbors, despising them as dull and stupid. Thus Truth himself admonishes us: *Have salt in yourselves and have peace among yourselves* [Mark 9:50]. Whoever is eager to have the salt of wisdom must take care never to withdraw from the peace of concord.[71]

Our statements about these two virtues ought to be understood as applicable to all the rest. Hence Paul admonishes us in a terrifying manner: *Strive for peace with all and for the holiness without which*

---

70. Here I read *corium* instead of *curvum*; see appendix 5, note 15.

71. Gregory's thought here is echoed in *Ep.* 7.29 to Anastasius, the priest in charge of Neas, one of the monasteries in Jerusalem, when he tries to reconcile him with Amos, the bishop of Jerusalem: "I know that both of you abstain, both of you are learned, both of you are humble; this is why it is necessary for the glory of our Lord to be praised, according to the text of the psalm, *with timbrel and choir* [Ps 150:4]. For on a timbrel a sound is produced from a dry membrane, but in a choir there is a concord of voices. Therefore, what is meant by the timbrel, if not abstinence? What is meant by the choir, if not unanimity? Therefore, since you praise the Lord with timbrel through abstinence, I beg you to praise him with choir through unanimity. Truth himself even said: *Have salt in yourselves, and have peace among yourselves* [Mark 9:50]. What is meant by salt, if not wisdom? Paul testified to this when he said: *Let your word always be gracious, seasoned with salt* [Col 4:6]. Therefore, since we know that you have the salt of the heavenly Word on account of your learning, it remains that you should also keep peace among yourselves with all your heart through the grace of love."

no one will see God [Heb 12:14]. Truth himself indicates that nothing is pleasing to God without concord when he says: *If you are offering*[72] *your gift at the altar, and there you remember that your brother has something against you, leave your gift there before the altar and go, first be reconciled with your brother and then come and offer your gift* [Matt 5:23-24]. See, he does not want to receive a sacrificial offering from those enmeshed in discord; he refuses to accept a holocaust from them. So then, ponder how great the evil of discord must be if on account of it the offering through which guilt is remitted is rejected. ³Therefore, it is right that the holy Church be called *terrifying as an army's front poised for battle* ⁴because the elect, ⁵who constitute an army, a spiritual military force that has ventured upon war against the powers of the air, ⁶are always joined together in charity. And this same charity of theirs strikes the punishment of fear into wicked spirits, which is to say their ancient enemies.[73]

Song 6:6. *Like the skin of a pomegranate are your cheeks, apart from what you hide.*

W42. ¹The 'cheeks' of the holy Church are the spiritual fathers ²who insofar as they are filled with charity, control their flesh by abstinence, enlighten the hearts of their hearers with the splendor of preaching, perform signs, work mighty deeds, ³glow with marvelous deeds. ⁴Because the good deeds they have done publicly become known to us, not undeservedly ⁵do they give a venerable appearance to the face of the holy Church. For when we see many perform wonders, prophesy future events, perfectly forsake world, ardently burn with heavenly desires, the holy Church's 'cheeks' are considered to be 'like the skin of a pomegranate.' But what is all this we admire in comparison to that reality of which it is written: *What eye has not seen, nor ear heard, nor entered into the heart of man, which God has prepared for those who love him* [1 Cor 2:9]? Therefore, when he admired the cheeks of the Church, it is good that he

---

72. Here I read *offeres* instead of *offers*; see appendix 5, note 16.
73. The Carthusian version (ms. D) omits verses 3-6, "Therefore, it is right . . . ancient enemies."

added: *apart from what you hide*. It is as if he were saying in plain speech: "Indeed, those things in you[74] which are not hidden are great, but those which are hidden are utterly inexpressible."

Song 6:9. *Who is this coming forth, rising like the dawn?*

W43. [1]The holy Church, [2]whom the Bridegroom admires here, [3]is fittingly[75] described by being compared with the 'dawn.' [4]Leaving the darkness of sin, she now bursts forth into the light of eternity. [5]By knowledge of the faith she exchanges the darkness of her sins for the clear light of righteousness. [6]Because dawn is changed from darkness into light, the name 'dawn' is not undeservedly applied to the whole Church of the elect. For when she is led from the night of unbelief to the light of faith, she is broken open with the splendor of heavenly brightness, as the dawn breaks open into day after the darkness. [7]The holy Church as she pursues the rewards of the heavenly life is called the 'dawn' because when she leaves the darkness of sin she shines with the light of righteousness. [8]She is 'rising like the dawn' since she has left the darkness of her former wickedness and turned herself to the radiance of the new light.

[9]Yet we have here something quite profound which ought to be pondered by considering the characteristics of the dawn. Now the dawn announces that night is past,[76] but does not yet put forward the full[77] brightness of day. Rather, while it dispels the night and takes on the day, it keeps the light intermingled with the darkness. And so, what are all of us who follow the truth in this life, if not the dawn? For in the present time we both do some things which belong to the light and yet are not free from the rest of the other things which still belong to the darkness. After all, it is said to God through the Prophet: *Every living man will not be justified in your sight* [Ps 142:2]. Again it is written: *All of us offend in many things* [Jas 3:2]. Paul too said: *I see another law in my members fighting against the law*

---

74. Here I read *te* instead of *ea*; see appendix 5, note 17.
75. Here I read *apte* instead of *aperte*; see appendix 5, note 18.
76. Here I read *praeterisse* instead of *interisse*; see appendix 5, note 19.
77. Here I add *integram* after *claritatem*; see appendix 5, note 20.

of my mind and leading me captive under the law of sin, which is in my members [Rom 7:23]. Where then the law of sin struggles with the law of the mind, there it is certainly still the dawn because the light which has already shone forth has still not entirely overcome the darkness that preceded it. It is still the dawn because, if the law of the flesh assails the law of the mind and the law of the mind assails the law of the flesh, light and darkness battle each other. Thus when Paul said, *The night is past* [Rom 13:12], he did not continue with "the day has arrived," but rather, *the day has drawn near* [Rom 13:12]. For he who teaches that the day has still not arrived after the night has departed but rather that it 'has drawn near' indisputably proves that he is still at dawn before the sun yet after the darkness.

But the holy Church of the elect will be fully day at that time when the darkness of sin is no longer associated with her. She will be fully day at that time when she has been brightened with the perfect fervor of interior light. She will be fully day at that time when, saddled no longer with the tempting memory of evil deeds, she has concealed from herself even all the remains of darkness. [10]But at present because the Church, enduring still the annoyance of temptations, hastens elsewhere by intention of heart, she progresses to her own place 'rising like the dawn.' [11]For what is the place of the dawn, if not the perfect brightness of interior vision? When after being guided there she arrives at this place, she will no longer have any darkness of the night that is past. [12]If she were not to perceive this place with her mind, she would remain in the darkness of this life. But by striving daily to be perfected and to be increased daily in light,[78] she already beholds her own place and seeks for the sun to shine fully on her. The dawn gazes upon its own place when a holy soul burns to contemplate the sight of her Creator. The dawn was consumed with reaching its proper place when David said: *My soul has thirsted for the living God. When shall I come and appear before the face of God?* [Ps 41:2]. [13]The dawn was

---

78. Here I add *contendit perfici et in lucem cotidie* after *cotidie*; see appendix 5, note 21.

hastening to arrive at this place, which it knew, when Paul said that he had a desire *to depart and to be with Christ* [Phil 1:23]. And again: *For me to live is Christ and to die is gain* [Phil 1:21]. And again: *We know that if our home of this earthly dwelling is destroyed, that we have a building from God, a home not made by hands, eternal in the heavens* [2 Cor 5:1]. ¹⁴The blessed Job spoke of this dawn: *May that night be solitary and not worthy of praise! May it look forward to the light and see neither it nor the breaking of the rising dawn!* [Job 3:7, 9].⁷⁹

¹⁵So then, in that light which is manifested at the coming of the strict Judge, the body of our enemy when condemned will not see the break of the rising dawn. For when the strict Judge comes for retribution, each wicked person, being oppressed by the blackness of his own deserts, is kept from knowing the wondrous splendor with which the holy Church rises to the interior light of the heart. At that time the mind of the elect is transported on high such that she is illumined with the rays of Divinity, and she is bathed in the light of his countenance to the extent that she is lifted up above herself in the refulgence of grace. At that time the holy Church becomes a full dawn since she has wholly parted with the darkness of her mortality and ignorance. So then, at the judgment she is still dawn but in the kingdom she is day. For though she already begins to behold the light at the judgment when bodies are resurrected, yet she attains a fuller vision of it in the kingdom. And so, the break of dawn is the beginning of the Church in splendor, which the reprobate cannot see. For oppressed by the weight of their evils, they are dragged from the sight of the strict Judge into darkness. Hence it is rightly said through the Prophet: *The impious man is borne away lest he see the glory of God* [Isa 26:10].

CHAPTER SEVEN

Song 7:4. *Your nose is like the tower of Lebanon.*

W44. ¹I ask you, dear brothers, what kind of praise is it for the Bride's nose to be compared by the voice of the Bridegroom to a

---

79. This verse is an addition by William.

'tower'? But since ²the thing which we cannot make out with our eyes is generally sensed beforehand by its smell, ³and we use our nose to distinguish between pleasant scents and foul odors, what then is meant by the Church's 'nose,' if not the farseeing discernment of the saints and ecclesiastical authorities? ⁴Now a watchtower is placed on high so that the approaching enemy may be spotted from afar. So then, the Church's 'nose' is rightly said to be 'like the tower which is in Lebanon' because as long as the farseeing discernment of the saints placed on high carefully monitors all possible places, it catches sight of sin before its arrival. And so, the greater the vigilance in detecting sin before its arrival, the greater the strength to avoid it.

⁵The Church's 'nose' is rightly said to be 'like the tower which is in Lebanon' clearly because the discerning foresight of the saints is situated on high in such a way that it can spot[80] the attacks of temptations even before they come and successfully withstand them when they do come. If future events can be sensed beforehand they become less potent when present. For when an enemy believes he is unexpected, but instead his quarry is ready for the blow, the same enemy is weakened to the very extent that he is sensed beforehand.

⁶The Church's 'nose' is rightly said to be 'like the tower which is in Lebanon' ⁷because clearly the discernment of superiors ought always be fortified with careful attention and be established on loftiness of conduct, which is to say they ought not lie in the valley of feeble effort. For as a tower is placed on a mountain to spot enemies coming from afar, so too ought the conduct of a preacher always to remain fixed on high. Thus like a nose he may distinguish between the foul odors of vices and the pleasing scents of virtues, perceive from afar the onslaughts of malicious spirits, and through his farsightedness safely return the souls entrusted to him.

⁸Therefore, the conduct of a watchman ought always be high and circumspect. ⁹It does not suffice for the watchman to live on

---

80. Here I add *videat* after *priusquam veniant*; see appendix 5, note 22.

high unless by persistent speaking he also attracts his hearers to the heights and by speaking ignites their minds with a love for the heavenly homeland. [10]Let it be high lest he succumb to the love of earthly things. Let it be circumspect on every side lest he be struck by the darts of a hidden enemy.[81]

Song 7:12. *Let us get up early to go to the vineyards. Let us see whether the vine has budded, whether the buds are ready to produce fruits.*

W45. [1]Vines have 'budded' when the minds of the faithful plan good works. But they do not 'produce fruits' if they falter in carrying out their plans when overcome by certain erring practices. We ought then not look to see if the vines have budded but if the buds are strong for producing fruits. For there is nothing to admire if someone begins good works, but there is much to admire if someone persists in a good work with the right intention. Accordingly it is generally the case that, if a right intention is not maintained in the course of a good work, even the very work itself, which is deemed good, is lost.

[2]We need to ponder how a vine *is spoilt when it first buds* [Job 15:33]. If a vine in bud is exposed to excessive cold due to variations in the air, all the moisture that gives it freshness is immediately sucked out of it. And there are some who after journeying along wicked roads yearn to pursue holy paths, but before good desires can gain strength in them, as we said,[82] some piece of good fortune in the present age comes upon them, which entangles them in outward affairs. And when it withdraws their mind from the warmth[83] of intimate love, which is snuffed out, as it were, by the cold, it also kills any bud of virtue that seemed to appear in them. For the soul grows very cold in earthly activities if she was not already strengthened by interior gifts.

---

81. On the order of verses 8-10, see appendix 5, note 32.

82. Here I insert *ut diximus*; see appendix 5, note 23. For another instance of William's retention of a Gregorian reference to an earlier discussion that he did not include in his florilegium see n. 42 above.

83. Here I read *a calore* instead of *calorem*; see appendix 5, note 24.

Hence it is essential that the administration of positions of great responsibility or the performance of exterior works, which help meet human need, should be taken on only by those who know by reason of their interior virtue how to judge them and not be overcome by them. When any weak person is summoned either to a position of leadership or the performance of exterior works, he is destroyed inasmuch as he has been raised above his capabilities. Even the tree which does not first plant deep roots is quickly knocked down by a gust of wind if it has raised itself too highly: the higher it grows in the air without roots, the more quickly it crashes to the ground.

But sometimes it is not cold that dries up a vine in bud but hot weather: when it is exposed to excessive heat, the bud is killed and the grape cluster withers. As for those who do not come to good works with the right intention, it generally comes to pass that when they realize that they are winning the approval of others, they are beset with a burning desire to do these same works. Though it makes them anxious, they are eager to do what will be popular in the eyes of others and become fervent as if for a holy pursuit. What then has come upon these whom the appetite for human praise has alienated from producing fruit, if not the hot weather that kills the bud? *³*But know that things such as these always happen to those who do not follow God with pure and undivided zeal.

Chapter Eight

Song 8:5. *Who is this ascending from the desert overflowing with an abundance of delights?*

W46. *¹*Surely if the holy Church were not 'overflowing with an abundance of delights,' which is to say with the words of God, she could not 'ascend from the desert' of the present life to the regions above. So then, she is 'overflowing with an abundance of delights' and 'ascending' because when she is nourished by mystical understandings she is lifted up daily in the contemplation of heavenly things. *²*To be 'overflowing with an abundance of delights' is to be filled as much as possible from the delicacies of Sacred Scripture when having love for the Almighty. In his words surely we find as many delights as we obtain varieties of understanding for our benefit. Thus now the bare historical narrative itself nourishes us, now the moral allegory veiled under the literal text refreshes us deep within, now contemplation attaches us to the higher regions, even now in the darkness of this present life shining some of the light of eternity upon us.

But know that she who is 'overflowing with an abundance of delights' relaxes a certain aspect of herself and slackens in her zeal for labor as if from weariness because surely when the soul begins to 'overflow with an abundance of delights' interiorly, she no longer agrees to occupy herself with earthly works. Rather, captivated by love of the Creator and by her very captivity now set free, she yearns though fading to contemplate his brightness and is invigorated as if by growing weary. For no longer able to bear loathsome burdens, she hastens through rest to him whom she loves within.

³Hence the Psalmist said: *And the night shall be my illumination in the midst of delights* [Ps 138:11]. For when mystical understanding renews the eager mind, then the darkness of the present life is dispersed in her by the illumination of the day to follow. Thus even in the darkness of this state of corruption, the force of the light to come may break into her understanding, and being fed with the delights of words she may learn by such a foretaste how she hungers for the sustenance of truth.

Song 8:5 (LXX). *Who is this who ascends made white?*

W47. ¹The holy Church does not have the heavenly life by nature but when the Spirit comes upon her she is adorned with the beautifulness of gifts. For this reason she is described by the voice of the Bridegroom not as "white" but as 'made white.' ²Thus also when rebuking arrogant heretics in the Church, the blessed Job called those faithful who were truly humble 'the purest dyeings,' saying: ³*Nor shall the purest dyeings be adorned* [Job 28:19]. They are called 'the purest dyeings' who are truly humble and truly holy, who know indeed that they do not have the beauty of virtues through their own efforts but that they hold this by the gift of grace which comes upon them. For they would not have been dyed if they had holiness by nature. But they are 'the purest dyeings' because when the grace of the virtues comes upon them they humbly guard this gift which they have received.

⁴Those are rightly called 'the purest dyeings' who were once foul through wicked deeds, yet when the Spirit comes upon them are clothed with the radiance of grace, so that they are seen to be far different from what they were. Hence our own descending into the water is also said to be a "baptism," that is, a "dyeing."[84] For we are dyed, and we, who were once hideous and black by the disfigurement of vices, upon accepting the faith are rendered beautiful and 'made white' by grace and the adornment of the virtues.[85]

Song 8:6a. *Set me as a seal upon your heart.*

W48. ¹Sacred Scripture is in the habit of using 'seal' for faith. For example, the younger brother who returned to his father after squandering all his property received a signet ring as a gift.[86] In addition, the Gentile people who returned to God through repentance after losing immortality is fortified by the seal of faith. ²Now a seal is set on things so that they may not be violated by any audacity of plunderers. So then, the Bridegroom, who here speaks to the Church, is 'set as a seal on our heart' when the mystery of faith in him is impressed upon us for the safekeeping of our thoughts. Hence when that faithless servant, namely our adversary, observes our hearts sealed by faith, he does not have the audacity to break into them with temptation.

Song 8:6b. *Strong as death is love.*

W49. ¹The strength of love[87] is praised by the true voice of the holy Church ²and love[88] is compared to the power of death ³because

---

84. Lat. *tinctio*, "dyeing." The use of this word for baptism was fairly common in early Christianity.
85. For textual comments on this line, see appendix 5, note 33.
86. See Luke 15:22.
87. Lat. *caritas*.
88. Lat. *dilectio*.

as death destroys the body, so love[89] for eternal life ⁴makes the mind seized by it wholly dead to the love[90] of corporeal things and the love[91] of the world. ⁵For him whom it perfectly consumes becomes indifferent to outward earthly desires. ⁶And the stronger the authority it confers upon him, the more it renders him indifferent to objects of terror. ⁷For whoever is rooted in the desire for eternity alone is neither exalted by prosperity nor shaken by adversity. When there is nothing in the world for which he seeks, nothing from the world makes him tremble. ⁸Did not Paul burn with the fire of this love?[92] For he said: *For I am certain that neither death nor life, nor angels, nor principalities, nor things present, nor things to come, nor strength, nor height, nor depth, nor anything else in all creation will be able to separate us from the love*[93] *of God that is in Christ Jesus our Lord* [Rom 8:38-39].

Song 8:8. *Our sister is little and she has no breasts.*

W50. ¹As the age of each individual person is described, so that of the holy Church. For she was 'little' when fresh from birth she could not preach the word of life ²because surely before she made progress by growth in virtue, she could not offer the 'breasts' of preaching to each of her weak listeners. But the Church is called "adult" when, being wedded to the Word of God and filled with the Holy Spirit, she conceives children through the ministry of preaching, enters into labor with them by exhortation, and gives birth to them by effecting conversion.

Song 8:13. *You who dwell in gardens, the friends are listening: make me hear your voice.*

W51. ¹The Church, to whom these words are said during the Bridegroom's conversation with her, 'dwells in gardens' because she has cultivated a state of inner greenness whereby she preserves

---

89. Lat. *caritas.*
90. Lat. *amor.*
91. Lat. *dilectio.*
92. Lat. *dilectio.*
93. Lat. *caritas.*

a place where virtues can be planted. ²Indeed,⁹⁴ 'in gardens' the holy Church, 'in gardens' every individual soul 'dwells' who in the present time is filled with the greenness of hope and the fruitfulness of good works. For hope in this age is barren because all things loved here hastily wither away. And so Peter the Apostle urges us to hasten *to an inheritance that never perishes, never spoils, and never withers* [1 Pet 1:4].

So then, she who already 'dwells in gardens' must 'make' her Bridegroom 'hear her voice,' which is to say she must sing the song of good preaching in which he whom she desires will delight. ³Clearly it is her voice that the Bridegroom desires to hear because he longs for her preaching through the souls of his elect, ⁴because 'the friends are listening,' namely, all the elect who in order to return to life again in the heavenly homeland desire to hear the word of life from her, ⁵the word of her preaching.

⁶Therefore, whoever makes progress in the holy Church by beholding spiritual things must offer them to others by recounting them. For she realizes that she must communicate them when, seeing that she makes progress in herself, she also preaches out of concern for her neighbor's progress. Hence it is written elsewhere: *Let the one who hears say: Come!* [Rev 22:17]. For the one who has already heard the voice of God speaking in her heart must unsilence her own voice on behalf of her neighbor through the office of preaching and thereby call another because she herself was already called.

Song 8:14. *Escape, my beloved, escape!*

W52. ¹We say "it escapes me" as often as what we want to remember does not come to mind. We say "it escapes me" when we do not retain in our memory what we want to remember. So the holy Church, after narrating the Lord's death, resurrection, and ascension, cries out to him, filled with a prophetic spirit: *Escape, my beloved, escape!* It is as if she were saying: "You who were made comprehensible to us by the flesh, transcend the grasp of our senses

---

94. Here I read *enim* instead of *est*; see appendix 5, note 25.

by your divinity and remain incomprehensible to us in your very own self!"

²Thus it is rightly said through the Psalmist: *Dark clouds were under his feet, and he mounted the Cherubim, and he flew: he flew on the wings of the winds, and he made the darkness his covering* [Ps 17:10-12]. Now he has 'dark clouds under his feet' because those beneath do not perceive him in that brightness in which he exercises dominion among those above. And *he mounted the Cherubim, and he flew*. Cherubim means "fullness of knowledge." Accordingly, it is related that 'he mounted the fullness of knowledge, and he flew' because no branch of knowledge can comprehend the loftiness of his majesty. So then, 'he flew' because he retreated on high, far from the reach of our understanding. 'He flew on the wings of the winds' because he transcends the knowledge that souls can have.[95] 'And he made the darkness his covering' because when the darkness of our mind[96] renders us incapable of comprehension, our ignorance conceals him from us lest we see him now in his eternal and interior glory. ³He hides the power of his majesty from mortal beings. ⁴In this life we do not perceive the glory of his kingdom, so great as it is within, and that glory of the heavenly kingdom is not seen such as it is.

⁵And so, dear brothers, it is appropriate for us to follow the Lord in our heart to that place where we believe he ascended in his body. Let us escape from earthly desires. Let nothing in the lower regions delight us now, for we have a Father in the heavens. And we need especially to ponder this, that he who ascended in peace will return in terror, that whatever he enjoined upon us with mildness he will exact from us with severity. Therefore, let no one disparage this grace-period for repentance. Let no one neglect to care for himself while he can. For the severity with which our

---

95. Lat. *scientiam transcendit animarum*. In his interpretation here, Gregory makes a connection between "wind" (*ventus*) and "soul" (*anima*) because *anima* can also mean "breath."

96. Here I read *mentis nostrae* instead of *nostrae infirmitatis*; see appendix 5, note 26.

Redeemer will come in the future for judgment stands in direct proportion to the great patience he accorded us before judgment. And so, brothers, do these things for your own benefit; carefully reflect upon them in your mind. Though your soul be agitated still by disturbing thoughts about these things, nonetheless fix the anchor of our hope now in your eternal homeland, focus the gaze of your mind on the true light. Indeed, we believe that the Lord has ascended into heaven. So let us keep what we believe as the subject of our meditation. Although here we are confined still by the weakness of our body, let us nonetheless follow him by the footsteps of our love. He who gave us our desire will not fail to fulfill it, Jesus Christ our Lord, who lives and reigns with the Father in the unity of the Holy Spirit, God forever and ever. Amen.

SUPPLEMENTAL TEXTS

Introduction

Paterius, Bede, and especially William of Saint Thierry exhibited remarkable industry in collecting Gregorian texts on the Song of Songs. Paterius found just under 50 percent of all such texts in Gregory's corpus, and Bede about 56 percent. In contrast, William located just under 90 percent of all possible passages—and this in the days before Scripture indices, let alone searchable databases. He failed to locate only nine of the eighty-nine passages. Three of these are from Gregory's letters, which William probably did not scour for discussions of verses of the Song of Songs. In fact, two of the passages from the letters are identical, the one letter being a later version of the other.[1] In addition, both Bede and William knew of the passage that cited Song 1:3, but since the same passage actually commented on Song 2:8, they listed it under the latter verse.[2] Accordingly, William really missed only five relevant sections in those Gregorian works that he probably read. Since this volume is intended to be a comprehensive resource for the study of Gregory's exegesis of the Song of Songs, the nine passages omitted by the excerpters are translated here for the sake of completeness. At the same time, one can understand why William (and the other excerpters) might have omitted these passages if indeed they knew of them. For they repeat interpretations found elsewhere or offer little substantial interpretation of verses from the Song of Songs.

---

1. *Reg. ep.* 9.148 and *Reg. ep.* appendix 10; see Martyn, *Letters*, 889.
2. See B13 and W17.

Translation

Song 1:3. *Draw me! After you we shall run in the odor of your ointments.*

1. From *H. Ev.* 29 [10–11], 226–40 (CCSL 141:251–52)[3]— Solomon says in the voice of the Church: *Behold! He comes leaping upon the mountains, springing across the hills* [Song 2:8]. Considering his great works to be like lofty peaks, she said: *Behold! He comes leaping upon the mountains.* For by coming for our redemption the Lord performed, if I may put it so, a certain number of leaps. Dear brothers, do you want to learn what these leaps of his were? From heaven he came into the womb. From the womb he came into the manger. From the manger he came onto the cross. From the cross he came into the tomb. From the tomb he returned to heaven. Behold! Truth manifested in the flesh performed for our benefit a certain number of leaps so as to make us run after him. *He exulted like a giant to run his course* [Ps 18:6] so that we might say to him from our heart: *Draw me! After you we shall run in the odor of your ointments* [Song 1:3]. And so, dear brothers, it is fitting that we follow him in our heart to where we believe he ascended in his body. Let us flee earthly desires. Let us no longer take delight in things here below, seeing that we have a Father in heaven.

2. From *Reg. ep.* 7.23, 1–15 (CCSL 140:474–75)—I give great thanks to Almighty God that Your Excellency,[4] though placed in such a great tumult, is filled with the richness of the Sacred Word and sighs ceaselessly for eternal joys. For I see fulfilled in you what was written about the elect fathers: *The sons of Israel walked on dry land in the midst of the sea* [Exod 15:19]. But in contrast: *I have entered the waters of the deep, and the waves have overwhelmed me* [Ps 68:3]. I see that you walk with dry steps to the promised land in the midst of the waves of worldly affairs. Therefore, let us give thanks to the Spirit who lifts up the hearts that he fills, who produces a solitary place in the mind in the midst of the tumults of men, and in whose presence every place becomes conducive for a soul to feel com-

---

3. Compare B13 and W17.
4. The letter is addressed to Theoctista, the emperor's sister.

punction. For you breathe in the odor of eternal sweetness and hence love the Bridegroom of your soul with such ardor that you can say to him, along with the heavenly Bride: *Draw me! After you we shall run in the odor of your ointments* [Song 1:3].

Song 2:3. *I sat under the shadow of him whom I had desired.*

3. From *Mor.* 18.20 [32], 1–30 (CCSL 143A:906–7)—The mind of each one of the elect is cooled down when the heat of evil inclinations is extinguished therein and the flame of carnal desires grows cold. Hence the holy Church, praising her spouse, cries out with joy: *I sat under the shadow of him whom I had desired* [Song 2:3]. The Lord speaks to her about the abatement of this heat, making this promise through Isaiah: *Instead of the bramble shall come up the cypress tree, and instead of the nettle shall come up the myrtle tree* [Isa 55:13]. For 'instead of the bramble' there 'comes up' in her 'the cypress tree' when in the heart of the saints, instead of the lowness of earthly thought, the elevation of heavenly contemplation rises up. Now the 'nettle' is altogether of a fiery nature and the 'myrtle tree' is said to have the power to cool. Therefore, 'instead of the nettle' there 'comes up the myrtle tree' when the minds of the righteous are brought from the itching and heat of evil inclinations to a coolness and quietness of the thoughts, no longer seeking earthly things, extinguishing the flames of the flesh by heavenly desires.

Song 2:5b. *I have been wounded by love.*

4. From *Mor.* 34.10 [21], 1–11 (CCSL 143B:1746–47)—*The archer shall not put him to flight* [Job 41:19]. What do we understand by arrows, if not the words of preachers? When the voice of those of upright life launch them, they pierce the hearts of their hearers. The holy Church had been struck with these arrows when she said: *I have been wounded by love* [Song 2:5b]. These arrows are mentioned by the voice of the Psalmist: *Their wounds have been caused by the arrows of children* [Ps 63:8]. For clearly the words of the humble have penetrated the souls of the proud. These arrows are mentioned to the Champion who is to come: *Your arrows are sharp, almighty one, peoples shall fall under you in their heart* [Ps 44:6]. And so, the archer is the one who by aiming his bow at a holy target plants the words of upright exhortation in the hearts of his hearers.

Song 2:10-12. *Arise, make haste, my love, my beautiful one, and come! For now the winter is past, the rains are over and gone.*

5. From *Mor.* 29.30 [65], 180–91 (CCSL 143B:1480)—Frost and ice[5] can also designate the adversity of the present life, whose harshness oppresses the saints but makes them stronger thereby. For when Almighty God lets us be troubled by annoyances, and conveys us to a better life condition by the mediation of sadness, he is carrying out a marvelous plan through which he gives birth to frost and ice as well as future fruit. This he does so that each of the elect may endure the adversities of wind and cold in this life, as though he were in winter, and in the future, as if he were in the calm of summer, display the fruits which he has conceived here in this life. Hence it is said by the voice of the Bridegroom to every soul hastening from the whirlwinds of this world to the charming delights of eternity: *Arise, make haste, my love, my beautiful one, and come! For now the winter is past, the rains are over and gone* [Song 2:10-12].

Song 4:2. *Your teeth are like a flock of shorn sheep coming up from a washing.*

6. From *Mor.* 11.33 [45], 1–51 (CCSL 143A: 610–12)—In the Sacred Scriptures 'teeth' are usually taken to mean either the holy preachers or the interior senses. As for the holy preachers, it is said to the Bride: *Your teeth are like a flock of shorn sheep coming up from a washing* [Song 4:2]. Hence it is said to one of them (here the Gentiles are represented figuratively): *Kill and eat* [Acts 10:13]. In other words, "masticate their oldness and change it into the body of the Church, which is to say into your own members." Then again, Jeremiah testifies that 'teeth' are usually taken to mean the interior senses. For he says: *He broke my teeth one by one* [Lam 3:16]. Now the teeth break down food that it may be swallowed. Hence not unworthily do we take the 'teeth' as the interior senses, for in

---

5. See Job 38:29.

a certain sense they chew and chomp on every thought that occurs to the mind, and transfer all of them to the belly of the memory. The Prophet says that these teeth are 'broken one by one' because the senses become blind to understanding in proportion to the quantity of each particular sin. According to the quantity of exterior sins committed, each one loses perception of those interior and invisible truths which he could have understood.

Song 6:8. *One alone is my dove, my perfect one.*

7. From *Reg. ep.* 9.148, 69–85 (CCSL 140A:701) and *Reg. ep.* App. 10, 70–86 (CCSL 140A:1106–7)—Your Belovedness,[6] who are most sweet to me because you live an especially upright life in good conduct, because you afflict yourself through abstinence, because you are wholeheartedly devoted to the doctrine of God, must reflect on this matter with even greater attention,[7] lest by following the error of schismatics a church be found divided from the holy, universal Church. And what would so many toils have brought forth, if it were not found in the unity of the faith, which in particular keeps the soul in good deeds before the eyes of Almighty God? Hence it is said: *One alone is my dove, my perfect one.* Hence the Lord says to Moses: *There is a place near me, and you shall stand upon the rock* [Exod 33:21]. What place is there which is not in God, seeing that all things are held together by him through whom they were created? And yet there is a place within him, namely the unity of the holy Church, which is where one stands upon the rock, humbly planting one's feet on the solid foundation of the Church's confession. Regarding this place, it is added: *Then you shall see my backsides* [Exod 33:23]. For by standing on the rock, which is to say in the holy Church, we shall see the backsides of God, when we contemplate the joys of the heavenly homeland, which have been promised us at the end of time.

---

6. This excerpt is from a letter to Secundinus, an anchorite, whom Gregory addresses with the title of politeness, "Your Belovedness."
7. The matter is the Three Chapters controversy.

Song 7:4. *Your nose is like the tower which is in Lebanon.*

8. From *Reg. past.* 11, 27–33 (SChr 381:166)—We use our nose to discern pleasant scents and foul odors. Therefore, the nose rightly represents discernment, through which we choose virtues and avoid transgressions. Thus it is said in praise of the Bride: *Your nose is like the tower which is in Lebanon* [Song 7:4]. For surely the holy Church though discretion monitors the places where any sort of temptation may enter and from on high apprehends the approaching attacks of vices.

APPENDICES

Appendix One

Gregory's Citations of the Song of Songs

The following table lists each of Gregory's citations of the Song of Songs outside of the *Exposition* (which comments on Song 1:1-8). Those references to passages of Gregory's works marked by an asterisk (*) indicate places where Gregory alluded to, but did not cite, the Song of Songs. Cross-references to the collections of Paterius, Bede, and William are provided. When a Gregorian passage has not been included by any of the excerpters, the reference number to the appropriate supplemental text is given.

Song 1:1					
Mor. 27.17, 45	CCSL 143:1356	-	B1	W1	
Mor. 14.43, 9	CCSL 143:729	P1	B2	W2	
H.Ev. 33, 165–66	CCSL 141:294	P1	-	W3	
Mor. 30.13, 57–58	CCSL 143:1524	-	B3	W4	
Song 1:2					
Mor. 19.12, 13	CCSL 143:970	-	-	W5	
Mor. 24.4, 26	CCSL 143:1194	P2	B4	W5	
Song 1:3					
Mor. 34.17, 13–14	CCSL 143:1757	-	-	W6	
H.Ev. 29, 236–37	CCSL 141:254	-	-	-	Supp. 1
Reg. ep. 7.23, 14–15	CCSL 140A:475	-	-	-	Supp. 2
Song 1:4					
Mor. 18.30, 66–67	CCSL 143:917	-	B5	W7	

Song 1:5					
H.Ev. 17, 314–15	CCSL 141:128	P3	B6	W8	
Song 1:6					
Mor. 30.26, 32–33	CCSL 143:1546	P5	B7	W9	
H.Ev. 33, 191–92	CCSL 141:295	–	–	W9	
Song 1:7					
Mor. 16.44, 11–13	CCSL143:832	–	–	W10	
Mor. 30.17, 10–12	CCSL143:1529	P6	B8	W10	
Song 1:11					
Mor. 35.17, 33–34	CCSL 143:1804	P7	B9	W11	
Song 2:2					
H.Ev. 38, 171–72	CCSL 141:366	–	–	W12	
Mor. 1.1, 25–26	CCSL 143:25	–	–	W12	
Mor. 20.39, 37–38	CCSL 143:1059	–	–	W12	
Song 2:3					
Mor. 18.20, 19–20	CCSL 143:906	–	–	–	Supp. 3
Mor. 33.3, 17–18	CCSL 143:1673	–	–	W13	
Song 2:5					
H.Ez. 2.3, 171	CCSL 142:242	–	–	W15	
H.Ez. 2.3, 185–86	CCSL 142:242	P8	B10	W14	
Mor. 6.25, 20	CCSL 143:315	P9	B11	W15	
Mor. 34.10, 5	CCSL 143:1746	–	–	–	Supp. 4
H.Ev. 25, 66–67	CCSL 141:207	–	–	W15	
Song 2:6					
Reg. past. 3.26, 39–40	SChr 382:440	P10	B12	W16	
H.Ev. 21, 32–33	CCSL 141:174	–	–	W16	
Song 2:8					
H.Ev. 29, 227–28	CCSL 141:253	P11	B13	W17	
H.Ev. 29, 229	CCSL 141:253	P11	B13	W17	
Song 2:9					
H.Ev. 33, 190★	CCSL 141:295	–	–	W18	
H.Ez. 2.1, 457–58	CCSL 142:220	P12	B14	W19	
Mor. 18.48, 46	CCSL 143:942	–	–	W19	

Song 2:10-11					
Mor. 27.24, 72–73	CCSL 143:1365	P13	B15	W20	
Mor. 29.30, 190–91	CCSL 143:1480	–	–	–	Supp. 5
Song 2:11					
H.Ez. 2.4, 419★	CCSL 142:269	–	B16	W20	
Song 2:10-12					
H.Ez. 2.4, 414–16	CCSL 142:269	–	B16	W20	
Song 2:12					
H.Ez. 2.4, 428–29	CCSL 142:269	–	B16	W20	
Song 3:1					
H.Ev. 25, 36	CCSL 141:206	P15	B17	W21	
H.Ez. 2.7, 353–55	CCSL 142:325	P17	B19	W21	
Mor. 8.24, 7–8	CCSL 143:412	–	–	W21	
Mor. 27.2, 23–24	CCSL 143:1333	P20	–	W21	
Song 3:1-2					
H.Ev. 25, 32–35	CCSL 141:206	P15	B17	W21	
Song 3:3					
Mor. 27.2, 25	CCSL 143:1333	P20	–	W21	
Song 3:3-4					
H.Ev. 25, 37–40	CCSL 141:206	P15	B17	W21	
Mor. 18.49, 27–30	CCSL 143:944	P19	B18	W21	
Mor. 27.2, 27–29	CCSL 143:1333	P20	–	W21	
Song 3:4					
Mor. 18.49, 35–36	CCSL 143:944	P19	B18	W21	
Mor. 27.2, 44–45	CCSL 143:1333	P20	–	W21	
Song 3:6					
H.Ez. 2.10, 576–78	CCSL 142:396	–	B20	W22	
H.Ez. 2.10, 581	CCSL 142:396	–	B20	W22	
Mor. 1.36, 148–50	CCSL 143:57	P21	–	W22	
Song 3:7					
Mor. 7.21, 21–22	CCSL 143:349	–	B21	W23	

Song 3:8					
Mor. 19.30, 92–93	CCSL 143:1001	P22	B22	W24	
Mor. 20.3, 78–79	CCSL 143:1007	P23	B23	W25	
Reg. past. 3.32, 49–50	SChr 382:492	-	B24	W25	
Song 3:9-10					
H.Ez. 2.3, 277–79	CCSL 142:245	P24	B25	W26	
Song 3:10					
H.Ez. 2.3, 308	CCSL 142:246	P24	B25	W26	
H.Ez. 2.3, 327	CCSL 142:247	P24	B25	W26	
H.Ez. 2.3, 331	CCSL 142:247	P24	B25	W26	
Song 4:1					
Mor. 9.11, 160–62	CCSL 143:469	-	B26	W27	
Mor. 9.11, 170–71	CCSL 143:469	-	B26	W27	
Mor. 9.11, 175	CCSL 143:469	-	B26	W27	
Song 4:2					
Mor. 11.33, 5–6	CCSL 143:610	-	-	-	Supp. 6
Mor. 33.27, 8–9	CCSL 143:1714	P25	B27	W28	
Song 4:3					
Mor. 2.52, 4	CCSL 143:109	P26	B28	W29	
Song 4:4					
H.Ez. 2.3, 449–51	CCSL 142:251	-	B29	W30	
H.Ez. 2.3, 561–62	CCSL 142:254	-	B29	W30	
Song 4:5-6					
Mor. 24.8, 73–75	CCSL 143:1199	P27	B30	W31	
Song 4:6					
Mor. 24.8, 92–93	CCSL 143:1200	P27	B30	W31	
Song 4:8					
Mor. 17.32, 42–43	CCSL 143:882	P28	B31	W32	
Song 4:11					
Mor. 15.11, 13–14	CCSL 143:756	P30	B32	W33	
Song 4:16					
H.Ez. 1.2, 185–86	CCSL 142:22	-	-	W34	
Mor. 9.11, 128–29	CCSL 143:468	P31	-	W34	
Mor. 27.38, 10–11	CCSL 143:1381	-	B34	W34	

Song 5:2					
H.Ez. 2.2, 315	CCSL 142:234	P32	B35	W35	
Mor. 5.31, 16	CCSL 143:256	-	-	W35	
Mor. 5.31, 67★	CCSL 143:257	-	-	W35	
Mor. 23.20, 53–54	CCSL 143:1173	P33	B36	W35	
Song 5:4					
H.Ez. 2.7, 302–4	CCSL 143:323	P34	B37	W36	
Song 5:5					
H.Ev. 10, 121	CCSL 141:70	-	-	W37	
Song 5:6					
H.Ev. 25, 69	CCSL 141:207	-	B38	W38	
Mor. 4.33, 48–49	CCSL 143:210	P34B	-	W38	
Song 5:7					
Mor. 27.2, 26–27	CCSL 143:1332	P35	B39	W39	
Song 5:8 (See Song 2:5)					
Mor. 6.25, 20	CCSL 143:315	P9	B11	W15	
Mor. 34.10, 5	CCSL 143:1746	-	-	-	Supp. 4
Song 5:11					
Mor. 34.15, 7	CCSL 143:1752	P36	B40	W40	
Song 6:3					
H.Ez. 1.8, 135–36	CCSL 142:105	P37	B41	W41	
H.Ez. 1.8, 145–46	CCSL 142:105	P37	B41	W41	
H.Ez. 1.8, 169–70	CCSL 142:105	P37	B41	W41	
Song 6:6					
Reg. ep. 9.148, 76	CCSL 140A:701	-	-	-	Supp. 7
Reg. ep. App. 10, 77	CCSL 140A:1106	-	-	-	Supp. 7
H.Ez. 2.4, 253–54	CCSL 142:264	P38	B42	W42	
Song 6:9					
Mor. 4.11, 39–40	CCSL 143:176	P39	-	W43	
Mor. 16:63, 20–21	CCSL 143:844	-	-	W43	
Mor. 18.29, 9–10	CCSL 143:915	-	-	W43	
Mor. 29.2, 16–17	CCSL 143:1435	P40	B43	W43	

Song 7:4					
Mor. 31.44, 7–8	CCSL 143:1609	P41	B44	W44	
H.Ez. 1.11, 136	CCSL 142:172	P42	B45	W44	
Reg. past. 1.11, 30–31	SChr 381:166	-	-	-	Supp. 8
Reg. past. 3.32, 58–59	SChr 382:494	-	-	W44	
Song 7:12					
Mor. 12.53, 46–47	CCSL 143:666	P43	B46	W45	
Song 8:5					
Mor. 16.19, 18	CCSL 143:813	-	B47	W46	
Mor. 18.53, 9–10	CCSL 143:950	P44	B48	W47	
Song 8:6					
Mor. 29.6, 33–34	CCSL 143:1441	P45	B49	W48	
H.Ev. 11, 37–38	CCSL 141:75	P46	B50	W49	
Mor. 10.21, 22	CCSL 143:565	-	-	W49	
Song 8:8					
Mor. 19.12, 6	CCSL 143:970	P47	B51	W50	
Song 8:13					
Reg. past. 3.25, 68–69	SChr 382:432	-	-	W51	
H.Ez. 2.2, 94–95	CCSL 142:227	P48	B52	W51	
Song 8:14					
Mor. 17.27, 24	CCSL 143:874	P49	B53	W52	
Mor. 17.27, 29	CCSL 143:874	P49	B53	W52	

APPENDIX TWO

Table of Correspondences among Paterius, Bede, and William

The following table compares the excerpts of Paterius, Bede, and William of Saint Thierry. The first column has the excerpt signal, which indicates the compiler of the excerpt (P = Paterius; B = Bede; and W = William) and its number in his collection. The second column has the corresponding reference to the excerpter's text. The third column has the reference to the corresponding text in Gregory. In order to save space, the following abbreviations are used:

L = CCSL
M = CCCM

Song 1:1a		
P1.1	*Test.* 13.1 (PL 79:905b)	*Mor.* 14.34 [51], 9–11 (L 143:729)
P1.2	*Test.* 13.1 (PL 79:905b)	*H.Ev.* 33 [6], 166–67 (L 141:294)
B1.1	*Cant.* 6, 25–28 (L 119B:359)	*Mor.* 27.17 [34], 34–39 (L 143:1356)
B1.2	*Cant.* 6, 28–31 (L 119B:359)	*Mor.* 27.17 [34], 40–44 (L 143:1356)
B1.3	*Cant.* 6, 32 (L 119B:359)	*Mor.* 27.17 [34], 40 (L 143:1356)
B1.4	*Cant.* 6, 32–33 (L 119B:359)	*Mor.* 27.17 [34], 39–40 (L 143:1356)
B1.5	*Cant.* 6, 33–35 (L 119B:359)	*Mor.* 27.17 [34], 44–47 (L 143:1356)
B2	*Cant.* 6, 36–42 (L 119B:359–60)	*Mor.* 14.43 [51], 4–11 (L 143:728–29)
W1.1	*Exc.* 1, 3–7 (M 87:395)	*Mor.* 27.17 [34], 34–39 (L 143:1356)
W1.2	*Exc.* 1, 7 (M 87:395)	*Mor.* 27.17 [34], 40 (L 143:1356)
W1.3	*Exc.* 1, 7–8 (M 87:395)	*Mor.* 27.17 [34], 39–40 (L 143:1356)
W1.4	*Exc.* 1, 8–15 (M 87:395)	*Mor.* 27.17 [34], 40–47 (L 143:1356)
W2.1	*Exc.* 1, 16–18 (M 87:396)	*Mor.* 14.43 [51], 1–4 (L 143:728)
W2.2	*Exc.* 1, 18–20 (M 87:396)	*Mor.* 14.43 [51], 9–11 (L 143:729)

W2.3	*Exc.* 1, 20–23 (M 87:396)	*Mor.* 14.43 [51], 4–7 (L 143:728–29)
W3.1	*Exc.* 1, 24–25 (M 87:396)	*H.Ev.* 33 [5], 108–9 (L 141:292)
W3.2	*Exc.* 1, 25–28 (M 87:396)	*H.Ev.* 33 [6], 159–60 (L 141:294)
W3.3	*Exc.* 1, 28–30 (M 87:396)	*H.Ev.* 33 [6], 141–43 (L 141:293)
W3.4	*Exc.* 1, 31–33 (M 87:396)	*H.Ev.* 33 [5], 104–6 (L 141:292)
W3.5	*Exc.* 1, 33–37 (M 87:396)	*H.Ev.* 33 [6], 161–64 (L 141:294)
W3.6	*Exc.* 1, 37–38 (M 87:396)	*H.Ev.* 33 [6], 144–45 (L 141:293)
W3.7	*Exc.* 1, 38–40 (M 87:396)	*H.Ev.* 33 [6], 166–67 (L 141:294)
Song 1:1b		
B3	*Cant.* 6, 44–46 (L 119B:360)	*Mor.* 30.13 [48], 58–60 (L 143:1524)
W4	*Exc.* 1, 42–45 (M 87:396)	*Mor.* 30.13 [48], 58–60 (L 143:1524)[1]
Song 1:2c		
P2	*Test.* 13.2 (PL 79:905b)	*Mor.* 24.4 [8], 24–28 (L 143:1194)
B4	*Cant.* 6, 48–52 (L 119B:360)	*Mor.* 24.4 [8], 24–28 (L 143:1194)
W5.1	*Exc.* 1, 46–47 (M 87:397)	*Mor.* 24.4 [8], 24–25 (L 143:1194)
W5.2	*Exc.* 1, 49–52 (M 87:397)	*Mor.* 19.12 [19], 13–17 (L 143:970)
W5.3	*Exc.* 1, 53–56 (M 87:397)	*Mor.* 24.4 [8], 25–28 (L 143:1194)
Song 1:3b		
W6.1	*Exc.* 1, 58 (M 87:397)	*Mor.* 34.17 [32], 12–13 (L 143:1757)
W6.2	*Exc.* 1, 58–59 (M 87:397)	*Mor.* 34.17 [32], 11–12 (L 143:1757)
W6.3	*Exc.* 1, 59–61 (M 87:397)	*Mor.* 34.17 [32], 14–16 (L 143:1757)
Song 1:4a		
B5	*Cant.* 6, 54–58 (L 119B:360)	*Mor.* 18.30 [49], 64–68 (L 143:917)
W7.1	*Exc.* 1, 63–65 (M 87:397)	*Mor.* 18.38 [59], 9–12 (L 143:925)
W7.2	*Exc.* 1, 66–67 (M 87:397)	*Mor.* 18.30 [49], 64–65 (L 143:917)
W7.3	*Exc.* 1, 68–69 (M 87:397)	*Mor.* 18.30 [49], 67–68 (L 143:917)
Song 1:5de		
P3	*Test.* 13.3 (PL 79:905bc)	*H.Ev.* 17 [14], 315–18 (L 141:128)
B6	*Cant.* 6, 60–64 (L 119B:360)	*H.Ev.* 17 [14], 314–18 (L 141:128)
W8	*Exc.* 1, 72–94 (M 87:398)	*H.Ev.* 17 [14], 296–318 (L 141:128)
Song 1:6a		
P5[2]	*Test.* 13.5 (PL 79:905d)	*Mor.* 30.26 [79], 33–36 (L 143:1546)
B7	*Cant.* 6, 66–69 (L 119B:360)	*Mor.* 30.26 [79], 33–36 (L 143:1546)

1. See P29.

2. Raymond Étaix ("Le *Liber testimonium* de Paterius," *Revue des Sciences Religieuses* 32 [1958]: 74) suppresses P4 as inauthentic.

| W9.1 | Exc. 1, 97–100 (M 87:398) | Mor. 30.26 [79], 33–36 (L 143:1546) |
| W9.2 | Exc. 1, 101–13 (M 87:398–99) | H.Ev. 33 [7], 193–206 (L 141:295) |

Song 1:7

P6	Test. 13.6 (PL 79:906b)[3]	Mor. 30.17 [56], 12–22 (L 143:1529)
B8	Cant. 6, 72–80 (L 119B:360–61)	Mor. 30.17 [56], 12–22 (L 143:1529)
W10.1	Exc. 1, 116–18 (M 87:399)	Mor. 30.17 [56], 7–9 (L 143:1529)
W10.2	Exc. 1, 118–22 (M 87:399)	Mor. 16.44 [56], 11–16 (L 143A:832)
W10.3	Exc. 1, 122–23 (M 87:399)	Mor. 16.44 [56], 9–10 (L 143A:832)
W10.4	Exc. 1, 124, 33 (M 87:399)	Mor. 30.17 [56], 12–22 (L 143:1529)

Song 1:11

P7	Test. 13.7 (PL 79:906bc)	Mor. 35.17 [43], 34–41 (L 143:1804)
B9	Cant. 6, 82–93 (L 119B:361)	Mor. 35.17 [43], 29–41 (L 143:1804)
W11.1	Exc. 1, 136 (M 87:400)	Mor. 35.17 [43], 34 (L 143:1804)
W11.2	Exc. 1, 136–37 (M 87:400)	Mor. 35.17 [43], 31–33 (L 143:1804)
W11.3	Exc. 1, 137–43 (M 87:400)	Mor. 35.17 [43], 34–41 (L 143:1804)
W11.4	Exc. 1, 144–46 (M 87:400)	Mor. 35.17 [43], 28–31 (L 143:1804)

Song 2:2

W12.1	Exc. 2, 3–4 (M 87:400)	H.Ev. 38 [7], 163–64 (L 141:366)
W12.2	Exc. 2, 4–28 (M 87:400–401)	H.Ev. 38 [7], 141–63 (L 141:365–66)[4]
W12.3	Exc. 2, 28–32 (M 87:401)	H.Ev. 38 [7], 165–68 (L 141:366)
W12.4	Exc. 2, 32–36 (87:401)	Mor. 1.1 [1], 7–12 (L 143:25)
W12.5	Exc. 2, 36–37 (M 87:401)	H.Ev. 38 [7], 168–70 (L 141:366)[5]
W12.6	Exc. 2, 37–46 (M 87:401–2)	Mor. 1.1 [1], 12–20 (L 143:25)[6]
W12.7	Exc. 2, 46–47 (M 87:402)	Mor. 1.1 [1], 26–27 (L 143:25)
W12.8	Exc. 2, 47–48 (M 87:402)	Mor. 1.1 [1], 2–3 (L 143:25)
W12.9	Exc. 2, 48–49 (M 87:402)	Mor. 1.1 [1], 6 (L 143:25)
W12.10	Exc. 2, 49–50 (M 87:402)	Mor. 1.1 [1], 27–28 (L 143:25)
W12.11	Exc. 2, 50–52 (M 87:402)	H.Ev. 38 [7], 177–79 (L 143:366)

3. Étaix ("Le *Liber testimonium*," 74) suppresses the first few lines of P6 as inauthentic: *id est . . . imitare populorum* (PL 79: 905d–906a).

4. William follows the text of *H.Ev.*, but fills out the excerpt with lines from *Mor.* 20.39 [76], 20–32 (CCSL 143A.1059), which is a slightly more expanded version of the same text.

5. Compare *Mor.* 1.1 [1], 10–12 (CCSL 143: 25).

6. Compare *H.Ev.* 38 [7], 174–177 (CCSL 141: 366).

W12.12	*Exc.* 2, 53–54 (M 87:402)	*H.Ev.* 38 [7], 182–84 (L 143:366–67)
W12.13	*Exc.* 2, 55–61 (M 87:402)	*H.Ez.* 1.9 [22], 460–66 (L 142:135)[7]
W12.14	*Exc.* 2, 62–64 (M 87:402)	*H.Ev.* 38 [7], 184–86 (L 141:367)
W12.15	*Exc.* 2, 65–70 (M 87:402–3)	*H.Ez.* 1.9 [22–23], 473–79 (L 142:136)
W12.16	*Exc.* 2, 70–94 (M 87:402–3)	*H.Ez.* 1.9 [22–23], 480–504 (L 142:136)
W12.17	*Exc.* 2, 95–98 (M 87:403)	*Mor.* 20.39 [76], 33–36 (L 143:1059)
Song 2:3		
W13.1	*Exc.* 2, 100–103 (M 87:403)	*Mor.* 33.3 [5], 2–5 (L 143:1673)
W13.2	*Exc.* 2, 103–6 (M 87:403–4)	*Mor.* 33.3 [5], 15–18 (L 143: 1673–74)
W13.3	*Exc.* 2, 106–7 (M 87:404)	*Mor.* 33.3 [5], 14–15, (L 143:1673)
W13.4	*Exc.* 2, 107–8 (M 87:404)	*Mor.* 33.3 [5], 18–19 (L 143:1674)
W13.5	*Exc.* 2, 109–15 (M 87:404)	*Mor.* 33.3 [5], 7–13 (L 143:1673)
Song 2:5a		
P8	*Test.* 13.8 (PL 79:906c)	*H.Ez.* 2.3 [9], 186–95 (L 142:242–43)
B10.1	*Cant.* 6, 95–98 (L 119B:361)	*H.Ez.* 2.3 [9], 176–79 (L 142:242)
B10.2	*Cant.* 6, 98–108 (L 119B:361)	*H.Ez.* 2.3 [9], 184–95 (L 142:242–43)
W14	*Exc.* 2, 118–47 (M 87:404–5)	*H.Ez.* 2.3 [9–10], 176–207 (L 142:242–43)
Song 2:5b		
P9	*Test.* 13.9 (PL 79:906d–7a)	*Mor.* 6.25 [42], 20–39 (L 143:315)
B11	*Cant.* 6, 110–27 (L 119B:361–62)	*Mor.* 6.25 [42], 20–28 (L 143:315)
W15.1	*Exc.* 2, 149–50 (M 87:405)	*Mor.* 6.25 [42], 2–3 (L 143:314)
W15.2	*Exc.* 2, 150–67 (M 87:405–6)	*Mor.* 6.25 [42], 9–26 (L 143:315)
W15.3	*Exc.* 2, 168–74 (M 87:406)	*H.Ez.* 2.3 [8], 164–70 (L 142:242)
W15.4	*Exc.* 2, 174–77 (M 87:406)	*H.Ez.* 2.3 [8], 171–75 (L 142:242)
W15.5	*Exc.* 2, 178–79 (M 87:406)	*Mor.* 6.25 [42], 26–28 (L 143:315)
W15.6	*Exc.* 2, 180–88 (M 87:406)	*H.Ev.* 25 [2], 60–69 (L 141:207)

---

7. Though *H.Ez.* 1.9 [22–23] shares both theme and scriptural citations with the other texts excerpted for W12, it does not actually cite Song 2:2.

Song 2:6		
P10	*Test.* 13.10 (PL 79:907ab)	*Reg. past.* 3.26, 40–43 (SChr 382:440)
B12.1	*Cant.* 6, 119–22 (L 119B:362)	*Reg. past.* 3.26, 40–43 (SChr 382:440)
B12.2	*Cant.* 6, 122–26 (L 119B:362)	*Reg. past.* 3.26, 50–54 (SChr 382:442)
W16.1	*Exc.* 2, 191–97 (M 87:406–7)	*Reg. past.* 3.26, 32–40 (SChr 382:442)
W16.2	*Exc.* 2, 197–99 (M 87:407)	*H.Ev.* 21 [2], 30–32 (L 141:174)
W16.3	*Exc.* 2, 199–211 (M 87:407)	*Reg. past.* 3.26, 40–54 (SChr 382:442–43)
Song 2:8		
P11.1	*Test.* 13.11 (PL 79:907b)	*H.Ev.* 29 [10], 228–30 (L 141:253)
P11.2	*Test.* 13.11 (PL 79:907b)	*H.Ev.* 29 [10], 230–35 (L 141:253–54)
B13	*Cant.* 6, 128–35 (L 119B:362)	*H.Ev.* 29 [10], 229–37 (L 141:253–54)
W17	*Exc.* 2, 213–23 (M 87:407)	*H.Ev.* 29 [10–11], 229–39 (L 141:253–54)
Song 2:9a		
W18.1	*Exc.* 2, 225–26 (M 87:408)	*H.Ev.* 33 [7], 192–93 (L 141:295)
W18.2	*Exc.* 2, 116–28 (M 87:408)	William[8]
Song 2:9b		
P12	*Test.* 13.12 (PL 79:907c)	*H.Ez.* 2.1 [15], 450–67 (L 142:219–20)
B14	*Cant.* 6, 136–53 (L 119B:362–63)	*H.Ez.* 2.1 [15], 449–67 (L 142:219–20)
W19.1	*Exc.* 2, 231–37 (M 87:408)	*H.Ez.* 2.1 [15], 430–36 (L 142:219–20)
W19.2	*Exc.* 2, 237–46 (M 87:408)	*H.Ez.* 2.1 [15], 439–49 (L 142:219–20)
W19.3	*Exc.* 2, 246–51 (M 87:408)	*Mor.* 18.48 [78], 42–48 (L 143:942)
W19.4	*Exc.* 2, 251–68 (M 87:408–9)	*H.Ez.* 2.1 [15], 450–67 (L 142:219–20)

8. Gregory cites Rom 9:5 twice in *H.Ez.*, but neither passage seems to be William's source.

Song 2:10-12		
P13	*Test.* 13.13 (PL 79:907d)	*Mor.* 27.24 [45], 73–78 (L 143:1365–66)
B15	*Cant.* 6, 155–63 (L 119B:363)	*Mor.* 27.24 [45], 69–78 (L 143:1365–66)
B16	*Cant.* 6, 167–82 (L 119B:363)	*H.Ez.* 2.4 [15], 416–33 (L 142:269–70)
W20.1	*Exc.* 2, 272–83 (M 87:409)	*Mor.* 27.24 [45], 50–62 (L 143:1365)
W20.2	*Exc.* 2, 284–86 (M 87:410)	*Mor.* 27.24 [45], 69–71 (L 143:1365)
W20.3	*Exc.* 2, 286–87 (M 87:410)	*H.Ez.* 2.4 [15], 412–13 (L 142:269)
W20.4	*Exc.* 2, 287–89 (M 87:410)	*Mor.* 27.24 [45], 71–73 (L 143:1365)
W20.5	*Exc.* 2, 290–97 (M 87:410)	*H.Ez.* 2.4 [15], 416–23 (L 142:269)
W20.6	*Exc.* 2, 297–302 (M 87:410)	*Mor.* 27.24 [45], 73–78 (L 143:1365–66)
W20.7	*Exc.* 2, 302–11 (M 87:410)	*H.Ez.* 2.4 [15], 424–34 (L 142:269–70)

Song 3:1-4		
P15[9]	*Test.* 13.15 (PL 79:908ab)	*H.Ev.* 25 [2], 40–58 (L 141:206–7)
P17[10]	*Test.* 13.17 (PL 79:908cd)	*H.Ez.* 2.7 [11], 355–60 (L 142:325)
P18	*Test.* 13.18 (PL 79:908d)	*Mor.* 5.4 [6], 31–34 (L 143:223)
P19	*Test.* 13.19 (PL 79:908d–9a)	*Mor.* 18.49 [80], 30–41 (L 143:944)
P20	*Test.* 13.20 (PL 79:909ab)	*Mor.* 27.2 [4], 45–52 (L 143:1333)
B17	*Cant.* 6, 188–206 (L 119B:364)	*H.Ev.* 25 [2], 40–58 (L 141:206–7)
B18	*Cant.* 6, 207–11 (L 119B:364)	*Mor.* 18.49 [80], 33–37 (L 143:944)
B19	*Cant.* 6, 212–20 (L 119B:364)	*H.Ez.* 2.7 [11], 352–60 (L 142:325)
W21.1	*Exc.* 3, 7–8 (M 87:411)	*Mor.* 8.24 [41], 5–7 (L 143:412)
W21.2	*Exc.* 3, 9–10 (M 87:411)	*Mor.* 8.24 [41], 4–5 (L 143:412)
W21.3	*Exc.* 3, 10–13 (M 87:411)	*Mor.* 8.24 [41], 8–11 (L 143:412)
W21.4	*Exc.* 3, 13–14 (M 87:411)	*Mor.* 27.2 [4], 30–31 (L 143:1332)
W21.5	*Exc.* 3, 15–18 (M 87:411)	*H.Ev.* 25 [2], 40–43 (L 141:206)
W21.6	*Exc.* 3, 18–19 (M 87:411)	*Mor.* 27.2 [4], 32–33 (L 143:1332)
W21.7	*Exc.* 3, 19–21 (M 87:411)	*H.Ez.* 2.7 [11], 356–58 (L 142:325)

9. Étaix ("Le *Liber testimonium*," 74) suppresses P14 as inauthentic.
10. Étaix ("Le *Liber testimonium*," 74) suppresses P16 as inauthentic.

W21.8	*Exc.* 3, 21–22 (M 87:411)	*H.Ez.* 2.7 [11], 359–60 (L 142:325)
W21.9	*Exc.* 3, 22–24 (M 87:411)	*H.Ez.* 2.7 [11], 347–49 (L 142:325)
W21.10	*Exc.* 3, 24–25 (M 87:411)	*H.Ev.* 25 [2], 30–31 (L 141:206)
W21.11	*Exc.* 3, 25–28 (M 87:411)	*H.Ev.* 25 [2], 57–60 (L 141:207)
W21.12	*Exc.* 3, 29–32 (M 87:412)	*Mor.* 5.4 [6], 31–34 (L 143:223)
W21.13	*Exc.* 3, 32–38 (M 87:412)	*H.Ev.* 25 [2], 43–49 (L 141:206)
W21.14	*Exc.* 3, 38–39 (M 87:412)	*H.Ev.* 25 [2], 28–29 (L 141:206)
W21.15	*Exc.* 3, 39–42 (M 87:412)	*H.Ev.* 25 [2], 35–38 (L 141:206)
W21.16	*Exc.* 3, 43–45 (M 87:412)	*Mor.* 18.49 [80], 30–33 (L 143:944)
W21.17	*Exc.* 3, 46–47 (M 87:412)	*Mor.* 27.2 [4], 39–40 (L 143:1333)
W21.18	*Exc.* 3, 47–49 (M 87:412)	*H.Ev.* 25 [2], 50–52 (L 141:206)
W21.19	*Exc.* 3, 49–58 (M 87:412–13)	*Mor.* 18.49 [80], 33–41 (L 143:944)
W21.20	*Exc.* 3, 59–62 (M 87:413)	*Mor.* 27.2 [4], 45–49 (L 143:1333)
W21.21	*Exc.* 3, 62–64 (M 87:413)	*H.Ev.* 25 [2], 53–54 (L 141:206)
W21.22	*Exc.* 3, 64–65 (M 87:413)	*Mor.* 27.2 [4], 49–50 (L 143:1333)
W21.23	*Exc.* 3, 65–66 (M 87:413)	*Mor.* 18.49 [80], 34–35 (L 143:944)
W21.24	*Exc.* 3, 66–69 (M 87:413)	*H.Ev.* 25 [2], 54–57 (L 141:206–7)
W21.25	*Exc.* 3, 69–70 (M 87:413)	*Mor.* 27.2 [4], 51–52 (L 143:1333)
Song 3:6		
P21	*Test.* 13.21 (PL 79:909b)	*Mor.* 1.36 [55], 150–56 (L 143:57)
B20	*Cant.* 6, 223–50 (L 119B:364–65)	*H.Ez.* 2.10 [22–23], 578–606 (L 142:396–97)
W22.1	*Exc.* 3, 74–83 (M 87:413)	*H.Ez.* 2.10 [22], 575–88 (L 142:396)
W22.2	*Exc.* 3, 84–87 (M 87:414)	*Mor.* 1.36 [55], 150–54 (L 143:57)
W22.3	*Exc.* 3, 88–104 (M 87:414)	*H.Ez.* 2.10 [22–23], 588–606 (L 142:396–97)
W22.4	*Exc.* 3, 105–7 (M 87:414)	*Mor.* 1.36 [55], 154–56 (L 143:57)
W22.5	*Exc.* 3, 108–13 (M 87:414)	*H.Ez.* 2.10 [21], 569–74 (L 142:396)
Song 3:7		
B21.1	*Cant.* 6, 252–56 (L 119B:365)	*Mor.* 7.21 [24], 4–8 (L 143:349)
B21.2	*Cant.* 6, 256–57 (L 119B:365)	*Mor.* 7.21 [24], 21–22 (L 143:349)
B21.3	*Cant.* 6, 257–58 (L 119B:365)	*Mor.* 7.21 [24], 19–21 (L 143:349)
W23.1	*Exc.* 3, 116–17 (M 87:415)	*Mor.* 7.21 [24], 19–21 (L 143:349)
W23.2	*Exc.* 3, 117–18 (M 87:415)	*Mor.* 7.21 [24], 15–17 (L 143:349)
W23.3	*Exc.* 3, 119–22 (M 87:415)	*Mor.* 7.21 [24], 4–8 (L 143:349)
W23.4	*Exc.* 3, 122–26 (M 87:415)	*Mor.* 7.21 [25], 41–45 (L 143:350)

Song 3:8a		
P22	*Test.* 13.22 (PL 79:909c)	*Mor.* 19.30 [56], 93–102 (L 143:1001)
B22	*Cant.* 6, 260–67 (L 119B:365:66)	*Mor.* 19.30 [56], 93–101 (L 143:1001)
W24.1	*Exc.* 3, 128–30 (M 87:415)	*Mor.* 19.30 [56], 93–95 (L 143:1001)
W24.2	*Exc.* 3, 130 (M 87:415)	*Mor.* 19.30 [56], 91–92 (L 143:1001)
W24.3	*Exc.* 3, 130–37 (M 87:415)	*Mor.* 19.30 [56], 95–102 (L 143:1001)
Song 3:8b		
P23	*Test.* 13.23 (PL 79:909c–d)	*Mor.* 20.3 [8], 79–86 (L 143:1007–8)
B23	*Cant.* 6, 269–76 (L 119B:366)	*Mor.* 20.3 [8], 79–87 (L 143:1007–8)
B24	*Cant.* 6, 278–83 (L 119B:366)	*Reg. past.* 3.32, 50–58 (SChr 382:492–94)
W25.1	*Exc.* 3, 140 (M 87:416)	*Reg. past.* 3.32, 48–49 (SChr 382:492)
W25.2	*Exc.* 3, 140–42 (M 87:416)	*Reg. past.* 3.32, 50–52 (SChr 382:492)
W25.3	*Exc.* 3, 143–44 (M 87:416)	*Mor.* 20.3 [8], 80–81 (L 143:1007)
W25.4	*Exc.* 3, 144–45 (M 87:416)	*Mor.* 20.3 [8], 79–80 (L 143:1007)
W25.5	*Exc.* 3, 146–50 (M 87:416)	*Reg. past.* 3.32, 52–58 (SChr 382:492–94)
W25.6	*Exc.* 3, 151–54 (M 87:416)	*Mor.* 20.3 [8], 84–87 (L 143:1008)
W25.7	*Exc.* 3, 154–56 (M 87:416)	*Mor.* 20.3 [8], 81–84 (L 143:1007–8)
Song 3:9–10		
P24.1	*Test.* 13.24 (PL 79:909d–910b)	*H.Ez.* 2.3 [13–14], 280–300 (L 142:245–46)
P24.2	*Test.* 13.24 (PL 79:910b–d)	*H.Ez.* 2.3 [14–15], 306–39 (L 142:246–47)
B25.1	*Cant.* 6, 287–305 (L 119B:366–67)	*H.Ez.* 2.3 [13–14], 280–300 (L 142:245–46)
B25.2	*Cant.* 6, 305–32 (L 119B:367)	*H.Ez.* 2.3 [14–15], 306–33 (L 142:246–47)
W26	*Exc.* 3, 161–215 (M 87:417–18)	*H.Ez.* 2.3 [13–15], 280–338 (L 142:245–47)

Song 4:1		
B26	*Cant.* 6, 325–33 (L 119B:367)	*Mor.* 9.11 [18], 162–72 (L 143:469)
W27.1	*Exc.* 4, 4–14 (M 87:419)	*Mor.* 9.11 [18], 162–72 (L 143:469)
W27.2	*Exc.* 4, 14–17 (M 87:419)	*Mor.* 9.11 [18], 157–59 (L 143:469)

Song 4:2		
P25	*Test.* 13.25 (PL 79:910d)	*Mor.* 33.27 [47], 6–7 (L 143:1714)
B27.1	*Cant.* 6, 335–37 (L 119B:367)	*Mor.* 33.27 [47], 6–7 (L 143:1714)
B27.1	*Cant.* 6, 337–39 (L 119B:367)	*Mor.* 33.27 [47], 9–12 (L 143:1714)
W28.1	*Exc.* 4, 20–21 (M 87:419)	*Mor.* 33.27 [47], 6–7 (L 143:1714)
W28.2	*Exc.* 4, 21–24 (M 87:419)	*Mor.* 33.27 [47], 9–12 (L 143:1714)
Song 4:3		
P26	*Test.* 13.26 (PL 79:910d–11a)	*Mor.* 2.52 [82], 5–16 (L 143:109)
B28	*Cant.* 6, 341–47 (L 119B:368)	*Mor.* 2.52 [82], 5–12 (L 143:109)
W29.1	*Exc.* 4, 26 (M 87:419)	*Mor.* 2.52 [82], 5 (L 143:109)
W29.2	*Exc.* 4, 26–27 (M 87:419)	*Mor.* 2.52 [82], 2–3 (L 143:109)
W29.3	*Exc.* 4, 27–35 (M 87:419–20)	*Mor.* 2.52 [82], 5–12 (L 143:109)
Song 4:4		
B29.1	*Cant.* 6, 350–55 (L 119B:368)	*H.Ez.* 2.3 [19–20], 451–58 (L 142:251)
B29.2	*Cant.* 6, 355–58 (L 119B:368)	*H.Ez.* 2.3 [20], 484–87 (L 142:252)
B29.3	*Cant.* 6, 358–62 (L 119B:368)	*H.Ez.* 2.3 [22], 566–70 (L 142:254)
B29.4	*Cant.* 6, 362–69 (L 119B:368)	*H.Ez.* 2.3 [23], 576–85 (L 142:254–55)
B29.5	*Cant.* 6, 369–72 (L 119B:368)	*H.Ez.* 2.3 [23], 591–95 (L 142:255)
B29.6	*Cant.* 6, 372–76 (L 119B:368)	*H.Ez.* 2.3 [23], 597–602 (L 142:255)
W30.1	*Exc.* 4, 39–186 (M 87:420–24)	*H.Ez.* 2.3 [19–23], 451–606 (L 142:251–55)
W30.2	*Exc.* 4, 187–94 (M 87:424)	*H.Ez.* 2.3 [18–19], 441–48 (L 142:251–52)
Song 4:5		
P27	*Test.* 13.27 (PL 79:911a–c)	*Mor.* 24.8 [15], 75–106 (L 143:1199–1200)
B30	*Cant.* 6, 380–403 (L 119B:369)	*Mor.* 24.8 [15], 75–100 (L 143:1199–1200)

W31.1	Exc. 4, 198–99 (M 87:425)	Mor. 24.8 [15], 52–54 (L 143:1199)
W31.2	Exc. 4, 199–201 (M 87:425)	Mor. 24.8 [16], 70–71 (L 143:1199)
W31.3	Exc. 4, 201–32 (M 87:425–26)	Mor. 24.8 [17], 75–106 (L 143:1199–1200)
W31.4	Exc. 4, 232–35 (M 87:426)	Mor. 24.8 [18], 123–26 (L 143:1201)

Song 4:8

P28	Test. 13.28 (PL 79:911d)	Mor. 17.32 [52], 43–51 (L 143:882–83)
B31	Cant. 6, 405–12 (L 119B:369)	Mor. 17.32 [52], 43–51 (L 143:882–83)
W32.1	Exc. 4, 238–40 (M87:426)	Mor. 17.32 [52], 41–45 (L 143:882–83)
W32.2	Exc. 4, 240–46 (M 87:426)	Mor. 17.32 [51], 12–18 (L 143:882)
W32.3	Exc. 4, 246–52 (M 87:426)	Mor. 17.32 [52], 45–51 (L 143:883)

Song 4:10

P29	Test. 13.29 (PL 79:911d–12a)	Mor. 30.13 [48], 58–60 (L 143:1524)[11]

Song 4:11

P30	Test. 13.30 (PL 79:912ab)[12]	Mor. 15.11 [13], 14–22 (L 143:756)
B32	Cant. 6, 414–23 (L 119B:369–70)	Mor. 15.11 [13], 10–20 (L 143:755–56)
W33.1	Exc. 4, 254–56 (M 87:426)	Mor. 15.11 [13], 10–12 (L 143:755–56)
W33.2	Exc. 4, 257–65 (M 87:426–27)	Mor. 15.11 [13], 14–22 (L 143:756)

Song 4:13

B33	Cant. 6, 425–28 (L 119B:370)	Reg. past. 2.4, 72–76 (SChr 381:192)[13]

---

11. Though Paterius excerpts this text for Song 4:10, it actually cites Song 1:1. See B3 and W4.

12. Étaix ("Le *Liber testimonium*," 74) suppresses the following lines of P30 as inauthentic: *sicut plerique . . . lingua tua* (PL 79:912a).

13. See Gregory, *Reg. ep.* 1.24, which has the same text.

Song 4:16		
P31	Test. 13.31 (PL 79:913bc)[14]	Mor. 9.11 [17], 125–49 (L 143:468)
B34	Cant. 6, 430–39 (L 119B:370)	Mor. 27.38 [63], 6–17 (L 143:1381)
W34.1	Exc. 4, 268–71 (M 87:427)	H.Ez. 1.2 [9], 176–80 (L 142:22)
W34.2	Exc. 4, 271–72 (M 87:427)	H.Ez. 1.2 [9], 183–84 (L 142:22)
W34.3	Exc. 4, 272–75 (M 87:427)	Mor. 27.38 [63], 6–9 (L 143:1380–81)
W34.4	Exc. 4, 275–76 (M 87:427)	Mor. 9.11 [17], 126–27 (L 143:468)
W34.5	Exc. 4, 276–77 (M 87:427)	Mor. 27.38 [63], 11–13 (L 143:1381)
W34.6	Exc. 4, 278–80 (M 87:427)	H.Ez. 1.2 [9], 186–90 (L 142:22)
W34.7	Exc. 4, 280–83 (M 87:427)	Mor. 9.11 [17], 133–35 (L 143:468)
W34.8	Exc. 4, 280–87 (M 87:427)	H.Ez. 1.2 [9], 189–93 (L 142:22)
W34.9	Exc. 4, 287–89 (M 87:427)	Mor. 27.38 [63], 15–17 (L 143:1381)

Song 5:2		
P32	★[15]	H.Ez. 2.2 [13–14], 315–24 (L 142:234)
P33	Test. 13.33 (PL 79:913a)[16]	Mor. 23.20 [38], 54–57 (L 143:1173)
B35	Cant. 6, 441–47 (L 119B:370)	H.Ez. 2.2 [13–14], 310–17 (L 142:234)
B36	Cant. 6, 448–52 (L 119B:370)	Mor. 23.20 [38], 54–57 (L 143:1173)
W35.1	Exc. 5, 3–14 (M 87:428)	Mor. 5.31 [54], 5–16 (L 143:255–56)
W35.2	Exc. 5, 15–18 (M 87:428)	Mor. 23.20 [38], 54–57 (L 143:1173)
W35.3	Exc. 5, 18–21 (M 87:428)	Mor. 5.31 [54], 16–19 (L 143:256)
W35.4	Exc. 5, 22–23 (M 87:428)	H.Ez. 2.2 [13–14], 315–17 (L 142:234)
W35.5	Exc. 5, 24–26 (M 87:428)	Mor. 5.31 [54], 2–4 (L 143:255)
Song 5:4		
P34	Test. 13.34 (PL 79:913ab)	H.Ez. 2.7 [10], 304–12 (L 142:323–24)

14. Étaix ("Le *Liber testimonium*," 74) adds lines from the *Moralia* (*Mor.* 9.11 [17], 135–49 [CCSL 143:468]) to the text of P31 (PL 79:912c).

15. Étaix ("Le *Liber testimonium*," 74) replaces the text of *Test.* 13.32 with *H.Ez.* 2.2 [13–14], 315–24 (CCSL 142:234).

16. Étaix ("Le *Liber testimonium*," 75) suppresses the following lines of P33 as inauthentic: *qui exterioribus . . . ac si diceret* (PL 79:912d–13a).

B37	*Cant.* 6, 455–61 (L 119B:371)	*H.Ez.* 2.7 [10], 304–10 (L 142:323–24)
W36.1	*Exc.* 5, 29 (M 87:429)	*H.Ez.* 2.7 [10], 291–92 (L 142:323)
W36.2	*Exc.* 5, 29–31 (M 87:429)	*H.Ez.* 2.7 [10], 289–91 (L 142:323)
W36.3	*Exc.* 5, 31–50 (M 87:429)	*H.Ez.* 2.7 [10], 293–312 (L 142:323–24)
Song 5:5		
W37.1	*Exc.* 5, 53–54 (M 87:429)	*H.Ev.* 10 [6], 120–21 (L 141:70)
W37.2	*Exc.* 5, 54–55 (M 87:429)	*H.Ev.* 10 [6], 119 (L 141:70)
W37.3	*Exc.* 5, 55–57 (CCSM 87:429–30)	William
W37.4	*Exc.* 5, 57–66 (M 87:430)	*H.Ev.* 10 [6], 125–33 (L 141:70–71)
Song 5:6		
P34B	★[17]	*Mor.* 4.33 [67], 49–53 (L 143:210)
B38	*Cant.* 6, 463–72 (L 119B:371)	*H.Ev.* 25 [2], 70–80 (L 141:207)
W38.1	*Exc.* 5, 68–69 (M 87:430)	*H.Ev.* 25 [2], 70–71 (L 141:207)
W38.2	*Exc.* 5, 69–71 (M 87:430)	*Mor.* 4.33 [67], 49–51 (L 143:210)
W38.3	*Exc.* 5, 71–73 (M 87:430)	*H.Ev.* 25 [2], 71–73 (L 141:207)
W38.4	*Exc.* 5, 73–74 (M 87:430)	*Mor.* 4.33 [67], 43–45 (L 143:210)
W38.5	*Exc.* 5, 74–81 (M 87:430)	*H.Ev.* 25 [2], 73–80 (L 141:207)
Song 5:7[18]		
P35	★[19]	*Mor.* 27.2 [4], 39–44 (L 143:1333)
B39	*Cant.* 6, 475–81 (L 119B:371)	*Mor.* 27.2 [4], 37–44 (L 143:1333)
W39	*Exc.* 5, 86–97 (M 87:431)	*Mor.* 27.2 [4], 32–44 (L 143:1332–33)

17. Étaix ("Le *Liber testimonium*," 75) adds an additional excerpt between *Test.* 13.34 and 13.35.

18. At *Mor.* 27.2 [3], 22–29 (CCSL 143:1332), Gregory cites Song 3:1; 3:3; 5:7; 3:3-4 in succession. The following commentary by Gregory (*Mor.* 27.2 [4], 30–62 [CCSL 143:1332–33]) was mined by both Paterius and William for the excerpt on Song 3:1-4; see P20 and W21. But all three excerpters also recognized that Gregory also cited Song 5:7. Accordingly, they excerpted the same text for this verse.

19. Étaix ("Le *Liber testimonium*," 75) replaces the text of *Test.* 13.35 with *Mor.* 27.2 [4], 39–44 (CCSL 143:1333).

Song 5:11		
P36	*Test.* 13.36 (PL 79:913c)[20]	*Mor.* 34.15 [26], 7–10 (L 143:1752–53)
B40	*Cant.* 6, 483–85 (L 119B:371)	*Mor.* 34.15 [26], 7–10 (L 143:1752)
W40.1	*Exc.* 5, 99–100 (M 87:431)	*Mor.* 34.15 [26], 5–7 (L 143:1752)
W40.2	*Exc.* 5, 100–103 (M 87:431)	*Mor.* 34.15 [26], 7–10 (L 143:1752)

Song 6:3		
P37	*Test.* 13.37 (PL 79:914a–c)	*H.Ez.* 1.8 [6–7], 136–72 (L 142:105)
B41	*Cant.* 6, 488–508 (L 119B:371–72)	*H.Ez.* 1.8 [6], 136–59 (L 142:105)
W41.1	*Exc.* 6, 4 (M 87:432)	*H.Ez.* 1.8 [6], 133–34 (L 142:104–6)
W41.2	*Exc.* 6, 5–68 (M 87:432–33)	*H.Ez.* 1.8 [6–9], 136–202 (L 142:104–6)
W41.3	*Exc.* 6, 68–69 (M 87:433–34)	William
W41.4	*Exc.* 6, 69 (M 87:434)	*H.Ez.* 1.8 [9], 203 (L 142:106)
W41.5	*Exc.* 6, 69–71 (M 87:434)	*H.Ez.* 1.8 [6], 132–33 (L 142:104)[21]
W41.6	*Exc.* 6, 71–73 (M 87:434)	*H.Ez.* 1.8 [9], 203–6 (L 142:106)

Song 6:6		
P38	*Test.* 13.38 (PL 79:914d)[22]	*H.Ez.* 2.4 [8], 254–65 (L 142:264)
B42	*Cant.* 6, 510–20 (L 119B:372)	*H.Ez.* 2.4 [8], 254–65 (L 142:264)
W42.1	*Exc.* 6, 76 (M 87:434)	*H.Ez.* 2.4 [8], 254 (L 142:264)
W42.2	*Exc.* 6, 77–79 (M 87:434)	*H.Ez.* 2.4 [8], 245–48 (L 142:264)
W42.3	*Exc.* 6, 79 (M 87:434)	*H.Ez.* 2.4 [8], 255 (L 142:264)
W42.4	*Exc.* 6, 79–80 (M 87:434)	*H.Ez.* 2.4 [8], 248–49 (L 142:264)
W42.5	*Exc.* 6, 80–90 (M 87:434)	*H.Ez.* 2.4 [8], 255–65 (L 142:264)

20. Étaix ("Le *Liber testimonium*," 75) retains only the following lines of P36 as authentic: *quia caput Christi . . . principatur* (PL 79:913c). He suppresses the remainder of P36 as inauthentic.

21. William alters this text considerably.

22. Étaix ("Le *Liber testimonium*," 75) adds *H.Ez.* 2.4 [8], 259–65 to the text of P38 at PL 79:914d.

Song 6:9		
P39	Test. 13.39 (PL 79:914d–15b)[23]	Mor. 4.11 [19], 40–58 (L 143:176–77)
P40	Test. 13.40 (PL 79:915b)	Mor. 29.2 [2], 17–28 (L 143:1435)
B43	Cant. 6, 522–31 (L 119B:372–73)	Mor. 29.2 [2], 17–28 (L 143:1435)
W43.1	Exc. 6, 93 (M 87:434)	Mor. 18.29 [46], 10 (L 143:915)
W43.2	Exc. 6, 93 (M 87:434)	Mor. 4.11 [19], 38–39 (L 143:176)
W43.3	Exc. 6, 93–94 (M 87:434)	Mor. 18.29 [46], 10–11 (L 143:915)
W43.4	Exc. 6, 94–95 (M 87:434)	Mor. 16.63 [77], 18–19 (L 143:844)
W43.5	Exc. 6, 95–96 (M 87:434)	Mor. 18.29 [46], 11–12 (L 143:915)
W43.6	Exc. 6, 97–101 (M 87:434–35)	Mor. 29.2 [2], 11–15 (L 143:1435)
W43.7	Exc. 6, 101–3 (M 87:435)	Mor. 29.2 [2], 17–19 (L 143:1435)
W43.8	Exc. 6, 103–5 (M 87:435)	Mor. 4.11 [19], 41–42 (L 143:177)
W43.9	Exc. 6, 106–31 (M 87:435)	Mor. 29.2 [3–4], 20–48 (L 143:1435–36)
W43.10	Exc. 6, 131–33 (M 87:435–36)	Mor. 29.2 [4], 53–55 (L 143:1436)
W43.11	Exc. 6, 133–36 (M 87:436)	Mor. 29.2 [4], 51–53 (L 143:1436)
W43.12	Exc. 6, 136–42 (M 87:436)	Mor. 29.2 [4], 56–63 (L 143:1436)
W43.13	Exc. 6, 142–48 (M 87:436)	Mor. 29.2 [4], 74–79 (L 143:1436–37)
W43.14	Exc. 6, 149–51 (M 87:436)	William
W43.15	Exc. 6, 152–67 (M 87:436)	Mor. 4.11 [19], 43–59 (L 143:177)

Song 7:4		
P41	Test. 13.41 (PL 79:915c)	Mor. 31.44 [85], 8–15 (L 143:1609)
P42	Test. 13.42 (PL 79:915d)	H.Ez. 1.11 [7], 138–48 (L 142:172)
B44	Cant. 6, 533–39 (L 119B:373)	Mor. 31.44 [85], 8–15 (L 143:1609)
B45	Cant. 6, 540–54 (L 119B:373)	H.Ez. 1.11 [7], 133–48 (L 142:172)
W44.1	Exc. 7, 3–4 (M 87:437)	H.Ez. 1.11 [7], 136–37 (L 142:172)
W44.2	Exc. 7, 4–5 (M 87:437)	Reg. past. 3.32, 59–60 (SChr 382:494)

23. Étaix ("Le *Liber testimonium*," 75) suppresses the following lines of P39 as inauthentic: *aurora ecclesia . . . quasi aurora consurgens* (PL 79:915a).

W44.3	Exc. 7, 5–7 (M 87:437)	Reg. past. 3.32, 60–63 (SChr 382:494)[24]
W44.4	Exc. 7, 7–13 (M 87:437)	Mor. 31.44 [85], 10–15 (L 143:1609)
W44.5	Exc. 7, 14–20 (M 87:437)	Reg. past. 3.32, 63–70 (SChr 382:494)
W44.6	Exc. 7, 21 (M 87:437)	Reg. past. 3.32, 63 (SChr 382:494)
W44.7	Exc. 7, 22–30 (M 87:437)	H.Ez. 1.11 [7], 140–48 (L 142:172)
W44.8	Exc. 7, 30–31 (M 87:437)	H.Ez. 1.11 [7], 123–24 (L 142:172)
W44.9	Exc. 7, 31–33 (M 87:437–38)	H.Ez. 1.11 [7], 126–29 (L 142:172)
W44.10	Exc. 7, 33–35 (M 87:438)	H.Ez. 1.11 [7], 124–26 (L 142:172)

Song 7:12		
P43	Test. 13.43 (PL 79:915d–16a)[25]	Mor. 12.53 [60–61], 47–53 (L 143:666)
B46	Cant. 6, 556–61 (L 119B:373)	Mor. 12.53 [60–61], 47–53 (L 143:666)
W45.1	Exc. 7, 38–45 (M 87:438)	Mor. 12.53 [60–61], 47–55 (L 143:666)
W45.2	Exc. 7, 46–72 (M 87:438–39)	Mor. 12.53 [60], 10–38 (L 143:665)
W45.3	Exc. 7, 72–74 (M 87:439)	Mor. 12.53 [61], 63–65 (L 143:666)

Song 8:5		
B47	Cant. 6, 563–67 (L 119B:373)	Mor. 16.19 [24], 18–22 (L 143:813)
W46.1	Exc. 8, 4–7 (M 87:439)	Mor. 16.19 [24], 19–22 (L 143:813)
W46.2	Exc. 8, 7–21 (M 87:439–40)	Mor. 16.19 [24], 2–17 (L 143:812–13)
W46.3	Exc. 8, 22–27 (M 87:440)	Mor. 16.19 [24], 22–28 (L 143:813)
Song 8:5 (LXX)		
P44	Test. 13.44 (PL 79:916a)	Mor. 18.53 [87], 10–13 (L 143:950)
B48	Cant. 6, 569–72 (L 119B:374)	Mor. 18.53 [87], 10–13 (L 143:950)
W47.1	Exc. 8, 29–31 (M 87:440)	Mor. 18.53 [87], 10–13 (L 143:950)

24. Compare *Mor.* 31.44 [85], 8–10 (CCSL 143B:1609) and *H.Ez.* 1.11 [7], 137–39 (CCSL 142:172), which are basically the same.

25. Étaix ("Le *Liber testimonium*," 75) suppresses the following lines of P43 as inauthentic: *unde fit . . . ammittur* (PL 79:915a).

W47.2	Exc. 8, 32–35 (M 87:440)	★[26]
W47.3	Exc. 8, 36–42 (M 87:440)	Mor. 18.53 [87], 1–8 (L 143:950)
W47.4	Exc. 8, 42–49 (M 87:440)	Mor. 18.53 [87], 17–24 (L 143:950)
Song 8:6a		
P45	Test. 13.45 (PL 79:916b)	Mor. 29.6 [12], 34–39 (L 143:1441)
B49	Cant. 6, 574–79 (L 119B:374)	Mor. 29.6 [12], 34–39 (L 143:1441)
W48.1	Exc. 8, 50–54 (M 87:441)	Mor. 29.6 [12], 28–32 (L 143:1440–41)
W48.2	Exc. 8, 54–59 (M 87:441)	Mor. 29.6 [12], 34–39 (L 143:1441)
Song 8:6b		
P46	Test. 13.46 (PL 79:916b)	H.Ev. 11 [2], 28–41 (L 141:75)
B50	Cant. 6, 581–83 (L119B:374)	H.Ev. 11 [2], 38–41 (L 141:75)
W49.1	Exc. 8, 61 (M 87:441)	Mor. 10.21 [39], 21 (L 143:565)
W49.2	Exc. 8, 62 (M 87:441)	Mor. 10.21 [39], 23 (L 143:565)
W49.3	Exc. 8, 62–63 (M 87:441)	H.Ev. 11 [2], 38–39 (L 141:75)
W49.4	Exc. 8, 63–64 (M 87:441)	Mor. 10.21 [39], 24 (L 143:565)
W49.5	Exc. 8, 64–67 (M 87:441)	H.Ev. 11 [2], 39 (L 141:75)
W49.6	Exc. 8, 68–69 (M 87:441)	Mor. 10.21 [39], 25–26 (L 143:565)
W49.7	Exc. 8, 69–72 (M 87:441)	Mor. 10.21 [39], 7–10 (L 143:565)
W49.8	Exc. 8, 72–77 (M 87:441)	Mor. 10.21 [39], 15–20 (L 143:565)
Song 8:8		
P47	Test. 13.47 (PL 79:916c)	Mor. 19.12 [19], 6–12 (L 143:970)
B51	Cant. 6, 585–97 (L 119B:374)	Mor. 19.12 [19], 2–17 (L 143:970)
W50.1	Exc. 8, 79–81 (M 87:442)	Mor. 19.12 [19], 2–5 (L 143:970)
W50.2	Exc. 8, 81–86 (M 87:442)	Mor. 19.12 [19], 6–12 (L 143:970)
Song 8:13		
P48	Test. 13.48 (PL 79:916cd)	H.Ez. 2.2 [4], 96–106 (L 142:227)
B52	Cant. 6, 599–608 (L 119B:374–75)	H.Ez. 2.2 [4], 95–106 (L 142:227)
W51.1	Exc. 8, 89–91 (M 87:442)	Reg. past. 3.25, 69–70 (SChr 382:432)
W51.2	Exc. 8, 92–100 (M 87:442)	H.Ez. 2.2 [4], 95–104 (L 142:227)

26. W47.2 is a combination of Mor. 18.52 [86], 88–89; 18.53 [87], 2–3; and 18.53 [87], 17–18 (CCSL 143A:949–50).

W51.3	Exc. 8, 101–2 (M 87:442)	Reg. past. 3.25, 72–74 (SChr 382:432)
W51.4	Exc. 8, 103–4 (M 87:442)	H.Ez. 2.2 [4], 104–6 (L 142:227)
W51.5	Exc. 8, 104–5 (M 87:442)	Reg. past. 3.25, 71–72 (SChr 382:432)
W51.6	Exc. 8, 105–13 (M 87:442–43)	H.Ez. 2.2 [4], 87–94 (L 142:227)

Song 8:14

P49	Test. 13.49 (PL 79:916d)	Mor. 17.27 [39], 24–32 (L 143:874)
B53	Cant. 6, 609–16 (L 119B:375)	Mor. 17.27 [39], 24–32 (L 143:874)
W52.1	Exc. 8, 114–21 (M 87:443–44)	Mor. 17.27 [39], 24–32 (L 143:874)
W52.2	Exc. 8, 122–35 (M 87:443–44)	Mor. 17.27 [39], 9–23 (L 143:873–74)
W52.3	Exc. 8, 136 (M 87:443–44)	Mor. 17.27 [39], 33 (L 143:874)
W52.4	Exc. 8, 136–38 (M 87:443–44)	Mor. 17.27 [39], 3–4 (L 143:873)
W52.5	Exc. 8, 138–58 (M 87:443–44)	H.Ev. 29 [11], 238–56 (L 141:254)

Appendix Three

Textual Notes on Gregory the Great's *Exposition on the Song of Songs*

The emendations employed in the translation found in this volume are presented below. The first column refers to the line number of Verbraken's edition.

Line #	Verbraken's Reading	Adopted Reading	Source
10	*infidelitatis*	*insensibilitatis*	Meyvaert/ Bélanger
14	*positae*	*infra positae*	Meyvaert
18	*separatur a terra*	*sperantur aeterna*	Meyvaert
45	*nuptiali, necesse est : ne, si*	*nuptiali. Necesse est, ne, si*	Waszink/ Bélanger
59	*utilis*	*utile*	Bélanger
109	*cum verba dei*	*cum verba dei audirent*	Meyvaert/ Bélanger
143	*figuram*	*figurate*	Meyvaert/ Bélanger
257	*per prophetarum*	*per ora prophetarum*	Meyvaert
268	*eum videre*	*eum subito videre*	Meyvaert/ Bélanger

306	unaquaeque	unaquaque	Waszink/Bélanger
321	humilliae incarnationis eius	humilliae praedictiones incarnationis eius	Meyvaert/Bélanger
326–27	humillimam praedictionis dominicae incarnationem	humillimam praedictionem dominicae incarnationis	Bélanger[1]
349	domino	deo	Meyvaert
351	proficit	prope fit	Meyvaert
371	suadenti is	sua danti is	Bélanger
485	et nonnulli	sed nonnulli	Meyvaert
512	tenditur	extenditur	Meyvaert
562	adherentium	adherentes	Bélanger
675–76	conversam . . . vocatam	conversa . . . vocata	Bélanger
680	quid facta est	considerat quid facta est	Meyvaert
685	cedar	cedar quippe	Meyvaert
722–23	mala mea	malis meis	Waszink/Bélanger
725	afferent	afferem	Meyvaert
810	~	Id est	Meyvaert
835	egredere id est exi	egredere id est foras exi	Meyvaert

I have rejected one of the punctuation changes that Bélanger adopted based on the suggestion of Waszink (*vocatur, ac si ei dicatur* for *vocatur. Ac si ei dicatur* at line 545) because Verbraken's reading reflects Gregory's usage.

I have rejected one of Waszink's suggested alternative readings that Bélanger adopted: *discretionis* for *discretione* at line 492. The full context is: *qui . . . pervenire ad eum sub digna operatione discretione*

---

1. Note that Bélanger does not print this text in his edition but recommends it; see Rodrigue Bélanger, *Grégoire Le Grand: Commentaire sur le Cantique des Cantiques*, SChr 314 (Paris: Cerf, 1984), 94 n. 31.

contendunt. I do not accept Waszink's preference for *discretionis* over *discretione* despite the frequency of the genitive elsewhere in the corpus of Gregory. I agree with him that *discretione* is the *lectio difficilior* and that the alternate readings (*ac discretione, cum discretione, per discretionem*) are attempts to make sense of the passage. But I think *discretionis* is as well. Since Gregory's use of *discretione* immediately before a verb is frequent enough in his writings, and both grammatical and logical sense can be made of *discretione* as it stands, I judge that there is no need for an emendation here.

Appendix Four

Textual Notes on the Compilations of Paterius and Bede

A comparison of Paterius's and Bede's texts with that of Gregory reveals that there are several divergences between the excerpters and their Gregorian source. Some of these divergences indicate that the editions of Paterius and Bede need to be emended. Such emendations represent necessary (in my opinion) corrections of scribal errors, whether on the part of Paterius or Bede themselves, or a later copyist. In the following notes, the emendations that I suggest for adoption in future editions of Paterius and Bede are marked with an asterisk (*). Other divergences are reflective of the Gregorian text available to Paterius or Bede. As such they provide clues about the transmission of Gregory's writings after his death. Still other divergences appear to be purposeful alterations. All these divergences are footnoted in the translation, but discussion of the textual issues involved is reserved for the following notes.

I. Paterius

I have identified fourteen cases in which Paterius has diverged from the text of Gregory. Eight of these represent scribal errors. The majority of these are the result of corruption or confusion (see notes 4P, 5P, 6P, 10P, and 11P), though there are a few instances of haplography (see notes 7P, 12P, and 14P). Only one divergence almost certainly reflects an alternative form of the Gregorian text that Paterius used (see note 2P). But there are five other cases where Paterius's text may bear witness to a primitive textual corruption (see notes 1P, 3P, 8P, 9P, and 13P). None the Paterian divergences seems to be the result of a willful alteration.

Note 1P. Gregory, *Mor.* 6.25 [42], 22 (CCSL 143:315): *nec videre requirebat*; Paterius, *Test.* 13.9 (PL 79:906d): *nec videri requirebat a Domino*. It may be the case that Paterius's text read *videri* instead of *videre*, prompting the addition of *a Domino*.

Note 2P. Gregory, *H.Ez.* 2.1 [15], 458–59 (CCSL 142:220): *nec totus videtur, nec totus non videtur*; Paterius, *Test.* 13.12 (PL 79:907): *nec totus latet nec totus videtur*. Paterius also omits the second *sic* at the beginning of the next sentence. These readings are also found in one of the early mss. of Gregory's *H.Ez.* Hence Paterius's reading represents the Gregorian text as he knew it.

Note 3P. Gregory, *H.Ez.* 2.3 [14], 296 (CCSL 142:246): *ergo*; Paterius, *Test.* 13.24 (PL 79:910a) omits this word, as does Bede; see note 10B. There is no evidence for this omission among the mss. of the *H.Ez.*, but the fact that both Paterius and Bede testify to it may indicate that it is primitive corruption.

★Note 4P. Gregory, *Mor.* 24.8 [15], 82 (CCSL 143B:1199): *contemplationis*; Paterius, *Test.* 13.27 (PL 79:911b): *contemplationum*. The nominal suffix of *contemplation-* seems to have been confused by Paterius or a later scribe. Hence the Paterian text should be emended to *contemplationis*.

★Note 5P. Gregory, *Mor.* 24.8 [15], 82–83 [CCSL 143B:1199): *Qui ut haec agant*; Paterius, *Test.* 13.27 (PL 79:911b): *Quia ut haec agant*. Both *qui* and *quia* were commonly abbreviated in mss., making them susceptible to confusion. The word *Qui* was miscopied as *Quia* by either Paterius or a copyist. Hence the Paterian text should be emended to *Qui*.

★Note 6P. Gregory, *Mor.* 17.32 [52], 44 (CCSL 143A:883); Paterius, *Test.* 13.28 (PL 79:911d): *signantur*. It appears that *signantur* is a corruption of *designantur*. Hence, the Paterian text should be emended to *designantur*.

Note 7P. Gregory, *Mor.* 17.32 [52], 46 (CCSL 143A:883): *quondam*; Paterius, *Test.* 13.28 (PL 79:911d) omits this word. This seems to be a case of haplography due to homoiarchton because of the word *quorum* that immediately preceded *quondam* in the original Gregorian text. Hence *quondam* should be inserted in the Paterian text.

Note 8P. Gregory, *H.Ez.* 2.7 [10], 309 (CCSL 142:324): *in laetitia*; Paterius, *Test.* 13.34 (PL 79:913a): *cum laetitia*; Bede, *Cant.* 6, 459 (CCSL 119B:371): *ac laetitia*. These variant readings seem to indicate that the original text lacked either a preposition or conjunction before *laetitia*, since *in*, *cum*, and *ac* appear to be attempts to construe *laetitia*.

Note 9P. Gregory, *H.Ez.* 2.7 [10], 309–10 (CCSL 142:324): *quia iam sentit quod de caelesti gaudio diligat, et adhuc*; Paterius, *Test.* 13.34 (PL 79:913a) reads *et si* in place of *quia* and omits the *et*. Paterius must have had corrupt text before him, prompting this alteration.

Note 10P. Gregory, *H.Ez.* 1.8 [6], 143 (CCSL 142:105): *quanto*; Paterius, *Test.* 13.37 (PL 79:914b): *quantum*. The Paterian text should be emended to *quanto*.

Note 11P. Gregory, *H.Ez.* 1.8 [7], 163 (CCSL 142:105): *qui*; Paterius, *Test.* 13.37 (PL 79:914c): *quia*. Both of these words were commonly abbreviated in the mss., making them susceptible to confusion. The Paterian text should be emended to *qui*.

Note 12P. Gregory, *H.Ez.* 2.4 [8], 258 (CCSL 142:264): *ecclesiae*; Paterius, *Test.* 13.38 (PL 79:914d) omits this word. This is probably an instance of haplography due to homoioteleuton (*sanctae ecclesiae genae*). Hence, the word *ecclesiae* should be inserted into the Paterian text.

Note 13P. Gregory, *Mor.* 29.6 [12], 38 (CCSL 143B:1441): *signata fide corda*; Paterius, *Test.* 13.45 (PL 79:916b): *signata corda*; Bede, *Cant.* 6, 578 (CCSL 119B:374): *signatam fidem*. The variations found in Paterius and Bede indicate some primitive textual corruption.

Note 14P. Gregory, *Mor.* 17.27 [39], 25–26 (CCSL 143A:874): *Fugit nos, dicimus, quotiens menti nostrae id quod reminisci volumus non* *occurrit. Fugit nos dicimus quando id quod volumus memoria non tenemus*; Paterius, *Test*. 13.49 (PL 79:916d): *Fugit nos, dicimus, quotiens id quod reminisci volumus memoria non tenemus.* There are two omissions: (1) *menti nostrae* and (2) *non occurrit. Fugit nos dicimus quando id quod volumus.* The second is likely an instance of haplography due to homoiarchton (*volumus . . . volumus*). The first may have been dropped in order to make sense after the second omission. Hence, the Paterian text should be emended to restore the omissions.

II. Bede

I have identified twenty-one cases in which Bede has diverged from the text of Gregory. Seven of these represent scribal errors. Some of these are the result of corruption or confusion (see notes 4B, 14B, 15B, and 17B), and there are a few instances of haplography (see notes 2B, 3B, and 5B). Three divergences almost certainly reflect an alternative form of the Gregorian text that Bede used (see notes 6B, 8B, and 11B). But there are three other cases where Bede's text may bear witness to a primitive textual corruption (see notes 10B, 16B, and 20B). Two additions on the part of Bede appear to be purposeful (see notes 1B and 19B). In five cases, the Bedan text contains an alteration, though it is not clear whether these are due to corruption or were done on purpose (see notes 7B, 9B, 13B, 18B, and 21B).

Note 1B. Bede, *Cant*. 6, 119 (CCSL 119B:362) inserts *ecclesia* as the subject of *posuit*; cf. Gregory, *Reg. past*. 3.26, 41 (SChr 382:440). This addition was probably meant as a clarification.

*Note 2B. Bede, *Cant*. 6, 139 (CCSL 119B:362) omits the *natura* found at Gregory, *H.Ez*. 2.1 [15], 451 (CCSL 142:219). It should probably be restored.

*Note 3B. Bede, *Cant*. 6, 146 (CCSL 119B:362) omits the *noster* found at Gregory, *H.Ez*. 2.1 [15], 460 (CCSL 142:220). This seems to be a case of haplography due to homoioteleuton (*-or . . . -er*). Hence, the Bedan text should be emended.

*Note 4B. Gregory, *H.Ez*. 2.1 [15], 461 (CCSL 142:220): *eis*; Bede, *Cant*. 6, 148 (CCSL 119B): *eius*. The word *eius* seems to be a corruption of *eis*. Hence, the Bedan text should be emended to *eis*.

*Note 5B. Gregory, *H.Ez.* 2.7 [11], 357 (CCSL 142:325): *iam carere*; Bede, *Cant.* 6, 217 (CCSL 119B:364): *carere*. Since Bede includes the other two instances of *iam* in this sentence, the omission of this one seems to be an oversight.

Note 6B. Bede, *Cant.* 6, 231–32 (CCSL 119B:365) adds *pro terreno studio* to Gregory, *H.Ez.* 2.10 [22], 587 (CCSL 142:396). This same addition is found in the Codex Longipontanus, one of the mss. of *H.Ez.*; see the critical apparatus for this line. The presence of this addition in Bede indicates that his text of the *H.Ez.* may have been of the same family as the Codex Longipontanus. There are other indications of this; see note 8B.

Note 7B. Gregory, *H.Ez.* 2.10 [22], 590 (CCSL 142:396): *subtilitatis*; Bede, *Cant.* 6, 233–34 (CCSL 119B:365) reads *simplicitatis*. Since there is no support for this reading among the Gregorian mss. of *H.Ez.*, this reading is either a corruption or a conscious alteration on the part of Bede (or a copyist).

Note 8B. Bede, *Cant.* 6, 240–43 (CCSL 119B:365) adds the parenthetical: *murram itaque quia se cruciant et cruciando a vitiis conservant, tus vero quia Dei visionem diligunt ad quam pervenire medullitus inardescunt*. This same addition is also found in the Codex Longipontanus; see the apparatus for *H.Ez.* 2.10 [22], 597 (CCSL 142:396). This is a second indication that Bede's copy of the *H.Ez.* may have been related to the Codex Longipontanus; see note 6B.

Note 9B. Gregory, *Mor.* 7.21 [24], 20 (CCSL 143:349): *ulla debilitate desiderii*; Bede, *Cant.* 6, 257–58 (CCSL 119B:365): *ulla dubietate desiderii*. Since there is no support for this reading among the Gregorian mss. of *Mor.*, this reading is either a corruption or a conscious alteration on the part of Bede (or a copyist).

Note 10B. Gregory, *H.Ez.* 2.3 [14], 296 (CCSL 142:246): *ergo*. Bede, *Cant.* 6, 301 (CCSL 119B:366) omits this word, as does Paterius. See note 3P for further discussion.

Note 11B. Gregory, *H.Ez.* 2.3 [14], 296 (CCSL 142:246): *eius*; Bede, *Cant.* 6, 301 (CCSL 119B:366) omits this word. This omission is also witnessed to by the thirteenth-century ms. *Palatinus latinus* 259; see the apparatus at Gregory, *H.Ez.* 2.3 [14], 296 (CCSL 142:246).

Note 12B. At Bede, *Cant.* 6, 312 (CCSL 119B:367), several lines have been omitted, namely, Gregory, *H.Ez.* 2.3 [15], 315–21 (CCSL 142:246–47). This is probably an accidental omission on the part of Bede or a copyist, an instance of haplography due to homoiarchton (*quid ergo . . . quid ergo*).

Note 13B. Gregory, *Mor.* 9.11 [18], 172 (CCSL 143:469): *remunerationis*; Bede, *Cant.* 6, 333 (CCSL 119B:367): *retributionis*. Since there is no support for this reading among the Gregorian mss. of *Mor.*, this reading is either a corruption or a conscious alteration on the part of Bede (or a copyist).

★Note 14B. Gregory, *H.Ez.* 2.2 [13], 316 (CCSL 142:234): *quia*; Bede, *Cant.* 6, 446 (CCSL 119B:370): *qui*. Though *qui* can be construed grammatically, it seems likely it is a corruption of *quia*. Both of these words were commonly abbreviated in the mss., making them susceptible to confusion. Hence the Bedan text should be emended to *quia*.

★Note 15B. Gregory, *Mor.* 23.20 [38], 57 (CCSL 143B:1173): *quasi*; Bede, *Cant.* 6, 451 (CCSL 119B:370): *suasi*. Since *suasi* is ungrammatical, it seems to be a corruption of *quasi*. Hence, the Bedan text should be emended to *quasi*.

Note 16B. Gregory, *H.Ez.* 2.7 [10], 309 (CCSL 142:324): *in laetitia*; Paterius, *Test.* 13.34 (PL 79:913a): *cum laetitia*; Bede, *Cant.* 6, 459 (CCSL 119B:371): *ac laetitia*. On the textual issue here, see note 8P.

★Note 17B. Gregory, *H.Ez.* 1.8 [6], 139 (CCSL 142:105): *eius vita et desiderium*; Bede, *Cant.* 6, 490 (CCSL 119B:371): *eius vitae desiderium*. It seems that Bede's *vitae* is a corruption of *vita et*. Hence, the Bedan text should be emended.

Note 18B. Gregory, *H.Ez.* 1.8 [6], 156 (CCSL 142:105): *et*; Bede, *Cant.* 6, 505 (CCSL 119B:372): *ut*. It is not clear whether *ut* is a mere corruption of *et*, or a purposeful alteration.

Note 19B. Bede, *Cant.* 6, 575 (CCSL 119B:374) adds an *ut* which is not found at Gregory, *Mor.* 29.6 [12], 36 (CCSL 143B:1441).

Note 20B. Gregory, *Mor.* 29.6 [12], 38 (CCSL 143B:1441): *signata fide corda*; Paterius, *Test.* 13.45 (PL 79:916b): *signata corda*; Bede, *Cant.* 6, 578 (CCSL 119B:374): *signatam fidem*. See note 13P.

Note 21B. At *Cant.* 6, 607 (CCSL 119B:375), Bede omits a *quia* found at Gregory, *H.Ez.* 2.2 [4], 104 (CCSL 142:227). There is no support for this omission among the Gregorian mss. of *H.Ez.* It is unclear whether this omission is accidental or purposeful.

Appendix Five

Textual Notes on William of St. Thierry's *Excerpts from the Books of Blessed Gregory on the Song of Songs*

I. Emendations to Verdeyen's Edition

My emendations to Verdeyen's edition are presented in the table below. The notes that follow this table justify these emendations. After these notes, I offer some concluding remarks about the character of the scribal errors in the manuscripts of William's *Excerpts*.

Note #	Exp.	Verdeyen's Reading	Adopted Reading
1	2, 114	*assumpsit*	*sumpsit*
2	2, 121	*merito*	*maeret*
3	2, 151	*intus delictorum vulnera*	*virus delictorum*
4	2, 152	*qui*	*quia*
5	2, 309	*hanc nos iam*	*ac noxiam*
6	3, 49	*solo*	*suo*
7	3, 82	*erecta*	*sic recta*
8	3, 100	*pulvis*	*pulveres*
9	3, 175–76	*occulta*	*luculente et*
10	4, 12	*aperte*	*apte*

11	5, 22	qui	quia
12	5, 31	solis	solum his
13	6, 11	quantum	quanto
14	6, 25	par	per
15	6, 47	coruum	corium
16	6, 61	offers	offeres
17	6, 89	ea	te
18	6, 93	aperte	apte
19	6, 107	interisse	praeterisse
20	6, 108	~	integram
21	6, 137	~	contendit perfici et in lucem cotidie
22	7, 16	~	videat
23	7, 50	~	ut diximus
24	7, 52	calorem	a calore
25	8, 92	est	enim
26	8, 133	nostrae infirmitatis	mentis nostrae

Note 1. The mss. R and A, as well as *Mor.* 33.3 [5], 12 (CCSL 143B:1673), support *sumpsit* instead of *assumpsit* (*Exc.* 2, 114 [CCCM 87:404]).

Note 2. I read *maeret* (*H.Ez.* 2.3 [9], 180 [CCSL 142:242]) for *merito* (*Exc.* 2, 121 [CCSM 87:404]). The word *merito* makes little sense in the context and thus seems to be a corruption of *maeret*.

Note 3. At *Exc.* 2, 151 [CCCM 87:405] I prefer the reading of ms. S (*ut virus delictorum curet*) to that of Verdeyen: *ut intus delictorum vulnera curet*, "to cure the wounds of sin inwardly." The reading of the other mss. and Verdeyen appear to be influenced by *Mor.* 6.25 [42], 2–26 (CCSL 143:314–15), which was employed in the Carthusian version (ms. D) of this passage; see p. 196, n. 20 for a translation. I prefer the reading of ms. S on the supposition that the Benedictine version (mss. R, V, and A) contains William's *summary* of this passage, rather than the exact words of Gregory. Gregory speaks of the "poison of sins" elsewhere (e.g., *Mor.* 7.18 [21], 23 [CCSL 143:348], and *H.Ev.* 40 [2], 25 [CCSL 141:395]), and William could have been borrowing this phraseology.

Note 4. I read *quia* (*Mor.* 6.25 [42], 11 [CCSL 143:315]) instead of *qui* (*Exc.* 2, 152 [CCCM 87:405]). Both of these words were commonly abbreviated in the mss., making them susceptible to confusion.

Note 5. I read *ac noxiam* (*H.Ez.* 2.4 [15], 432 [CCSL 142:270]) instead of *hanc nos iam* (*Exc.* 2, 309 [CCCM 87:410]). The incorrect reading appears to be an error of mishearing. First, the aspiration *h* was added where none was intended, probably causing the scribe to hear the word *ac* as *hanc* (the presence of the *n* is harder to explain). Second, the *x* of *noxiam* was heard as an *s*, resulting in *nos iam*.

Note 6. I read *suo* (*H.Ev.* 25 [2], 51 [CCSL 141:206]) instead of *solo* (*Exc.* 3, 49 [CCCM 87:412]). The word *solo* makes little sense and thus seems to be a corruption of *suo*. This could also be an error of hearing.

Note 7. I read *sic recta* (*H.Ez.* 2.10 [22], 586–87 [CCSL 142:396]) instead of *erecta* (*Exc.* 3, 82 [CCSL 87:413]). The word *erecta* seems to be a corruption of *sic recta*, possibly an error of hearing.

Note 8. I read *pulveres* (*H.Ez.* 2.10 [23], 601 [CCSL 142:397]) instead of *pulvis* (*Exc.* 3, 100 [CCSL 87:414]). The verb *dicuntur* requires a nominative plural predicate noun (*pulveres*) instead of the nominative singular *pulvis*. Hence *pulvis* seems to be a corruption of *pulveres*.

Note 9. I read *quod luculente et aperte audiunt* (*H.Ez.* 2.3 [14], 295 [CCSL 142:246]) instead of *quod occulta aperte audiunt* (*Exc.* 3, 175–76 [CCCM 87:417]). The incorrect reading appears to be an error of hearing: *luculente et* was heard as *occulta*. If the initial *l-* was not heard for some reason, one could see how *-uculente et* might be heard as *occulta*.

Note 10. I read *apte* (*Mor.* 9.11 [18], 170 [CCSL 143:469]) instead of *aperte* (*Exc.* 4, 12 [CCCM 87:419]). Both of these words were commonly abbreviated in the mss., making them susceptible to confusion.

Note 11. I read *quia* (*H.Ez.* 2.2 [13], 316 [CCSL 142:234]) instead of *qui* (*Exc.* 5, 22 [CCCM 87:428]). See note 4.

Note 12. I read *solum his* (*H.Ez.* 2.7 [10], 293 [CCSL 142:323]) instead of *solis* (*Exc.* 5, 31 [CCCM 87:429]). The two words *solum his* were probably contracted into *solis* due to an error of hearing. By the medieval period, it was common for nominal endings such as -*um* not to be fully pronounced. Hence one can see how *sol- his* was heard as *solis*.

Note 13. I read *quanto* (*H.Ez.* 1.8 [6], 143 [CCSL 142:105]) instead of *quantum* (*Exc.* 6, 11 [CCCM 87:432]). As these two words were abbreviated in mss., they could be easily confused. Note that William's reading reflects that of the *Mor.* ms. G (see the critical apparatus on line 143 on CCSL 142:105). Hence, it would appear that William did not make this change on purpose.

Note 14. I read *per* (*H.Ez.* 1.7 [6], 158 [CCSL 142:105]) instead of *par* (*Exc.* 6, 25 [CCCM 87:432]). The word *par* is a misprint.

Note 15. I read *corium* (mss. S, A, and D; *H.Ez.* 1.8 [8], 181 [CCSL 142:106]) instead of *curvum* (*Exc.* 6, 47 [CCCM 87:433]). At first glance, the version of ms. S printed in Migne appears to read *curvum* at PL 180:466. Such is the reading of the electronic *Patrologia Latina Database*. But on close inspection of a printed copy of PL 180, the *v* is a *y* printed so lightly that its tail is nearly undetectable. Accordingly, ms. S witnesses to *curyum*, found also in A D, but spelled differently, as *corium*.

Note 16. I read *offeres* (*H.Ez.* 1.8 [9], 196 [CCSL 142:106]) instead of *offers* (*Exc.* 6, 61 [CCCM 87:433]). The word *offers* is a misprint.

Note 17. I read *te* (*H.Ez.* 2.4 [8], 265 [CCSL 142:264]) instead of *ea* (*Exc.* 6, 89 [CCCM 87:434]). The difficulty of construing the word *ea* motivates this correction. The reading *te* also seems preserved in the *in se* of ms. S.

Note 18. I read *apte* (*Mor.* 18.29 [46], 10 [CCSL 143:915]) instead of *aperte* (*Exc.* 6, 93 [CCCM 87:434]).

Note 19. I read *praeterisse* (*Mor.* 29.2 [3], 22 [CCSL 143:1435]) instead of *interisse* (*Exc.* 6, 107 [CCCM 87:435]). The word *interisse* does not make sense in the context and appears to be a corruption of *praeterisse*.

Note 20. I add *integram* (*Mor.* 29.2 [3–4], 23 [CCSL 143B:1435]) after *claritatem* (*Exc.* 6, 108 [CCCM 87:435]). The word *integram* was accidentally omitted due to homoioteleuton (*-em . . . -am*).

Note 21. I add *contendit perfici et in lucem cotidie* (*Mor.* 29.2 [4], 57 [CCSL 143:1436]) after *cotidie* at *Exc.* 6, 137 (CCSL 87:436). These words were omitted due to homoioteleuton (*cotidie . . . cotidie*).

Note 22. I add *videat* (*Reg. past.* 3.32, 65 [SChr 382:494]) after *priusquam veniant* at *Exc.* 7, 16 (CCCM 87:437). The word *videat* was omitted due to a combination of homoiarchton (*v- . . . v-*) and homoioteleuton (*-t . . . -t*).

Note 23. I insert *ut diximus* at *Exc.* 7, 50 based on ms. S and *Mor.* 12.53 [60], 15–16 (CCSL 143:665). William was not immune to retaining Gregorian references to earlier discussions that he did not include in his own florilegium; see W30. It is possible that *ut diximus* was omitted after *in eis* because of homoioteleuton (*-s . . . -s*).

Note 24. Here I read *a calore* (*Mor.* 12.53 [60], 18 [CCSL 143:665]) instead of *calorem* (*Exc.* 7, 52 [CCCM 87:438]). The presence of the accusative *calorem* gives *retrahit* two direct objects, making it difficult to construe the sentence. Hence, the word *calorem* is best viewed as a corruption of *a calore*.

Note 25. I read *enim* (*H.Ez.* 2.2 [4], 96 [CCSL 142:227]) instead of *est* (*Exc.* 8, 92 [CCCM 87:442]). Though the sentence is grammatically correct with *est*, it makes better sense if it is replaced with the original *enim*. The error could also be due to a confusion of abbreviations.

Note 26. I read *mentis nostrae* (ms. S) instead of *nostrae infirmitatis* (*Exc.* 8, 133 [CCCM 87:443]. If ms. S testifies to the autograph of William, then the phrase *mentis nostrae* represents a conscious departure from Gregory on the part of William.

Concluding Remarks. The emendations explained above can be classified into six categories. The first two categories comprise corrections to readings offered by Verdeyen; the remaining four categories contain corrections made to errors in William's text that were introduced by scribes.

1. Reversion to ms. readings. In four cases I have preferred readings of ms. S (in two cases based on ms. S alone, in two cases along with other textual support): see notes 3, 15, 17, and 26. In one case I have preferred the readings of mss. R and A; see note 1.
2. Correction of misprints introduced by Verdeyen: see notes 14 and 16.
3. Confusion of abbreviations; see notes 4, 10, 11, 13, 18, and 25.
4. Errors of mishearing; see notes 5, 7 (possibly), 9, and 12. These errors are significant because they provide clues regarding the process of manuscript copying (see also note 30 below). They demonstrate that, at least on some occasions, a scribe could copy a text by having it read to him.
5. Omissions: see notes 20, 21, 22, and 23. The presence of these errors, which occurred because of faulty reading, indicates that scribes also continued to copy texts by reading them. What is interesting about the errors of omission in the mss. of William's text is that they are clustered together, at the end of *Exc.* 6 and the beginning of *Exc.* 7. This may indicate that the scribe was particularly tired on the day that this section of text was copied.
6. Corruptions not otherwise explained; see notes 2, 6, 8, 19, and 24.

II. OTHER TEXTUAL COMMENTS

The following seven notes comment on significant textual issues that present themselves in William's text.

Note 27. On *Exc.* 2, 161–62 (CCCM 87:405). William's Latin text here reads *in huius exsilii statum caeca securitate prostrata*. His version inserts the word *statum*, which is not found in Gregory's *in huius exsilii caeca securitate prostrata* (*Mor.* 6.25 [42], 20–21 [CCSL 143:315]). Both Paterius (P9; *Test.* 13.9 [PL 70:906d]) and Bede (B11; *Cant.* 6, 111 [CCSL 119B:361]) follow Gregory's text. The critical apparatus of *Mor.* 6.25 [42], 20–21 indicates that various words such as *statim*, *stratum*, and *statu* were inserted between *exsilii* and *caeca*, and William's text testifies to the mss. family that contains this textual tradition. Though the insertion of *statum* is not original to Gregory, it is retained as it represents the text that William knew. The translation of the uncorrupted text is: "lays prostrate in the blind security of this exile."

Note 28. On *Exc.* 2, 173 (CCCM 87:406). For this line, all the mss. are corrupt: *Ipsa salus sui corporis quae transfixa est vulnere amoris* (mss. S, R, A, V, D). Verdeyen has restored this text to *Vilis ei fit ipsa salus sui corporis, quia transfixa est vulnere amoris* based on *H.Ez.* 2.3 [8], 169–70 (CCSL 142:242). The apparatus of *H.Ez.* for this line indicates evidence for the omission of *vilis ei*, an omission that seems reflected in William's text.

Note 29. On *Exc.* 2, 246–47 (CCCM 87:408). The full Latin text of this line is *Unde sancta ecclesia sub sponsi voce aperte speciem eius videre desiderans in divinitate*. Though the original Guillelmian text is surely *sponsi* (*Exc.* 2, 246 [CCCM 87:408]), it should be corrected to *sponsae* for two reasons. First, *sponsi* makes little sense in the context. Second, *sponsi* seems to be a mistake on the part of William when combining *Unde sancta ecclesia sub sponsae voce hunc aperte iam videre desiderans* (*H.Ez.* 2.1 [15], 449–50 [CCSL 142:219]) and *Unde sancta ecclesia sponsi sui speciem videre in divinitate desiderans* (*Mor.* 18.48 [78], 42–43 [CCSL 143:942]). The *sponsi* modifies *speciem*, whereas the *sponsae* modifies *voce*.

Note 30. On *Exc.* 3, 150 (CCCM 87:416). At this point all the mss. contain a primitive corruption: *ad intentionem certam in his parati* (mss. S, R, A, V) or *ad intentionem etiam in his parati* (ms. D). Based on *Reg. past.* 3.32, 57 (SChr 382:494), Verdeyen corrected the text to read: *ad intentionem certaminis parati*. Interestingly, this primitive corruption gives us insight into the methods of the copyist of R. Apparently there was an assistant reading the exemplar aloud to him, and he misheard *certaminis* as *certam in his*, adding an aspiration *h* where none was intended. On this corruption, see CCCM 87:391.

Note 31. On *Exc.* 4, 216–17 (CCCM 87:425). William's Latin here is *praecedentium interim patrum exemplis pascuntur*. Gregory reads: *per praecedentium interim patrum exempla pascuntur* (*Mor.* 24.8 [18], 90–91 [CCSL 143:1200]), which has the same meaning. It is likely that in William's copy of *Mor.* the *per* was omitted, necessitating the change of *exempla* to *exemplis*.

Note 32. On *Exc.* 7, 30–35 (CCCM 87:437–38). It may be the case that William accidentally omitted v. 10 (*ne enim terrenarum rerum amori succumbat alta sit; ne occulti hostis iaculis feriatur ex omni latere circumspecta*), which in its original context was located between v. 8 (*esse ergo speculatoris vita et alta debet semper et circumspecta*) and v. 9 (*neque hoc speculatori sufficit ut altum vivat . . .*). William's eye could have skipped from the *circumspecta* of v. 8, not to the *ne enim* of v. 10 as he should have done, but, misled by the *circumspecta* of v. 10, to the similar *neque hoc* of v. 9, thereby omitting v. 10. See *H.Ez.* 1.11 [7], 123–26. Interestingly, William seems to have caught his error and appended the missing verse to the end of his collation.

Note 33. On *Exc.* 8, 47–48 (CCCM 87:440). Ms. S omits *et nigri*, "and black," and *et dealbati*, "and 'made white,'" which are not original to Gregory's text (*Mor.* 18.53 [87], 22–23 [CCSL 143:950]).

BIBLIOGRAPHY

I. Primary Sources

AMBROSE OF MILAN

The Exposition on Psalm 118 (Expositio psalmi cxviii). Edition: Michael Petschenig. *Expositio psalmi cxviii*. CSEL 62. Vienna: Tempsky; Leipzig: Freytag, 1913.

Epistles (Epistulae). Edition: Otto Faller. *Epistvlae et acta, tom. I. Epistvlarvm libri I-VI*. CSEL 82/1. Vienna: Hoelder-Pichler-Tempsky, 1964.

On the Holy Spirit (De spiritu sancto). Edition: Otto Faller. *De spiritu sancto libri tres; De incarnationis dominicae sacramento*. CSEL 79. Vienna: Hoelder-Pichler-Tempsky, 1968.

ANONYMOUS

The Book of Pontiffs (Liber pontificalis). Edition: L. Duchesne. *Le Liber Pontificalis, Texte, introduction et commentaire*. 2nd ed., 3 vols. Paris: E. de Boccard, 1955–57. English translation (to 715): Raymond Davis. *The Book of Pontiffs (Liber Pontificalis)*. Translated Texts for Historians Latin Series V. Liverpool: Liverpool University Press, 1989.

ANONYMOUS

The Whitby Life of Gregory (Liber beati et laudabilis viri Gregorii papae urbis Romae de vita atque eius virtutibus). Edition and English translation: Bertram Colgrave. *The Earliest Life of Gregory the Great by an Anonymous Monk of Whitby*. Lawerence: University of Kansas Press, 1968.

Apponius

Commentary on the Song of Songs (In Canticum canticorum expositio). Edition and French translation: Bernard de Vregille and Louis Neyrand. *Apponius: Commentaire sue le cantique des cantiques.* 3 vols. SChr 420, 421, and 430. Paris: Cerf, 1997–98.

Augustine

Sermons (Sermones). Edition: PL 38–39.

Explanations of the Psalms (Enarrationes in Psalmos). Edition: Eligius Dekkers. *Sancti Avrelii Avgvstini Enarrationes in Psalmos.* CCSL 38–40. Turnhout: Brepols, 1956.

On Christian Teaching (De doctrina christana). Edition: Paul Tombeur. *Sanctus Aurelius Augustinus: De doctrina Christiana.* CCSL 32. Turnhout: Brepols, 1982.

Bede

Commentary on the Song of Songs (In Cantica Canticorum). Edition: D. Hurst and J. E. Hudson. *Bedae Venerabilis Opera. Pars II, Opera exegetica. 2B: in Tobiam, in Proverbia, in Cantica Canticorum, in Habacuc.* CCSL 119B. Turnhout: Brepols, 1983, 165–375.

Ecclesiastical History of the English People (Historia ecclesiastica gentis anglorum). Edition and English translation: Bertram Colgrave and R. A. B. Mynors. *Bede's Ecclesiastical History of the English People.* Oxford Medieval Texts. Oxford: Clarendon Press, 1969.

Excerpts from the Works of Saint Augustine on the Letters of the Blessed Apostle Paul (In apostolum quaecumque in opusculis sancti Augustini exposita inueni). English translation: David Hurst. *Bede the Venerable: Excerpts from the Works of Saint Augustine on the Letters of the Blessed Apostle Paul.* CS 183. Kalamazoo, MI: Cistercian, 1999.

Homiles on the Gospels (Omeliarum euangelii libros II). English translation: Lawrence T. Martin and David Hurst. *Bede the Venerable: Homilies on the Gospels.* 2 vols. CS 110, CS 111. Kalamazoo, MI: Cistercian, 1989–90.

Bernard of Clairvaux

Sermons on the Song of Songs (Sermones super Cantica canticorum). English translation: Killian Walsh and Irene Edmonds. *Bernard of Clairvaux: Sermons on the Song of Songs.* 4 vols. CF 4, 7, 31, and 40. Spencer, MA: Cistercian Publications, 1971–80.

Columbanus

Letters (Epistulae). Edition and English translation: G. S. M. Walker. *Sancti Columani Opera*, Scriptores Latini Hiberniae, vol. 2. Dublin: Dublin Institute for Advanced Studies, 1957, 2–59.

Didymus the Blind

On the Holy Spirit (De spiritu sancto). Edition: Louis Doutreleau. *Didyme l'Aveugle: Traité du saint-Esprit*. SChr 386. Paris: Cerf, 1992. English translation: Mark DelCogliano, Andrew Radde-Gallwitz, and Lewis Ayres. *Works on the Spirit: Athanasius the Great and Didymus the Blind*. Popular Patristics Series 43. Crestwood, NY: St. Vladimir's Seminary Press, 2011.

Gilbert of Hoyland

Sermons on the Song of Songs (Sermones super Cantica canticorum). English translation: Lawrence C. Braceland, *Gilbert of Hoyland: Sermons on the Song of Songs*. 3 vols. CF 14, 20, and 26. Kalamazoo, MI: Cistercian Publications, 1978–79.

Gregory of Tours

The History of the Franks (Historiarum libri X). Editions: W. Arndt and Bruno Krusch. *Gregorii Turonensis Opera. Teil 1: Libri historiarum X*. MGH, SrM 1/1 Hannover, 1885; and Rudolf Buchner. *Zehn Bücher Geschichten*. 2 vols. Berlin: Rütten & Loening, 1955. English translation: Lewis Thorpe. *Gregory of Tours. The History of the Franks*. London: Penguin, 1974.

Gregory the Great

Commentary on First Kings (Commentarius in Librum Primum Regum) [spurious] Edition: Adalbert de Vogüé. *Grégoire le Grand (Pierre de Cava): Commentaire sur les Premier Livre des Rois*. 6 vols. SChr 351, 391, 432, 449, 469, and 482. Paris: Cerf, 1989–2004.

Dialogues (Dialogorum libri IV de miraculis patrum italicorum). Edition: Adalbert de Vogüé and Paul Antin. *Grégoire le Grand. Dialogues*. 3 vols. SChr 251, 260, and 265. Paris: Cerf, 1978–80. English translation: Odo Zimmerman. *St. Gregory the Great: Dialogues*. Fathers of the Church 39. New York: Fathers of the Church, 1959.

Exposition on the Song of Songs (Expositio in Canticis canticorum). Editions: Patrick Verbraken. *Sancti Gregorii Magni Expositiones in Canticum Canticorum, in Librum Primum Regum*, CCSL 144. Turnhout: Brepols, 1963, 387–444; and Rodrigue Bélanger. *Grégoire le Grand. Commentaire Sur Le Cantique Des*

Cantiques. SChr 314. Paris: Cerf, 1984. German translation: K. Suso Frank. *Origenes und Gregor der Grosse. Das Hohelied.* Christliche Meister 29. Einsiedeln: Johannes, 1987, 79–129. Italian translation: Emilio Gandolfo. *Gregorio Magno. Commento al Cantico dei Cantici.* Magnano: Qiqajon, 1997. English translation: Denys Turner. *Eros and Allegory: Medieval Exegesis of the Song of Songs.* CS 156. Kalamazoo, MI: Cistercian, 1995, 215–55.

Homilies on the Gospels (Homiliae in Evangelia). Edition: Raymond Étaix. *Gregorius Magnus. Homiliae in Evangelia.* CCSL 141. Turnhout: Brepols, 1999. English translation: David Hurst. *Gregory the Great: Forty Gospel Homilies.* CS 123. Kalamazoo, MI: Cistercian, 1990.

Homilies on the Prophet Ezekiel (Homiliae in Hiezechihelem prophetem). Edition: Marcus Adriaen. *Sancti Gregorii Magni Homiliae in Hiezechihelem prophetem.* CCSL 142. Turnhout: Brepols, 1971. English translation: Theodosia Grey. *The Homilies of Saint Gregory the Great on the Book of the Prophet Ezekiel.* Etna, CA: Center for Traditionalist Orthodox Studies, 1990.

Letters (Registrum epistularum). Edition: Dag Norberg. *S. Gregorii Magni Registrum epistularum.* 2 vols. CCSL 140 and 140A. Turnhout: Brepols, 1982. English translation: John R. C. Martyn. *The Letters of Gregory the Great.* 3 vols. Medieval Sources in Translation 40. Toronto: Pontifical Institute of Mediaeval Studies, 2004.

Morals on Job (Moralia in Iob). Edition: Marcus Adriaen. *S. Gregorii Magni Moralia in Iob.* 3 vols. CCSL 143, 143A, and 143B. Turnhout: Brepols, 1979–85. English translation: *Gregory the Great: Morals on the Book of Job.* 4 vols. Library of Fathers of the Holy Catholic Church 18, 21, 23, and 31. Oxford: J. H. Parker, 1844–50.

Pastoral Care (Regula pastoralis). Edition: Bruno Judic, Floribert Rommel, and Charles Morel. *Grégoire le Grand. Règle pastorale.* 2 vols. SChr 381 and 382. Paris: Cerf, 1992. English translations: Henry Davis. *St. Gregory the Great: Pastoral Care.* Ancient Christian Writers 11. New York and Mahwah, NJ: Newman Press, 1950; and George E. Demacopoulos. *St. Gregory the Great: The Book of Pastoral Rule.* Popular Patristics Series 34. Crestwood, NY: St. Vladimir's Seminary Press, 2007.

HIPPOLYTUS OF ROME

Commentary on the Song of Songs. Edition (preserved only in Georgian) and Latin translation: G. Garitte, *Traités d'Hippolyte sur David et Goliath, sur le Cantique des cantiques et sur l'Antéchrist.* Corpus scriptorum Christianorum orientalium 263–64. Scriptores Iberici 15–16. Louvain: Sécretariat du CorpusSCO, 1965.

John Cassian

The Conferences (Conlationes). Edition: Michael Petschenig. *Iohannis Cassiani Conlationes XXIIII*, CSEL 13. Vienna: Geroldus, 1886. English translation: Boniface Ramsey. *John Cassian: The Conferences*. Ancient Christian Writers 57. New York and Mahwah, NJ: Paulist Press, 1997.

John the Deacon

The Life of Pope Saint Gregory (Sancti Gregorii papae vita). Edition: PL 75:59–242.

John of Ford

Sermons on the Song of Songs (Sermones super Cantica canticorum). English translation: Wendy Mary Beckett. *John of Ford: Sermons on the Song of Songs*. 7 vols. CF 29, 39, 43, 44, 45, 46, and 47. Kalamazoo, MI: Cistercian, 1978–84.

Idefonsus of Toledo

On the Writings of Illustrious Men (De virorum illustrium scriptis). Edition: PL 96:195–206.

Isiodore of Seville

On Illustrious Men (De viris illustribus). Edition: PL 83:1081–1106.

Origen

Commentary on the Song of Songs (In Cantico canticorum). Edition: W. A. Baehrens. *Origenes Werke*. 8. Bd. *Homilien zu Samuel I, zum Hohelied und zu den Propheten. Kommentar zum Hohelied, in Rufins und Hieronymus' Übersetzung*. Die griechischen christlichen Schriftsteller 33. Leipzig: J. C. Hinrichs, 1925. English translation: R. P. Lawson. *Origen. The Song of Songs Commentary and Homilies*. Ancient Christian Writers 26. New York and Mahwah, NJ: Newman Press, 1956.

Homiles on the Song of Songs (Homiliae in Canticum Canticorum). Editions: W. A. Baehrens. *Origenes Werke*. 8. Bd. *Homilien zu Samuel I, zum Hohelied und zu den Propheten. Kommentar zum Hohelied, in Rufins und Hieronymus' Übersetzung*. Die griechischen christlichen Schriftsteller 33. Leipzig: J. C. Hinrichs, 1925; and O. Rousseau. *Origène. Homélies sur le Cantique des Cantiques*. SChr 37. Paris: Cerf, 1954. English translation: R. P. Lawson. *Origen: The Song of Songs Commentary and Homilies*. Ancient Christian Writers 26. New York and Mahwah, NJ: Newman Press, 1956.

PAUL THE DEACON

The Life of Gregory (Vita Gregorii). Editions: PL 75:41–59 [interpolated version]; H. Grisar. *Zeitschrift für katholische Theologie* 11 (1888): 162–73; Walter Stuhlfath, *Gregor I, der Große. Sein Leben bis zu seiner Wahl zum Papste nebst einer Untersuchung der ältesten Viten.* Heidelberger Abhandlungen zur mittleren und neueren Geschichte, 39 (Heidelberg: C. Winter, 1913), 98–108.

The History of the Lombards (Historia Langobardorum). Edition: L. Bethmann and G. Waitz. *Monumenta Germaniae Historica, Scriptores rerum Langobardicarum et Italicarum.* Tome 1. *Scriptores rerum Langobardicarum et Italicarum saec. VI–IX* (Hannover, 1878), 12–187.

PATERIUS

Book of Testimonies (Liber testimonium). Edition: PL 79:683–916, with emendations by Raymond Étaix. "Le *Liber testimonium* de Paterius." *Revue des Sciences Religieuses* 32 (1958): 66–78.

TAIO OF SARAGOSSA

Sentences (Liber sententiarum). Edition: PL 80:727–990.

WILLIAM OF ST. THIERRY

Excerpts from the Books of Blessed Gregory on the Song of Songs (Excerpta de libris beati Gregorii super Cantica canticorum). Paul Verdeyen, Stanislaw Ceglar, and Antonius van Burink. *Guillelmi a Sancto Theodorico Expositio super Cantica canticorum, Brevis commentatio, Excerpta de libris beati Ambrosii et Gregorii super Cantica canticorum.* CCCM 87. Turnholt: Brepols, 1997, 387–444.

The Life of Saint Bernard (Vita Bernardi). Edition: PL 185:246b–247d.

The Golden Epistle (Epistola ad fratres de Monte Dei). Edition: Jean Déchanet. *Guillaume de saint-Thierry. Lettre aux frères du Mont-Dieu.* 1st ed. rev. et corr. SChr 223. Cerf: Paris, 2004. English translation: Theodore Berkeley. *William of Saint Thierry: The Golden Epistle.* CF 12. Kalamazoo, MI: Cistercian, 1971.

II. SECONDARY SOURCES

Amory, Patrick. *People and Identity in Ostrogothic Italy.* Cambridge: Cambridge University Press, 1997.

Astell, Ann W. *The Song of Songs in the Middle Ages.* Ithaca, NY: Cornell University Press, 1990.

Ayres, Lewis. *Nicaea and Its Legacy: An Approach to Fourth-Century Trinitarian Theology*. Oxford: Oxford University Press, 2004.
Bartelink, G. J. M. "Pope Gregory the Great's Knowledge of Greek." In *Gregory the Great: A Symposium*, edited by John C. Cavadini, 117–36. Notre Dame, IN: University of Notre Dame Press, 1995.
Batiffol, Pierre. *Saint Grégoire le Grand*. 2nd ed. Paris: J. Gabalda, 1928.
Bélanger, Rodrigue. "Anthropologie et parole de Dieu dans le commentaire de Grégoire le Grand sur la cantique des cantiques." In *Grégoire le Grand*, edited by Jacques Fontaine, Robert Gillet, and Stan Pellistrandi, 245–54. Paris: Éditions du CNRS, 1986.
Bell, David N. *Image and Likeness: The Augustinian Spirituality of William of St. Thierry*. CS 78. Kalamazoo, MI: Cistercian, 1984.
Bergant, Dianne. *The Song of Songs*. Berit Olam. Collegeville, MN: Liturgical Press, 2001.
Bloch, Ariel, and Chana Bloch. *The Song of Songs: A New Translation with an Introduction and Commentary*. New York: Random House, 1995.
Bloom, Harold, ed. *The Song of Songs*. New York: Chelsea House Publishers, 1988.
Bouyer, Louis. *The Cistercian Heritage*. London: Mowbray, 1958.
Boyarin, Daniel. "The Song of Songs: Lock or Key? Intertextuality, Allegory, and Midrash." In *The Book and the Text: Bible and Literary Theory*, edited by Regina M. Schwartz, 214–30. Cambridge, MA: Basil Blackwell, 1990.
Brenner, Athalya, ed. *A Feminist Companion to the Song of Songs*. Sheffield: Sheffield Academic Press, 1993.
———. and Carole R. Fontaine, eds. *The Song of Songs: A Feminist Companion to the Bible*. Sheffield: Sheffield Academic Press, 2000.
Burns, Thomas S. *Barbarians within the Gates of Rome*. Bloomington: Indiana University Press, 1994.
———. *Rome and the Barbarians, 100 B.C.–A.D. 400*. Baltimore, MD: Johns Hopkins University Press, 2003.
Bynum, Caroline Walker. "Seeing and Seeing Beyond: The Mass of St. Gregory in the Fifteenth Century." In *The Mind's Eye: Art and Theological Argument in the Middle Ages*, edited by Jeffrey F. Hamburger and Anne-Marie Bouché, 208–40. Princeton, NJ: Department of Art and Archaeology, Princeton University in association with Princeton University Press, 2005.
Cameron, Averil. *The Later Roman Empire. AD 284–430*. Cambridge, MA: Harvard University Press, 1993.
———. *The Mediterranean World in Late Antiquity. AD 395–600*. London: Routledge, 1993.

Cameron, Michael. "Augustine's Use of the Song of Songs against the Donatists." In *Augustine: Biblical Exegete*, edited by Frederick Van Fleteren and Joseph C. Schnaubelt, 99–127. New York: Peter Lang, 2001.

Capelle, Bernard. "Les homélies de saint Grégoire sur le Cantique." *Revue Bénédictine* 41 (1929): 209–17.

Cavadini, John C., ed. *Gregory the Great. A Symposium*. Notre Dame, IN: University of Notre Dame Press, 1995.

Christman, Angela Russell. *What did Ezekiel See? Christian Exegesis of Ezekiel's Vision of the Chariot from Irenaeus to Gregory the Great*. Leiden: Brill, 2005.

Clark, Elizabeth A. "The Uses of the Song of Songs: Origen and the Later Latin Fathers." In *Ascetic Piety and Women's Faith*, edited by Elizabeth A. Clark, 386–427. Lewiston, NY: E. Mellen Press, 1986.

———. "The Celibate Bridegroom and His Virginal Brides: Metaphor and the Marriage of Jesus in Early Christian Ascetic Exegesis." *Chuch History* 77, no. 1 (March 2008): 1–25.

Clark, Francis. *The Pseudo-Gregorian Dialogues*. Leiden: Brill, 1987.

———. *The "Gregorian" Dialogues and the Origins of Benedictine Monasticism*. Leiden: Brill, 2003.

Collins, Gregory. "Saint Gregory the Great as Mystical Theologian." In *L'eredità spirituale di Gregorio Magno tra Occidente e Oriente*, edited by Guido Innocenzo Gargano, 181–200. Verona: Gabrielli Editori, 2005.

Collins, Roger. *Early Medieval Europe*. 2nd ed. New York: St. Martin's Press, 1999.

Cremascoli, Giuseppe. *L'esegesi biblica di Gregorio Magno*. Brescia: Queriniana, 2001.

Cribiore, Raffaella. *Gymnastics of the Mind: Greek Education in Hellenistic and Roman Egypt*. Princeton, NJ: Princeton University Press, 2001.

Dagens, Claude. *Saint Grégoire le Grand: culture et expérience chrétiennes*. Paris: Études augustiniennes, 1977.

Dawson, David. *Allegorical Readers and Cultural Revision in Ancient Alexandria*. Berkeley: University of California Press, 1992.

———. *Christian Figural Reading and the Fashioning of Identity*. Berkeley: University of California Press, 2002.

Déchanet, Jean Marie. *William of St. Thierry: The Man and His Work*. CS 10. Kalamazoo, MI: Cistercian, 1972.

DelCogliano, Mark. "The Composition of William of St. Thierry's *Excerpts from the Books of Blessed Gregory on the Song of Songs*." *Cîteaux: Commentarii cistercienses* 58 (2007): 57–77.

———. "Basil of Caesarea, Didymus the Blind, and the Anti-Pneumatomachian Exegesis of Amos 4:13 and John 1:3." *Journal of Theological Studies* n.s. 61 (2010): 644–58.

DeLeeuw, Patricia. "Unde et Memores, Domine: Memory and Time and the Mass of St. Gregory." In *Memory and the Middle Ages*, edited by Nancy Netzer and Virginia Reunburg, 33–42. Boston, MA: Boston College Museum of Art, 1995.

D'Imperio, Francesca Sara. *Gregorio Magno. Bibliografiia per gli anni 1980–2003*. Firenze: Sismel, 2005.

Drobner, Hubertus R. *Person-Exegese und Christologie bei Augustinus*. Leiden: Brill, 1986.

———. "Grammatical Exegesis and Christology in St. Augustine." *Studia Patristica* 18 (1990): 49–63.

———. *The Fathers of the Church: A Comprehensive Introduction*. Translated by Siegfried S. Schatzmann with bibliographies updated and expanded for the English edition by William Harmless and Hubertus R. Drobner. Peabody, MA: Hendrickson Publishers, 2007.

Dudden, F. Homes. *Gregory the Great: His Place in History and Thought*. 2 vols. London: Longmans, Green, and Co., 1905.

Duval, Yves-Marie. "La discussion entre l'aprocrisaire Grégoire et la patriarche Eutychios a sujet de la réssurrection de la chair: l'arrière-plan doctrinal oriental et occidental." In *Grégoire le Grand*, edited by Jacques Fontaine, Robert Gillet, and Stan Pellistrandi, 347–66. Paris: CNRS, 1986.

Ekonomou, Andrew J. *Byzantine Rome and the Greek Popes: Eastern Influences on Rome and the Papacy from Gregory the Great to Zacharias, A.D. 590–752*. Lanham, MD: Lexington Books, 2007.

Elliott, Mark W. *The Song of Songs and Christology in the Early Church 381–451*. Studien und Texte zu Antike und Christentum 7. Tübingen: Mohr Siebeck, 2000.

Étaix, Raymond. "Le *Liber testimonium* de Paterius." *Revue des Sciences Religieuses* 32 (1958): 66–78.

Exum, J. Cheryl. *The Song of Songs*. Old Testament Library. Louisville, KY: Westminster John Knox Press, 2005.

Feuillet, André. *Comment lire le Cantique des Cantiques: Étude de théologie biblique et réflexions sur une méthode d'exégèse*. Paris: Téqui, 1999.

Fontaine, Jacques, Robert Gillet, and Stan Pellistrandi, eds. *Grégoire le Grand*. Paris: CNRS, 1986.

Fox, Michael V. *The Song of Songs and the Ancient Egyptian Love Songs*. Madison: University of Wisconsin Press, 1985.

Garrett, Duane. *Song of Songs*. Word Biblical Commentary 23B. Nashville, TN: Thomas Nelson Publishers, 2004.

Gillet, Robert, "Introduction." In *Grégoire le Grand: Morals sur Job I–II*, edited by *idem* and André de Gaudemaris, 7–133. SChr 32 bis. Paris: Cerf, 1975.

Godding, Robert. *Bibliografia di Gregorio Magno (1890/1989)*. Roma: Città Nuova Editrice, 1990.

Goulder, Michael D. *The Song of Fourteen Songs*. Journal for the Study of the Old Testament. Supplement Series 36. Sheffield: JSOT, 1986.

Goussainville, Pierre de. *Sancti Gregorii Papae Primi cognomenato Magni Opera in tres tomos distributa*. Lutetiae Parisiorum: impensis Societatis Typographicae, 1675.

Grant, Robert M., with David Tracy. *A Short History of the Interpretation of the Bible*. 2nd ed. Revised and enlarged. Philadelphia, PA: Fortress Press, 1984.

Hauréau, J. Barthélemy. *Notices et extraits de quelques manuscrits latins de la Bibliothèque Nationale*. Paris: Klincksieck, 1890–93.

Heine, Gotth. *Bibliotheca Anecdotorum seu Veterum Monumentum ecclesiasticorum Collectio novissima. Pars I. Monumenta regni Gothorum et Arabum in Hispaniis*. Leipzig: Weigel, 1848.

Humphries, Mark. "Italy, A.D. 425–605." In *Late Antiquity: Empire and Successors, A.D. 425–605*, edited by Averil Cameron, Bryan Ward-Perkins, and Michael Whitby, 525–51. The Cambridge Ancient History, vol. 14. Cambridge: Cambridge University Press, 2000.

Irvine, Martin. *The Making of Textual Culture: Grammatical and Literary Theory 350–1100*. Cambridge: Cambridge University Press, 1994.

Jones, A. H. M. *The Later Roman Empire, 284–602*. Baltimore, MD: Johns Hopkins University Press, 1986.

Kallas, E. "Martin Luther as Expositor of the Song of Songs." *Lutheran Quarterly* 2 (1988): 323–41.

Kardong, Terrence. "Who Wrote the *Dialogues of Saint Gregory?* A Report on a Controversy." *Cistercian Studies Quarterly* 39, no. 1 (2004): 31–39.

Kaster, Robert A. *Guardians of Language: The Grammarian and Society in Late Antiquity*. Berkeley: University of California Press, 1988.

Kessler, Stephan Ch. *Gregor der Grosse als Exeget : eine theologische Interpretation der Ezechielhomilien*. Innsbruck: Tyrolia, 1995.

Kinder, Terryl. *Cistercian Europe: Architecture of Contemplation*. Kalamazoo, MI: Cisterician, 2002.

Kugel, James L., and Rowan A. Greer. *Early Biblical Interpretation*. Philadelphia, PA: Westminster Press, 1986.

La Bonnardière, A. M. "Le Cantique des Cantiques dans l'œuvre de saint Augustin." *Revue des Études Augustiniennes* 1 (1955): 225–37.

LaCocque, André. *Romance She Wrote: A Hermeneutical Essay on Song of Songs*. Harrisburg, PA: Trinity International Press, 1998.

Leclerq, Jean. *The Love of Learning and the Desire for God*. 3rd ed. New York: Fordham University Press, 1982.

Lubac, Henri de. *Medieval Exegesis*, 2 vols. Translated by Mark Sebanc. Grand Rapids, MI: Eerdmans, 1998.

Lyke, Larry L. *I Will Espouse You Forever: The Song of Songs and the Theology of Love in the Hebrew Bible*. Nashville, TN: Abdingdon Press, 2007.

Margerie, Bertrand de. *Introduction to the History of Exegesis*. Petersham: St. Bede's Press, 1993–94.

Markus, R. A. *Gregory the Great and His World*. Cambridge: Cambridge University Press, 1997.

Marrou, H. I. *Education in Antiquity*. Madison: University of Wisconsin Press, 1956.

Martens, Peter W. "Revisiting the Allegory/Typology Distinction: The Case of Origen." *Journal of Early Christian Studies* 16 (2008): 283–317.

Martyn, John R. C. "Six Notes on Gregory the Great." *Medievalia et Humanistica*, n.s. 29 (2003): 1–25.

———. "Pope Gregory the Great and the Irish." *Journal of Australian Early Medieval Association* 1 (2005): 65–83.

Matter, E. Ann. *The Voice of My Beloved: The Song of Songs in Western Medieval Christianity*. Philadelphia: University of Pennsylvania Press, 1990.

———. "Song of Songs, Book of." in *Dictionary of Biblical Interpretation*. Vol. 2, edited by John H. Hayes, 492–96. Nashville, TN: Abingdon, 1999.

McCready, William D. *Signs of Sanctity: Miracles in the Thought of Gregory the Great*. Studies and Texts/Pontifical Institute of Mediaeval Studies 91. Toronto: Pontifical Institute of Mediaeval Studies, 1989.

Meyvaert, Paul. "A New Edition of Gregory the Great's Commentaries on the Canticle and I Kings." *Journal of Theological Studies* n.s. 19 (1968): 215–25.

———. "The Date of Gregory the Great's Commentaries on the Canticle of Canticles and on I Kings." *Sacris Erudiri* 23 (1978–79): 191–216.

———. "Uncovering a Lost Work of Gregory the Great: Fragments of the Early Commentary on Job." *Traditio* 50 (1995): 55–74.

Moorhead, John. *Gregory the Great*. The Early Church Fathers. London and New York: Routledge, 2005.

Morgan, Teresa. *Literate Education in the Hellenistic and Roman Worlds*. Cambridge: Cambridge University Press, 1998.

Müller, Susanne. *"Fervorem discamus amoris": das Hohelied und seine Auslegung bei Gregor dem Grossen*. St. Ottilien: EOS Verlag, 1991.

Murphy, Roland E. "The Canticle of Canticles and the Virgin Mary." *Carmelus* 1 (1954): 18–28.

———. "Patristic and Medieval Exegesis—Help or Hindrance?" *Catholic Biblical Quarterly* 43 (1981): 505–16.

———. *The Song of Songs: A Commentary on the Book of Canticles or the Song of Songs.* Hermeneia. Minneapolis, MN: Fortress Press, 1990.

Neuschafer, Bernhardt. *Origenes als Philologe.* 2 vols. Basle: Friedrich Reinhardt, 1987.

Ohly, Friedrich. *Hohelied-Studien: Grundzüge einer Geschichte der Hoheliedauslegung des Abendlandes bis um 1200.* Wiesbaden: Franz Steiner, 1958.

O'Keefe, John J., and J. J. Reno. *Sanctified Vision: An Introduction to Early Christian Interpretation of the Bible.* Baltimore, MD: The Johns Hopkins University Press, 2005.

Oudin, Casimir. *Commentarius de Scriptoribus Ecclesiae Antiquis.* Frankfort and Leipzig, 1722.

Parente, Paschal P. "The Canticle of Canticles in Mystical Theology." *Catholic Biblical Quarterly* 6 (1944): 142–58.

Pennington, M. Basil. *The Last of the Fathers.* Studies in Monasticism 1. Still River, MA: St. Bede's Publications, 1983.

Petersen, Joan M. *The Dialogues of Gregory the Great in the Late Antique Cultural Background.* Studies and Texts/Pontifical Institute of Mediaeval Studies 69. Toronto: Pontifical Institute of Mediaeval Studies, 1984.

———. "The Influence of Origen upon Gregory the Great's Exegesis of the Song of Songs." *Studia Patristica* 17 (1985): 343–47.

Phipps, William E. "The Plight of the Song of Songs." *Journal of the American Academy of Religion* 42 (1974): 82–100. Reprinted in Bloom, *The Song of Songs,* 5–23.

Pope, Marvin H. *Song of Songs.* The Anchor Bible 7C. Garden City, NY: Doubleday, 1977.

Porcel, O. *La doctrina monastica de San Gregorio Magno y la 'Regula Monachorum.'* Washington, DC: Catholic University of America Press, 1951.

Provan, Iain W. *Ecclesiastes, Song of Songs.* Grand Rapids, MI: Zondervan, 2001.

Ramos-Lisson, Domingo. "En torno a la exégesis de San Gregorio Magno sobre el 'Cantar de los Cantares'." *Teología y vida* 42 (2001): 241–65.

Recchia, Vincenzo. *L'esegesi di Gregorio Magno al cantico dei cantici.* Torino: Società Editrice Internationale, 1967.

———. *Gregorio Magno papa ed esegeta biblico.* Bari: Edipuglia, 1996.

———. "*Invigilata Lucernis*: L'esegesi di Gregorio Magno ai simboli del «Cantico dei Cantici»," *Invigilata Lucernis* 23 (2001): 207–21.

———. *Lettera e profezia nell'esegesi di Gregorio Magno*. Quaderni di "Invigilata Lucernis," Dipartamento di Studi Classici e Cristiani, Università degli Studi di Bari, vol. 20. Bari: Edipuglia, 2003.

Richards, Jeffery. *Consul of God: The Life and Times of Gregory the Great*. London: Routledge and Kegan Paul, 1980.

Riché, Pierre. *Education and Culture in the Barbarian West*. Translated by John J. Contreni. Columbia: University of South Carolina Press, 1976.

———. *Petite vie de saint Grégoire le Grand (540–604)*. Paris: Desclée de Brouwer, 1995.

Riedlinger, Helmut. *Die Makellosigkeit der Kirche in den Lateinischen Hoheliedkommentaren des Mittelalters*. Beiträge zur Geschichte der Philosophie und Theologie des Mittelalters 38, 3. Münster: West. Aschendorff, 1958.

Rivera, Alfonso de. "Sentido mariológico del Cantar de los Cantares." *Ephemerides mariológicas* 1 (1951): 437–68; and 2 (1952): 25–42.

Robert, André, and Raymond J. Tournay, with André Feuillet. *Le Cantique des Cantiques: Traduction et commentaire*. Paris: J. Gabalda, 1963.

Rönnegård, Per. *Threads and Images: The Use of Scripture in Apophthegmata Patrum*. Lund: Lund University, 2007.

Rowley, H. H. "Interpretation of the Song of Songs." *The Servant of the Lord and Other Essays on the Old Testament*. Rev. ed. Oxford: Basil Blackwell, 1965, 197–245.

Rudolph, Conrad. *Violence and Daily Life: Reading, Art, and Polemics in the Cîteaux Moralia in Job*. Princeton, NJ: Princeton University Press, 1997.

Saint-Marthe, Dom Denys de. *Histoire de S. Grégoire le Grand, Pape et Docteur de l'Église*. Rouen: Behourt, 1697.

Simonetti, Manilo. *Biblical Interpretation in the Early Church*. Edinburgh: T & T Clark, 1994.

Slusser, Michael. "The Exegetical Roots of Trinitarian Theology." *Theological Studies* 49 (1988): 461–76.

Straw, Carole. *Gregory the Great: Perfection in Imperfection*. Berkeley: University of California Press, 1988.

———. *Gregory the Great*. Authors of the Middle Ages 12. Historical and Religious Writers of the Latin West. Aldershot: Variorum, 1996.

Tournay, Raymond J. *Word of God, Song of Love: A Commentary on the Song of Songs*. New York: Paulist, 1988. English translation of *Quand Dieu parle aux hommes le langage de l'amour: études sur Le Cantique des Cantiques*. Cahiers de La Revue Biblique 21. Paris: J. Gabalda, 1982.

Trible, Phyllis. "Love's Lyrics Redeemed." *God and the Rhetoric of Sexuality*. Minneapolis, MN: Fortress Press, 1978, 144–65. Reprinted in Bloom, *The Song of Songs*, 49–66.

Turner, Denys. *Eros and Allegory: Medieval Exegesis of the Song of Songs.* CS 156. Kalamazoo, MI: Cistercian, 1995.

Vaccari, P. A. "De scriptis S. Gregorii Magni in Canticum Canticorum." *Verbum Domini* 9 (1929): 304–7.

Verbraken, Patrick. "Le commentaire de Saint Gregoire sur le Premier Livre des Rois." *Revue Bénédictine* 66 (*1956*): 159–217.

———. "La tradition manuscrite du commentaire de saint Grégoire sur le Cantique des cantiques." *Revue Bénédictine* 73 (1963): 277–88.

———. "Un nouveau manuscript du Commentaire de saint Grégoire sur le Cantique des Cantiques." *Revue Bénédictine* 75 (1965): 143–45.

Vogüé, Adalbert de. "Les vues de Grégoire le Grand sur la vie religieuse dans son commentaire des Rois." *Studia Monastica* 20 (1978): 17–63; English translation: "The Views of St Gregory the Great on the Religious Life in his Commentary on the Book of Kings." *Cistercian Studies Quarterly* 17 (1982): 40–64 and 212–32.

———. *The Life of St. Benedict—Gregory the Great.* Translated by Hilary Costello and Eoin de Bhaldraithe. Petersham, MA: St. Bede's Publications, 1993.

———. "L'auteur du Commentaire des Rois attribué à saint Grégoire: un moine de Cava?" *Revue Bénédictine* 106 (1996): 319–31.

———. "Is Gregory the Great the Author of the *Dialogues*?" *American Benedictine Review* 56, no. 3 (Sept. 2005): 309–14.

Walsh, Corey Ellen. *Exquisite Desire: Religion, the Erotic and the Song of Songs.* Minneapolis, MN: Fortress Press, 2000.

Ward, Benedicta. *The Venerable Bede.* CS 169. Kalamazoo, MI: Cistercian, 1998.

Waszink, J. H. "Sancti Gregorii Magni Expositiones in Canticum Canticorum, in Librum Primum Regum." *Vigliae Christianae* 27 (1973): 72–74.

Weems, Renita J. "Song of Songs." In *Women's Bible Commentary*, edited by Carol A. Newsom and Sharon H. Ringe, 156–60. Louisville, KY: Westminster John Knox Press, 1992.

———. "Song of Songs." *The New Interpreter's Bible*, vol. 5. Nashville, TN: Abingdon, 1997, 361–434.

Wilmart, André. "Le recueil grégorien de Paterius et les fragments wisigothiques de Paris." *Revue Bénédictine* 39 (1927): 81–104.

Yannaras, Christos. *Variations on the Song of Songs.* Brookline: Holy Cross Orthodox Press, 2005.

Young, Frances. *Biblical Exegesis and the Formation of Christian Culture.* Cambridge: Cambridge University Press, 1997.

SCRIPTURAL INDEX

Old Testament

Genesis
4:8	213n
5:24	213
6:13f.	214n
12:4	116n
22:16-17	214n
25:13	133n
26:14-22	116n
28:12	116n
29:20	214n
29:25	214n
30:29	214n
32:25	214n
39:12-20	214n

Exodus
12:21-29	217n
14:28	143n
15:1-28	90
15:6	155, 199
15:19	244
15:21	90, 113
19:12-13	112
20:17	212
33:11	120n
33:17-23	120n
33:21	247
33:23	247

Leviticus
19:18	212

Numbers
12:3	214
12:6-8	120
21:17-18	90
25:7-11	214n

Deuteronomy
32:1	114
32:1-43	90
33:2	113, 201

Joshua
10:12-14	217n

Judges
5:1-31	90

1 Samuel
2:1	114
2:1-10	90
2:5	114
12:23	215
16:1	215
16:2	215

26:11	215	59:7	199
		62:9	127–28
2 Samuel		63:8	245
22:1-51	90	67:14	209, 209n
1 Kings		67:18	143
10:21	162n, 208n	68:3	244
17:17-24	217n	75:1	97
		83:6	128
2 Kings		104:4	198
4:18-37	217n	117:19	128
		117:27	123
1 Chronicles		118:96	128
1:29	133n	118:140	112
16:8-36	90	137:6	188
Job		138:11	235
3:7	231	140:2	160, 205
3:9	231	142:2	229
9:9	170	150:4	227, 227n
26:13	220	*Proverbs*	
28:19	235	3:16	87, 199
30:29	192	5:1	116
38:29	246	10:14	111
41:19	245	13:14	117n
Psalms		16:22	117n
2:11	162, 208, 208n	22:24-25	194
16:8	194	25:2	111
17:2	114	*Ecclesiastes*	
17:10-12	239	1:2	116
18:6	93, 94, 155, 199, 244	9:8	166
30:3	194		
30:20	132	*Song of Songs*	
30:25	207	1:1	94, 95, 96
35:10	117n	1:1a	99, 118, 120, 123, 150, 151, 186, 187
41:2	230		
41:3	198, 223	1:1b	99, 119, 120, 121, 123, 151, 187
44:6	245		
44:8	119		
48:13	141	1:1b-2a	118

Scriptural Index

1:1-8	30, 31, 32, 43, 45, 46, 47, 48, 99	1:6ab	140
1:1–4:5	44, 46	1:7	41n, 80, 100, 141, 190
1:2	179	1:8	100, 142, 143, 144
1:2a	99, 119, 121, 124	1:9f.	30, 31, 32, 45, 48
1:2b	99, 82, 83, 96, 97, 98, 98n, 125	1:11	86, 152, 191
		2:2	89, 191, 193
1:2bc	126	2:3	86, 194, 195, 245
1:2c	99, 125, 151, 188	2:5	80, 152, 195, 196, 197, 198, 245
1:3	46, 50n, 155, 199, 243, 244, 245	2:6	87, 198
1:3a	99, 100, 126	2:8	93, 94, 155, 199, 243, 244
1:3b	98, 99, 100, 127, 128, 188, 188n	2:9	50n, 80, 86, 155, 199, 200
1:3c	100, 129	2:10-12	156, 201, 202, 246
1:3cd	128	2:12	157
1:3c-f	30	2:19	139
1:3d	100, 130	3:1	59, 158, 204
1:3e	100, 131	3:1-2	50n
1:3f	100, 131, 132	3:1-4	50n, 157, 202–3
1:4a	100, 135, 137, 151, 188	3:1–5:10	59
1:4b	100, 135	3:3	204
1:4bc	137	3:3-4	50n
1:4c	100, 135	3:4	159, 204
1:4-5	81	3:6	159, 160, 161, 205, 206
1:4-5a	133		
1:5a	100, 136	3:7	161, 206
1:5ab	134, 138	3:8	80, 81, 82, 161, 162, 207
1:5b	100, 136		
1:5c	81, 100, 134, 136, 138	3:9	163, 208n, 209
		3:9-10	162, 164n, 208
1:5d	100, 137	3:10	163, 164, 210
1:5de	134, 138, 188, 189	4:1	164, 165, 211
1:5e	100, 137	4:2	88, 165, 211, 246
1:6	40, 41, 41n, 88	4:3	82, 165, 211
1:6a	100, 139, 189	4:4	80, 166, 212, 216
1:6b	100, 139	4:5	45, 46

4:5-6	167, 218	55:13	245
4:6	43, 168, 219	58:14	151, 186
4:6–8:14	44, 45, 46	*Jeremiah*	
4:8	116, 168, 219	2:2	92, 114
4:10	169		
4:11	169, 220	*Lamentations*	
4:13	82, 170	3:16	246
4:16	88, 170, 171, 221, 221n	*Ezekiel*	
		1:1–4:3	23
5:2	81, 171, 222	40:1-47	23
5:4	172, 223	40:7	164, 164n
5:5	223	*Hosea*	
5:6	173, 224	2:19-20	92, 114
5:7	50n, 173, 224	*Joel*	
5:11	173, 225	1:17	224
6:3	174, 175, 225, 226, 228	*Habakkuk*	
6:6	175, 228	3:3	112
6:8	247	3:5-6	127
6:9	176, 229	3:15	142
7:4	50n, 177, 231, 248	*Malachi*	
7:12	177, 233	1:6	92, 114
8:5	178, 234, 235		
8:6	178, 179, 236		
8:8	179, 237		
8:13	179, 237	**New Testament**	
8:14	45, 83, 180, 238	*Matthew*	
Wisdom		2:11	224
9:15	201	5:2	118, 150, 187
		5:23-24	228
Isaiah		5:28	212
1:20	151, 186	5:44	213
5:1-7	90	6:24	213
14:13	221	7:13	152n, 191n
24:16	129	9:15	115
26:9	198	10:5	133, 134n
26:10	231	16:13	111
53:1	150, 186		

16:15	112	13:26	134–35
16:23	128	13:46	135
16:24	213n	19:12	217n
22:1-14	110n	21:13	216n
22:37	212	26:14	142
22:39	212		

Mark

8:33	128
9:50	227, 227n

Luke

1:35	86, 190, 195
7:44-45	122
7:45	94, 95, 96, 123, 187
9:23	213n
11:23	213
12:33	213
14:33	213
15:22	236n
23:13-35	118n
24:32	113
24:39	12

John

1:3	150, 186
1:14	187
3:29	115
4:14	117n
10:13	246
12:31	220
14:6	216n
14:27	95

Acts

5:15	217n
6:5	192n
9:32-34	217n
10:1–11:18	136n
11:1	136

Romans

5:5	97
7:23	127, 229–30
7:25	127
8:38-39	237
9:5	199
13:11	81, 222
13:12	230

1 Corinthians

1:25	121
2:9	175, 228
3:3-4	111
8:1	131
9:24	98, 127
9:26-27	98
11:3	173, 225
15:33	194
15:34	81, 222

2 Corinthians

2:15	86, 89, 124, 153, 167, 171, 188, 191, 218, 221
3:6	111
5:1	231
5:17	112
10:4-5	136
11:2	115
12:14	129

Galatians

2:17	134
4:26	136n

Ephesians
4:24	151, 188
5:8	135
5:27	115
6:17	82, 161, 207

Philippians
1:21	196, 231
1:23	196, 223, 231
1:24	196
2:6-7	83, 98n, 125
2:15	193

Colossians
4:6	227n

1 Thessalonians
2:19	196
4:13	222
4:13-14	81
4:14	222

2 Timothy
4:8	132

Hebrews
11:5	213
11:8	214
11:17-18	214n
12:14	227–28
12:20	112

James
3:2	229

1 Peter
1:4	179, 238
1:12	174, 225

2 Peter
2:7-8	192–93

1 John
1:8	151, 188
5:6	215–16, 216n

Revelation
2:6	192n
2:15	192n
7:17	117n
19:9	115
21:2	115
22:17	238

GENERAL INDEX

Abel, 192, 194, 213
Abraham, 116, 192, 214
abstinence, 175, 226–27, 228, 247
Ælred of Rievaulx, 54
Æmiliana, 6
Æthelbert, King, 18
affection, 115, 154
Agapitus, Pope, 6
Agilulf, 17, 23n
Alaric, 2
Alberic, 54
Alexandria, 18, 22
allegory, 60, 63–64, 75, 76n, 84, 109, 235. *See also* allegory; interpretation, figural
Amana, 168, 219
Ambrose of Milan, 8, 49, 52, 55, 56, 68, 92–98
Anastasius (priest of Neas), 227n
Anastasius (Roman emperor), 3
ancient enemy, 170, 175, 220, 226. *See also* Devil; Satan
angels, 72, 81, 88, 116–19, 126, 138, 170–71, 174, 195, 214, 225, 237. *See also* Cherubim
Antioch, 18, 22, 192n

apostle(s), 19, 81, 112, 129, 130, 134, 136, 142, 158, 179, 188, 192, 199, 204, 205, 238. *See also* Paul; Peter
Apponius, 89–92
Aquileia, 5
ardor; ardent, 113, 123, 124, 125, 138, 153, 158, 160, 165, 175, 191, 203, 205, 206, 212, 215, 224, 228, 245. *See also* fervor, fervent; burning (spiritual); warmth (spiritual)
Arius, 139
arm(s), 150, 186
ascension (of Christ), 83, 94, 180, 199, 238, 239, 240, 244
ascension (of mind), 167, 178, 218, 234–35
Augustine of Canterbury, 18
Augustine of Hippo, 8, 41, 49, 50n, 52, 68, 73, 85, 87–89, 89n, 92, 93, 149n, 184, 198n
Ayres, Lewis, 68

baptism, 125, 143, 151, 165, 188, 211, 236

barbarians, 2–5. *See also* Franks; Lombards; Ostrogoths; Vandals; Visigoths

bed, 73, 116, 117, 157–58, 161, 202–3, 206

Bede, 28, 29, 50, 52–3, 56, 57, 147–48, 150n, 154n, 155n, 156n, 158n, 160n, 161n, 163n, 164n, 165n, 171n, 172n, 174n, 178n, 180n, 208n, 243, 251, 257, 279, 280, 281, 282–85, 293
Commentary on the Song of Songs, 52–53

Bélanger, Rodrigue, 40n, 41n, 42, 86, 88, 89, 108, 275–76

Benedict I, Pope, 10

Benedict of Nursia, 20, 22, 23

Benevento, 17

Bergant, Dianne, 63

Bernard of Clairvaux, 54, 55, 59

body; bodily, 25, 61, 78, 110, 112, 133n, 171, 175, 176, 179, 190, 194, 195, 197, 199, 201, 224, 226, 231, 237, 239, 240, 244, 246

body of Christ (Church), 167, 218

Body of Christ (Eucharist), 26

Boethius, 7

breast(s), 99–100, 110, 118–19, 120–21, 123–24, 130, 131, 151, 167, 169, 179, 187, 218, 237

Bride, 72–73, 80, 81, 86, 95, 110, 114, 115, 117, 118, 125, 141, 143, 150–51, 153, 155, 158, 165, 167, 173, 186, 188, 190, 194–95, 197, 198n, 203–4, 205, 209, 211, 212, 218, 222, 223, 224, 225, 245, 246, 248. *See also* Church; soul

Bridegroom. *See* Jesus Christ

Britain, 18

burning (spiritual), 78, 95, 110, 112–13, 125, 139, 140, 152, 153, 154, 160–61, 165, 168, 170, 173, 175, 189–90, 191, 197–98, 206, 212, 216, 219, 224, 228, 230, 234, 237. *See also* charity; desire; love; panting; yearning

Cain, 192, 194

Capelle, Bernard, 30–33, 40–42, 47,

charity, 41, 78, 95, 110, 113, 121, 122, 128–29, 131, 139, 140, 142, 174–75, 187, 197, 215–16, 226–28. *See also* love

Cassiodorus, 7

cheek(s), 110, 175, 228

Cherubim, 239

chilliness (spiritual), 88, 89, 170, 171, 221. *See also* coldness (spiritual)

Christ. *See* Jesus Christ

Church, 10, 20, 58, 63, 64, 72–73, 75–76, 80–83, 86, 88–89, 92, 95–96, 114, 115, 116, 117, 118, 119, 120, 121, 124, 128–29, 130, 133, 134, 135, 136–37, 140, 141–42, 150, 151, 152, 153, 155, 157–59, 159–60, 163, 165, 166, 167, 169, 170, 171, 174, 175, 176, 177, 178, 179, 180, 187, 188, 189, 191, 198, 200, 201–2, 204, 205, 209, 210, 211, 212, 213, 216, 218, 221, 223, 225, 226, 228, 229–31, 232, 234, 235, 236, 237, 238,

244, 245, 246, 247, 248. *See also*
   Bride; Church, English;
   Church, Roman
Church, English, 26, 52–53
Church, Roman, 6, 14, 18, 19, 28,
   50
Cicero, 7
Claudius, 31, 33–43
Cleopas, 118
Clovis, 3
coldness (spiritual), 109, 110, 125,
   128, 157, 201, 202, 212, 218,
   221, 233, 245, 246. *See also*
   chilliness (spiritual)
Columbanus, 29, 434–35, 46
compunction, 67, 122–23, 160,
   205–6
concord, 175, 226–28
condescension, divine, 110, 119
Constantia, 13
Constantine, 1, 4
Constantinople, 1, 3, 8, 10, 11, 13,
   14, 18, 19, 21, 22, 48n, 87n
contemplation, 10, 13, 14, 16, 22,
   67, 77, 113, 116, 123, 124, 129,
   130, 151, 154, 157, 167–68, 169,
   170, 171, 178, 187, 190, 197,
   202, 218, 219, 222, 234, 235, 245
coolness (spiritual), 152, 189,
   195n, 224, 245. *See also*
   refreshment
Cornelius, 136
Creator, 118, 124, 136, 139, 142,
   150, 152, 163, 165, 166, 170,
   173, 174, 187, 190, 203, 209,
   211, 212, 216, 223, 224, 225,
   230, 235
crown; crowning, 168–69, 196,
   219–20

Dalmatia, 18
Dante, 26
David, 90, 91, 93, 114, 166, 198,
   212, 213, 215, 216, 230
death, 81, 112, 169, 179, 216,
   220, 222, 223, 236–37
death (of Christ), 83, 169, 180,
   220, 238
Deborah, 90
Defensor of Ligugé, 49
demon(s); demonic, 143, 168,
   200, 219, 220. *See also* spirit(s),
   evil
desire, 7, 9, 61–62, 64, 73, 76, 78,
   80, 81, 87, 95–96, 99, 111, 116,
   118, 120, 122–23, 125, 127,
   132, 138, 139, 141, 150, 152,
   153, 154, 155, 157, 158, 161,
   161n, 173, 174, 175, 179, 180,
   187, 189, 190, 191, 194–95,
   196–98, 200, 203, 206, 212,
   213, 219, 222–25, 228, 231,
   233, 234, 237, 238, 239, 240,
   244, 246. *See also* burning
   (spiritual); charity; love; panting; yearning
Devil, 88, 142, 221. *See also*
   ancient enemy; Satan
Didymus the Blind, 98
discord, 174–75, 226, 228
divinity, 78, 82, 83, 96–98, 110,
   111, 119, 125, 156, 158, 174,
   176, 180, 187, 200, 205, 225,
   231, 239
drunkenness, 121, 124, 131

ear(s), 193, 228
Ecclesiastes, book of, 32, 78, 116
Egypt, 214

Ekonomou, Andrew, 11–12
elect, 113, 122, 125, 141, 143, 144, 151, 152, 153, 157, 158, 160, 165, 167, 175, 176, 180, 188, 189, 190, 191, 192, 196n, 198, 202, 203, 204, 205, 211, 218, 224, 226, 228, 229, 230, 231, 238, 244, 245, 246
England, 18, 28, 52. *See also* Church, English
enigma(s), 77, 79, 84, 109. *See also* allegory; interpretation, figural
enjoyment, 61, 118, 120, 213
enkindling (spiritual), 78, 110, 122, 168, 170, 214, 216, 218, 219, 221. *See also* burning (spiritual)
Enoch, 213
Esau, 133
Étaix, Raymond, 147, 258n, 259n, 262n, 266n, 267n, 268n, 269n, 270n, 271n
eternal life, 87, 132, 179, 237
Eutychius of Constantinople, 11–12
examples (*exempla*), 13, 25, 140, 141, 152, 166, 167–68, 191–93, 212, 216, 218–19
exarch, 4, 8, 17
exteriority, 77–79, 84, 97, 109, 110, 111, 113, 115, 121, 123, 125, 138–39, 152, 171–72, 189, 190, 222, 234, 247. *See also* interiority
Exum, J. Cheryl, 61, 64
eye(s), 118, 120, 122, 138, 155, 156, 157, 158, 164, 165, 171, 175, 193, 199, 200, 201, 202, 203, 211, 212, 213, 214, 216, 228, 232, 234, 247, 294

Ezekiel, 129
Ezekiel, book of, 23, 27, 43, 44, 45, 48n, 67, 92

faith, 77, 82, 124, 128, 129, 141, 159, 163, 169, 170, 177, 178, 192, 204, 210, 217, 220, 221, 227, 229, 233, 235, 236, 247
Father (God), 79, 91–92, 94, 114–15, 118, 150, 186, 239, 240, 244
fathers; forefathers, 45, 49, 54, 73, 78, 85, 93, 149, 158, 159, 163, 166, 168, 175, 185, 199, 204, 209, 216–19, 228, 244
Felix III, Pope, 6
fervor; fervent, 41, 73, 88, 117, 126, 127, 128, 139, 140, 142, 170, 195, 217, 221, 230, 234. *See also* ardor, ardent; burning (spiritual); warmth (spiritual)
flesh (of Christ), 12, 86, 93, 94, 118, 119, 121, 155, 180, 187, 199, 200, 238, 244
flesh, 80, 81, 83, 111, 112, 115, 127, 135–36, 152, 154, 157, 160, 161, 162, 171, 175, 191, 196, 196n, 202, 206, 207, 208n, 212, 214, 216, 222, 223, 224, 226, 228, 230, 245
forgiveness, 15, 130
fragrance, 119. *See also* odor; scent; smell; stench
Franks, 3, 11, 19, 27

Gaul, 3, 18, 43,
Gentile(s), 81, 95, 96, 133–37, 167, 187, 193, 218, 223, 236, 246
Gilbert of Hoyland, 59

Gillet, Robert, 84
Gordiana, 6
Gordianus, 6, 6n
Goussainville, Pierre de, 31–32
grace, 9, 118, 119, 120, 122, 129, 130, 131, 133, 134, 135, 139, 149, 151, 163, 167, 176, 179, 188, 190, 209, 215, 217, 220, 227n, 231, 236
Gregory of Tours, 7, 27
Gregory the Great
    achievements as Pope, 17–20
    approach to figural interpretation, 73–79
    conversion of, 9–10
    deacon, 10–14
    death of, 24–25
    debate with Eutychius, 11–13
    Dialogues, 20, 23–24, 36n
    early life of, 5–10
    education of, 7–8
    election as pope, 15–16
    Exposition on the Song of Songs, 29–48; authenticity of, 29–33; date of, 33–43; circumstances of composition of, 33–43; scope of, 43–48
    family of, 5–7
    Homilies on Ezekiel, 23, 27, 44, 67, 86, 92
    Homilies on the Gospels, 22–23, 86
    legacy of, 26–28
    monastic life of, 10, 14
    Moralia in Iob, 14, 21, 21n, 37, 38, 48n, 49, 51, 66, 86, 101, 184
    motivation for figural interpretation, 65–67
    papal *apocrisiarius*, 10–14, 21
    Pastoral Care, 21, 44, 48n, 86
    political career of, 8–9
    practice of figural interpretation, 79–84
    Registrum epistularum, 20
    residence in Constantinople, 11–14
    writings of, 20–24
Guerric of Igny, 54

hair(s), 82, 165, 187, 211
Hannah, 90–91
head(s), 82, 154–55, 165–66, 173, 198, 211, 225
headband, 82, 165, 211–12
heaven, 9, 93–94, 114, 115, 155, 175, 191, 193, 199, 211, 226, 231, 239, 240, 244. *See also* homeland, heavenly; homeland, spiritual; kingdom, heavenly
Heine, Gotthard, 108
Hellinus of Saint Thierry, 184
Hermon, 168, 219
Herod, 215
Hippolytus of Rome, 94
holiness, 23, 128, 227, 236
Holy Spirit, 27, 75, 82, 88, 89, 96–98, 119, 120n, 161, 170, 178, 179, 190, 193, 207, 216n, 221, 235, 236, 237, 240, 244
    as Spirit of grace, 88
    as Spirit of truth, 170, 221
homeland, heavenly, 170, 172, 174, 180, 207, 223, 225, 233, 238, 247; *see also* heaven; homeland, spiritual; kingdom, heavenly

homeland, spiritual, 170, 221; *see also* heaven; homeland, heavenly; kingdom, heavenly
hope, 109, 128–29, 130, 132, 132n, 159, 162, 164, 179, 196, 201, 204–5, 207, 208, 208n, 210, 215, 238, 240
human condition, 80, 109, 111, 127, 155–56, 171, 193, 221, 234
human nature, 94, 97, 111, 126, 138, 159
human nature (of Christ), 86, 119, 156, 158, 159, 174, 200–205, 225
human race. *See* humanity
humanity, 49, 60, 109, 118, 125, 193
humility, 23, 121, 124, 129, 131, 142, 151, 167, 175, 188, 192, 213, 217, 218, 226, 235–36, 245, 247
humility (of Christ), 120, 121, 125, 158, 205

Ildefonus of Toledo, 28, 29, 47
Illyricum, 3, 18
image of God, 141, 152, 190
immortality, 11, 236
impassibility, 110
incarnation, 49, 75, 76n, 82, 86, 87, 94, 97, 98, 118, 119, 121, 125, 126, 187, 194–95, 199, 220
interiority, 22, 77–78, 84, 109, 110, 111, 112, 113, 115, 116, 120, 123, 138–39, 152, 159, 161, 163–65, 170, 171, 172, 176, 189, 190, 198, 205, 206, 209, 210, 211, 222, 223, 230–31, 233, 234, 235, 239, 246–47. *See also* exteriority

interpretation, allegorical. *See* interpretation, figural
interpretation, figural, 70, 79, 80, 82
   allegory vs. typology, 74–75
   grammatical reading techniques and, 67–73
   Gregory's approach to, 73–79
   Gregory's motivation for, 65–67
   Gregory's practice of, 79–84
   modern disdain for, 62–64
   Song of Songs and, history of, 57–65
Isaac, 116, 192, 214
Isaiah, 198, 221, 245
Isidore of Seville, 13, 28, 29, 48n, 49
Italy, 2, 3, 4, 5, 7, 8, 11, 14, 18, 19, 20, 89

Jacob, 116, 192, 214
Jeremiah, 246
Jerome, 8, 32, 43, 52, 68, 85, 92, 98n, 129n
Jerusalem, 18, 22, 100, 133, 135, 136, 162, 164, 174, 208, 210, 225, 227n
Jesus, 75, 118, 196, 222, 237, 240. *See also* Jesus Christ
Jesus Christ, 75, 196, 240
   as Beloved, 157–58, 172, 173, 180, 199, 203–5, 223, 224, 238
   as Bridegroom, 72–73, 79, 80, 91–92, 93–94, 110, 114–15, 116, 117, 118, 119, 122, 123, 124, 129, 130, 138, 139, 141, 143, 151, 153, 156, 157, 158,

169, 170, 173, 177, 178, 179, 186, 187, 188, 190, 193, 195, 197, 198n, 201, 202, 203, 205, 212, 218, 219, 221, 225, 229, 231, 235, 236, 237, 238, 245, 246
- as Christ, 12, 25, 26, 43, 49, 58, 63, 64, 72, 76, 83, 95, 97, 98, 112, 115, 122, 123, 124, 134, 135, 153, 159, 167, 171, 173, 188, 191, 196, 198n, 199, 204, 215, 216, 218, 221, 223, 225, 231, 237
- as Judge, 99, 132, 176, 231
- as Mediator, 118, 119
- as Only-Begotten Son, 150, 151, 186
- as Redeemer, 95–96, 118, 121, 133, 139, 151, 156, 157, 158, 159, 164, 173, 186, 187, 190, 199, 200, 203, 204, 210, 218, 225, 240
- as Son of God, 118, 151, 159, 186, 204
- as Son of man, 111
- as Truth, 93, 155, 199, 216, 216n, 220, 220n, 227, 227n, 228, 244
- as Word of God, 59, 86, 87, 92, 94, 115, 150, 179, 186, 187, 237
- *See also* ascension (of Christ); death (of Christ); flesh (of Christ); human nature (of Christ); humility (of Christ); Incarnation; resurrection

Jew(s), Jewish, 81, 95–97, 133–34, 167, 187, 200, 218, 223

Job, 192, 193, 231, 235

Job, Book of, 14, 21, 45, 48n, 67
John (subdeacon), 33, 38
John VIII, Pope, 28
John Cassian, 8, 85, 98–99
John of Ford, 59
John of Ravenna, 35n
John of the Cross, 60
John the Baptist, 215–16
John the Deacon, 8n, 25, 26, 28, 29, 43, 51
John the Evangelist, 115, 150, 151, 186, 188, 216
Jordan River, 90, 91, 93
Joseph, 214
Joshua, 215
joy(s), 153, 196, 245
- of heaven, 172, 223, 244, 247
- of paradise, 109

Judaea, 133, 134, 136
Judge. *See* Jesus Christ
Julian of Eclanum, 149
Justinian, 4, 7
Juvenal, 7

Kedar, 100, 133–35, 137
kingdom, heavenly, 163–64, 176, 210, 223, 231, 239. *See also* heaven; homeland, heavenly; homeland, spiritual
kiss(es); kissing, 94–96, 99, 110, 118, 120, 122, 123, 150–51, 186–87
knowledge, 7, 66, 77, 85, 87, 118, 123–25, 126, 129, 131, 136, 141–42, 185, 214, 222, 229, 239. *See also* understanding; wisdom

Lactantius, 92

Leander of Seville, 13, 48n, 66
Lebanon, 112, 116, 162–63, 177, 208–9, 231–32, 248
letter (as opposed to spirit), 69, 77, 111. *See also* spirit (as opposed to letter)
lip(s), 82, 165, 211
Lombards, 5, 7, 7n, 8, 10, 11, 14, 15, 17, 19, 23n, 28
Lot, 192–93
love, 9, 13, 23, 49, 59, 60–64, 72–73, 76, 78, 79, 80, 88, 92, 95–96, 99–100, 109, 110, 112, 114, 115, 117, 122, 123, 124, 125–26, 127, 128, 130, 131–32, 138, 139, 140, 149, 150, 151, 152, 153–54, 154–55, 156–57, 157–59, 160–61, 161, 162, 164, 165, 166, 167, 168, 170, 172, 173, 174, 175, 179, 187, 188, 189, 190, 191, 195–96, 196–98, 198, 199, 201–2, 202–5, 205–6, 207, 208, 210, 211, 212, 213, 218–19, 221, 223, 224, 225, 226, 227n, 228, 233, 235, 236, 237, 238, 240, 245, 246. *See also* charity; desire; panting; yearning
lowering. *See* condescension, divine
Lubac, Henri de, 85
Luther, Martin, 60

Magi, 223
Marinianus of Ravenna, 35n, 36, 92
Markus, Robert, 16, 22, 28
marriage-bed. *See* bed
Mary (Mother of God), 59, 94, 190, 195, 195n

Mary (repentant sinner), 190
Matthew the Evangelist, 150, 187
Maurice, 11, 13, 15, 16
Maurists, 31, 31n, 34n, 39n, 107, 147
Maximian, 10
Mediator. *See* Jesus Christ
Mediterranean Sea, 4
mercy, 78, 110, 124, 130, 36, 167, 199, 217, 223
Meyvaert, Paul, 35, 37, 39, 40, 42, 86, 108, 275–76
Milan, 5, 25, 55, 92
Miriam, 90–91, 113
Montanus, 139
mortality, 11–12, 155, 168, 170, 171, 176, 200, 201, 219, 221, 224, 231, 239
Moses, 90, 91, 113, 120, 196n, 201, 214, 247
mouth, 95, 99, 114, 118, 120, 123, 150–51, 186–87
Müller, Suzanne, 50
Murphy, Roland, 63

Narses, 13
New Testament, 51, 52, 75, 115, 131
Noah, 192, 213
North Africa. 3, 4, 18
nose(s), 121, 177, 231–32, 248
numbness (spiritual), 81, 109, 110, 157, 170, 171, 201, 202, 218, 221, 222

obtuseness (spiritual), 109, 127
Odoacer, 3
odor, 97, 99, 118–20, 121, 124, 125, 127–28, 153, 155, 167,

171, 188, 191, 199, 206, 218, 221, 244–45. *See also* fragrance; scent; smell; stench
Old Testament, 34, 36, 37, 51, 52, 63, 75, 76, 79, 113
Origen, 58, 59, 60, 68, 76, 77n, 80, 85–87, 87, 88, 90, 91, 98
Ostrogoths, 3
Oudin, Casimir, 32, 183n

Palatinus, 6
Pannonia, 3
panting, 154, 197. *See also* burning (spiritual); charity; desire; love; yearning
passion(s), 41, 112
pastor(s), 20, 22, 25, 84, 123, 188
Pateria, 6
Paterius, 31n, 50–52, 53, 56, 57, 147–48, 149, 150n, 154n, 156n, 163n, 164n, 167n, 168n, 169n, 172n, 174n, 175n, 178n, 180n, 243, 251, 257, 266n, 268n, 279–82, 283, 284, 285, 293
Book of Testimonies, 50–52
patience, 167, 217, 240
Patriarch(s), 116, 118, 159, 204
Paul the Apostle, 82, 83, 98, 111, 124, 125, 127, 132, 134, 136, 153, 161, 188, 191, 193, 194, 196, 207, 216, 222, 227, 227n, 229, 230, 231, 237
Paul the Deacon, 7, 28, 29
Pavia, 5
Pelagius II, Pope, 10, 11, 14
perfection, 72, 73, 89, 116, 117, 127, 128, 129, 130, 131–32, 153, 166, 168, 172, 175, 194, 195, 212, 219, 223, 228, 230, 237, 247

Peter (subdeacon), 23, 27, 36n
Peter Abelard, 49n
Peter of Cava, 24, 34n
Peter Oldradus, 25
Peter Lombard, 49n
Peter the Apostle, 128, 136, 159, 179, 192, 204, 216, 238
Peterson, Joan M., 86
Pharaoh, 101, 142–44
Pharisee(s), 96, 122, 187, 190
philosophy; philosophers, 7, 12, 121
Phineas, 214
Phipps, William E., 62
preacher(s); preaching, 15, 22, 23n, 67, 73, 80, 117, 118, 119, 120–21, 130, 133, 134, 136, 143, 150, 151, 152n, 156, 157, 159, 162–64, 165, 166, 169, 173, 177, 179, 187, 189, 189n, 201, 202, 204, 207, 208n, 209, 210, 211, 212, 213, 217, 223, 225, 228, 232, 237, 238, 245, 246
Preacher to the Gentiles, 223. *See also* Paul the Apostle
predestination, 142–44
presence, divine, 117–18, 119–20, 120, 124, 150–51, 160, 186, 205–6, 244
prophet(s), 33, 91, 112, 114, 118, 119, 120, 123, 127, 129, 130, 142, 150, 151, 158, 159, 180, 186, 187, 198, 200, 204, 205, 221, 224, 229, 231, 247. *See also* Isaiah; Ezekiel; Jeremiah
Proverbs, book of, 33, 52n, 78, 115–16
prudence, 116

Psalmist, 160, 193, 194, 199, 205, 206, 227, 235, 239, 245. *See also* David

Ravenna, 4, 5, 8, 17, 33, 35, 36, 38, 39, 92
Recchia, Vincenzo, 65, 67n
Red Sea, 90, 91, 113, 143
Redeemer. *See* Jesus Christ
refreshment (spiritual), 152, 189, 235. *See also* coolness (spiritual)
reprobate, 143, 152, 176, 189, 192, 231
resurrection, 83, 94, 112, 169, 180, 220, 238
resurrection body, 11–12, 112, 176, 231
righteousness; righteous, 114, 134, 137, 151, 161, 166, 168, 169, 176, 187, 188, 192–94, 207, 212, 218–19, 220, 222, 223, 229, 245
Robert of Molesme, 54
Robert of Tombelaine, 30, 30n, 32
Roman Empire, 1–4
Rome, 1–2, 4, 5, 6, 8, 9, 10, 11, 12, 13, 14, 16–18, 19, 21, 22, 23n, 27, 34–36, 38–39, 43, 49, 89, 109, 144n. *See also* Church, Roman
Romulus Augustus, 3
Rufinus, 85

Sabellius, 139
Sabinian, Pope, 19
Saint Andrew (monastery), 10, 13, 14, 34, 35
saint(s), 119, 124, 153, 157, 161, 165, 167, 170, 171, 177, 191, 193, 201, 202, 206, 212, 218, 221, 232, 245, 246
Samuel, 215
Satan, 128, 193. *See also* ancient enemy; Devil
Saul, 90, 215
scent, 119, 127. *See also* fragrance; odor; smell; stench
self-control, 175, 224, 226
self-indulgence, 141, 142, 143, 175, 224, 226
self-love, 154, 198
Seneca, 7
Senir, 168, 219
Sicily, 6, 10, 18, 22n
Silvia, 6
sin(s), 15, 88, 125, 127, 130, 136, 151, 173, 176, 177, 179, 188, 196, 215, 222, 223, 224, 227, 229, 230, 232, 247
sinner(s), 88–89, 96, 99, 133, 134, 136, 137, 152, 154, 165, 169, 187, 190, 194, 211, 220, 223
smell, 232. *See also* fragrance; odor; scent; stench
Solomon, 47, 78, 82, 83, 100, 115, 125, 133–34, 135–36, 137, 161, 162, 163, 194, 199, 206, 207, 208, 209, 244
soul, 9, 26, 59, 64, 72, 76, 77, 86, 100, 109, 110, 116, 120, 122, 123, 124, 127, 129, 137–41, 152–54, 156–57, 158–59, 160, 163, 171–73, 179, 189, 190, 193–98, 201–6, 209, 212–13, 215, 218, 223, 224–25, 230, 233, 235, 238–40, 244–45, 246, 247
Spain, 3, 13, 18, 28, 48n

Spanish Church, 48
spirit (as opposed to letter), 77, 111. *See also* letter
spirit(s), evil, 88, 171, 174, 175, 177, 221, 225, 226, 228, 232. *See also* demon(s)
Spirit, Holy. *See* Holy Spirit
spirit, human, 25, 112, 157, 198, 202, 203
spirit, prophetic, 83, 180, 238
Spoleto, 17
stench, 224. *See also* fragrance; odor; scent; smell
Stephen Harding, 21n, 54
sun, 100, 133–34, 136, 138, 139, 170, 217, 230

Taio of Saragossa, 49, 50n
Tarsilla, 6
teacher(s); teaching, 78–79, 84, 88, 119, 129, 131, 137, 139–40, 142, 151, 173, 204, 205, 225
tear(s), 123, 160, 187, 205, 206
Theoctista, 13, 16n, 244n
Theoderic, 3–4
Theodosius the Great, 2
Theodosius (son of Maurice), 13
thigh(s), 80, 110, 162, 207–8
Thomas Aquinas, 26, 26n
Tiberius (Roman emperor 578–582), 11, 12
Toledo, 3, 28, 29, 47, 48
Totila, 4, 6
Toulouse, 2
Trajan, 1, 26
Truth. *See* Jesus Christ
Turner, Denys, 47, 75, 76

understanding, 33, 37–38, 66–67, 70, 75–78, 83, 85, 109–10, 112, 119–20, 120–21, 122, 126, 131, 133, 141, 164, 167, 172, 198, 209n, 210, 218, 223, 235, 239, 245, 247. *See also* knowledge; wisdom

Valentio, 10
Vandals, 3, 4
vice(s), 12, 114, 137, 144, 154, 160, 161n, 177, 190, 206, 214, 216, 224, 232, 236, 248
Virgil, 7
virtue(s), 12, 23, 86, 110, 114, 121–22, 124, 128, 137, 139, 140, 153, 158, 159, 160–61, 164, 166–67, 170, 171, 177, 179, 188, 189, 190, 191, 193, 204, 205, 206, 210, 214, 216, 217, 221, 226, 227, 232, 233, 234, 235, 236, 237, 238, 248
Visigoths, 2–3
vision of God, 119, 135, 171–72, 174, 176, 197, 198, 202, 225, 230, 231
Vogüé, Adalbert de, 24, 35, 39
Vouillé, 3

warmth (spiritual), 88, 110, 170–71, 218, 221, 233. *See also* ardor, ardent; burning (spiritual); fervor, fervent
Waszink, J. H., 108, 275–77
William of Saint Thierry, xii, 50, 54–57, 57n, 59, 183–85, 208n, 212n, 231n, 233n, 243, 251, 257, 259n, 261, 261n, 268, 268n, 269, 269n, 270, 287–94

Excerpts from the Books of Blessed Gregory on the Song of Songs, 54–57
Wilmart, André, 147
wine, 99–100, 118–19, 120–21, 123–24, 130, 131, 151, 169, 187
wisdom; wise, 65, 66, 77, 111, 116, 118–19, 120–22, 128, 130, 131, 143, 167, 209n, 218, 227, 227n; *see also* knowledge; understanding
Word of God. *See* Jesus Christ
works, 7, 21n, 23, 24, 28, 29–30, 33, 39, 43, 45–46, 48n, 48–49, 52–53, 55, 59, 63, 86, 87, 98, 101, 115, 132, 136, 142, 149, 171, 184, 243, 251

bad works, 132, 143, 193, 194, 222, 234–35
good works, 73, 86, 99, 117, 122, 131–32, 155, 161, 166, 170, 174, 177–79, 206, 217, 218, 221, 226, 233, 234, 238, 244
works of penance, 135–36

yearning, 7, 76, 78, 110, 154, 158, 174, 197, 203, 215, 222, 225, 233, 235. *See also* burning (spiritual); charity; desire; love; panting
Young, Frances, 70, 71

Zeno (Roman emperor), 3

www.ingramcontent.com/pod-product-compliance
Lightning Source LLC
Chambersburg PA
CBHW031232290426
44109CB00012B/257